SHADOWS OF THE ENGLIGHTENMENT

Shadows *of the* Enlightenment

*The Hidden Politics and Ideology of
the Natural and Social Sciences*

George E. McCarthy

MONTHLY REVIEW PRESS

New York

Copyright © 2025 by George E. McCarthy
All Rights Reserved

Library of Congress Cataloging-in-Publication Data
available from the publisher

ISBN 978-158367-111-0 paperback
ISBN 978-158367-112-7 cloth

Typeset in Minion Pro

MONTHLY REVIEW PRESS, NEW YORK
monthlyreview.org

5 4 3 2 1

Contents

For my children
Devin and Alexa

and my grandchildren
Eliana, Warren, and Sylvia

May your world be
more enlightened and free,
more creative and inspired,
and more open and happy,
informed by the spirit of kindness,
wisdom, and social justice.

Acknowledgments

I would like to thank my close colleagues and friends in Gambier, Ohio for their support and encouragement with special gratitude to Patricia Keane, Royal Rhodes, and Hays Stone. Their help over many years has been invaluable in maintaining my intellectual focus and political hopes for the future. I would also like to recognize the importance of my students at Kenyon College for their hard work, serious discussions, and dedication to learning new and exciting ideas and traditions and for the invaluable technical support of Kenyon employees In Helpline and the Information Technology Department. And most important of all is the gratitude I feel to my immediate and extended family for providing me with the dreams, inspiration, and ideals to continue writing and teaching in difficult social and political times.

"From the beginning people like this have never managed, whether on their own or with the help by others, to see anything besides the shadows that are [continually] projected on the wall opposite them by the glow of the fire."—PLATO, *THE REPUBLIC*, 380 BC

"After Buddha was dead, his shadow was still shown for centuries in a cave—a tremendous, gruesome shadow. God is dead; but given the way of men, there may still be caves for thousands of years in which his shadow will be shown. . . . There are no eternally enduring substances; matter is as much of an error as the God of the Eleatics. But when shall we ever be done with our caution and care? When will all these shadows of God cease to darken our minds? When will we complete our de-deification of nature?"—FRIEDRICH NIETZSCHE, *THE GAY SCIENCE*, 1882

"Reason has liquidated itself as an agency of ethical, moral, and religious insight. Bishop Berkeley, legitimate son of nominalism, Protestant zealot, and positivist enlightener all in one, directed an attack against such general concepts. . . . Justice, equality, happiness, tolerance, all the concepts that, as mentioned, were in the preceding centuries supposed to be inherent in or sanctioned by reason, have lost their intellectual roots [and their connection] to an objective reality. Domination of nature involves domination of man."—MAX HORKHEIMER, *ECLIPSE OF REASON*, 1947

"The technological a priori is a political a priori inasmuch as the transformation of nature involves that of man, and inasmuch as the 'man-made creations' issue from and reenter a societal ensemble." —HERBERT MARCUSE, *ONE-DIMENSIONAL MAN*, 1964

"For the master's tools will never dismantle the master's house. They may allow us to temporarily beat him at his own game, but they will never enable us to bring about genuine change."—AUDRE LORDE, SECOND SEX CONFERENCE, NEW YORK, 1979

Epistemology, the Crisis of Science, and the Twilight of Reason

THIS BOOK EXAMINES the hidden metaphysics and politics of the modern natural and social sciences and their implications for diagnosing and resolving social and ecological crises and for developing a comprehensive theory of social justice. In it I outline the underlying and forgotten politics of science by tracing the main critical traditions in modern European philosophy and social theory. The central goal is to uncover the unconscious assumptions, values, and ideologies lying deeply buried and hidden beneath the surface of scientific theories of knowledge and methods that direct and even distort inquiries into the systems, structures, and processes of nature and society. In order to undertake this task, it is necessary to inquire into the underlying theoretical imperatives of science to dominate nature (*Herrschaftswissen*), humanity (scientific and workplace technology), and human reason (rationalization and disenchantment). These interconnected imperatives of domination result in a dialectic of enlightenment and the loss of critical or substantive faculties of human reason that are then incapable of calling into question the role of science in modern industrial society. The emphasis of this work is not on the usual technological use or potential abuse of science in its formal and operational applications to nature and society. Rather, it is about the underlying concepts, theories, and methods of both natural and social science that are themselves political and heavily value-laden both in immediate construction and technical application, both in abstract theory and concrete practice. However, these values and assumptions are unarticulated and repressed, hidden deep within the methods and theories of the natural and social sciences as researchers search for knowledge that focuses on the domination of their physical and social worlds. The following chapters trace the evolution of these dark shadows of the Enlightenment as they evolve in our understanding of the natural and social sciences.

The first part of this work, which focuses on the history, epistemology, and methodology of post-analytic and neo-Kantian philosophy of science within European and American philosophy, examines the logic and limits of the natural sciences, whereas the second part considers the historical and political economic foundations of natural science in historical materialism. "Politics" is the term used here to connote any set of values or value system that unconsciously permeates modern science in ways that affect or distort our perception of reality and understanding of nature, as well as distorting science's application to the study of the economy, production, and society as a whole. The politics of natural science has become a very recognizable issue in our explanation of the economy and industrial production, medical science and health care, modern psychology and the treatment of mental disorders, and the depletion of natural resources and the ecological deterioration of nature.[1] However, perhaps as important, it also becomes a political issue when considering the very interconnected elements of the principles of empirical research and the logic of scientific discovery in the construction of inductive theories, hypothetical conjectures, deductive predictions, empirical observations, explanatory laws, and scientific theories.[2] The scientific method begins with systematic observation, hypothesis formulation, and concludes with the empirical experiments to verify or falsify the initial hypothesis and theory. These very connections also unsuspectingly affect our interdependent social relations with each other and with our broader organic environment. The manner in which both the natural and social sciences are created and validated is political for a number of complex reasons that will be examined in this text.

The third, and final, part of this work details the political dimensions of science as they influence our understanding of the social sciences and the evolution of the methodological and theoretical debates about the relationship between sociology and science, the problems of democracy and the environment, and the options available to solve them. The aim of this work is to recover these lost connections and the dialectic between science and politics that have been hidden for years behind the epistemological curtain and Enlightenment shadows of rational objectivity, formal neutrality, and universal truth.[3] The political dimensions of the principles and logic of science are embedded in a complex web of metatheory and normative assumptions about the world, including the following: (1) metaphysics and constructivism of a formal, mechanical, and deterministic physical nature; (2) methodology and ethics of the domination and control of nature; (3) positivist theory of knowledge based upon empiricism, realism, and the factual validation of an apparent objective reality; (4) ethical silence of disenchantment, nominalism, and nihilism in the philosophy of science and the scientific method; (5) instrumental politics of positivism in its formal application in technological rationality and industrial production; and (6) critical social theory and comprehensive sociology of knowledge with its examination of the causal foundations and interrelated value systems of nature, science, and liberal society. The metatheory makes science possible as it frames the potential issues to be raised in theory at the same time that it limits and legitimates the scientific responses to these questions within the traditional definition of science. Once these foundational principles of science are excavated, it then becomes possible to build a more comprehensive and holistic theory of society and social justice.

In both the natural and the social sciences, the actual structures of society are suppressed and immunized against critical reflection in the various analyses of nature, ecology, and the economy. Thus, the epistemology and methodology of the natural and social sciences hide and repress the underlying politics of science because they do not reflect upon their foundations in metaphysics, methodology, ethics, and unarticulated cultural and social values. They make a substantive ethical and political critique nearly impossible because traditional reason prior to the Enlightenment is viewed as unscientific, non-empirical, and decadent, and because science examines only the phenomenal or surface appearances of the social world. Finally, the political underpinnings of the sciences go unrecognized because they are themselves sociological reflections and historical manifestations of the deeper structures of the social system and cultural values of Western civilization. This critique of modern reason, which begins with the philosophy of Immanuel Kant and Friedrich Nietzsche and the social epistemology of Max Weber, Edmund Husserl, and Max Scheler, extends into the Critical Theory of the Frankfurt School and beyond.

Approaching the end of the eighteenth century, Kant wrote in the *Critique of Pure Reason* (1781 and 1787) that the mind consists of a priori transcendental categories of the understanding, while nearly two centuries later Herbert Marcuse wrote in *One-Dimensional Man* (1964) that science consists of a priori political concepts. Kant meant that the mind is so structured through the mental categories of substance, accidents, and causality and the sensuous forms of intuition of time and space that it is constitutive in the process of perceiving and thinking about the world. The world of phenomena, the world we see and recognize every day, is actually created and formed through the mind; we can never get behind these appearances (*Erscheinungen*) and representations (*Vorstellungen*) to see the actual empirical reality or thing-in-itself (*Ding an sich*). The worlds of our everyday experience and our theoretical science are both constructs and representations of the human mind. Marcuse looked at science in a similar way but within the general framework of a critical social theory that expanded his interpretation of the meaning of these formative concepts and categories of the human mind. The concepts by which science organizes our understanding and knowledge of the world in empirical inquiry are not neutral and objective reflections of reality but are the product of the broader social system. These concepts, which originally began with metaphysics and transcendental logic, are now filtered through political and economic institutions and relationships. Society, and not transcendental consciousness, mediates and transforms our perception of the world. That is, the Enlightenment and science create a world of experience and theories that contain in them values and principles reflective of society at large. Thus, the apparent a priori and philosophical categories of Kant that structure our perception and experience of the world are not transcendental and universal, but historical and social.[4] The concepts and ideas that frame and validate the scientific method and theories are themselves a product of modern industrial society. In the end, we will uncover that science is an historical and social construct and form of political ideology; that is, it is a cultural representation and reflection of the substructures, institutions, and values of Western liberalism and political economy. The logic of Western reason and science reflects the underlying logic and principles of capital production. Our goal is to trace the sociogenic connections between the Enlightenment and industrial capitalism to better appreciate the true nature of modern science and its possible role and limitations in responding to the social problems of class inequality, poverty, human suffering, loss of democracy, environmental crises, etc., that we face in the twenty-first century.

One of the more important aspects of modern society has been the rise of Enlightenment science along with its practical application in Western technology and industry since the seventeenth century. Science has occupied a central and, for the most part, unassailed and unquestioned position with the advent of modernity, especially in the form of the natural sciences and to a lesser extent the social sciences. Although the philosophical justification for Enlightenment science rests in the traditions of both empiricism and rationalism, there have been areas critical of this development, including the empiricist skepticism of Hume, critical idealism of Kant and Hegel, romantic *Naturphilosophie* of Goethe, Fichte, Schelling, and Hegel, existentialism of Schopenhauer, Nietzsche, and Heidegger, phenomenology and hermeneutics of Rickert, Scheler, Husserl, Ellul, Borkenau, and Berman, classical social theory of Marx, Weber, and Durkheim, critical theory of Horkheimer, Adorno, Marcuse, and Habermas, Marxist social theory and history of science of Sohn-Rethel, C. W. Mills, Berman, and Braverman, and the neo-Kantian historicism and post-analytic pragmatism of Quine, Duhem, Sellars, Feyerabend, Lakatos, Kuhn, and Rorty. The complex and various philosophies of knowledge and science articulated by romanticism, idealism, existentialism, classical social theory, phenomenology, hermeneutics, post-analytic philosophy, pragmatism, critical theory, and neo-Marxism will be integrated into a general social critique of the natural and social sciences for the purposes of understanding the nature of modern science and its relationship to society and the environment.

Phenomenology, understood in its broadest parameters as drawing upon European idealism and existentialism, is the neo-Kantian study of the nature and structure of subjectivity/consciousness and its construction of the objects of thought in human perception, understanding, reason, spirit, and culture. It provides us with a crucial theory of knowledge and consciousness because it connects early German idealism with later critical schools of thought including hermeneutics, existentialism, and pragmatism. It also provides us with a connecting link between philosophy and social theory. According to this tradition, the objectivity of experience and knowledge is never given, but is a construct of the human mind and value relations (*Wertbeziehung*). That is, it is the interpretive and social consciousness that constructs the world we experience and inhabit, and it is through this consciousness that the objects of nature, culture, and social institutions appear to us as phenomenal forms of the projection of the human mind. Much of contemporary European philosophy and social theory from Georg Friedrich Hegel's theory of the spirit to Thomas Kuhn's theory of scientific consensus involves the analysis of the implications of this mental reconstruction of objective reality. Finally, these various schools of philosophy will, in turn, be incorporated into a critical social theory grounded in a history and sociology of science and historical materialism.

The following work will begin with the examination of the construction of the phenomenal world in modern thought. It will trace in detail the "shadows of God" and the Enlightenment or the negative implications and ideology of the dark side of Western rationality. Science has provided a justification for the great transformation and domination of nature. Will it also provide an avenue of critical evaluation and escape from the contemporary crises of both nature and society? Or is science so embedded in the values and ideals of modernity that it cannot distance itself from political liberalism and industrial capitalism, especially if the causes of the social crises lie in these human-made social institutions? By reintroducing these European theoretical traditions into the heart of today's practical problems of the structures and institutions of the social system we can see how they are again made relevant.

Enlightenment science has traditionally attempted to break away from magic, religion, and superstition as it searched for the universals and absolutes in nature, whether they were articulated in a theory of knowledge as substance, matter, causality, time, space, laws of nature, order, and truth or in moral philosophy as human nature, natural rights, absolute ideas, categorical imperatives, and social justice. The underlying presupposition of these positions is that there is some essentialism or eternal natural law or moral order, reality in itself, or objective scientific truth independent and outside of our perception of it. As we shall see in

Nietzsche's writings, this turns science into a "shadow of God."
Science has become a shadow or form of replacement of God in
the natural world order:

> After Buddha was dead, his shadow was still shown for centuries
> in a cave—a tremendous, gruesome shadow. God is dead; but
> given the way of men, there may still be caves for thousands of
> years in which his shadow will be shown. . . . There are no eter-
> nally enduring substances; matter is as much of an error as the
> God of the Eleatics. But when shall we ever be done with our
> caution and care? When will all these shadows of God cease to
> darken our minds? When will we complete our de-deification
> of nature?[5]

Nietzsche proclaimed that "God is dead," but the ideal of a transcendent universal and eternal truth continued to live on in the
form of the idolatry and worship of philosophy, politics, theology,
art, and the natural sciences. According to Nietzsche, these forms
of reason or shadows of God were illegitimate claims to objective
truth and Apollonian universality because they confused epistemological and moral nihilism for universal validity; Dionysian
existentialism for Apollonian reality; and Heraclitean change
and becoming for Platonic essence, being, and form. In the following work on nature, science, and reason, a similar perspective
will be taken. According to Nietzsche, in the Western traditions
these dark shadows were worshipped as false gods. Applying this
dynamic metaphor to a critical social analysis of modern natural
science we can see that the latter, too, has been mistaken by many
for expressing a universal, if not divine, truth rather than a particular and limited form of knowledge that reflects, not the empirical
reality, but the dominant politics and ideology of society. From
this perspective, Enlightenment reason and science rise above the
historically specific moment as they claim a universal validity in
epistemology and metaphysics for their categories, theories, and
laws. This immunizes science from a truly critical and creative

review as epistemology is reduced to methodology, metaphysics to physics, knowledge to technical science, and *episteme* to *techne*. That is, debates about the nature of knowledge, truth, and science are replaced by the immediate acceptance of the legitimacy of science and by reflection on its formal procedures and technical method—how science acquires and validates its facts, laws, and theories. From Max Weber's perspective in his essay "Science as a Vocation" (1917), discussions about objective reason and substantive knowledge have been replaced by the study of the actual method and techniques of natural science. The present status of knowledge is no longer open to question and analysis; this issue has been settled with the rise of the Enlightenment and modern positivism.

The important paths opened by the Enlightenment and modern reason should be appreciated, but the conceptual and theoretical limits of science should also be recognized.. This investigation undertakes a critical approach by reflecting on the general criticisms of science's absolutist and essentialist claims to truth (critique of foundationalism) and by examining the social, political, and historical context of scientific inquiry. From these perspectives, science turns from being a manifestation of ultimate and objective reality into a political form for the domination of nature and humanity. Thus, we move from traditional epistemology and philosophy of science to metaphysics (first principles, values, and assumptions about nature and the immediate physical environment) and politics (values and assumptions about ethics and society), and, finally, to a sociology of knowledge and critical social theory. Once science is understood as a shadow of God and natural law, and thus a questionable quest for universal and absolute truth, we can begin to recognize that it only conceals a deeper truth about the death of God, science, and nature. These are the true shadows of disenchantment or the dialectic of Enlightenment. With this recognition of shadows, science becomes an historical and social phenomenon expressing the hidden values and institutions of modern liberalism and capitalism. It loses its independent and ontological status as it becomes another object of investigation within the history and sociology of knowledge. The term "Shadows of the Enlightenment" is simply another way of expressing the rationalization and disenchantment of substantive reason (Weber), the formalization and liquidation of objective reason (Max Horkheimer), the dialectic of enlightenment (Theodor Adorno and Max Horkheimer), the alienation of nature (Karl Marx), and the alienation of reason (Leszek Kolakowski).[6]

Behind the realm of physics is the world of metaphysics—the philosophical and ontological principles and unarticulated a priori values and assumptions about nature and humanity. Metaphysics grounds the natural sciences in their material, spatial, temporal, and causal assumptions about the laws of nature, but they themselves are never empirically verified, but only theologically assumed to be real and valid. It is metaphysics that allows physics to function as a science, hypotheses to be created, and laws to be empirically validated. However, because of their meta-physical or ontological nature, metaphysics also acts as another form of technological rationality and political philosophy. Beyond metaphysics are the social and political institutions that created this distinctive and deceptively complex Western concept of reason and science. Both Nietzsche and Weber saw this distorted development as leading to the decadence of the "last man" and the twilight of reason.

Both empiricism and rationalism defended scientific inquiry as unbiased and objective. Its formal method freed it from all personal prejudices, cultural biases, and political ideologies; it freed science to investigate concrete, physical reality using an objective, value-free method. Although empiricism and rationalism used different approaches and theories of nature, they both agreed that there existed an external empirical reality that was knowable using the rational scientific method whether it utilized inductive or deductive reasoning, empirical evidence or mathematical truths. The debate between the ideas of René Descartes and David Hume occupied much of the later philosophical controversies in the eighteenth and nineteenth centuries. However, with the recognition that science, objectivity, and empirical reality are created by the transcendental subject and the categories of human perception and the understanding, theories no longer reflected the absolute truth of the thing-in-itself. The early skepticism and critique of empiricism of Hume and the later constructivism and idealist subjectivity of Kant ultimately led to the critical breakdown of science in romanticism, existentialism, and historicism, and later to a consideration of the historical and social context of the rise of Western consciousness and reason in historical materialism and critical theory. With the critique of traditional epistemology there is an awareness that science and its corresponding empirical reality are social constructs that leave us with the question: "Why and how did science develop the way it did?" The obvious linear argument is that science peers into reality and each generation gets progressively closer and closer to ultimate truth. However, once the impenetrability and universality of traditional theories of science are called into question, the investigation of science moves into the historical and social analyses of the conditions and context of scientific inquiry. Using this approach, the Enlightenment is then tied to the broader social system, just as objective reason is reduced to technical and instrumental reason for social purposes.

Part I of this work, titled "Natural Science, Technology, and the Domination of Nature," contains the first two chapters on politics, epistemology, and metaphysics. Chapter 1, "Social Epistemology and the Radical Pragmatism of Postmodernism," examines the works of Willard Van Orman Quine, Thomas Kuhn, and Richard Rorty. These authors reject the objectivist and essentialist view of knowledge articulated by Descartes and Hume. For them, knowledge is always a provisional interpretation of reality whose validity rests upon its pragmatic usefulness to the scientific community. Issues of foundationalism—essential being and external reality— are replaced by the central focus of science on issues of puzzle solving, technical utility, and formal manageability. This new approach of pragmatism rejects the various forms of traditional objectivity of science in realism, naturalism, and positivism.[7] The idea that there is an objective reality that the subjective mind and objective science can reflect (realism) and whose only legitimate method of explanation and study is that of the natural sciences (naturalism) is the hallmark of positivism.

Thomas Kuhn in his pathbreaking work *The Structure of Scientific Revolutions* (1962) begins to undertake his analysis by returning to the history of science, that is, to the astronomy of Copernicus and Kepler, the physics of Galileo, Newton, and Einstein, and the chemistry of Priestley and Lavoisier. But he does so by rejecting the traditional theories of science and creating a new theory of normal science and scientific paradigms based on the insights of Gestalt psychology, linguistic anthropology, and post-analytic philosophy. By drawing upon different disciplines and theories of knowledge outside of positivist philosophy, Kuhn undertakes a direct assault on the citadel of Western science, objectivity, and truth in rationalism, empiricism, and idealism. Science is the product of the social construction of theoretical paradigms through a consensus within the scientific community over questions of problems, research, and theories. Universality does not exist independent of human perception, nor is it revealed by discovering the true being or formal essence of reality. It is only by forming a consensus within the community about the scientific issues and hypotheses of central theoretical importance that scientific truth is maintained. Objectivity is reached by methodological and theoretical consensus, not by traditional forms of epistemological objectivity. In fact, the objectivity of method, reality, and science is a construct; that is, it is created and not discovered or reflected in the mind. History, society, and theoretical consensus are now the foundation stones of modern science, which only broaden our understanding of its true nature. Although he never pushed his arguments to the social extreme, Kuhn is partly responsible for moving our understanding of science away from the exclusivity of philosophy and its theories of knowledge to sociology and social consensus.

Paradigms cannot be grounded in reality or epistemology in ontology since there is no independent access to an autonomous, external world of objects. The existential need for paradigms makes such a reality impossible. The validity of a theory is ultimately based on its usefulness for solving particular problems raised within the scientific community. And since consensus about the truth of a theory is not anchored in objective reality, theories cannot be compared with each other to determine which is more accurate or valid, nor can they be compared with some abstract and independent reality. There is no third party that can be the basis for comparison of ideas and paradigms nor provide the foundation for truth between conflicting theories within the natural sciences since all perception is filtered through a paradigm. This is the myth of physical objects developed by Wilfred Sellars, Quine, and Kuhn. Without any underlying base, essence, or objective reality there is no right or wrong explanation of empirical evidence or facts; truth is ultimately a question of utility, not ontology. It is the paradigm itself that produces its own ontological reality and scientific facts; truth is particular, hermeneutical, and interpretive. It is this singular and revised neo-Kantian insight that unleashes existentialism, nominalism, and pragmatism. The adjudication of the validity of any particular theory was traditionally based on empirical evidence (Hume), explanatory predictions (Descartes), or predictive falsifications (Popper). Kuhn will borrow from Quine's theories of the myth of objectivity and critique of the distinction between synthetic and analytic statements. The latter form of statements is inherently systematic and logical, and concludes that science cannot be empirically justified or validated since there is no empirical evidence or proof for any scientific paradigm or theory. All theories are ultimately analytic and logically coherent statements that touch experience only at the periphery of thought. The objects of both religion and science—gods and nature—are constructs and thus cannot be verified or falsified by perception or experience. There is no privileged access to truth through thought and science. According to Kuhn, in the end verification is achieved by non-ontological criteria, such as scientific agreement and problem solving, community and utility. Because of this, different or competing paradigms are what Kuhn calls "incommensurable"; there is no basis for comparison or epistemological judgment. Theories are not verified or falsified, only provisionally agreed upon because of pragmatic convenience and consciousness.

Richard Rorty continues Kuhn's pragmatism by elegantly tracing its philosophical origins in his major writing, *Philosophy and the Mirror of Nature* (1979). While Kuhn was trained as a physicist at Harvard, Rorty was educated in philosophy at the universities of Chicago and Yale and began to follow in the tradition of the American pragmatists Charles Peirce, William James, and John Dewey. Rorty continues to push Kuhn's argument against both epistemology and ontology, and against foundationalism and the ocular metaphor that the mind is the mental mirror or presentation of nature and reality.[8] Paralleling Kuhn's critique of epistemology and the correspondence theory of truth, as well as his theory of paradigms, Rorty, with the help of Sellars and Quine, sees the relationship between the mind and nature expressed as a contingent vocabulary, social practice, and cultural conversation. The whole ontological basis of Western thought and epistemology has been undermined by the skepticism and relativism of pragmatism. There is no thing-in-itself or true world behind the appearances of perception and the experience of phenomena. Knowledge is displaced from objective reality, epistemology is split off from ontology, thought is separated from experience, and subjectivity from objectivity, as science becomes not a reflection of reality, but an expression of pragmatic usefulness and consequences for Kuhn and hermeneutical understanding and conversation for Rorty. Although both Kuhn and Rorty would like to break with representational epistemology, both philosophers ultimately view the world and objectivity as a product of consciousness and subjectivity. Pragmatism never truly develops far from the parental tree of neo-Kantian phenomenology.

Kuhn and Rorty have laid the foundations for a deeper and more profound understanding of the nature of modern science by moving beyond the simple dichotomy of subjectivity and objectivity. Science has become a limited historical and social product no longer tied to representations or to objective and empirical reality. It is a product of social consensus or scientific conversation. However, the next step in our analysis is to uncover, through a deeper hermeneutics and critique of political economy, the unconscious grounding of science in a broader array of cultural and political values. Emancipated from its bond to ontology and representational knowledge, a new theory of science emerges that includes the idea that it is the deep structures of political economy that form the basis for scientific objectivity.

Rejecting traditional or subjective scientific truth as the "mirror of nature," Kuhn and Rorty develop a relatively brief and idealist analysis of the social dimension within the context of intersubjective consciousness and consensus. However, to fully appreciate and take advantage of their intellectual revolution, it is necessary to move beyond their writings to examine the social component of their respective epistemologies. Once the transcendence and immutability of science is called into question by Kuhn and Rorty, the next crucial question is about the history of science: If the philosophical foundations of traditional epistemology have been dismantled, and there are no real core principles or reality to science, then the sociological question arises by necessity as to why and how a particular view of the world and a series of coherent theoretical paradigms evolved since the seventeenth century. If Kuhn argues that there are different possible paradigms, then what criteria are decisive in determining which theory is generally accepted as valid? Why was the Cartesian paradigm so successful?

Chapter 2 in Part I continues the analysis of chapter 1 and critique of the traditional theories of knowledge with a central focus on the modern evolution within German phenomenology and its views of consciousness, knowledge, and science. The major representatives of this epistemological tradition view science as a distinct form of knowledge—*Herrschaftswissen*. In this analysis we begin to see a deeper level of hidden values and principles that characterize modern physics. Knowledge is not objective in the

traditional sense, but it is now ladened with the normative imperative to dominate and control nature. Formal mathematical and
empirical studies are not neutral; they contain a cultural drive to
interpret nature in a way that makes explanation and prediction,
control and domination, the driving forces of science. This idea
of science as domination develops out of the writings of Bacon,
Nietzsche, Weber, Scheler, Husserl, and Heidegger.

The term *"Herrschaftswissen"* was first coined by Max Scheler
in 1924 in his work *Society and Forms of Knowledge,* but the
idea behind it had been used extensively by Weber in his writings on science.[9] Scheler used the term to refer to the domination
of both the physical nature of the external world and the inner
nature of humanity; it also referred specifically to the technical
and positive knowledge of causes, effects, and the specific method
of science that produces the practical results of explanations and
predictions. Weber's theory of the "iron cage" and rationalization of society is the product of a long history of the evolution of
Western consciousness from Hegel's analysis of the phenomenology of the mind from consciousness, self-consciousness, reason,
and absolute spirit to Nietzsche's theory of the twilight of the idols
of human reason from Platonic rationalism to Kantian idealism.
According to Nietzsche, this long history of the devaluation and
decline of human reason ends in the nihilism of the iron cage of the
last man without hope, vision, or dreams. It is this tradition that
Weber builds upon for his understanding of the degradation and
dismantling of human reason from substantive (*Wertrationalität*)
to formal, technical reason (*Zweckrationalität*). Humanity is no
longer capable of asking the profound questions about the meaning and purpose of human life, being and truth, ethics and justice,
or art and aesthetics. It is now only capable of solving technical
problems and utilitarian issues under the imperative of the domination of nature. We live in an iron cage without self-consciousness
and reason. We can no longer raise the important questions in
philosophy, theology, ethics, and art about reality, truth, morality,
and beauty. The world is an existentially empty and meaningless

place brought about by the rise of Enlightenment science and utilitarian economics. This is what Weber means by decadence and disenchantment—"a world of specialists without spirit (*Geist*), sensualists without heart (*Herz*)." This is a world inhabited by technical and scientific experts who have lost the ability and will to imagine or create a self-conscious, free, and just society; there are also the economic specialists who, caught in the desires for market pleasures and money accumulation, have lost the ability to make moral and virtuous judgments about their lives. The domination of nature has spilled over to the domination of a humanity that has lost its reason (virtue) and spirit (politics) for existence. From Hegel's perspective, the dangers of modernity were caused by a form of reason divorced from the Spirit of the ethical and political community in the form of the Terror of the French Revolution unrestrained by the political constitution and the state and the inner violence and oppression of Kant's categorical imperative. Now with Nietzsche, Weber, and Heidegger the problem is one of nominalism and relativism—the twilight or decline of human reason into moral nihilism. Weber will expand these issues to include science and positivism. Science has replaced the traditional forms of substantive reason and can no longer legitimately raise questions about the nature and purpose of social research or society itself; it can no longer raise questions about ethics and social justice.

Production has replaced metaphysics and nature as the physical reality reflected in the "transcendental" categories of the mind. The Enlightenment does not represent truth per se, but a form of truth produced at a particular historical moment in time in Western society that transforms nature from a living organism into a technical machine that is mathematically, formally, and predictably quantifiable. This approach to nature simply reflects the destruction of the integrated medieval guild and craft system through the rational calculation and bookkeeping (Weber) and the quantification and commodification of human labor power in the modern workplace (Marx). This is why today the natural sciences and social sciences are bound to the same methodological principles of reified objectivity and technical positivism. This leads us into chapter 3, where we will move beyond the domination of nature to a review of the application of science in the production process itself and the resulting domination and alienation of humanity.

In order to move beyond phenomenology and postmodern philosophy of science to a critical sociology, it is essential to see that science is not a reflection of the objective truth and universal laws of the external, real world, but is rather a "mirror of production" or a reflection of the institutions and values of the total social system of modern industrial society.[10] The term "mirror of production" refers here to the laws and logic of political economy and the fetishism of capitalist production unconsciously embedded in the theories, method, metaphysics, and epistemology of natural science. Science is more a reflection of the technical knowledge and class interests of capitalism as an economic and political system than a neutral unprejudiced knowledge of and correspondence to the external world or thing-in-itself. Marcuse has summarized this idea with the statement that "the technological a priori is a political a priori. . . . The evolution of scientific method merely 'reflects' the transformation of nature into technical reality in the process of industrial civilization."[11] Alfred Sohn-Rethel in *Intellectual and Manual Labor* (1970) was arguably the first to connect Kant's epistemology to Marx's historical materialism: Kant's philosophy of knowledge and science (categories of the understanding) with Marx's theory of value and commodity exchange (money); and Kant's theory of transcendental subjectivity and the forms of experience with Marx's theory of alienated labor, commodity exchange, wage labor, labor power, and the capitalist mode of production.[12] To help articulate and answer these issues, it will be necessary to inquire into the values, norms, and principles of modern science that both justify and make science possible.

In Part II, "Natural Science, Political Economy, and the Domination of Nature," two chapters examine in more detail the metaphysics and politics of natural science in sociology and political economy as they inquire into the broad nature of science as the "mirror of production and politics" and as it questions the non-scientific values of this new worldview of modern science. These values of Enlightenment and production are articulated in four distinct areas. Each area expresses a particular aspect of scientific rationality that contains displaced and repressed forms of political values that unconsciously affect our relations with nature and society as a whole; each area reflects the complex relationships between science and politics, reason and society. The a priori forms of political rationality and alienated consciousness contained in modern science include the following: a new subjective reason and formal technology—the utility, domination, and rationalization of nature in chapter 2; a new philosophy and ontology of nature—metaphysics of science and disenchanted reason in chapter 3; a new view of formal technology, economics, and scientific management—the domination of humanity for control over nature, surplus value, and human labor in chapter 4; and a new view of formal realism and positivism in the social sciences—the rise of a non-reflective and positivistic social science that is incapable and unwilling to question the underlying normative assumptions of modern society or scientific application, thereby immunizing the status quo and structures of power from critical reflection, in chapter 5. It is by these approaches that science becomes a "mirror of production" and a mirror of alienated consciousness reflecting the deeper values of Enlightenment rationality, which, in turn, are themselves concrete expressions of the fetishism, alienation, and exploitation of the logic of capital and the capitalist mode of production. Science is no longer the "mirror of nature" but the "mirror of production" and capitalist rationality and technology.

We will follow how the fundamental categories of science begin with the claim to universal rationality but quickly devolve into a priori politics in the form of metaphysics, technology, production, formal rationality, and positivism and thereby replace substantive reason, truth, and reality to create a new social consensus about objectivity. Behind the world of appearances and phenomena, behind the logical formalism, mathematical certainty, and theoretical predictions, and behind the ethical neutrality, phenomenal objectivity, and moral nominalism of science lie the distinct political and social shadows—the values and agendas hidden in their scientific theories, method, and technical applications. From this perspective science remains a form of political ideology because it imposes a metaphysics and political worldview on humanity which it makes real in its ideas and institutions under the guise of a transcendent reason and universal truth. It is for this reason that science is a priori technological in its application and a priori political in its forms of domination. In the process of application, science reduces objective and substantive reason to technical reason and purposive-rational action. This recognition is the beginning of a process that will end in later and more radical social theorists who will tie science, society, and nature together in the context of the wider political and economic systems and the cultural lifeworld; this will necessarily involve the decolonization of science itself by the recognition of its relationship to the social system and the lifeworld in the writings of Jürgen Habermas.

The chapters in Part II focus on the topic of science and politics. This section articulates the political character of both the natural and the social sciences since both forms of science are products of a certain worldview generated by the political economy and, in turn, both forms reinforce that worldview in the academy and in industry. In very subtle and complex ways, the sciences for the study of nature and society reinforce the political and ideological values of the society that created them. This is accomplished behind a non-reflective and deceptive facade of objectivity, neutrality, and nominalism. But science, as is the case with any other social phenomenon, replicates and reaffirms the underlying values and institutions of an advanced capitalist society. These political values, as discussed in the following chapters, are buried deep within the concepts, method, theories, and meta-theories (epistemology and ontology) of modern science. Science and rationality are inherently technological and political.

The first chapter in Part II examines the relationship between modern science and metaphysics found in Descartes' *Meditations on First Philosophy* (1641) by beginning with an analysis of the Cartesian metaphysics of natural science. In chapter 3, we will examine the metaphysics of science as the underlying and unconscious foundations of our knowledge of the physical environment, which are usually not viewed as needing justification. The metaphysics of science entails an analysis of Descartes' philosophy of nature and his method of scientific inquiry in the seventeenth century. The nature of space, time, matter, force, and motion is understood as a functioning, deterministic, and self-contained machine to be explained by mathematical relationships, methodical calculation, and the quantification of physical experience. Humanity's relationship to this quantifiable world (metaphysics) and knowledge of this world (epistemology) is the basis for the grand debates in the seventeenth and eighteenth centuries. Reducing the natural world to its mechanical parts permits humans to view it in terms of mathematics, utilitarianism, and functionalism. The world is a dead machine that functions efficiently and can be explained by its natural works and the functional interrelationship of its component parts. It is this approach that allows for the human domination and exploitation of nature. Nature is split among the dualism of the mind and the body or *res cogitans* and *res extensa*, thinking substance (consciousness) and extended substance (matter), and primary (thought) and secondary (sensations) qualities. Descartes in his *Discourse on Method* (1637) is also perceptively aware that this dualistic and formalistic view of nature is simply the externalization of the structure and organization of the division of labor and technical specialization within the workplace.[13] The values and institutions of work and production are projected onto nature and form its underlying metaphors for understanding the physical world as we move further and further away from the organic and ethical view of nature articulated by the ancient Greeks and medieval Christians. The method of science is built upon this metaphor with Descartes' ideas of clear and distinct

ideas, analytic and synthetic reason, and the reduction of knowledge to its simplest technical components and statements. Carolyn
Merchant has referred to this view as "the death of nature."[14]

Continuing this line of reasoning, E. A. Burtt, in his work *The
Metaphysical Foundations of Modern Physical Science* (1924),
writes, referring to Galileo: "With him, the physical world begins
to be conceived as a perfect machine whose future happenings can
be fully predicted and controlled by one who has full knowledge
and control of the present motions. With man eliminated from
the real world, the latter appeared bounded by mechanical necessity."[15] According to Burtt, it is the study of nature and politics,
epistemology and morality, that forms this comprehensive view
of our physical and social environment. This chapter examines
Descartes' philosophy of nature, its indifference to more ancient
and scholastic views of nature as a living and ethical organism,
and its broader implications for epistemology and politics. After
reviewing Burtt's analysis of the metaphysics of science, we see
that metaphysics is a set of a priori principles and postulates of
science that are necessary for an adequate interpretation of nature
but are not open to empirical or scientific inquiry and justification. In Burtt's theory of knowledge, the traditional concentration
of epistemology on ontology has been replaced by metaphysics.
The application of the scientific method and theory are made possible only by a pre-understanding and acceptance of fundamental
non-scientific metaphysical principles about the reality, being, and
existence of a particular view of nature. Philosophical metaphysics and ontology precede scientific methodology and theory. The
next series of chapters will replace metaphysics and ontology with
politics.

Part II, chapter 4 focuses on the relationship between science
and technology, productive forces and the social relations of production, and Marx and historical materialism. After Marx, the
technical application of science to production becomes more
socially and psychologically sophisticated with the introduction
of new techniques for the rationalization and legitimation of

production. These new forms of the social organization of production included Taylorism, scientific management, human relations technology, and consumer psychology and advertising that only intensify work production and the extraction of surplus and profits at the same time they validate the exploitation of human labor through science, technology, and business management. The goal of production is not the satisfaction of human needs and the common good but the creation of a more profitable economy for the accumulation of private property and class power over nature and humanity. The metaphysical principles of the domination of nature are extended into the domination of humanity through the division of labor, scientific management, restructuring the organization of production, rationalized bureaucracy, and the hidden values of science. Here again science acts as a political ideology as it legitimates the intensification and exploitation of human labor at the expense of human potentiality. Science, as part of the technical and productive forces of society, also reflects the broader social relations or social organization of production. Science is used to justify the modernization and reorganization of industrial production in order to further rationalize the specialization, class division of labor, and the managerial control over the workplace in order to further ensure the appropriate redistribution of power and profits in production. At first, what appears to be merely the rational technology of modern society also includes the political and social dimensions of the very organization of capitalist production.

Of special interest of study in this chapter is the dialectical relationship within Marx's theory of historical materialism and the economic mode of production between the scientific and technological forces of production on the one hand and the social relationships and structural organization of production on the other. One aspect of the mode of production is intimately connected with and inseparable from the other; they both exist in a dialectical relationship with each other. To initiate the application of the instrumental and productive forces in production, that is, to rationalize production itself, it is also necessary to

restructure the social and class relations of power and organization. To export these technical innovations today in production
to foreign countries is to also export the social forms of capitalism
and neoliberalism. Being a product of modern society, the science
and technology of industrial production include the foundational
principles of modern capitalism. That is, science is not neutral
or objective since it reflects and imposes an a priori political and
economic dimension that includes both the technical and social
aspects of the capitalist mode of production. The rationalization
and alienation of work always contain both elements of production—the technical and social features of work. Science appears
to introduce rational technology, greater efficiency, and increased
productivity, but it does so through corporate centralized control,
the de-skilling of workers, labor market fragmentation, and the
centralization and monopolization of knowledge in production.
Science thereby both legitimates and rationalizes the further alienation of the existing class structure and its monopoly control over
production.

Part III, "Social Science, Positivism, and the Domination of
Reason and Society," establishes that the political imperative
and drive to dominate is not just a characteristic of natural science. It is also found in the study and application of positivism
and the social sciences. The section begins with an analysis of
David Hume's initial defense of positivism and empirical science,
but also includes later epistemological skepticism and critique of
the internal logical errors of empiricism and induction; rationalism, causality, and deduction; and realism and objective reality.
Neither the senses, perception, or reason can justify the objects of
perception through induction or through deduction (billiard ball
thesis); nor can they justify the existence of an objective reality
(realism). We can only perceive and know our impressions of the
world, but not the world itself. This radical skepticism will shape
questions about the nature of science over the next two and a half
centuries well into the positivist dispute in German sociology. It
will continue into the mid-twentieth century to inform Weber's

theory of rationalization, Max Horkheimer's theory of the dialectic of enlightenment and the eclipse of reason, and C. Wright Mills's critique of abstracted positivism in the form of quantitative and qualitative sociology. According to Mills, sociology, because of its underlying positivist theory of knowledge and science, has been unable to make any truly critical advances or insights into the nature of modern capitalism and its corresponding theory of liberal democracy.

In chapter 5 the discussion of the domination of humanity shifts from the natural sciences to the social sciences, from nature and production to the academy and social theory. Horkheimer in his work *Eclipse of Reason* (1947) follows the odyssey of the loss of reason and social theory in the tradition of German idealism, existentialism, and phenomenology by tracing the history of Western reason from the objective reason of Greek philosophy, medieval scholasticism, English and French Enlightenment, and German idealism to the "liquidation of reason" by narcissism, Nazism, and positivism. The modern crisis of reason is a long by-product of the Protestant Reformation and the nominalism and relativism produced by rationalism, empiricism, and idealism. Horkheimer pushes the argument of the dialectic and crisis of reason to include both positivism in the social sciences and the loss of ethics and democracy with the rise of fascism. The debate in the 1950s and 1960s between the positivists and critical theorists of the Frankfurt School over the nature of science parallels some of the discussion we have already seen about the natural sciences. With the application of the latter's theories and method to the social sciences, the ability to critically examine the epistemology and methodology of science is greatly weakened as is its ability to criticize the institutions and structures of modern industrial society.

The form of objective or substantive reason is no longer seen as a legitimate form of knowledge in the social sciences; what is lost is the ability to judge the real by the ideal, historical reality and political economy by the ethical and political principles of traditional social and political thought. Horkheimer replaced the

Terror of the French Revolution with the terror of German fascism, the iron cage with the barbed wire of concentration camps. Existentialism, fascism, and positivism are just the modern forms of the domination of humanity filtered through the social sciences. The end result is existentially isolated pleasure seekers without virtue and reason and positivistic scientists without spirit and justice; the traditional values of individual freedom, liberty, rights, and justice are reduced to utilitarian and market qualities. The objective reality of social science has repressed the need for critical reflection and social justice that only further turns science into a form of political ideology. There are no longer social and political ideals by which history can be measured and evaluated. Positivism has silenced Western reason and completed the project begun by existentialism to produce a world empty of critical ideas and moral values. This silencing of reason is also a characteristic of the inner nature of the modern personality whose ideals are now those of the leader, nation, and traditions, thereby replacing those of freedom, democracy, and objective reason. These latter ideals are displaced into the collective unconscious of society. In his analysis, Horkheimer integrates Weber's theory of scientific rationalization with Marx's theory of alienation of labor and consciousness and Freud's theory of psychological repression of the unconscious mind.

The dialectic of natural science and modern capitalism has helped produce a society and cultural lifeworld that has lost a rich assortment of traditional and classical values and principles, including the loss of a metaphysics of a dynamic, organic, and spiritual physical nature; a moral philosophy of natural law, individual responsibility, and existential meaning with the rise of nihilism and the domination of nature; a creative world of productive self-determination, political rights, economic freedom, and human labor with the domination of the workplace; a critical and reflective social science that integrates empirical research and social ethics, science and social justice in an academy imprisoned in an iron cage of positivism that is unable to make moral decisions about the structure and future of modern society; and a loss of ethics (*Sittlichkeit*) and community (*Gemeinschaft*), self-consciousness and critical reflection, and political and economic democracy through the rise of authoritarianism and fascism, the rationalization and disenchantment of nature, and the alienation and derangement of society. The natural and social sciences play a key role in the evolution of these various forms of political displacement as they attempt to suppress the critical responses of the various schools of non-positivistic and non-analytic philosophy and sociology. With the rationalization of science, natural science has participated directly and indirectly in the loss of these traditional forms of substantive reason from individual moral principles and action to the building of integrative social structures and collective institutions. In this disenchanted and dehumanized universe we live without social direction, individual purpose, or existential meaning; we live without creative control and freedom, without spirit and heart, and without a collective conscience and ethical solidarity as we inhabit an empty, homeless world in continuous despair, unquenchable market longing, and anomic industrial production. These conditions and the devolution of Western rationality represent the twilight of Enlightenment reason and social ethics. This chapter ends with a hint of a possible answer to the question of disenchantment, nominalism, and the dialectic of enlightenment with their corresponding loss of reflective and substantive reason. Where Marcuse turned to art as a means of bypassing the failures and loss of substantive and critical reason, Habermas turned to a social theory emphasizing the distinctions between the productive forces and social relations of production (Marx) and systems of political economy and the cultural lifeworld (Parsons) with the development of his theory of intersubjectivity and communicative action. These are important expansions of the methodological debates within the social sciences. However, members of the Frankfurt School overlooked the central importance of political economy and justice in Marx's own theory of social justice, which included civil and human rights

of free speech and public assembly, worker control and ownership, ecological balance and symbiotic relationship with nature,
distributive justice based on human needs and grace, political
freedom and communal democracy, and economic rationality and
democracy.

In chapter 6, on the positivism debate within German sociology, the analysis of the previous chapter in the history of
modern sociology continues, but now goes into the theoretical and practical study of human society within the positivist
debate (*Positivismusstreit*) in the writings of Adorno, Horkheimer,
Popper, Albert, Marcuse, and Habermas. It was Herbert Marcuse
who wrote in his *One-Dimensional Man* (1964): "It is my purpose
to demonstrate the internal instrumentalist character of modern
scientific rationality by virtue of which it is a priori technology and
the a priori of a *specific* technology—namely, technology as a form
of social control and domination."[16] This chapter attempts to show
the interconnection between rationality, technology, and domination. The central question is whether Western science and reason
are a priori technological resulting in the domination of nature
and humanity and whether human and environmental emancipation require a new social and classless context for science or a
new form of science entirely with a new metaphysics and a priori
value system based on social justice. That is, does science necessarily entail an objectivity, neutrality, and domination of nature and
society or does the problem lie in the social context; that is, does
it lie in the use and abuse of science itself? Are Western science
and reason forms of capitalist consciousness or do they transcend
the historical context and are thus applicable in any social system?
This is the fundamental and classic debate between Marcuse and
Habermas.

This discussion within German social theory between Marcuse
and Habermas leads to an analysis of the contemporary Marxist
debate between the Instrumental and the Structural Marxists over
the nature of science, technology, and the social organization of
production. This debate, in turn, leads us to a reconsideration of

Marx's theory of the logic and contradictions within political economy between labor and capital, human needs and surplus value, as well as the contradictions within nature between alienated labor and the metabolic rift and within science between a metaphysics of death and a politics of worker control. Marx's theories of the alienation, contradictions, and the logic of nature are grounded in his prior analyses of human nature and work (*Economic and Philosophic Manuscripts of 1844*), political liberalism and natural rights (*On the Jewish Question*), and capitalism and economic crises (*Grundrisse* and *Capital*). Modern capitalism is fractured by unresolvable and structural divisions that make the realization of its social and political ideals impossible: the divisions between creative and self-defining labor and alienated labor, the political and democratic rights to freedom of speech and assembly and the economic and market rights to private property and economic liberty, and the economic growth to satisfy human needs and the common good as opposed to the exploitation of labor and the private accumulation of surplus value and property. Distortions in the modern industrial system appear in the logic of industrial work, liberal rights, and capital production because the total social system in Marx's view is internally inconsistent and structurally contradictory, thus making it both irrational and unethical.

There has been an extensive debate among Marxist scholars over the roles of science in Marx's thought. In order to transform society into a democratic and free moral economy must science transcend the historical context of production and the social relations of production? That is, can science and technology be used as the basis for this revolutionary transformation toward democratic socialism and worker ownership and control over production? This is the position taken by Instrumental Marxists with their theory of technical or dialectical materialism. This school of thought has been supported by Alfred Schmidt, Jürgen Habermas, William Leiss, Charles Taylor, Jeremy Shapiro, and Anthony Wilden. This latter group, although extensively criticizing the implications and conclusions of the Structural Marxists, has argued that Marx did in fact have an instrumentalist view of science, believing that science is independent of society and thus applicable in both capitalist and socialist societies,

A second tradition within Marxist social theory argues for an alternative to this technological and dialectical determinism. It takes a more historical and structuralist approach, contending that Marx viewed the natural sciences more critically as a form of *Herrschaftswissen* and, therefore, as a product of the class system, alienated labor, and the social organization of production of capitalist society (André Gorz, Herbert Marcuse, Ernst Bloch, Ben Agger, and William Ophuls). A more radical approach to the ecological crisis would necessarily involve a more profound understanding of the complexity of the social totality consisting of issues of science, technology, and democracy, as well as those of social justice. The critical discussion between the two approaches to Marx's view of science expresses the relationship and priority between science as a neutral productive force and rational technology and science as a reflection of the deeper social relations and oppressive organization of capitalist production. This latter structuralist position maintains that the domination of humanity in the social relations of production precedes the actual domination of nature by the productive forces. Thus, science and technology are the product of capitalist domination as its method and theories evolved from its social structures and broader cultural values. Science in the first instance is viewed as a narrow economic and formal category and in the second instance is seen as a sociological and political force. The instrumentalists claim that science is a neutral technology that can be the basis for radical social change in both capitalism and socialism, whereas the structuralist approach emphasizes the historical boundedness, class structure, and social relations of production that underlie scientific categories. In the latter case, science and technology are part of the broader process of production and logic of capital and thus cannot be conceptually divorced from it.

In summary, this section undertakes an in-depth critical investigation into the modern crisis of Western science with its hidden and often unconscious metaphysical and political foundations and its technical applications in the fields of the domination of nature and the ecology, the economy and production, and society and democracy. Both the natural and the social sciences are social constructs and products of the structures, institutions, and cultural values of European industrial society. They are, therefore, grounded in the fundamental metaphysical and political value systems of that society that, in turn, direct the formulation of their distinctive epistemologies, method, and theories. Science is thus a priori political and ideological, not only in its technical application, but in its theoretical construction. Science reflects the hidden and unconscious values of Western capitalism in its mechanical and materialist metaphysics, testable hypothesis construction, natural theory formulation, and methodical verification of empiricism and nominalism. Even before its technical and formal application to the environment, economic production, and academic disciplines, science as pure theory is not objective and neutral but guided by fundamental social and political values that are rarely articulated and even less often recognized. Science is a political philosophy that must be carefully deconstructed; it is a priori political because of the numerous features built into its conceptual, methodological, and theoretical framework and substructures.

These hidden political assumptions make the application of science to social, as well as environmental and ecological issues, extremely problematic and open to further public discussion. Therefore, the goal of this work is to examine in detail the complex relationships among Enlightenment science, liberalism, and capitalism in order to capture the underlying rationality of natural and social science as a manifestation of a particular historical and social moment in time and ultimately a product of post-seventeenth-century Western society. This leads us to the key question, discussed in the last two chapters in this book: If science is a reflection of the social organization of production, can the products of capitalism—Western science and technology—solve the ecological problems originally created by capitalism itself? That is, can the master's tools solve the master's problems (Audre Lorde)? Traditionally, these issues have remained repressed and unacknowledged, hidden in the blind shadows of the Enlightenment or summarily dismissed as operational or technical anomalies.

To adequately consider the politics of science—the metaphysics, methodology, and technology of science—along with the corresponding crisis of the organic environment, we must also reflect upon a social critique of political economy and the principles and structures of a true democracy. Ecological justice necessarily entails social justice since one without the other is meaningless.

The critical theorists took the position that advanced monopoly capitalism changed in many ways that undermined the traditional Marxist criticism of modernity. Nineteenth- and early twentieth-century liberal values and ideals no longer could be used as the basis for immanent and dialectical critique. The rationality of objective or substantive reason had been replaced by Enlightenment science, technology, and rationality, which could not be used to criticize the social system that they only reinforced and expanded. The critical theorists spent their academic lives looking for legitimate mechanisms that would justify criticisms of advanced capitalist societies and neoliberalism. It was an exciting period in the second half of the twentieth century as they looked for new ways by which they could call capitalism into question: (1) with the loss of objective reason and its historical traditions going back to ancient Greek philosophy and its replacement by positivism and naturalism there was a corresponding loss of critical social theory, resulting in the dialectic of enlightenment and moral disenchantment (Adorno and Horkheimer); (2) with the rise of scientific and technological rationality, there was a loss of the need for cultural, ethical, and political legitimation that provided the theoretical foundations for social critique (Marcuse); (3) in contemporary society the rationality and expansion of science, technology, and production replaced the need for the political ideology and social ideals of liberalism stressing natural and political rights and personal freedom, resulting in a crisis of legitimation and loss of immanent critique (Marcuse and Habermas); and (4) with the rise of technological rationality in a one-dimensional society, the possibility of a dialectical critique of the internal structural contradictions of political economy and capital was viewed as no longer relevant, resulting in the loss of political economy and economic theory (Habermas). The end result was the transformation of critical social theory based on the ethical and economic contradictions of modern capitalism into a critique of the culture industry (Adorno and Horkheimer), the aesthetic critique of Marcuse, and the theory of communicative action and colonization of the cultural lifeworld of Habermas. They all looked for alternative approaches to social criticism that went beyond Marx. The heart of the latter's social theory was replaced by a critique of the culture industry, epistemology, and metatheory.

The goal of this book is to recognize these lost traditions and integrate the critique of the system of political economy and the culture of the lifeworld into a dialectical history of the evolution of human consciousness beyond Kantian philosophy and the French Revolution (Hegel) to present possibilities of a free and democratic society. This undertaking would be an extremely difficult and daunting one. Fortunately, however, this project was already started in the writings of Marx, as he had already integrated a comprehensive phenomenology of the spirit and collective consciousness based on Hegel's phenomenology and theory of the state, an extensive integration of ethics (virtue and happiness) and politics (political democracy and moral economy), classical and modern humanism and political economy based on Aristotle's theory and major works, and a broad overview of the historical and institutional possibilities for democratic socialism that rested in the Athenian polity of classical Greece, the French Revolution and the French Constitutions of 1789 (declaration of the rights of man), 1791, 1793, and 1795, the Paris Commune of 1871, and the Iroquois Confederacy of Nations of the seventeenth and eighteenth centuries in Indigenous America. This integration of Greek philosophy, German Idealism, French socialism, British political economy, and British and German Romanticism and poetry provided Marx with the political and civil ideals and social institutions that could build upon the insights of Aristotle, Kant, Hegel, and Schiller.

But Marx did not stop there, as he integrated these modern insights into an even broader and more comprehensive understanding of the history of Western thought, reason, and consciousness. Although never part of a scholarly work or academic presentation because of his life and political commitments in exile, there was in Marx's social theory, however implicit and unrecognized for many years, a theory of the self-constitution of the collective spirit. He accomplished this by borrowing from the ancient Hebrews and Mosaic code of law from Deuteronomy, Leviticus, and the Prophets, the Hellenes of classical Greece, the Hellenists of the Followers of the Way and early Christians, and modern poetry, art, philosophy, and political economy. These traditions provided him with the context and content for his ethics and politics that framed the whole structure of his early and later writings on ethical humanism and political democracy. In this manner Marx was able to connect Aristotle's social ethics and political democracy with Hegel's phenomenology of the ethical community and spirit of the family, civil society, and the state (*Sittlichkeit*) within which the essential moral life of individuals develops. He was able to integrate ethics and politics into his theory of social justice and critique of industrial capitalism. The result is a form of human experience and existence that represents a synthesis of beauty and ideals—grace, harmony, elegance, and inspiration expressed in their highest forms of aesthetics and politics.

True beauty is a production of imaginative and creative human labor in art, material well-being, and economic democracy; it is the realization of the potentiality of the human heart, reason, and community. It is a form of Western consciousness and spirit from the ancients to the moderns that exalts a political existence based on individual freedom, self-determination, human creativity, aesthetic and poetic labor, communal and moral economy, public dialogue and discursive reason, a common concern for the weakest members of society, satisfaction of human needs, and democratic socialism. Ultimately, beauty is public happiness and social justice in action. It is a society imagined by Marx that not only recapitulates the phenomenal history of Western consciousness and Athenian ideals (Hegel), the classical integration of ethics and politics (Aristotle), and the potentially emancipatory and historical structures of political economy (modern economic and political theory) into a comprehensive theory of social justice, but it also becomes the foundation for a later theory of communication and social critique of advanced capitalism in the twenty-first century.

To summarize this introduction, we turn to Kant's fundamental insight that what we know in perception and experience are only "representations" of reality, but not objective reality or the thing-in-itself. Once the Kantian revolution in epistemology is established in the eighteenth century and the radical nature of Kant's critique of pure reason and theory of knowledge is fully appreciated, much of the following history of Western thought is an attempt to clarify the nature of "representations" as constructs of transcendental subjectivity, phenomenal consciousness, the metaphysics of science, the methodological imperative for the domination of nature, the existential crisis of nothingness, nihilism, and the iron cage, and, finally, the logic of capitalist production and historical materialism. Each one of these traditions is featured as a chapter in this book, tracing the evolution of Kantian thought from idealism, phenomenology, pragmatism, neo-Kantian and postmodern philosophy of science, existentialism, Marxism, and critical social theory of the Frankfurt School. Each chapter discusses a different intellectual tradition that defines and delineates a different means by which "representations" are translated and understood in philosophy, political economy, and sociology. What begins as a constitution of objectivity and reality through consciousness and the mind ends with a constitution of objectivity through the logic of capital. Tracing this evolution of various epistemological and social theories of science and knowledge will reveal how they have been understood using the metaphors of the mirror of nature, the mirror of production, and the mirror of social justice.

The historical form of unarticulated and hidden assumptions, values, and ideologies that are deeply embedded in modern natural and social sciences—the shadows of the Enlightenment—are reflected in the following areas:

Chapters 1–3: Hidden Assumptions of Science in Metaphysics, Metatheory, and Methodology and the Domination of Nature and the Environment

a. *Metaphysics and Machines*: the natural world has no meaning or teleological purpose as it is a dead, deterministic machine which is amenable to predictive measurement and analysis of the material world of time, space, matter, and motion.

b. *Metatheory and Domination*: the distinctive philosophy of knowledge and science maintains that scientific inquiry consists of the development of mathematical, quantitative, and deterministic laws for the expressed purpose of the domination of nature (*Herrschaftswissen*). The traditional epistemological approaches in empiricism, rationalism, analytic philosophy, and the modern forms of positivism with their search for objective truth and reality (ontology) are replaced by issues of technical usefulness and scientific predictability (utility).

c. *Methodology and Objectivity*: the distinctive form of scientific inquiry begins with the universal laws of science, recognition of a particular problem, hypothesis construction, scientific experimentation and testing, observation of the results, and the empirical verification or falsification of the original hypothesis. In science, method creates the objectivity of both research and reality, methodology and the objects of experience and knowledge. Every important issue and method related to the environment, ecological crises, and the social pathologies of political economy that do not conform to this approach are repressed, forgotten, or lost in an eclipse of reason. This results in the loss of critical theory in classical and contemporary European and American social thought.

Chapters 4–6: Science as A Priori Technological, Political, and Economic and the Domination of Nature, Political Economy, Society, and Reason

d. *Technology and Utility*: the utility and technical application of science for industrial expansion and increased formal efficiency in work for the purpose of the domination and control of nature. The very concepts, theories, and method of natural science, found in a, b, and c above, contain an a priori technological imperative for the domination of nature (*Herrschaftswissen*).

e. *Politics, Ideology, and the Domination of Humanity and Reason*: the ideological application of formal reason and science to justify and maintain the power of private property and the class organization of production within a capitalist society for the purposes of the rationalization of work and the domination of human beings. Human alienation and exploitation become rationalized and validated through formal reason, modern science, and industrial technology. The a priori technological aspect of science thus contains a social imperative in the form of an a priori political element to rationalize and justify not only the productive/technical forces of modern industry—science and technology—but also the historically specific form of capitalism and class structure in the workplace. When the same set of categories, theories, and method are applied in the social sciences in the various forms of positivism in order to examine social and political issues, the main result is the domination of reason and the loss of critical and substantive thought, that is, the loss of social theory itself.

f. *Economics and the Class Structure of Capitalist Society*: the historical and materialist understanding of the origins of Western consciousness, thought, and science as abstract and theoretical reflections of the social relations and class organization of capitalist production of abstract and surplus labor and the bureaucracy and calculation of market and commodity exchange. The historical origins of natural science lie in the inner rationalization, logic, and abstractions (balance sheets, costs, prices, wages, profits, etc.) of commercial and industrial capitalism and the class system. Science reflects the shadows, hidden assumptions, and inner logic of capital as it introduces through its method, concepts, theories, and experiments the a priori political and a priori economic imperatives toward the capitalist domination of nature, work, industry, humanity, and reason, whether consciously intended or not. These are the hidden and unrecognized "shadows of the Enlightenment."

Each of these areas of the hidden assumptions and normative values found in metaphysics, epistemology, methodology, technology, and political economy will be further examined and developed in the chapters that follow. The concluding chapter will attempt to move beyond these shadows and shades of modern reason by laying the foundations for an emancipatory postmodern science and technology by placing the natural and social sciences within the structural and historical framework of Habermas's theory of communicative action and public discourse and Marx's theory of economic democracy and social justice. This will also recreate the classical Greek vision and dreams of Aristotelian democracy and social ecology within the institutions of modern industrial society in an attempt to provide us with the potentiality for a new and liberating future. This integration of the Frankfurt School and Marx's political economy is an attempt to revive the critical imagination and economic dreams that move beyond the eclipse of positivism, the loss of objective and ethical reason, and the twilight of American social theory.

PART I

The Crisis of Natural Science, Technology, and the Domination of Nature

Social Epistemology and Radical Pragmatism of Postmodernism: Thomas Kuhn and Richard Rorty

IN THIS CHAPTER WE EXAMINE the contemporary discussions in American pragmatic thought regarding the nature of knowledge, science, and society. Contemporary philosophers of science Willard Van Quine, Thomas Kuhn, and Richard Rorty, building on the late nineteenth- and early twentieth-century tradition of pragmatism founded by William James, Charles Peirce, John Dewey, and George Herbert Mead,[1] have opened new doors of scientific inquiry based on their break with analytic philosophy and their dialogue with European thought. The pragmatists pushed the epistemological arguments of the nineteenth century to their logical extreme and ultimately rejected both empiricism and rationalism as adequate foundations for truth claims. Instead, they turned to a consensus within the scientific community to justify the appropriate method of objective knowledge. What they accomplished was a reintegration of science and politics, truth and democracy. The result was that another avenue of methodological discussion was reopened which sought to reconstruct the relationships between science and ethics.

Here we will trace the development of contemporary pragmatism from Quine's theory of the underdetermination of experience and myth of objectivity and Kuhn's theory of paradigms and scientific revolutions to Rorty's theory of epistemological privilege and political nihilism. Contemporary American pragmatism has responded to the question of objectivity in science in a variety of interesting ways. The nature of objectivity has been transformed over time from a philosophical question about the nature of truth and reality to a sociological question about the interests and priorities of society, that is, it has been transformed from an epistemological (universality) and ontological (being) category into a question of scientific method (Popper), technical utility (Quine), puzzle-solving and consensus (Kuhn), and social practice (Rorty). The Duhem-Quine thesis and the Popper-Quine debates provide crucial foundations for the development of this transformation in the way science is viewed within the history and philosophy of science.

POPPER-QUINE DISPUTE AND THE CRITIQUE OF EMPIRICISM

In 1934 Karl Popper published his famous work, *The Logic of Scientific Discovery*, in which he attempted to provide the natural sciences with clear methodological foundations. It produced a profound effect in the philosophical community as he read past Hume's defense of positivism and revived the latter's skeptical arguments about the justification of science in *An Enquiry Concerning Human Understanding* (1748).[2] Popper's assault on both empiricism and inductive logic was grounded in Hume's own original problem of justification that had been conveniently misplaced for nearly two hundred years. There had always been a tension between Hume's empiricism and skepticism, but the history of philosophy had tended to rely merely on the former. Replying to the generally accepted view of the natural sciences, Popper revisits Hume's epistemology when he argues that universal statements cannot be derived from the accumulation of many singular experiences. The example of "All swans are white" is derived in just this manner and Popper, following David Hume, argues that it is not logically justifiable. No matter how many observed instances of white swans there may have been in the past, there is no logical justification for this universal statement. It may correspond to all the rules of common sense, but there remains a problem of how one philosophically justifies the obvious. Hume argues that "even after the observation of the frequent or constant conjunction of objects, we have no reason to draw any inference concerning any object beyond those of which we have had experience."[3] Hume concludes that in the final analysis causality is simply a psychological connection that the mind makes through subjective habit. Popper is aware of Hume's refutation of inductive reasoning and the logical problem of infinite regress.[4] In the end, he too concludes that inductive inferences are logically unjustifiable since they must incorporate inductive reasoning into the proof of induction itself which commits a logical fallacy of infinite regress—utilizing the very thing that requires justification. Induction is used as the basis for justifying inductive inferences. The statement "All swans are white" is true, because all previous observations of swans have shown them to be white.

Popper concludes by arguing that the principle of induction cannot provide science with the secure logical and methodological foundation that it requires. He recognizes the immensity of the issue at stake. Quoting from H. Reichenbach, he writes, "To eliminate it [the principle of induction] from science would mean nothing less than to deprive science of its power to decide the truth or falsity of its theories. Without it, clearly, science would no longer have the right to distinguish its theories from the fanciful and arbitrary creations of the poet's mind."[5] Against the overwhelming acceptance of this principle by science, Popper concludes that it is superfluous and logically inconsistent. Experience and induction can never be the foundation for universal statements or scientific knowledge. Instead, he argues that the origins of ideas or theories making claims to universal validity is a psychological question and not an epistemological or logical one. Science begins where history, imagination, and inspiration leave off. He is no longer concerned with the older approaches of epistemology, which begin by tracing ideas back to their origins in impressions or experience. Rather, he begins with these ideas and seeks answers to their justification or validity in practice by deducing predictive statements from their original insights and testing them against experience. Ideas cannot be verified as absolutely true by showing how they mirror impressions, but can, in fact, be falsified when their predictions are shown not to come true. Popper has transplanted the logical justification of science from induction to deduction, from the logic of inquiry to the logic of justification. "But I shall certainly admit a system as empirical or scientific only if it is capable of being *tested* by experience. These considerations suggest that not the *verifiability* but the *falsifiability* of a system is to be taken as a criterion of demarcation."[6] It is the scientific method and practice of theoretical conjecture, deductive hypothesis formation, competition of ideas, predictive explanations, testability, and potential refutation that defines theories as scientific, not their reduction to or verification by experience. Objectivity is a function of the rules of method and logic. "The so-called objectivity of science lies in the objectivity of the critical method."[7]

Popper was instrumental in weakening the hold of logical positivism of the Vienna School on philosophy of science. His critique of empiricism and Hume's dilemma was an important step in the later development of even more critical theories of knowledge. Years later Willard Van Quine wrote his famous essay titled "Two Dogmas of Empiricism" (1951) that further radicalizes the critique of positivism. In this essay he articulates a number of different critical theses about the nature of science that include: (1) the breakdown of the distinction between analytical and synthetic statements; (2) the underdetermination of theory by experience; (3) the difference between the theoretical core and empirical periphery; (4) uncovering the myth of objectivity; (5) critique of Popper and his theory of falsification; and (6) the development of *ad hoc* scientific theories to explain anomalies.[8] These attempts to reframe the nature of empiricism would later be very important in Kuhn's *Theory of Scientific Revolutions* (1962).

According to Quine, the two dogmas of empiricism are represented by the doctrine of the distinction between analytic and synthetic truths and the theory of radical reductionism (radical empiricism). The former asserts that there are two distinct kinds of truths: analytic and synthetic statements. Analytic truths are not based on experience, but are logical or tautological in nature. In analytic statements the predicate is derived from the subject and adds no more information than is already contained in the subject itself. Their truth comes not from matters of fact, but from logical or mathematical relations of ideas independent of experience. Thus these statements can never be self-contradictory, nor can they add to our understanding of the experiential world. He offers two examples of such types of truths. The statement "No unmarried man is married" is logically true, whereas "No bachelor is married" is synonymously true. The second type of statement is a synthetic truth that is grounded in experiential facts and can only be derived from sense perception. It expands our knowledge of the world through the accumulation of empirical information.

The second dogma of empiricism is that of radical reductionism or empirical verification which refers to the belief that every meaningful statement can ultimately be traced back to immediate experience. Truth must be the result of direct empirical confirmation of statements by experience. Quine undertakes a general critique of empiricism by arguing that the distinction between analytic and synthetic statements, accepted since Immanuel Kant, is a false distinction.[9] In the actual course of acquiring scientific knowledge the differences between logic and experience, universal and contingent statements of meaning break down. "Furthermore, it becomes folly to seek a boundary between synthetic statements which hold contingently on experience, and analytic statements which hold come what may. Any statement can be held true come what may, if we make drastic enough adjustments elsewhere in the system."[10]

Quine divides science into the core and periphery. The core of science contains the fully developed theory, which is built on complex abstractions, subtle ideas, mathematical relationships, and logical connections, whereas the periphery contains the experiential element that lies at the edge of a theoretical model. Experience and theory touch only at the outer reaches or margins of a theory. "The totality of our so-called knowledge or beliefs, from the most casual matters of geography and history to the profoundest laws of atomic physics or even of pure mathematics and logic, is a man-made fabric which impinges on experience only along the edges."[11] Though Quine argues that science is a "linguistic structure that is keyed to observation at some points," not every sentence in science has an observational reference or empirical content; can be reduced to or verified by empirical impressions; or has an independent, synthetic meaning all its own.[12] From his theory of language (publicly shared sensory stimulations, observations, and inductions, and similarity and analogical synthesis) and science (holism and indeterminism), Quine contends that observations and experience only touch scientific laws along the empirical edges and therefore cannot be the only foundation of science.[13] One cannot move immediately between concept and reality, theory and experience, since the boundary conditions of analytic and synthetic statements have disappeared. As one gets closer to the theoretical heart of science, one is farthest removed from experience. Roger Gibson summarizes Quine's position:

> From a Quinian perspective, the three hundred years from Descartes to Carnap (Idealism aside) were dominated by a forlorn squabble revolving around the comparative foundationalist merits of innate ideas and sense data. . . . Both the *deduction* of and the *reconstruction* of knowledge of the external world on the basis of some epistemologically prior footing are impossible dreams.[14]

Quine concludes from this underdetermination of scientific knowledge by experience that when there is a conflict between the core and periphery, ideas and experience, adjustments within the system can be made that will explain away the recalcitrant factual information or readjust its theoretical explanation. As a result of this understanding of scientific inquiry, the traditional distinction between analytic and synthetic statements can no longer be held. Scientific statements based on empirical evidence or theoretical laws have the same logical content. Since empirical information can be manipulated to appear as analytic statements, so, too, may abstract universals be altered to have contingent properties. This is, in turn, connected with Quine's other thesis that scientific theories are learned as whole unities and any disputed sentence within the theory cannot represent a disputation of the whole. This is the famous Duhem-Quine thesis of holism which states that adverse observations cannot disprove a physical theory as other elements within a theory can be revised. Theories and language are learned as totalities and are not reducible to simple impressions of observations. As Paul Roth has written, "One consequence of the Duhem thesis, however, is the denial that there exist any clear-cut observational notions. The notions of truth and of facticity seem, on Quine's account, to be purely internal (immanent) to the theory with which one is working."[15]

Concomitant with this position runs the argument that because a theory is underdetermined, there can be multiple conflicting theories applicable to the natural world that although logically incompatible are empirically equivalent and acceptable.[16] Despite his rejection of traditional empiricism and rationalism and his critical reservations about science, Quine does hold to a transformed view of empiricism as a naturalized epistemology or empirical psychology. Since all evidence for truth claims in science ultimately comes from sensory evidence, epistemology must examine the process of learning, socialization, and the acquisition of language, experience, and knowledge.[17]

The traditional philosophical foundations of science are

unraveling further. Quine's holism, his rejection of the analytic-synthetic distinction, and the underdetermination of theory lead to his scientific pragmatism. Cornel West writes that Quine's rejection of the analytic and synthetic distinction is a result of his leaning on the anti-dualistic pragmatism of Emerson, James, and Dewey.[18] Gibson and J. Smart have both argued that Quine's empiricism and naturalism integrate instrumentalism and realism. Science is to be used as a tool for quantitative measurement, precise predictions, and hypothesis refutation, at the same time that it confirms the existence of real physical objects.[19]

What then becomes of the "foundation" of science? For Quine, it lies in the evidence provided by our sensory experience (realism and naturalism) and in the utility of science for predicting future events based on past experiences. Epistemology has been replaced by psychology and sociology—the examination of the influence of the external world on our sensory mechanisms and by the technical application of science in society. Both replace the traditional concerns about first philosophy and the truth and falsity of knowledge. As mentioned above, physical reality is a social construct comparable to the gods of Homer. Truth is measured not by empirical reality, but by its management of experience and its usefulness in prediction. Within this theory of knowledge, the mythology of the Homeric pantheon with its competing gods and empirical reality have the same ontological status. Science cannot mediate between the truth claims of either approach in order to determine the reality of the external world. What distinguishes science from Homeric mythology in the end is the ability of the former to create explanatory and predictive theories. Science is more adept at organizing and systematizing experience into a coherent unity. It posits a world of manageable objects, forces, and laws used for predicting future occurrences. The Homer myths cannot do this with the regularity and universality necessary in the modern world. Therefore, they must be rejected as epistemologically untrue. The basis for verification comes not from a term or statement, but from the whole of science itself and its pragmatic ability to organize our experience about the world around us. According to West, Quine never radically pushes these criticisms of epistemology to their logical conclusion. He is still caught in the "residues of logical positivism," that is, he is still caught in the epistemological principles and ontological realism of physics and foundationalism.[20] Despite Quine's criticism of traditional theories of knowledge, he remains committed to new forms of naturalism, scientism, realism, and non-dogmatic empiricism.[21]

Whatever later criticism of Popper and Quine might develop, both attack directly the foundations of traditional epistemology in rationalism and empiricism—the grounding of a first philosophy in a priori, synthetic truths or in immediate sense perception, and the deduction of science from these points of certitude. In the process, they sought alternatives to truth claims and verification in fallibilism and the reliability of the hypothetical-deductive method.

From Epistemology to the History of Science and Paradigms

In 1962 Thomas Kuhn published his famous work, *The Structure of Scientific Revolutions*. Written for the flagship journal of Anglo-American analytic philosophy, *International Encyclopedia of Unified Science*, it represented a fundamental and irreparable break with the positivist tradition. It challenged its assumptions and values about the nature of the logic and method of science and moved the discussion about these issues from philosophy of science to the history and sociology of science. Metatheoretical reflections on the nature of science were to be replaced by an historical understanding of the practice and revolutionary changes within science itself. In the preface, Kuhn acknowledges his reliance on many key figures within the history of science, including Alexandre Koyré, Emile Meyerson, Hélène Metzger, Anneliese Maier, and A. O. Lovejoy, the psychology of perception of Jean Piaget and gestalt psychology, the linguistic anthropology of B.

Benjamin Whorf, the epistemology of Willard Quine and Paul Feyerabend, and the sociology and philosophy of Ludwik Fleck.[22]

Kuhn's work is extremely important because it introduces ideas into American philosophy that are very new and exciting. Though these same ideas were part of the philosophical tradition in Germany for a hundred years, they call into question the American belief in positivism and scientific objectivity. Kuhn, following Popper, makes the distinction between the context of discovery and the context of justification. Unlike Popper, however, he is critical of any philosophy of science that contains a mythic idealization of the logic and method of the natural sciences. It also means that the strict differentiation in German philosophy between *Naturwissenschaften* and *Geisteswissenschaften* (natural and social sciences) is no longer tenable. Kuhn directly confronts both empiricism and rationalism as inadequate to the study of the method of science because they are grounded upon a faulty understanding of the way science actually functions in history. Epistemology has treated science as something in a social and historical vacuum and instead formulates ideal-type categories about the way it must rationally work. Moving beyond epistemology, Kuhn rejects the notion that science represents an incremental and piecemeal development of universal knowledge. He also refuses to accept the idea that it has clear rules of logical procedures and methodological practice; its theories and laws could be verified or falsified; its theories are reflections of absolute truth; it develops through accumulated conjectures and refutation; it is grounded in self-reflection and empirical fact; and its claim to objectivity is based on observation, accumulated experience, and the scientific method. Kuhn is skeptical that these traditional positivist perspectives could explain how science actually develops. Therefore he argues for the need to introduce an historical and sociological analysis of the context in which science develops to combat the one-sidedness of the context of justification.

Kuhn calls for the creation of a "new image of science" which he introduces with his concept of "paradigm."[23] Though shifting metaphors throughout his work as he attempts to explain his new ideas, scientific paradigms are essentially conceptual frameworks or theoretical models within which science organizes the massive amount of empirical information that accumulates over time.[24] The whole scientific process of observation, experimentation, and hypothesis construction is filtered through the prevailing historical paradigms. The choice of empirical data, measurement techniques, and the systematic collection of evidence is mediated by the scientific model. Kuhn argues that the "paradigm is prerequisite to perception itself. What a man sees depends both upon what he looks at and also upon what his previous visual-conceptual experience has taught him to see."[25] These paradigms function quite differently from the orthodox view of scientific theories and laws. Their development does not result from the application of rational methods and procedures over time, but are produced through arbitrary and contingent changes that have structural similarities to mythical beliefs, ideological commitments, religious conversions, and political subversions. They are grounded in irrational social forces which Kuhn explains using political, religious, and cultural metaphors that determine what is acceptable scientific knowledge. Objectivity no longer reflects ontological truths but a consensus within the scientific community about which issues and problems are important to solve. Kuhn's analysis of the history of science and critique of traditional epistemology represents an epistemological revolution in American thought in the mid-1960s.

Kuhn's theory of scientific paradigms is informed by his readings in gestalt psychology. Its theory of perception and consciousness is Kantian in orientation and directly undermines the positivist view of objectivity. It assumes that the mind is actively engaged in the constitution of the objects of experience. Kuhn sees direct parallels between shifts in perception in gestalt psychology and paradigm shifts in scientific discovery. In the famous gestalt experiment of differing perceptions, individuals are asked to look at two drawings: one a drawing of a duck and the other a drawing of a box.

In the drawing of a duck, some participants see ducks and others see rabbits; some see the box from below, others see it from above. Perception of reality is filtered through the forms of consciousness. There is never a direct access to an empirically given world independent of the process of perception. Kuhn believes that these experiments in psychology reflect the reality of scientific observation, since different theoretical configurations cause scientists to see different realities.

He refers to two other well-known psychology experiments. The first is the anomalous card experiment in which a red six of spades and a black four of hearts are substituted in a deck of playing cards. The second experiment involves an individual who is fitted with goggles having inverted lenses thereby seeing everything upside down. In the second experiment of inverted perception, the individual, after initial disorientation of seeing an upside-down world, readjusts his perception and returns to normal. The world is seen right-side up while still wearing the goggles. In the first case, the perceiver does not recognize the anomaly and substitutes a correct perception of a black six of spades, while actually looking at a red card. If given more time, the subject in the experiment still does not recognize the anomaly but feels uncomfortable that something is wrong without recognizing the cause. Only after prolonged exposure to the card does the subject begin to identify the problem. Normal perception, or that which is generally anticipated over time, reestablishes itself even in the face of contrary and inconsistent observations. Later, in the postscript to his work, Kuhn writes with more Kantian flavor that we have no direct access to the objects of our knowledge. Though we may share the same stimuli, our sensations and perceptions are mediated through an interpretive process of the mind that involves the socialization and education of individuals in a shared, unconscious language of reality. Stimuli make sense only through abstract thought and, though the stimuli may be the same, the perceptions of reality will be quite different in different scientific communities sharing different theories and paradigms. The form or structure of the mind organizes our perception of reality. This theory of gestalt perception has direct application for Kuhn's theory of paradigms and normal science since in both cases it is the theoretical expectation of the paradigm that defines and limits the content and interpretation of experience.

Kuhn draws a few conclusions from this application of psychology to epistemology. Perception in everyday life and scientific observation are both determined by paradigms, and anomalies arise only with difficulty. There is no immediate access to objectivity or to the thing-in-itself. Thus an explanation of terrestrial motion and a falling object is filtered through Aristotle's theory of constrained fall or Galileo's theory of pendulum motion; a theory of celestial physics through Ptolemy's epicycles and eccentrics or Copernicus's heliocentric theory of astronomy; a theory of air through Presley's theory of phlogiston or Lavoisier's theory of oxygen; and a theory of time and space through Newton's mechanistic ideas of finite time and space or Einstein's theory of relativity. These are all examples of gestalt shifts in scientific observation in which the empirically given is formed through the conceptual framework of the paradigm. Individuals with different paradigms see different phenomena and interpret the natural world through a set of different lenses. And the available data may be consistently and objectively interpreted through different paradigms. There is usually more than one paradigm that can explain the same facts of observation particularly at the early stages of development of normal science.

The conceptual paradigms representing the logic, method, ideas, theories, and laws of science are not the result of accumulated knowledge about the natural world, but rather the form in which the accumulation takes place. Theories precede facts, invention comes before discovery as paradigms pre-select the relevant observations and experiences that would be part of scientific knowledge. The traditional separation of theory and facts is no longer viable. Kuhn is developing ideas that Kant and the neo-Kantians had argued about in the previous century. With Kuhn's

ideas about objectivity, theoretical paradigms, and scientific revolutions, the whole edifice of the logic and method of science
appears to come tumbling down. Paradigms filter the manifold
of experience; they decide on what questions are to be asked
and what issues are important in science. Paradigms represent a
maturation over time of a consensus within the scientific community regarding the important physical objects, theories, laws,
and methods of scientific inquiry. This is what Kuhn calls "normal
science," which he characterizes as an enterprise that attempts "to
force nature into the preformed and relatively inflexible box that
the paradigm supplies."[26]

Kuhn rejects the idea that science evolves through accumulated experiments and fact-gathering in an objective, value-free
environment. He contends that Boyle's law of gas, pressure, and
volume required the prior invention of air as an elastic fluid,
whereas Coulomb's law of electrical attraction could take place
only after electricity was viewed as particles of electric fluid acting
at a distance on other particles. That is, Boyle's law of gas and
Coulomb's theory of electricity both required a prior articulation
of theoretical concepts that helped systematically and coherently
to organize our perception of the world into universal laws. Even
the measuring equipment designed for the experiments, whose
purpose is to prove the validity of these theories, is contingent
upon the conceptual framework of the theories themselves. The
result, according to Kuhn, is that theories guide experimentation,
observation, and the accumulation of empirical evidence. It does
not happen haphazardly or casually. "In the absence of a paradigm
or some candidate for paradigm, all of the facts that could possibly pertain to the development of a given science are likely to
seem equally relevant. . . . No natural history can be interpreted in
the absence of at least some implicit body of intertwined theoretical and methodological belief that permits selection, evaluation,
and criticism."[27] Kuhn's critique of empiricism lies in his historical
understanding that without theoretical models pre-selecting the
relevant empirical facts there can be no science.

At the early stages of development of normal or paradigmatic science, there are usually a number of competing and justifiable theoretical perspectives which are in general agreement with the facts. In astronomy, for example, Nicholas Copernicus published *De Revolutionibus* in 1543 and permanently changed the landscape of European thought. Kuhn has written a work on the Copernican Revolution in terrestrial and celestial physics, but offers a different interpretation of its importance and meaning to the development of Western science. He is aware that the revolutionary transformation of science from the Aristotelian and medieval worldview of Ptolemaic astronomy to the modern perspective of Copernicus was not precipitated by the dramatically superior, factually more accurate, or more predictive theory of Copernicus. "So far the conceptual scheme developed by Copernicus is just as effective as Ptolemy's, but it is surely no more so, and it seems a good deal more cumbersome."[28] In fact, Kuhn contends that even with its complex astronomical categories of equants, epicycles, eccentrics, and deferents, there was no appreciable difference between Ptolemy and Copernicus in terms of observation and measurement. He even takes the unusual position that Aristotle and Ptolemy were as objective and accurate in their observations as Copernicus and Galileo.[29] Kuhn attributes the remarkable success of Copernicus to a revolution in aesthetic consciousness since the superiority of the new system lay not in its technical precision or improved predictive capacity. The decision in favor of Copernicus over Ptolemy was the result of personal taste for an astronomical system based on mathematical elegance, geometric harmony, unified coherence, and planetary symmetry. There were fewer *ad hoc* assumptions about the orbital periods and motion of particular planets since all were now harmoniously linked into a coherent system of planetary motion around the sun. By explaining planetary motion within a sun-centered universe without the need to resort to complex theories of retrograde motion, epicycles, and eccentrics, Copernicus was able to develop an alternative system based on the cosmological heresy of different aesthetic values of harmony, symmetry, and coherence. As Kuhn writes, "Copernicus's arguments are not pragmatic. They appeal, if at all, not to the utilitarian sense of the practicing astronomer but to his aesthetic sense and to that alone. . . . New harmonies did not increase accuracy or simplicity."[30] Others have argued that the change to a Copernican worldview was precipitated by a technical revolution in explanatory prediction of planetary movement.[31] Kuhn states, on the other hand, that the appeal of this new mathematical system was to a small group of Renaissance neo-Platonists who were prepared to accept a geometrical view of the universe.

Though they were attempting to describe planetary motion, they saw "the same constellation of objects" within entirely different interpretations. Kuhn, on the other hand, thinks that the objects themselves are different since Priestley's phlogiston is not Lavoisier's oxygen and Aristotle's theory of natural fall is not Galileo's theory of pendulum movement. Kuhn seems to vacillate over whether normal science creates its own objects and empirical data or simply interprets the same observations differently.

Kuhn rejects an epistemology of empiricism and a theory of verification as an adequate basis for the logic of scientific inquiry because it misconstrues the relationship between concepts and reality. "To the historian, at least, it makes little sense to suggest that verification is establishing the agreement of fact with theory. All historically significant theories have agreed with the facts, but only more or less."[32] There are always multiple paradigms that correspond to and fit reality in some general sense. Kuhn also rejects the rationalism of Popper as an adequate basis for a theory of knowledge.[33] Even a revised theory of falsification or negative de-confirmation of a theory cannot be justified because every paradigm is incomplete and imperfect and thus never entirely fits experience. Ultimately, all theories are subject to falsification since they never entirely fit the existing facts. There are always anomalous observations. This is what constitutes the game of science and its attempt to solve the puzzles each paradigm was constructed to resolve.

Kuhn views the problems associated with Popper's theory of falsification as a variation of the logical problems of verification. Both
rest on similar shifting epistemological grounds; both are built on
systems of thought and non-empirical assumptions which argue
that the criterion for truth as verification or falsification lies within
contingent conceptual paradigms. There is no value-neutral van-
tage point within the system of language which would permit an
objective interpretation for the justification or confirmation of a
theory. That is, there is no external or transcendent position from
which to verify or falsify a theory other than a paradigm's own
standards of meaning. Paradigms cannot be compared to an objective standard or objective reality that decides the relative value of a
particular theoretical claim to truth. The choice between competing paradigms cannot be made on a basis that approximates the
truth of empirical reality. Each conceptual framework provides its
own criteria for evaluation. The history of science is not the history
of truth; nor does the development of scientific categories represent greater approximation to true being. Kuhn has disconnected
the relationship between concepts and reality, epistemology and
ontology. Science is no longer making claims about the world in
the traditional sense. Truth claims are based on other criteria here
than that of traditional objectivity and verification.

As in the case with Quine's critique of Popper, Kuhn argues
that anomalous or conflicting observations that could potentially
call into question the validity of a paradigm are either ignored or
explained away. "They [scientists] will devise numerous articula-
tions and *ad hoc* modifications of their theory in order to eliminate
any apparent conflict."[34] These "epistemological counterinstances"
are only "minor irritants" within the history of science. Over time
there is always a possibility that an accumulation of these irritants
could result in a paradigm shift, but these are very unusual events.
Anomalies are not used to falsify theories. Kuhn accepts two of
Quine's arguments here. First, that synthetic statements can also
act as analytic or tautologically closed statements and second,
that theories cannot be falsified because of their flexible ability to

adjust to and absorb any conflicting information. Kuhn provides examples of this process when he mentions Newton's second law of motion and Dalton's chemical law of fixed proportion. Both were treated for many years as logical statements that could not be dislodged or refuted by conflicting observations. Paradigms never explain all reality about nature and the toleration of crisis is part of what it means to be a scientist. Most of the practitioners of normal science, especially the young initiates, accept the validity of a paradigm on the basis of the authority of teachers and text-books and not on the authority of experience. Kuhn also relies upon Quine's theory of the underdetermination by experience when he writes that "there are seldom areas in which a scientific theory, particularly if it is cast in a predominantly mathematical form, can be directly compared with nature."[35] Scientific theories within paradigms are not easily verifiable or falsifiable because of the distance and abstraction from direct experience. In many instances only approximate agreement between facts and reality can be obtained.

This leads us to a discussion of Kuhn's analysis of normal science. Since he has already rejected empiricism and rationalism, inductive and deductive logic, what is the foundation upon which science makes truth claims about reality? At this point we see Kuhn's major contribution to contemporary philosophy and the history of science. By rejecting epistemology as capable of establishing the ground of scientific knowledge, he is forced to move beyond the traditional debates within philosophy to an analysis of the praxis of science. That which is important is not the philosophical inquiry into an idealized methodology, but the actual methods employed by which theories are created and accepted as true. The justification of paradigms lies not in a verification of their truth or falsification of their ideas, but in a general acceptance within the scientific community on the basis of technical criteria of their adequacy for problem solving. *Episteme* is reduced to *techne*; the criterion of truth is displaced outside of epistemology to the technical interests of the scientific community. Puzzle-solving and technological advancement become the criteria by which truth claims are measured.

The limits of concept formation in natural science are to be found in the paradigm itself. Observations, experiments, and measurements are important to the extent that facts are accumulated and predictions are projected that conform to patterns already contained within the paradigms. Epistemology remains important in establishing the foundations of the activity of normal science but not the foundations of truth itself. The role of normal science is to clarify the theoretical configuration of the paradigm, further the match between facts and theory, observation and prediction, and develop the theoretical and experiential possibilities inherent in the paradigm itself. This is what Kuhn calls the "mopping-up operation," which is supposed to draw out the implications contained within the limits of every paradigm. Its goal is not to question the accepted theoretical construct or create new phenomena or new paradigms. Kuhn characterizes the activity of paradigm articulation as a mechanical improvement and development of what is already implicitly there. The positive side of this approach is that it permits a very detailed and precise study of nature, theory, and empirical evidence. The exploration of empirical facts and the prediction of future occurrences are refined and focused.

Paradigms define the issues to be examined and problems to be solved, select and collect data, perform appropriate experiments and develop instrumental aids and apparatus, offer theoretical and technical solutions, pursue residual inconsistencies and ambiguities in theory, and, in application, bring together a better fit between concepts and reality. "These three classes of problems—determination of significant fact, matching of facts with theory, and articulation of theory—exhaust, I think, the literature of normal science, both empirical and theoretical."[36] Kuhn maintains that once the Newtonian paradigm was accepted the further development of its implications and application resulted in dramatic advances in mathematical physics, mechanical theory, thermodynamics, wave theory of light, and electromagnetic theory. All these advances helped articulate a better fit between Newtonian ideas and their potential application to nature.

Kuhn's theories of scientific paradigms and theoretical and technical problem solving, his critique of epistemology and rejection of empiricism and rationalism lead to a rethinking of the nature of science and its claims to truth. If its goal is not the search for universal truth or absolute certainty, what is the purpose of modern science and what kind of knowledge does it seek? Kuhn's answer is that science searches for answers to puzzles and problems raised by the constructed paradigms. The conclusions are always anticipated and even known in great detail in advance. It is the solution to the puzzle, the means to the end, that invites the enthusiasm of the scientist. Kuhn uses the term "puzzle-solving" to describe the normal process of paradigm articulation since puzzles are constructed from already finished products. The picture or design of a jigsaw puzzle is already known. What is fascinating and exciting is its reconstruction using new techniques and approaches. Only those problems contained within the paradigm are accepted by the scientific community as relevant. All others are viewed as unimportant, metaphysical distractions. Other important elements for Kuhn are that scientists only undertake the analysis of problems that are technically solvable within the paradigm and they do so according to an established set of rules determined by the concepts, theories, and laws of science.

Kuhn mentions that during the eighteenth and nineteenth centuries, Newtonian physics set the ontological rules by defining the central questions around matter and force, whereas in chemistry a quantitative boundary was established that defined reality in terms of atoms, atomic weights, and molecular structure. In the seventeenth century, Descartes limited the range of puzzle-solving questions by his ontology of microscopic corpuscles. All primary reality was constructed of quantitative phenomena and science was methodologically and theoretically limited to the study of their shape, size, motion, and force (primary qualities). Kuhn outlines this whole process as a religious commitment to a set of metaphysical beliefs about the world that shape our description of reality, the definition of problems to be solved, the methodological rules of the game, and the instruments and theories with which this is to be accomplished. Within this perspective of knowledge as theoretical construction, science is reduced to technical solutions to specifically defined paradigm problems.

Over time, minor anomalies, resistant and unassimilable facts, unanticipated novelties, and inconsistencies within paradigms can become serious problems and lead to acute crises or "pronounced professional insecurities." When paradigms no longer solve the problems they generate or when new problem-solving issues arise to which they cannot adequately respond, a revolution in consciousness and ideas might be necessary. New facts and predictions arise that cannot be explained within the framework of the old metaphors of science. When this occurs, there is always a possibility of a scientific revolution or shift in paradigms. This is how Kuhn describes the birth of the new scientific theories of Copernicus's astronomy, Lavoisier's theory of oxygen, Maxwell's electromagnetic theory, Bohr's quantum physics, Einstein's theory of relativity, and so forth. At first *ad hoc* adjustments in dynamic, astronomical, and chemical theory can readily solve initial discrepancies, but they sometimes accumulate to the point where these adjustments become inadequate.

Kuhn argues that paradigms are never rejected because of inconsistent empirical evidence, but may be replaced by paradigms better able to handle those problems that the scientific community deems important. Since there is no neutral observation language to which competing parties may appeal, no traditional view of objectivity, the struggle between competing paradigms looks like a struggle within a political revolution. Neither logic, nature, nor science alone can adjudicate the debate—they "provide no ground for discrimination."[37] The future is open to the powers of persuasion within the scientific community. "Like the choice between competing political institutions, that between competing paradigms proves to be a choice between incompatible modes of community life. . . . As in political revolutions, so in paradigm choice—there is no standard higher than the assent of the relevant community."[38] This is similar to the situation in a jury deliberation about the law: there is no decision that can ultimately prove the innocence of a defendant. The jury can only decide the issue of whether the defendant is guilty or not guilty. It accepts the version of truth of the prosecutor or defense attorney. But there is no objective position from which to make the judgment about innocence or absolute truth.

Kuhn expands his discussion by arguing that all debate about paradigm selection is necessarily circular since each party defends itself using its own theories, methods, and facts. Thus only the power of persuasion becomes the foundation for science and the arbiter between conflicting theoretical perspectives. The Popperian view of piecemeal refinement and progressive improvement of science through accumulation toward objective reality is rejected by Kuhn as inadequate to the historical evidence of how new paradigms evolve over time. The replacement of one construct by another is not an indication that one is more correct than another. It is just that one is more adequate to the problems raised at the time. With Kuhn's theory of paradigms, revolutions in science are no longer epistemological or metaphysical issues but sociological and historical ones. He does not consider the question of whether consensus can be the basis for truth; he only considers that social consensus is the basis for the acceptance of one paradigm over another. Thus Copernican astronomy and Einsteinian physics are not any truer than Ptolemaic astronomy or Newtonian physics. They just responded more adequately to the unexplainable anomalies and perceived problems of their historical periods.

Since there is no neutral language and since competing paradigms are incommensurable conceptual configurations that view the world so differently, there is no basis for a comparison or judgment between them. They represent different language communities with different worldviews, metaphysics, observations, and problems to be solved. Validation, justification, and verification are not terms that can be used when discussing scientific theories. Each paradigm has its own standards, definitions of reality, assumptions, values, and metaphorical references, which are not capable of being translated into one another. The medieval world of organic and teleological substances and efficient and formal causes is not a world that can be readily understood by individuals within a deterministic and mechanical universe described by the concepts of matter, force, and motion.[39] Because paradigms are communally shared value systems with different languages, customs, categories, and understandings of reality, they each have a distinctive "language community." They thereby help form the scientific perception of reality as they socialize the community into a particular way of looking at the world. Paradigms are thus interpretive and deliberative processes within a special gestalt in which reality is made conceptually visible to its adherents.

Kuhn argues that the process of transformation is neither rational nor evolutionary. Even though Kuhn develops his arguments about the nature of science as a social phenomenon, there is little consideration of the social context of scientific revolutions. The question of why there are paradigm shifts and revolutions receives a vague response that change is dependent upon the personal idiosyncrasies and nationality of scientists, as well as the adequacy of the new paradigm to solve specific problems, predict new phenomena, or provide mystical and aesthetic appeal by creating theories that are more simple and suitable. Kuhn contends that Copernicus had solved the problem of the length of the calendar year, Newton the integration of terrestrial and celestial mechanics and the prediction of astronomical observations, Lavoisier the problem of the identification of oxygen, and Einstein the integration of electrodynamics and dynamics. In a change from his earlier work, *The Copernican Revolution* (1957), Kuhn maintains in *The Structure of Scientific Revolutions* that it was the transcending values of mathematical precision and quantitative superiority of these new theories which were the determining factors in their gestalt shifts.

"Usually the opponents of a new paradigm can legitimately claim that even in the area of crisis it is little superior to its traditional rival. Of course, it handles some problems better, and has disclosed some new regularities."[40] Revolutions are not as simple as they appear in textbooks since in many cases the older paradigm is able to respond adequately and adjust to the new intruder and the latter may have difficulty solving problems already considered solved. Kuhn is very clear that problem-solving techniques are themselves not adequate to produce a scientific revolution. It is the excitement generated within the scientific community about future research areas and problems that contains the key to its eventual general acceptance. This was the case with Copernicus and Einstein. In the end, Kuhn concludes that paradigm conversion is a complex phenomenon that involves many different and, at times, irrational elements.

In an interesting way Kuhn rejects the logical implications of his own arguments in the postscript to his book written seven years after its first publication. He refuses to accept the relativism that apparently lies beneath the surface of his position. From his perspective, science is not concerned with the nature of objective reality, but with solving certain problems articulated within the scientific community. If this is true, he contends, then he cannot be accused of being a relativist since certain paradigms are more successful and better suited to solving certain types of problems. Since paradigms are not concerned with issues of ontology and reality, but with issues of utility, the epistemological notion of relativism simply no longer applies. Kuhn restates his position developed earlier in his book when he writes: "I do not doubt, for example, that Newton's mechanics improves on Aristotle's and that Einstein's improves on Newton's as instruments for puzzle-solving. But I can see in their succession no coherent direction of ontological development."[41] The full epistemological implications of Kuhn's approach to science must wait until Rorty develops the relativistic and nihilistic implications that lie beneath the phenomenal surface of normal science. On the other hand, there is another direction this discussion has taken. The radical implications of the critique of epistemology developed by Quine and Kuhn have been developed in the United States by practitioners of the sociology of knowledge and in Germany by followers of the Frankfurt School. They have attempted to investigate the deeper social, political, and economic structures of social practice that have affected the development and legitimation of modern science.[42]

RORTY AGAINST DESCARTES AND KANT

In 1979 Richard Rorty wrote his major work, *Philosophy and the Mirror of Nature*, which expands upon some of the main themes examined by Quine and Kuhn in their philosophy and history of science. It was a major intellectual breakthrough in post-analytic philosophy, as he integrates the writings of Willard Quine's critique of epistemology and holism and Wilfrid Sellars's anti-foundationalism into a devastating critique of traditional theories of knowledge, realism, and foundationalism.[43] Rorty rejects the idea of a Cartesian thinking ego and a Kantian transcendental subject as possible bases for knowledge, the privileging of physical or mental representations as absolute truth, and the existence of a theory of knowledge in which impressions and ideas of consciousness or language mirror objective reality. Continuing the work of Wittgenstein, Heidegger, and Dewey, he challenges the accepted views of consciousness, objectivity, and rationality in logical positivism by developing a radical pragmatism based on anti-realism and anti-foundationalism.[44] It represents a direct assault on Cartesian, Kantian, and analytic philosophy.

Traditionally, modern philosophy since the seventeenth century had searched for the foundations of knowledge in the cognitive processes of the mind as it constructs accurate representations of the external world in the senses and thought.[45] Its central concern was building a theory of representations and consciousness. Within the history of philosophy, it had been Descartes, Locke, and Kant who were its major practitioners and it is just their works

that Rorty wishes to call into question. Developing a philosophical theory of knowledge, privileging certain representations of the
mind as truth, and deconstructing the a priori nature of the mind
that imposes itself on nature are all rejected by him.[46] Rorty turns
his criticisms against epistemology and foundational science as he
rejects the search for truth in both subjectivity and objectivity. He
clearly makes this point when he writes that "the attempt . . . to
explicate 'rationality' and 'objectivity' in terms of conditions of
accurate representation is a self-deceptive effort to externalize
the normal discourse of the day."[47] But having said this, Rorty
turns around and uses the norms of everyday social practice and
our conformity to them as the basis for his view of rationality
and objectivity.[48] Instead of assuming a priori structures of the
mind, he turns to the workings of the mind in social practice
as a philosophy of mind that is replaced by a social theory of
knowledge. Rorty is aware of the impossibility and ideological
implications of privileging one set of assumptions about the
nature of knowledge over another. In the end, he rejects all claims
to epistemological and scientific truth that are grounded on the
inner representations of the mind, accurate reflection of reality,
or objective truth. Instead he articulates a social pragmatism
of useful and discursive knowledge that integrates *theoria* and
praxis by expanding upon Kuhn's distinction between normal
and revolutionary science. He accomplishes this by introducing
the notions of normal and abnormal discourse.[49]

   As Rorty reconstructs the history of Western philosophy and
the origins of human knowledge, he argues that truth has been
expressed in metaphysical and epistemological traditions. Whether
it is a question of being and becoming in classical antiquity or sensation and intellect in modern post-Cartesian philosophy, truth
has been viewed as a thing or object reflected in the mind. The
articulation of a special branch of philosophy along with its search
for the foundations of knowledge, separate from both science and
metaphysics, is a distinctively modern phenomenon. Rorty traces
this perspective back to Platonic philosophy which made claims

that truth was grounded in causes defined as a compulsion of objects claiming objective validity. Certainty about these claims was determined by the metaphysical nature of the objects them-selves—universal certainty for pure forms and ideas and claims of contingency for the empirical world. Epistemology turns to exam-ining the faculties of the mind and the types of corresponding representations. By analyzing perception and thinking, ideas of the senses or the intellect make claims on the mind for recognition of their necessity and universality. Truth then lies in the privileged representations of experience or concepts. Thus in the traditional theory of knowledge, objectivity imposes itself on subjectivity: "The idea of 'necessary truth' is just the idea of a proposition which is believed because the 'grip' of the object upon us is ineluc-table."[50] It is within the power of perception and compulsion of the senses or the force of the mind to define the objects of truth. This has given rise to rival claims to knowledge of both empiricism and rationalism and their later integration in the Kantian critique of pure reason.

Rorty summarizes the conflicting elements in the modern theory of knowledge when he writes, "Before Kant, an inquiry into 'the nature and origin of knowledge' had been a search for privileged inner representations [senses or ideas]. With Kant, it became a search for the rules which the mind had set up for itself."[51] Kant's theory of knowledge was a scholastic reformula-tion of seventeenth-century philosophy of mind; he transformed Descartes' inner representations of space and motion into a priori structures of the mind or pure reason. Access to objectivity and knowledge was to be achieved through the examination of the physiological structure and transcendental operation of human consciousness. With empiricism this objectivity exists external to the self, whereas with rationalism it lies already innately in the mind. The objectivity of empiricism involves the perception of and reflection upon an external reality by a passive self, whereas the objectivity of rationalism is created by the interior reality of the Cartesian ego. Kant moved beyond both by arguing that the mind neither finds a preexisting objectivity nor creates its own, but constitutes reality by integrating the manifold of representations with the structural categories of the mind. The time and space of reality was viewed as part of the transcendental subject and the method of critique examined the origins and limits of the a priori concepts and structure of pure reason. Rationalism and idealism shared the belief that absolute certainty resulted from self-reflection on a priori ideas. "The Copernican revolution was based on the notion that we can only know about objects a priori if we 'constituted' them."[52]

Rorty sees the problem of objective validity as the heart of modern epistemology—the justification of the objective reality, theoretical accuracy, and universal certainty of our impressions and ideas. How do we know the external world corresponds to the way in which we perceive and understand it? This is the question at the heart of Cartesian and Humean skepticism. What was once so easily accepted by Locke with his simple and complex ideas becomes the source of concerned investigation in later philosophy. The goal was to get behind the inner representation of innate ideas in the Cartesian mind and the empirical impressions of the perceiving self of Hume to the underlying reality that caused them. Were the inner representations reflections of a true external reality? With Hume, there was a profound skepticism that we could ever get beyond the perceptions, and the nagging concern that scientific judgments built on inductive and deductive logic were illusions. Kant built upon this skepticism with his idea of the thing-in-itself and then chose to ignore it by examining the a priori structure of the transcendental mind.

According to Rorty, there is one other problem within these early epistemologists—an inadequate understanding of the relationship between seeing and knowing, perception and reason. There is a confusion among those who accept the ocular metaphor that the mind mirrors nature. It is not clear what the relationship between perception and knowledge is, that is, between the impression of nature on the mind in seeing and the act of knowing and judging something in reason. The former relates to the physiological process of receiving physical images and impulses from the external world. Rorty borrows from Wilfrid Sellars's analysis of the confusion surrounding the act of seeing a red triangle. There is a difference between seeing something immediately as red and triangular and knowing that the object seen is a red triangle. The ambiguity revolves around the difficulty of distinguishing between the mechanical receptivity of external material impressions on the brain and their transformation into ideas of the mind—a faculty of the mind that receives impressions and a faculty that grounds thought and judgment about their relationships to each other. Locke unconvincingly combines both elements in the same moment of receiving impressions in the *tabula rasa* and in the process recapitulates Aristotle's theory of phantasms. The impression of a frog in perception is quite different from the attribution and judgment of frogness in a representation of ideas. Rorty sees the distinction as one between a "physiological fact and speculative metaphor." The question remains open as to where knowledge exists—in the senses or thought, in the particular or in the universal. This confusion would later lead to Hume's skepticism and Kant's distinction between intuition and understanding, the transcendental aesthetic and the transcendental analytic.

Kant attempted to overcome the dualism of the inner representations of the mind, that is, the dualism between sensuous intuition and concepts, perception and thought, particular and universal, by synthesizing them in the mind as the manifold received by the intuition is reconfigured into a unified object. He continued the line of argument initially developed by Descartes that the world is formed through the projection of the inner representations of the mind onto the external world. Rorty also believes that tracing the origins and causal explanations of knowledge is not an adequate basis for the justification of that knowledge. By confusing causation and physiology, on the one hand, with justification and validity on the other, Kant was recapitulating the same logical errors as his philosophical predecessors. Objectivity is consciously formed through the synthesis of intuitions and, without this process, we cannot be conscious of our perception.

Troubled by some of the same problems of his time, Rorty raises the fascinating question of how we can discuss the issue of unsynthesized intuitions or the existence of the manifold of representations, as well as concepts before their application in knowing. These issues have been central to debates within the neo-Kantian community. Rorty's answer is very Quinean—the Kantian notions of intuition and concept do not stand on their own, but make sense only within the context of the totality of Kant's theory of knowledge in the same way that the categories of electron and proton have explanatory power only within the total framework of modern physics. They have only "contextual definitions." The synthetic activity of the mind is used to explain the possibility of a priori synthetic knowledge as the integration of intuition and concepts. But, for Rorty, this quasi-psychological explanation has no justification on its own: "But if it is not an evident pre-analytic fact that such a manifold exists, how can we use the claim that sensibility presents us with a manifold as a premise? How, in other words, do we know that a manifold which cannot be represented as a manifold is a manifold . . . how do we get our information about intuitions prior to synthesis?"[53] But since we do not have direct access to the manifold or to concepts outside of experience, Rorty rejects the validity of this argument. They are all unwarranted and unjustified epistemological postulates based on the anthropological assumptions that we have a privileged knowledge of that which is internally created by human beings and projected onto external space. This past critical philosophy also assumes that we have a privileged access to the constitutive process itself. Rorty rejects this also. The traditional foundations of knowledge and science in objectivity had moved to the a priori structure of the mind, as this too was rejected.

According to Rorty, the Kantian view of knowledge has been universally accepted in the twentieth century. The search for a privileged access to truth has been directed to the inner structure of the mind by Continental philosophers and to propositions and language by Anglo-American Analytic philosophers. Dewey, Wittgenstein, and Heidegger represent early exceptions to this neo-Kantian consensus and Quine and Sellars represent its latest critics.

SELLARS, QUINE, AND THE ASSAULT ON EPISTEMOLOGY

In his analysis of their critique of epistemology, Rorty stresses Sellars's psychological nominalism and anti-foundationalism and Quine's holism and behaviorism. Sellars moves beyond the logical positivist argument based on the empiricist "myth of the given" by arguing that all true awareness or knowledge is ultimately a linguistic affair of using nominalist concepts and words. However, he distinguishes between an initial and primitive awareness of "raw feels" from knowledge of what a thing is, since concepts are always linked to other concepts. That is, a child's consciousness of pain (or sense redness) is different from knowing the nature of pain, since the recognition of the latter involves the use of concepts and propositions. Sensation is not a cognitive act. Many unpleasant experiences are directly known prior to acquired linguistic activity and concept formation. Children can have primitive feelings of pain, anger, pleasure, etc., that are pre-linguistically felt without having the categories that could provide the conceptual knowledge and experiential framework for that experience. They may feel pain, but they do not know it.[54]

Conversely, Rorty contends that we are capable of having knowledge about something without having a concomitant raw feeling about it. We can have knowledge and true belief about pain or redness without the necessity of experiencing either. Sellars is attempting to avoid the confusion in Western epistemology between feelings and empirical awareness, on the one hand, and conceptual knowledge on the other. The latter does not add anything new to experience, broaden our consciousness, or synthesize the manifold into a coherent unity. What it does do is it permits us to enter into a linguistic community that attempts the justification of our claims to knowledge through discourse. Rorty views this approach to the critique of the "myth of the given" and positivism as overcoming the Lockean dualism between explanation and justification, acquisition and validation. The justification of knowledge does not lie in knowing its origins in inner or outer representations, that is, in a theory of privileged objectivity or subjectivity. Sellars does not search for the origins of knowledge in sensations, matters of fact, innate ideas, concepts, or the rules of pure reason. He explicitly argues against confusing the conditions of knowledge in initial stimulation and awareness and the grounding of knowledge in communication.

The connection between sensuous feelings and conceptual knowledge, which had been part of modern epistemology from Descartes to Kant, is broken and with it the naturalistic and genetic fallacy at the heart of empiricist theory of knowledge. The need for grounding truth is no longer tied to an ontological analysis of the empirical conditions and origins of knowledge. By challenging the ocular metaphor in epistemology, the underlying assumptions of modern philosophy have been called into question. In the end, justification is accomplished only through social practice and learning the language game of the community. The dualism that characterizes Sellars's argument is not that between feelings and knowledge, sensations and ideas, but between facts and linguistic rules of a language community. Rorty draws the analogy between gaining linguistic competence through the use of concepts and logic and gaining political competence and acquiring rights and responsibilities upon reaching the age of eighteen. It doesn't change individuals internally; it only changes their relation to the wider community.

Rorty continues to reinforce this split between ontological grounding and communal justification by turning to Quine's notions of the "indeterminacy of translation" and the "inscrutability of reference." These ideas become a further basis upon which to reject the idea of privileged representations of knowledge. Quine argues that when two different linguists translate a foreign language into the same language, the result can be two entirely different, consistent, and justifiable translations of that language. There is no original language or behavioral sources the linguists can turn to in order to settle their differences; there is no independent evidence to verify the truth claims of each translator; there is no basis for the claim that this is what the foreigners really meant by their linguistic expressions. "Then when I say there is no fact of the matter, as regards, say, the two rival manuals of translation, what I mean is that both manuals are compatible with all the same distributions of states and relationships over elementary particles. In a word, they are physically equivalent."[55] In a conflict between competing translations, there is no objective basis, hidden fact, or original source to fall back upon for determining the uniquely correct meaning of a term. It is always possible to have multiple and correct translations of a foreign language. That is, there are no ontological facts or empirical objects that ground the meaning of propositions, moral values, or cultural beliefs. Quine rejects the "'idea' idea" or the search for the inner representation or rules of thought that could justify the meaning of an utterance. He, in turn, also rejects the Kantian distinction between necessary or mathematical truths and contingent or empirical truths. Blending together necessary and contingent truths, concepts and intuitions represents a continued assault on the metaphysical and epistemological foundations of knowledge as there is no longer any basis upon which to distinguish universal and particular truth, absolute certainty and changing opinion.

The translations of texts from one language to another offers another insight into these epistemological problems as well as a clarification of Quine's critique of the two dogmas of empiricism as it relates to translation—that is, critique of essentialism and neutral observation language. Language does not express an inner meaning that reflects an external truth; concepts do not have ontological reference. Concepts have meaning within a holistic pattern of language itself which makes translation difficult. There is no third party or God's-eye view to ensure a correct reference or translation. To say, " '*Hund*' is German for 'dog,' " does not refer to an empirical fact, since there are no given facts outside of language that could steer a translator to the correct words of expression. Rather, it expresses a useful technique or social utility when translating or communicating between languages. Quine rejects the notion that this expresses a truth by correspondence and argues instead that it is only a truth by convenience. One will not go wrong or commit mistakes that lead to problems by translating *Hund* as dog, especially if a person goes into a pet store to purchase an animal.

The use of the term "rabbit" to refer to an external object is only an imposition of a linguistic term for the purpose of communication in an indeterminate world with indeterminate translations. Quine rejects the notions of ontology, reference, identity, and meaning in this context. A correct translation does not make ontological commitments, but performs a service by making two languages coherent and gives the translator useable knowledge in another linguistic community. It enables us to cope with the world by using socially agreed-upon conventions. By not having a neutral objectivity to fall back upon for empirical confirmation, a good translation is a practical convenience that helps us move in another world with limited difficulties. Truth is not about the world or about a reference to meaning, but rather about the nature of social practice. According to Rorty, Quine's fear of the implications of his own work and his unwillingness to make a full break with epistemology forces him to replace epistemology by empirical psychology and thereby salvage some elements of empiricism.

The other idea of Quine's to which Rorty refers and which continues this line of argument is that of the "inscrutability of reference." Rorty quotes from Quine's essay, "Ontological Relativity": "What makes sense is to say not what the objects of a theory are, absolutely speaking, but how one theory of objects is interpretable or reinterpretable in another."[56] Language is a social construction whose words are meaningful not because they are references to ontological entities but because they are conventional constructs that facilitate expression of intentions, communication, and action (behaviorism). Quine explicitly argues, but never with complete conviction or consistently, that we can dispense with meaning as reference. There is no direct access to empirical reality except through conventional language and theories and there is no possibility of verification through objectivity. With this Quine rejects positivism and the correspondence theory of truth. Rorty concludes that because of this position "epistemology and ontology never meet."[57] Similar ideas have already been expressed in this chapter in the analysis of the relation between scientific theories and their underdetermination by experience.

The radical implications Rorty draws from his analysis of the behaviorism of Quine and Sellars is the necessity to abandon the epistemological quest for first principles and privileged representations of truth. Philosophy can no longer mediate between competing claims to universal knowledge and absolute certainty; it cannot direct our way between truth and falsity, necessity and contingency. Both Quine and Sellars conclude that it is the community that has the authority to validate intersubjective claims to epistemic truth. After rejecting traditional epistemology, Rorty looks to the psychology of Norman Malcolm and Gilbert Ryle and the philosophy of language of Hilary Putnam, but to no avail. Beginning first with Dewey, Wittgenstein, and Heidegger, then following the philosophical criticisms of Quine and Sellars, Rorty's argument leads him to the history and sociology of science of Michael Polanyi, Thomas Kuhn, Paul Feyerabend, Rom Harré, and Mary Hesse. He is fully aware of the implications of Kuhn's argument even when Kuhn retreats from the edge of the relativity abyss. If there is no ontological or realist foundation that could mediate between the differing truth claims of Aristotle and Newton, and if the only basis for arguing in favor of the latter over the former rests on technical questions of puzzle-solving and control, then the floodgates to historicism and relativism are open. But this does not end Rorty's own concern about these issues. They have been transformed into another level of philosophical discourse.

From Objectivity to Social Practice, From Epistemology to Hermeneutics

The search for a commensurable language or common ground in the forms of Plato or ideas of Descartes, the inner representations of the mind of Locke and Hume, the structure of the transcendental subject of Kant, or the rules and grammar of language of the logical positivists, has been a philosophical failure and needs to be rethought. The split between sensation and thought, concepts and reality, and explanation and justification was called into question by Sellars's critique of the myth of the given and his distinction between awareness and knowledge and Quine's critique of the dogmas of empiricism, meaning, observation, and necessary truths, as well as his theory of analyticity. By questioning the distinctions between analytic and synthetic statements, universal and particular, and language and fact; by blurring the differences between observation and theory, facts and thought; and dropping the notions of sense data and pure intuitions, a new language of inquiry beyond objectivity and subjectivity was being opened that rejected prior epistemic foundations to knowledge and moved into the history and sociology of scientific practice.

Rorty radicalizes the criticisms of Sellars and Quine and moves away from causal explanations, privileged impressions or concepts, compulsion to truth acceptance by the object, and foundational knowledge prior to science. As he characterizes it, explanation is replaced by justification, causes by reasons, and compulsion of objectivity by conversation and persuasion.[58] By surrendering foundations and objectivity, knowledge has returned to the older Sophist tradition of discourse and debate. There is no longer any quest for truth by looking for hidden forms, essences, universals, or sense impressions. Rorty concludes that an analysis of Sellars and Quine leads to the conclusion that "justification is not a matter of a special relation between ideas (or words) and objects, but of conversation, of social practice."[59] Truth is no longer to be understood as a mirroring of nature or reflection of empirical reality, an accuracy of representations and ideas, a correspondence between concepts and reality, or an objectivity of method and ontology. Truth reflects the range of conversation within society about specific issues of science, art, morality, and so forth. Reason and truth become expressions for social interaction and public discourse. Rorty maintains that rationality is explained "by reference to what society lets us say" and "by reference to what we already accept."[60] He is adamant that this is not another form of foundationalism that has been removed from philosophical inquiry and displaced into sociology.

Because there is no neutral observational language, no privileged representations, and no universal standards that arbitrate between conflicting perceptions and ideas, there is no truth other than that decided upon by the members of the community. "For the Quine-Sellars approach to epistemology, to say that truth and knowledge can only be judged by the standards of the inquirers of our own day is not to say. . . . It is merely to say that nothing counts as justification unless by reference to what we already accept, and that there is no way to get outside our beliefs and our language so as to find some test other than coherence."[61] Questions of truth and morality become adjudicated within the community without recourse to some objective moral standard, since moral imperatives are a matter of the taste and standards of the community. There are no higher or inner forums for validation of truth. This form of nihilism and relativism that underlies Rorty's thinking has important implications for both philosophy and sociology. Though he doesn't examine the issue here, Rorty certainly raises the question as to the nature and structure of the society in which the conversation takes place. Though he denies it, the argument about the foundations of knowledge has, in fact, been displaced to questions about the structural foundations of society. If conversation has replaced compulsion and the structures of society have replaced the structures of reason and language, then what is the nature of the modern social system within which this conversation takes place? What are the structures of power and class in society; how does socialization, consciousness formation, and personality development take place?; are participation and conversation open to all equally?; what is the nature of democracy in an advanced capitalist society? Privileged representations turn into privileged social relations. Rorty has not gotten rid of the ghost of episte-mology; he has merely transformed it into the spirit of political economy and sociology.

At this stage in the development of his argument, Rorty attempts to clarify his notions of social practice and conversation by analyz-ing both hermeneutics and the history of science. By examining the nature of understanding and conversation in hermeneutics and the nature of deliberation within the scientific community over differing theoretical paradigms, he offers us an opportunity to inspect forms of knowledge that go beyond the authoritarian imposition of Platonic truth based on a special access to forms, observation, mind, or language. In turn, we are able to examine truth as a conversation without a common ground or intended common goal or ideal. There is an openness, contingency, and will-ingness to listen to the dialogue in which there is no coercion by a privileged objectivity or narrow rationality. Rorty borrows Kuhn's distinction between normal science and revolutionary science in order to aid in supporting this view of truth by discourse and con-sensus. Normal science involves a consensus about the acceptable method, theory, and factual information, whereas revolutionary science represents a gestalt shift in scientific consciousness and explanation. In history new problems arise that demand solu-tions and a new paradigmatic structure. As in normal science, the guidelines for normal discourse and agreement are clearly laid out. Rorty's description of the difference between normal and revolutionary science resonates with the Nietzschean distinction between the Apollonian and Dionysian drives—life and death, rational order and destructive creativity.

Epistemology involves the rationalization and codification—the grounding—of normal science. Consensus has already been reached and science systematically organizes the conventional practices of inquiry. Hermeneutics, on the other hand, becomes important when there is a breakdown in communication due to abnormal or revolutionary discourse. There develops a need for further understanding and conversation within the scientific community over differing interpretations and approaches. Though *The Structure of Scientific Revolutions* provides an important avenue of investigation that leads from epistemology to hermeneutics, Rorty is critical of Kuhn's inability to transcend the dichotomy between realism and idealism. We have already seen in this chapter that Kuhn's notion of paradigm was a very fluid and, at times, obscure term with multiple meanings. Rorty sees Kuhn as caught between two contradictory positions. Either paradigms are the theoretical constructs through which different worlds and different *Weltanschauungen* are created or they are different interpretations of neutral observations and given empirical facts. Kuhn's problem was that he had different definitions of paradigms that reflected an ambiguity about his critique of empiricism. Though finally siding with the idealist view, he never escaped epistemology itself but fell into a Kantian theory of knowledge based on the subjective constitution of perception and objectivity. In response to these inadequacies, Rorty wants to develop a behaviorism beyond epistemology.

Central to Rorty's evaluation of Kuhn is his analysis of the deliberative process itself. He accepts the basic idea that paradigm shifts involve different language games and conversations among its scientific participants. However, he disagrees strongly with Kuhn about whether there exist specific scientific values and criteria about what constitutes rational and objective choice within a scientific discussion. Kuhn has argued that values such as accuracy, simplicity, precision, etc., were important in determining the successful acceptance of a particular theory. Rorty feels that this is another example of displaced foundationalism and realism, since Kuhn is arguing for a series of values that ground the deliberative process or the choice of what constitutes scientific results. This will be important later in his critique of Jürgen Habermas's communications theory of truth and discourse ethics.

Rorty rejects any prior recognition of scientific values that would ground the deliberative process before its start. This would just be another form of epistemological foundationalism. Objectivity and rationality cannot be defined before the discourse within the scientific community about the nature and validity of competing theoretical models. This issue comes to light in Kuhn's analysis of the Bellarmine-Galileo debate over celestial physics. Cardinal Bellarmine introduced scriptural references and theological arguments in his attempt to refute the scientific proposals and methodology of Copernicus and Galileo. Rorty asks if this tactic was itself scientific, disinterested, and logical. Were there scientific values and methods, or a "disciplinary matrix," which could ground the discussion about the distinction between science and non-science that would invalidate Bellarmine's argument? What privileges Enlightenment standards of rationality over alternative views of reason and justification? Rorty asks, "Whether there is some antecedent way of determining the relevance of one statement to another, some 'grid' (to use Foucault's term) which determines what sorts of evidence there *could* be for statements about the movements of planets."[62] All Rorty is willing to admit is that during the debate there was no consensus about scientific rationality and after the debate Galileo's view was victorious. But there was no prior justification for the latter's scientific method lying within the realm of rationality and objectivity, nor was there a justification, after the fact, through a rational reconstruction.

Rorty relies heavily upon Hans Gadamer's and Martin Heidegger's notion of hermeneutics in *Truth and Method*.[63] He had used the Aristotelian notion of *phronesis* or political wisdom to describe the hermeneutical process, since, with Rorty, hermeneutics as discourse and edification replaces epistemology. After realism and ontology disappear, objectivity is redefined in terms of personal taste and "consensus of rational discussants." In his later works, he refers to it as solidarity. Though discourse and conversation become the new metaphor of science, the purpose of philosophy is to keep the conversation about truth going. However,

Rorty never raises the troubling questions about the nature of discourse. He never asks what keeps the conversation going or what distinguishes between a good and bad, legitimate or illegitimate, a serious or distorted conversation.[64] What is the difference between a conversation and babble or a conversation within a free democratic society and propaganda within a repressive totalitarian system? But suspicions arise about Rorty's political and social thought when he states that authority and rationality are defined through what the given society lets us say and the given beliefs we already accept. Though he agrees with Jean-Paul Sartre's critique of objective truth as restraining discursive rationality and conversation, he nowhere examines whether discourse itself could become fetishized, ideological, or repressive. Rorty's critique of epistemology and foundationalism has overflowed into his theory of wisdom as edification. *Philosophy and the Mirror of Nature* ends with an urging to continue "the conversation of the West," which is picked up in his later works as he expands upon the political and social nature of rational consensus by connecting pragmatism to liberalism, epistemology to politics.

IRONIC LIBERALISM WITHOUT ENLIGHTENMENT METAPHYSICS

Rorty begins to detail his political ideas about postmodern pragmatism and the liberal community in his work *Contingency, Irony, and Solidarity* (1989).[65] Having rejected "metaphysical liberalism" with its search for universal foundations in human nature, rationality, God, and objectivity, he instead turns to an ungrounded, playful, and aesthetic liberalism that Rorty calls "ironic liberalism." This conservative liberalism is characterized as pluralistic, diverse, progressive, and individualistic—a postmodern democracy.[66] This type of society will permit individuals to search for their own personal language and unique identity in their own way through aesthetic self-enrichment and private self-fulfillment. It represents a variant of rugged individualism and Nietzschean aestheticism for the postmodern period.[67] Enlightenment rationalism and realism have been replaced by aesthetic freedom and individual autonomy, universalism and objectivity by Romantic historicism and nominalism. There is no transcendent world of theology, metaphysics, science, or anthropology that secures and ensures the search for truth. Since there is no independent, objective reality or absolute form to fall back upon philosophically, truth can only result from a communal conversation in a free and democratic society. There exist only perspectival traditions, narrative vocabularies, and constantly changing metaphors of self-expression. "A liberal society is one which is content to call 'true' whatever the upshot of [free and open conversational] encounters turns out to be."[68]

Since metaphysics has been replaced by a dualistic world of contingent suffering and creativity held together by changing linguistic metaphors applied to an indifferent reality, there can be no rational justification for a defense of liberalism. Joining together his philosophy of science and political theory, Rorty maintains, against stiff opposition, that liberalism needs no foundations and can provide none.[69] Its defense lies in the personal self-definitions and metaphoric constructions of the critical poet and ironist that lie beyond good and evil and beyond the values of the Enlightenment and classical liberalism. There is a real split between the public and private sphere as issues of social virtue and justice are quite distinct from those of self-development. This split reflects Rorty's distinction between liberalism and aestheticism. He defines an ironic liberal as one who "thinks that cruelty is the worst thing we do," but can't justify any particular definitions or describe any forms of cruelty, since all vocabulary is contingent and ethnocentric.[70] Individual taste and an empathetic vocabulary that sensitively incorporates more and more people in opposition to cruelty and humiliation is the only protection of liberal democracy. On the other hand, it has been recognized that Rorty refuses to believe that victims can speak for themselves, since, for him, there can be no "voice of the oppressed."[71]

Rorty describes the public sphere in terms of negative freedoms, laissez-faire economics, and a depoliticized state. In describing the modern welfare state, he accepts that the public sphere is necessary, since "without the protection of something like the institutions of bourgeois liberal society, people will be less able to work out their private salvation, create their private self-images, reweave their webs of belief and desire in the light of whatever new people and books they happen to encounter."[72] The state is necessary to protect the alienated and disenchanted in their search for new contingent vocabularies and self-images, and also protect the marginal against humiliation and suffering. New poetic expressions of utopian visions are necessary in the ever-intensifying quest for moral autonomy and human dignity as ironic poets search for new linguistic and artistic forms of self-expression and self-creation. He has replaced Dewey and Peirce with Isaiah Berlin and Milton Friedman. The public sphere has been eclipsed in order for it to protect the radical freedoms of individual self-fulfillment within a consumer society. Negative liberty in the market has replaced positive self-realization in both the public and private spheres. Ronald Beiner has commented that this view of the individual and society "offers [us] not a promise of emancipation but the prospect of a postmodernist nightmare of confused roles and incoherent identities."[73] There are no foundations to science and no foundations to the self; truth and individuality are throwaway commodities in a consumer culture. Rorty believes he has redefined liberalism based upon "our loyalty to other human beings clinging together against the dark, not our hope for getting things right."[74] Despite this attempt at redescribing liberalism in postmetaphysical language, however, the result is an incoherence of liberalism that produces an aestheticized public sphere that undermines the very possibility of self-realization. The pragmatic individual destroys the polity. By creating a pragmatism without principles or structures, Rorty has undermined the very system he wishes to defend. We have moved from the eighteenth-century Enlightenment view of the individual as a bundle of sense impressions to the twentieth-century personality as a self within a centerless web of beliefs, desires, and hopes.[75] This is Camus's description in *The Fall* of humanity in the deepest levels of its own middle-class hell within the concentric circles of Amsterdam as a place of suffering, loneliness, and unwavering despair.

The philosophical and metaphysical foundations of possessive individualism and the "economic man" have been replaced by a narcissistic, historically decentered, and psychologically fragmented individual—the state of nature replaced by the tragic culture of a deconstructed and deformed narcissism. Society is constituted by a "band of eccentrics" and each postmodern *Übermensch* continually seeks his or her own new self-definition and meaningful life through the poetry of private utopian dreams or a self-perfected playful hell. Nietzsche's philosophical search for self-determination and moral autonomy takes on a different form when applied to the practical world of politics and personality development. Richard Shusterman writes: "Rorty's view of the self as a random composite of incompatible quasi selves constantly seeking new possibilities and multiple changing vocabularies seems indeed the ideal self for postmodern consumer society: a fragmented, confused self, hungrily enjoying as many new commodities as it can, but lacking the firm integrity to challenge either its habits of consumption or the system that manipulates and profits from them."[76] The danger here is that aesthetic irony displaces any public language capable of resisting oppression or demanding emancipation.[77] It is the purpose of the little that remains left in the public sphere to guarantee legally this idiosyncratic activity of the ironist, so long as it does not impinge upon the protected narcissism of others. Is this not a new ironic metaphysics formed around the altered relationship between the private and public? Gone in Rorty is a concern for the common good, community, positive self-realization, democratic ideals of public space, political participation, open discourse and criticism, and a sensitivity to the underlying structural features of the social and economic conditions that make a just society possible.[78] And gone, too, is the possibility of resistance to political elitism, hierarchy, and oppression.[79] In contrasting Dewey and Rorty, Shusterman writes: "Dewey thus aims at harmonizing liberty and equality with fraternity; Rorty instead seeks 'to dissociate liberty and equality from fraternity.' "[80] The postmodernist critique of Western metaphysics and Enlightenment rationalism has not resulted in a fundamental challenge to the political and economic system. Rather, Rorty has insulated and isolated liberalism from any kind of radical social criticism and praxis by depleting the public sphere of any ethical possibilities and reducing self-realization to an existential expression of artistic uniqueness. The metaphysics of Enlightenment rationalism has been replaced by the metaphysics of postmodern aestheticism.

At first, Rorty appears to be in initial agreement with Jürgen Habermas that issues of moral and political truths are decided on the basis of a general consensus about the accepted social standards within the community. "We shall call 'true' or 'good' whatever is the outcome of free discussion."[81] This is the public world as seen through the eyes of J. S. Mill, Dewey, and Rawls. He disagrees with Habermas's metaphysical attempts to ground liberalism in an ideal speech community and transcendental intersubjectivity. Rorty seeks to bridge the political differences between himself and Habermas by arguing that there are no real differences concerning their views on democracy, the necessity for social change, and the nature of "freedom from domination" and "undistorted communication." This hides more than it reveals, since his view of liberalism is tied to a disenchantment and indifference to positive liberal values and a replacement of the public sphere of democratic discourse by a decision-making process based on instrumental rationality and the pragmatic end of ideology.[82] This severely strains any democratic element in Rorty's ironic liberalism and limits the use of theoretical and conceptual frameworks which place emphasis on the structural conditions for liberal democracy. In the process, the real critical and substantive content of the ideals of American pragmatism of Peirce and Dewey have been lost.

There is, therefore, no possible standard of evaluation by which
to ask whether the institutions of modern liberal society support or
undermine the ideal of "undistorted communication." Asking this
question would require falling back into a metaphysical foundationalism. Liberalism with its tolerance and pluralism, its private
narcissism and public pragmatism, needs no justification[83] and in
constructing his image of a playful society, he excludes the possibility of a critique of ideology and distorted consciousness. There
are no internal social contradictions for Rorty between ideals and
structures of power and class, no contradictions between participatory democracy and corporate capitalism.[84] According to
Richard Bernstein, "Rorty's defense of liberalism is little more than
an *apologia* for the status quo—the very idea of liberalism that
Dewey judged to be 'irrelevant and doomed.' "[85] Rorty argues that
if there is such a standard of rationality, it lies within the ethnocentric ethos and shared values of the liberal community. Consensus
within liberalism provides the only necessary basis for valid moral
and political arguments. There is no discussion of the nature of
domination or distorted communication beyond vague references to social and individual cruelty and humiliation expressed
in terms of slavery, poverty, and prejudice at the institutional level
and coercion of socialization, language, and self-definition at the
personal level.

Though they may, at times, use similar terminology, there is
no agreement of meaning between Rorty and Habermas. For the
former, logical argumentation has been displaced by rhetoric and
redescription as the individual searches for a new vocabulary of
poetic metaphors and linguistic images to redefine their life and
hopes. It is not the better and more rational argument that wins but
the more attractive metaphors that sway others and these are not
grounded in absolute validity but in the freedom of contingency.[86]
Any position can be redescribed to look good or bad because of
the frailty and contingency of language. A cultural revolution must
take place in which a "deep metaphysical need" is replaced by the
acceptance of the contingency of vocabulary—the scientist and

philosopher by the cultural hero and poet. Rorty rejects the older liberal tradition of grounding ideas in metaphysical constants. "For the attempt to supply such foundations presupposes a natural order of topics and arguments which is prior to, and overrides the results of, encounters between old and new vocabularies."[87] This is a contingent world in which liberalism cannot be rationally justified and, for that matter, Nazism criticized. Since there are no correct descriptions of reality, Rorty contends that we are incapable of asking the question of whether our society is moral or not. The ironic poet is interested in redescriptions of reality to offer new insights and paradigms in order to help in the process of self-creation and self-definition.

In his integration of liberalism and postmodernism, Rorty sounds close to the radical individualism and striving "Overman" of Nietzsche or the charismatic leader of Weber who persuades by the power of linguistic expression and personality. This is also the language of Heidegger, Derrida, and Foucault. There is no public sphere or real exchange of ideas, there is only the ability to deconstruct language and influence others through the power and excitement of words on a relatively passive citizenry who hear their utopian hopes and needs expressed in the exciting new fantasies and metaphorically rich language of the ironist. The individual is defined as "incarnated vocabularies." Arguments look good, are expressed elegantly, and strike unconscious needs deep within the individual, but they don't rationally convince by traditional arguments based on first principles. Rorty says that this world of the ironist is one of continuous self-doubt and insecurity over the reliability of their private linguistic worlds that are historical and nominalistic. In the end, the public sphere disappears with only the private language of its citizens expressing its lost hopes in poetic images. From Habermas's perspective this would represent a private nightmare within a narcissistic world and depoliticized polity.[88]

The critique of epistemology and foundationalism, the contingency of language and metaphors, and the poetry and dialectic of discourse define the public in terms of the priority of private narratives, final vocabulary, or idiosyncratic fantasies. However, from Rorty's perspective, it is the ultimate goal of liberalism to encourage solidarity, diminish cruelty, avoid humiliation of others, recognize and respect individuals, and assume equal responsibility for the pain of others. In the essay "Private Irony and Liberal Hope," he defines respect and humiliation in terms of the language of the poet. Because of the radical dualism between the public and private spheres, he cannot say that the liberal goal is to ensure personal freedom and social diversity of self-definition in the private sphere. Rorty fears political authority making universal or essentialist claims to truth that only humiliate its citizens, who are no longer free to apply their own edifying vocabulary or articulate their own ironic needs. In much the same way as expressed in Isaiah Berlin's political philosophy but with the flare of postmodern language, Rorty describes political oppression as the external imposition of positive freedoms and metaphysical ideals. They undermine and humiliate our negative freedoms to self-determination by suppressing individual final vocabularies by which individuals make sense of their worlds.

Borrowing from both Popper and Berlin,[89] Rorty is fearful of a totalitarianism that imposes its reasons on citizens by enshrining transcendent metaphysical categories of truth resting in rights, humanity, God, nature, or history that undermine both public discourse and private redescriptions of reality. As in the case of most defenders of negative freedom and a market economy, he is less concerned with the possibility that ironic historicism will be unable to resist totalitarianism in the future. The danger is that by running away from metaphysics, he runs into political oppression—the dialectic of postmodernism. Individual humiliation occurs when a person "becomes incapable of weaving a coherent web of belief and desire" in order to define and express their creativity and autonomy in a meaningful fashion.[90] This inability to tell one's own story in one's own language becomes the basis for totalitarian abuse. The individual is robbed of their own redescriptive language and interpretive memory, leaving them with a past and future outlined by an external other and not by their own contingent actions. Idiosyncratic desires, memories, and hopes are distorted by a need to conform to the givenness of an accepted reality. By liberating us from an enslavement to Platonic rationalism, Enlightenment freedoms, and positive ideologies, Rorty's view of a utopian aesthetic culture follows Nietzsche's critique of idolatry in the hope of freeing the individual from externally imposed obligations and beliefs. There are no foundations to ideas, action, and discourse; there is nothing outside of the radical contingency and attractiveness of our own personal lives and rhetorical language; nothing outside our beliefs and desires. The philosophical critique of objective reality and truth is only the epistemological side of Rorty's political critique of totalitarianism.

But there is an apparent clash between the private narcissism of our idiosyncratic vocabulary and the need for solidarity and virtue in liberal democracy. The former is based on personal narratives and ethnocentric behavior and the latter on the utopian ideals of persuasion, argumentation, and the elimination of cruelty. But because there is no neutral or non-circular argument in language—no metaphysical ground—there is no possibility of justifying the meaning of these terms outside of Rorty's own ironic language and "final vocabulary." Bernstein has said that these are incommensurable and contradictory ideas: "Irony and liberalism appear to be mutually antagonistic—at war with each other."[91] Because of the contingency of our descriptive vocabulary and self-narrative language, there is no reason or objectivity to fall back upon in our confusion and arguments; because reason has become poeticized and indifferent, there is no basis for giving priority to one final vocabulary over another; and because there are no foundations, our ideas and actions are without rational justification. The rationality of liberalism is shown to be shallow and meaningless. We cannot be too discriminating about the nature of cruelty. We cannot demand a clear description or characterization of it and cannot ask, "Why not be cruel?" There is a real dilemma to define ironic and utopian liberalism in terms of its fight against cruelty, but be unable to state what it is and why it is better to have a non-cruel society than a cruel society.

In this form of liberalism, there is no public sphere in which to debate and discuss common issues; there are no reasons or arguments to convince and persuade other citizens of the virtue or morality of one course of action over another; and there is no descriptive language that could help us articulate the meaning of what is meant by cruelty and humiliation. The iron cage has been destroyed, only to be rebuilt in the narcissism of our own souls. The need to define and articulate political ideas, to make moral decisions, and to act intentionally founders upon the critique of epistemology and the contingency of experience. Under these conditions in liberal democracy, reason falls silent.[92] We are truly caught in the prison of our own language, unable to communicate or exchange meaning except with those who share our own nightmare. Only relative cynicism and an indifferent world remain, and we must adjust to our own silence. Rorty is expressing an advanced stage of bourgeois rationalization in which the self is even more isolated and fragmented from a community without reason or principles. Morality has become a matter of personal taste in a pluralistic and tolerant political marketplace. And the excommunication of language has moved from Freud's unconscious into Rorty's polity.

In the essay "Private Irony and Liberal Hope," Rorty schematically outlines the basic structural features of bourgeois liberalism: freedom of press, universities, and the political process, social mobility, universal literacy, peace and wealth, leisure to listen and think about social issues, negative freedom, and democratic political institutions and their functional prerequisites. The goal of such a liberal democracy is to permit each individual the opportunity to express their ability and potentiality at self-creation. However, he never really defines the structural features of ironic liberalism in any detail. Nor does he offer criteria or standards by which to choose between a liberalism which

encourages and protects natural rights (Thomas Hobbes and John
Locke), moral autonomy and individual respect (Kant), utilitar-
ian pleasure (Jeremy Bentham and James Mill), self-realization
(John Stuart Mill), equilibrium and circulation of elites (Max
Weber and Joseph Schumpeter), rational choice (Gary Becker
and Allen Buchanan), individual merit and market rationality (Friedrich Hayek and Milton Friedman), negative freedoms
(Isaiah Berlin), individual liberty and libertarian rights (Robert
Nozick), egalitarianism (Ronald Dworkin and Brian Barry), or
the veil of ignorance and social principles of justice and fairness
(John Rawls). Part of this is explained by his critique of epistemology. Having already rejected foundationalism, he cannot now
proceed to ground politics in some other universal principle. But
neither can he leave the reader hanging by vague references to a
liberalism that may or may not structurally facilitate democratic
values and undistorted communication. Though he is prevented
by his epistemology from articulating a universal ground to
politics, he is forced by his political philosophy to give some substance to his views on ironic liberalism. Combining elements of
both liberalism and postmodernism, he presents a picture of its
main characteristics as negative liberty, market rationality, split
between public and private, aesthetic self-fulfillment, and the
freedom of a postmodern self seen as narcissistic, decentered,
and fragmented. Bernstein has accused Rorty of replacing an
epistemological myth of the given with an historical myth of the
given—foundational epistemology with an ahistorical essentialist social theory. The stage has now been set for chapter 6 of this
book and Habermas's response to the debates over the nature of
science and objectivity raging on the continent of Europe and in
the pragmatism and post-analytic philosophy of science in the
United States. Responding directly to the Hegelian and pragmatist critiques of epistemology, foundationalism, and positivism, he
attempts to revive the Enlightenment project by delving into the
structures of language and communicative action. Along the way,
he stops to reflect on the logics of inquiry, forms of rationality,

and methods of social science, as he criticizes positivism, historicism, hermeneutics, and functional system theory.

Phenomenology of Scientific Consciousness and the Domination of Nature: Edmund Husserl, Max Scheler, and Max Weber

IN THIS CHAPTER WE EXAMINE the evolution of modern German epistemology and philosophy of science from the eighteenth to the twentieth century as it evolved through idealism, phenomenology, existentialism, and classical social theory. Its goal is to reveal the complex web of discussion relating to the nature of the natural sciences and positivism, and their place in the development of our understanding of the history and limits of human consciousness in relation to the physical world and external environment. It will not follow a chronological order, but will emphasize the evolution of a critical theory of knowledge from Edmund Husserl and Max Scheler to Friedrich Nietzsche and Max Weber. It will follow the evolution of philosophy and its phenomenological and existential theory of knowledge to an expanded critical theory of technical science, rationalization, disenchantment, and capitalism. By organizing the chapter in this manner, the importance of the development of phenomenology and existentialism in philosophy for the creation of classical sociology and a later critical social theory will become clearer and more visible.

Chapter 1 critically examined the traditional theories of knowledge based on objectivism and subjectivism while also opening up new avenues of investigation about the nature and foundation of phenomenal knowledge, experience, and consciousness. Following the critique of reason in Kantian and post-Kantian philosophy, Edmund Husserl will focus his attention on a number of issues that stress the central role of consciousness in the formation of knowledge and science. This chapter moves beyond traditional epistemology and postmodern philosophy of science to examine the continuing importance of consciousness and science in the domination and control of the physical environment. The traditional correspondence theory of truth in empiricism and rationalism is now replaced by a technical, if not political, perspective at the heart of modern physical science, as it includes the examination of social and political consciousness. In this manner, epistemology expands to include issues beyond the philosophy of science, that is, to examine the relationship between epistemology and social theory, and between philosophy and sociology. New questions therefore arise about the central importance of scientific inquiry, its relation to nature and traditional objectivity, and the importance of human consciousness and life itself. Husserl's phenomenology represents a philosophical uncovering of the radical implications of Kantian epistemology as he unravels the central importance and role of human consciousness (subjectivity) for our knowledge of the natural world. With his focus on the central importance of epistemological constructivism in our experience and knowledge of the objective world, he also begins to broaden his intellectual horizons to include issues of ethics, politics, and the meaning of human life. Moving beyond the postmodern philosophy of science of the previous chapter, we will explore the critique of reason and consciousness as it evolved from the phenomenology of Husserl and Scheler and the existentialism of Arthur Schopenhauer and Nietzsche, and on into the classical social theory of Max Weber.

In very complex and exciting but not so obvious ways,

phenomenology and existentialism begin with the revolution created by Immanuel Kant's critical idealism in the *Critique of Pure Reason* (1781 and 1787). It can never by overstated how crucial this work is to our understanding of the relationship between subjectivity (consciousness) and objectivity (natural objects). Responding to the inadequacies of both empiricism (Hume and Locke) and rationalism (Descartes)—to their understanding of our awareness and knowledge of the world through sense experience and natural science, through observation and reason—Kant rejected knowledge of an independent world through immediate sensation or innate ideas. Instead, he argued that it is the transcendental subject and its forms of intuition (time and space) and the concepts of the understanding (substance and causality) which order our experience and knowledge of the world around us. It is the interconnection between consciousness and nature that produces our knowledge of the physical reality as containing a world of distinct objects and their accidental qualities within a time-space continuum. These objects, in turn, interact with one another in mechanical and formal relationship reducible to causal and mathematical rules, which produce technical and predictable laws. The natural world is not reflected in the representations of our immediate experience or in our reflections of innate ideas.

This position represented a fundamental shift in Western consciousness about the nature of human experience, knowledge, and science. The world we observe and understand is not given to us immediately through experience or observation, but is the result of our construction of that world through the interaction between subjectivity and objectivity. This Kantian revolution in his theory of a priori pure reason and the analytical organization of the human mind would initiate a continuous dialogue over the next several centuries that continues to this day.

At the time Kant thought he was integrating elements of both empiricism and rationalism, experience and reason, into a comprehensive critique of pure reason and the role of human consciousness in the creation of our immediate experience and formal knowledge

of the physical world. Kant integrated both epistemological traditions into a comprehensive and critical theory of human cognition.
From empiricism, he maintained two central tenets: the principle
that knowledge begins with sense impressions and the principle
of metaphysical realism or the existence of an external physical
world independent of the human mind. From rationalism, he borrowed the idea of the central importance of the a priori forms of
cognition—that the human mind is active itself in the process of
knowing, since natural objects and human experience are formed
through a synthesis of matter and form, sensations and the mind.
However, the exciting element in Kant's revolution is that later
thinkers would separate and stress different aspects of his theory
of knowledge. They recognized that the natural world and modern
science are creative, imaginative, and artificial constructs of the
human mind; that our experience and understanding of the world
produce only representations and the appearances of reality, but not
the facts, reality, or "thing in itself" of the world beyond our knowledge. There is not a direct correspondence between consciousness
and the physical world. They continued to argue that if we can
never get behind the appearances of observable evidence to the
reality in itself beyond human experience, then a whole host of new
issues and questions arise which explain the later development of
modern German philosophy of knowledge and science. Some later
theorists would radicalize this Kantian perspective as a rejection of
realism and the correspondence theory of truth.[1] This led to a further critique of the foundations of Western science as grounded not
in reality, but in other value systems or cognitive interests, forcing a
new consideration of the nature of modern science. The traditional
view was that Kant believed in some form of realism, since objects
exist independently of our act of perception.[2] However, the manner
in which Kant develops his theory of the mind later led to a radical epistemological constructivism and eventually to the notion
that perception, experience, and science do not reflect reality but
instead existential relativism and nihilism or specific social cognitive interests (Rickert, Weber, and Habermas).

Georg Friedrich Hegel expanded Kant's theory of the mind beyond the transcendental subjectivity to incorporate not only human consciousness and nature, but the human *Geist* or Spirit of self-consciousness, reason, culture, the ethical community, and the Greek polis. It is the spirit which binds together morality, social ethics, the family, local community, and the government into a unified and distinct social and political entity. Its fullest representation is the family and polis in Hegel's *Phenomenology of Spirit* (1807) and the Greek polis and modern government in *The Philosophy of Right* (1820). The idea of human consciousness is expanded beyond subjectivity and nature in Kant's writings to the Objective Spirit of Aristotle and the ancient Greeks, medieval natural law, Kantian morality, and the French Revolution. The Greek spirit is initially lost in the *Phenomenology* with the turn to the Absolute Spirit (religion, art, and philosophy) as the means for the realization of the ethical community in the mind, but later becomes a central element in his political theory of the modern state in his philosophy of law, right, and the state. After Hegel, the forms of human consciousness expand, especially in the understanding of humanity's relationship to nature and the natural sciences.

Hegel expanded Kant's critical theory of knowledge by introducing the role of consciousness, not only in our experience of nature, but as self-consciousness evolving over time, from classical Greece and the master-slave relationship to the modern ethical community and the French Revolution. Hegel also expanded the role of moral subjectivity, practical reason, and the categorical imperative beyond morality to include history, community, and the modern state, thereby expanding classical humanism into the modern world. With the writings of Max Scheler and Max Weber, the notion of subjectivity in knowledge and ethics was extended further to include both phenomenology and sociology. Weber would continue this trend by broadening his analysis to include a sociology of knowledge in his writings on Christianity and capitalism and in his understanding of the nature of modern science and technology. Scheler began his pathbreaking work *Problems of a Sociology of Knowledge* (1926) with an analysis of the social foundations and origins of subjectivity in the various historical forms of consciousness. Moving beyond Kant's theory of pure and practical reason, he attempted to incorporate the history of Western consciousness in his "philosophical anthropology." This dramatically moved German idealism into a new critical theory of historical reason and knowledge that focused on the forms of consciousness in science, religion, technology, and metaphysics.

PHENOMENOLOGY, SKEPTICISM, AND THE MEANING AND CRISIS OF MODERN REASON: EDMUND HUSSERL

During the mid-1930s, Edmund Husserl wrote his major work on phenomenology, *The Crisis of European Sciences and Transcendental Phenomenology*, based on his lectures in Prague and Vienna (1935) and essays in the international yearbook *Philosophia* (1936). It is viewed as a significant contribution to phenomenology, but incomplete and uneven. In spite of these literary problems, the work is an important introduction to his view of the crisis of modern society and European civilization at a very difficult time in German history.

Husserl's two main goals are to examine both the crisis of European science and the meaning of European science. The first part of this major work moves beyond the phenomenology and history of consciousness in order to connect the mechanical method and mathematical laws of modern science to the cultural and existential crisis of the loss of meaning and substantive values in a society overwhelmed by positivism, science, and technology. Husserl refers to this as the mathematization and crisis of Western science. Science has created a self-enclosed universe of nature that has been subsumed under an infinite number of moving and causally interacting physical objects or bodies within a spatial and temporal framework of rational and mathematical relationships: this is the true being-in-itself. He clarified the distinctive aspect of natural science by comparing it to the humanistic science of ancient and medieval metaphysics and their forms of knowledge. The distinctive and defining aspect of modern consciousness is its loss of reason and existential meaning resulting in the severe cultural crisis of modernity. Husserl connects positive science to the broader cultural problems of modern society. He helps move phenomenology to a more comprehensive critical social theory. Scheler's writings will provide a more detailed examination of the underlying nature of science itself and its origins in the value orientation of modern society.

The second major part of *The Crisis of European Sciences* examines the meaning of science, including Husserl's analysis of the history of the cultural values and development of Western consciousness in religion, metaphysics, and science, and analysis of the origins and technical methods of positive science. His purpose is to establish a phenomenological and historical reconstruction and overview of the evolution of Western thought from Descartes (rationalism) and Hume (empiricism) to the subjectivity of Kantian idealism in order to understand the changes in the meaning and valuation of modern positive science. Husserl emphasizes the importance of Hume's *A Treatise of Human Nature* (1739) and his radical skepticism about Cartesian rationalism. It was Hume who pushed Descartes' own arguments about the ego and consciousness toward a radical skepticism about grounding all scientific knowledge, and its subsequent validation, in the subject. But this argument from Descartes quickly evolved into a solipsistic skepticism and isolation of the subject from objective knowledge and truth. In fact, for Hume, scientific knowledge was only appearances and fictions. Both Descartes and Hume recognized to different degrees that "the goal of tracing genuine scientific knowledge back to the ultimate sources of validity and of grounding it absolutely upon them, required reflections directed toward the subject."[3] This proved a dilemma for Kant, and awakened him from his own dogmatic slumber by undermining the logic and one-sidedness of both empiricism and rationalism. Husserl raises this central issue again in modern thought in its attempt to justify science: "Was it, then, the historical mission of Kant to experience the shaking of objectivism. . . . and to undertake in his transcendental philosophy the solution of the task before which Hume drew back?"[4] Husserl is skeptical and disappointed that Kant did not fully undertake this adventure, but Kant's radical transcendental subjectivism did indirectly address and undermine these traditions. As a response to the weaknesses of both empiricism and rationalism, Kant searched for a new approach to a critical theory of knowledge in his work *The Critique of Pure Reason* (1781) based on his critique of objectivism and radical skepticism—the belief that objective reality and objective truth are irrational illusions. And it is upon Kant's critique of reason that Husserl builds his own crisis of reason and phenomenology.

Many scholars have argued that Kant transcended the skepticism of the Cartesian radical doubt and Hume's theory of substance and causality with his introduction of a priori synthetic categories and judgments existing within the subject. However, Husserl rejects the solutions of both empiricism and rationalism, as he radically and systematically continues this skepticism about the nature and justification of knowledge and science when he maintains that "all categories of objectivity . . . are illusions."[5] He uses terms like psychologism and objectivism to emphasize that both traditions relied on the mythical and dogmatic fictions of the power of the ego or soul (knower) along with the importance of objective reality and truth (realism and naturalism). He calls into question the belief in objective truth (epistemology) about the possibility of objective knowledge in the form of mathematical science and everyday life, along with a similar belief in the existence of an objective reality (ontology) independent of consciousness (realism) that is reflected in scientific and pre-scientific knowledge. Husserl traces the changes within a phenomenology and philosophy of science as to the meaning of both the sensuous and intuitive nature of everyday perception and the realism and constructed objectivism of science within the various philosophical traditions and theories of knowledge.[6] This approach moves beyond a formal analysis of the technical method and mathematical science to a deeper meaning of science underlying the history of Western consciousness and knowledge. This is crucial for Husserl, since up to his time "no one possessed a real understanding of the actual meaning and the internal necessity of such accomplishments" of the scientific method and theories.[7] They were simply accepted by the various schools of epistemology and taken for granted by virtue of their technical success and machine-like predictions.

Husserl understood his central and most important writing to be an examination of the history of scientific consciousness and the meaning of epistemology, methodology, and science after the philosophical critique of traditional objectivism (objectivity of nature) and realism (independent external reality), beginning with the eighteenth century in Parts II and III of his work. It is quite clear that he is not attempting to reestablish a justification or validation of the scientific method, but rather, to explain the psychological motivation and epistemological meaning of these new schools of thought and their impact on Western science and method since Galileo and Descartes. Instead of analyzing and justifying positive science, he undertakes an extensive study of the meaning, evaluation, and motivation behind major advances in scientific and epistemological inquiry. Once the traditional foundations of science in empiricism and rationalism came under critical scrutiny in Kant's critique of pure reason—which led, according to Husserl, to idealism, skepticism, existentialism, and phenomenology—the goal of Kant's analysis was not to reestablish the foundations and validation of science, but to examine its meaning and implications for the phenomenal evolution of Western consciousness and reason. Thus Husserl's major question about the crisis of European reason: In the modern history of Western thought, what were the meaning, purpose, and goals of the search for truth in science and the everyday experiential lifeworld?

Once the universal and traditional validity and truth claims of science came under critical scrutiny, science was no longer the standard of universal knowledge and truth. New questions arose about positivism and positive science: (1) What is the meaning of epistemology and science in a constructed universe and what role do they play in modern thought? (2) What is the relationship between science and the constructed objective world after Hume's skepticism and Kant's critique of reason? (3) What does science mean if there is no objective reality? (4) What is the relationship between science and the universal philosophy of ethics, politics, and the humanities? (5) What is the purpose of science, if it no longer involves the search for objective reality and truth? (6) What are the a priori assumptions and hidden values of modern science buried deep within its concepts, theories, and method? And (7) what are the connections among the broader critique of reason, the meaning of science, and the crisis of science? For phenomenology, questions about epistemology and philosophy of science become questions about the meaning of truth and life and the relationship among humanity, science, and nature. Science becomes the basis for the modern crisis of reason with the dissolution in the belief in its absolute and unchallenged universality, objectivism, and correspondence theory of truth. These questions open up for Husserl a more comprehensive and radical understanding and appreciation of the forms and history of human consciousness and reason. They become the foundation stones for building his theory of philosophy and phenomenology.

Husserl begins his phenomenology with the historical conflicts and contradictions of the ideas and ideals of the cultural lifeworld and the method and axiomatic laws of positive science in modern consciousness. He articulates the central questions for *The Crisis of European Sciences* at the very beginning of his work: What is the nature, origin, and meaning of modern science and what is its relevance for our understanding of science, physical nature, and human existence within the history of Western consciousness?[8] These are the main existential questions understood by Husserl. Because of the central importance of the Cartesian and Kantian revolutions in epistemology, the issue of transcendental

subjectivity and psychology play an important part in the formation of objectivity and the phenomenal world of experience and
knowledge. Husserl refers to this as the "rational totality of being."[9]
He notes that Thomas Hobbes and John Locke play a parallel role
in their analyses of human nature in the state of nature. As the
title of Husserl's work indicates, there is a profound crisis in the
European sciences because they have left the modern world in a
state of confusion and silence in which "science has nothing to
say to us" regarding the nature of reason, freedom, self-determination, creativity, and human dignity; that is, it has nothing to say
regarding the religious or ethical meaning of human life.[10] These
questions of human subjectivity, historicity, and spirituality—
what Husserl calls the cultural "spirit of philosophy" and "goals of
reason"—have been lost in a reductionist and mechanical world
of scientific and mathematical objectivism, naturalism, and nominalism. According to Husserl, modernity only provides us with
"illusory progress" and "bitter disappointment."[11]

The physical and spiritual world that we see, experience, and
know is a world of constructed objectivity, legitimated by the ideology of positivism, which has its origins in the Renaissance. By
juxtaposing the ancient and medieval world on one side and the
modern consciousness on the other, Husserl highlights the startling differences in the ethical, social, and political values and
orientation of ancient universal knowledge (theoretical philosophy and metaphysics) and the modern lifeworld (*Lebenswelt*) of
positivism and science. The broad universal principles and questions in ethics, politics, and metaphysics that give meaning and
purpose to human life are no longer considered valid scientific
issues. Everything relevant is reduced to empirical observation and
objective facts. "Positivism decapitates philosophy" and absolute
reason and, in the process, creates an existential crisis of meaning
in Western consciousness. With the loss of the validity of universal
philosophy and metaphysics (questions of being and reality), there
is a loss of all the important questions that give humanity its freedom and dignity. Universal and philosophical questions about the

meaning of human life, its purpose, and its ideals are not viewed as legitimate because they do not conform to the method, concepts, and logic of the positive sciences.

   Husserl recognizes that the attempted revival of the absolute and philosophical spirit of ancient Greece during the Renaissance (14th–17th centuries) and the Enlightenment (18th century) could not survive the overwhelming power and skepticism of modern science. He views the important epistemological and philosophical discourses in philosophy since Hume and Kant as attempts to revive the spirit of philosophy and the power of human reason (*episteme*), but even that, he argues, eventually fails to counter the impact of the scientific revolution and the reduction of philosophy to its present subservient position in empiricism and positivism. With modernity, positive science "replaces" classical humanism and the search for meaning and values in human life in its philosophical and metaphysical forms. This replacement results in skepticism and existentialism. With this expansion of the Kantian transcendental philosophy and Hegelian phenomenology, Husserl recognizes that subjectivity and constructivism will eventually lead to the existential crisis of modern science and the nothingness of human experience and reason, that is, a world without meaning and values. He views modern philosophy as a continuous critical response to the impenetrable forces of modern science and its crisis of humanity and of reason.[12] The answer to this present crisis is to create a new renaissance and revival of universal reason through phenomenology and the recognition of the importance of a self-understanding and knowledge of the history of Western consciousness and true being or the meaning and purpose of humanity. It is a contest for the spirit of Western consciousness and the true being and inner essence (*telos*) of humanity itself, being fought between two opposing philosophies and forms of consciousness—the existential contradictions and dialectic of history between science and philosophy, between quantitative and mechanical objectivism (the physicalism and empiricism of Locke and Hume) on one side and a transcendental or universal subjectivism (emancipatory ethic of Kant) on the other. This is the conflict between the quantitative and mathematical world of the mechanical, predictive, and causal laws of science and the qualitative search for universal meaning and social ideals in an empty world of decaying matter.[13]

In Part II of *The Crisis of European Sciences*, Husserl turns to a more detailed examination of his idealism and phenomenological theory of science with his analysis of the "mathematization of nature" begun by Descartes (rationalism). He then proceeds to study the epistemological and ontological evolution of positive science into the existential dilemma of modern times. Husserl's answer is similar in many ways to Hegel's phenomenology, likewise retreating into a radical philosophy of the mind.[14] Husserl examines this modern relationship between nature and mathematics as the lived and observable world of experience and understanding is reduced to an objective world of mathematical relationships in a time-space lifeworld. Objective reality is no longer viewed as an independent and external world of physical objects. It is not a being-in-itself; it becomes the idealized mathematical world of artificial and abstract symbols as the scientific method creates true being, ideas, and empirical reality. Objectivity does not lie in itself, nor in nature itself, but is an expression of the method, theories, and objective facts of science, which create the physical world of nature. From this perspective, objectivity is seen as a construct of the objective scientific method and is not the result of the measurement and analysis of an independent and external reality. Methodology creates ontology in an anti-naturalistic science since it is a product of universal subjectivity. Phenomenology argues that nature is not given as a thing or object in sensibility, but is an a priori product of human consciousness and mathematical intentionality. Following in the footsteps of Hegel's idealism, Husserl argues that subjectivity or method constitutes objectivity. Or in the latter's categories, physicalistic objectivism (ontology) is, in fact, constituted by transcendental subjectivism (scientific method), just as sensuous perception of the external empirical reality and physical objects is constituted by human consciousness and experience.

The world of time, space, and motion that we perceive through experience and know through mathematical science is a constructed universe that does not exist independent of human consciousness; scientific facts are not objective in themselves. The objectivity of beings and facts does not lie in itself, but in the natural attitude and creations of human intentionality, consciousness, and positive science. Objectivity is a cultural phenomenon produced in the values and meaning of the pre-given lifeworld of sense experience and in the causal mechanics and technical inductions and predictions of science. He likens science and its method to efficient and productive machines. There is no being-in-itself or independent physical reality, only the creative impulse of the scientific method and its idealized world of mathematics. In fact, Husserl argues that method is mistaken for objective reality itself. But the meaning, origins, and ultimate source of the method are never investigated or called into question. The world is a constructed ideality or invention of ideal being—the idealized nature of mathematics—created by the ideal mathematical method which becomes the only valid way of understanding nature and the world of everyday life. Husserl pushes traditional theories of knowledge to their extreme within the realm of philosophy by maintaining that the world we experience as phenomena and the world constructed by the scientific method are products of subjectivity.[15] Husserl's belief in the idea that method constitutes the objects of experience and axiomatic science represents a fundamental critique of traditional theories of knowledge based on objectivism and naturalism.

> Mathematics and mathematical science, as a garb of ideas or the garb of symbols of the symbolic mathematical theories, encompasses everything which, for scientists and the educated generally, *represents* the life world, *dresses it up* as "objectively actual and true" nature. It is through the garb of ideas that we take for *true being* what is actually a method.[16]

The real world is a construct, since it is not discovered or uncovered as an external reality. Rather, it is a measurement of the lifeworld using the scientific method, analytical and quantitative concepts, and predictive theories. It is this world constructed from a "garb of ideas" that is real. Husserl is aware that this modern scientific accomplishment has not been investigated in any relevant detail, and philosophers have little understanding of its meaning and the inner structure of its a priori forms, concepts, theories, and mathematical laws. There is no comprehensive study of a philosophy of science, its relations to the history and phenomena of consciousness, or the origins of the modern spirit, especially since "no one possessed a real understanding of the actual meaning and the internal necessity of such [scientific] accomplishments."[17]

Part II and the early sections of Part III of the *Crisis of European Sciences* appear to be the book's central chapters, since they search for the root cause of the crisis of Western reason in the underlying and hidden meaning of science and reason in the history of the evolution of Western consciousness and its philosophies of science. That is, they search for the origin and meaning of science in the philosophical debates, and the corresponding changes within the various traditions on the meaning of knowledge and truth, as a way to access the development of the modern spirit or consciousness of nature.[18] Husserl begins with an analysis of the meaning of the new science as understood by Galileo and Descartes, and "the original motivation and movement of thought which led to the conceiving of their idea of nature and from there to the movement of its realization in the actual development of natural science itself."[19] The transformation of our understanding of Western reason is the goal of a phenomenology of science, as a critical and historical analysis of human consciousness and historical forms of scientific thought that will liberate us from our philosophical and methodological prejudices about the nature of mathematical science. Its purpose is to get beyond "the original meaning of science" in objectivism and realism found in both rationalism and empiricism. It seeks to move beyond the naive and false idea that natural science and its mathematical method reflect the truth about nature in its objectivity, as an independent and external reality to the true meaning of science, which lies in its transcendental subjectivity or the a priori structure of the human mind in its sensibility and understanding. The world we know through our senses and reason is a "meaning-construct" (*Sinngebilde*) of human subjectivity.[20] The lifeworld and science itself are constructs of subjective meaning, intentional life, and human consciousness within a community of others, and it is this idea which contains the true meaning of science. Only by moving beyond a theory of knowledge and method can one begin to raise the question about the meaning of science and method in the history of Western consciousness.[21] Husserl does hint at a possible source of the original meaning and motivation of pure science in his brief and tantalizing statement that the goal of science is the "mastery over mankind as belonging to the real surrounding world, i.e., mastery over himself and his fellow man" for the purposes of greater control over life and happiness.[22] However, he does not expand or develop this idea, which is left for the writings of Scheler and others.

Toward the end of this major undertaking, Husserl begins to move away from a narrow psychologism and self-consciousness toward a recognition of the importance of intersubjectivity and community in the process of subjective knowing.[23] To study the subjective forms of experience and consciousness, of which science is only one form, is Husserl's goal. To undertake this more radical view of phenomenology, he critically analyzes the meaning of reason along with its traditional objectivistic philosophy of science. This is a major epistemological prejudice for Husserl, who maintains that science cannot justify itself through its technical rationality and success. It also results in the "shaking of objectivism" or the radicalizing and expanding of the critique of pure reason to a transcendental subjectivity, one that examines the a priori structure of consciousness and its universal characteristics. This, in the end, "frees us from the old objectivistic ideal of the scientific system, the theoretical form of mathematical natural science, and frees us accordingly from the idea of an ontology of the soul which could be analogous to physics."[24]

According to Husserl, the underlying cause of the crisis of science is the singular and profound failure of modern thought to uncover adequately the meaning of its own epistemology and history, or to see that the traditional distinctions between universal philosophy (values of beauty, right, ethics, politics, metaphysics, etc.) and mathematical science are based on false premises and distinctions. Both traditions are grounded in a "transcendental subjectivity" of human reason. He is aware that both the rationalism of Descartes and the empiricism of Locke argue for an objective truth grounded in a belief in an objective reality (objectivism) and a psychology of the ego (sensationalism), neither of which are questioned. Locke in particular never doubted the nature or origin of sensibility, sensations, or the very objects of experience that undergird his theory of knowledge. As a result, he never raised the issue of their origin or formation, just as Descartes never raised the issue of the origin or source of the knowing self.[25] Both rationalism and empiricism abstracted themselves from consideration of the nature of subjectivity. By beginning his philosophical turn at this point in his analysis, Husserl hopes to free philosophers from epistemological prejudices that view nature as a given reality or being-in-itself. Thus, Part I traces the evolution of his understanding of the epistemology and philosophy of science from rationalism and empiricism to the critical idealism of Kant. The failure to see the subjective element in the earlier epistemologies led to an inability to appreciate the true meaning and relevance of scientific inquiry. "All previous discussions of idealism and realism have failed to penetrate to the consciousness of the genuine problem which lies, sought for but undiscovered, behind all theories of knowledge."[26] And with this failure to understand the origins and meaning of science, the naturalistic and mathematical method began to be universalized and applied to all forms of knowledge outside the boundaries of nature.

The goal of Husserl's phenomenology and the history of human

experience and consciousness, the everyday lifeworld, and positive science is to critically understand the foundations of modern
science beyond its mathematical and formal method. Its ultimate
purpose is to see that science, as with the experiences of the presci-
entific lifeworld, are constructs of human reason and subjectivity.
Thus, there is no break in the link between the lifeworld and science itself. They are both products of human consciousness, and
there is no unbridgeable division between the sensible world and
science. It is not a study of the evolution of scientific and technical methods, but a critical understanding of those methods within
a phenomenology of the mind in perception, experience, and
reason. It is an examination of the meaning of science and reason
in order to make a fundamental break with realism and objectivism as standing outside and independent of human consciousness.
What we see, hear, observe, and think about are all empirical or
mathematical constructs. Questions about the meaning of human
life, its values, and ideals are not secondary to the power of scientific reason and mathematical science.

It is important to note that, according to Husserl, the reality that
we experience in the modern world is an artificially constructed
objectivity of conceptual illusions and theoretical fictions created
for improving scientific predictions. He refers to this as "academic skepticism" and the "bankruptcy of objective knowledge."[27]
In their analysis of pure mathematical science, philosophers did
not look into the nature of creating subjectivity, reason, or created objectivity, since these were hidden by the doctrines of
realism and naturalism; from the start of their analyses, philosophers simply accepted the underlying dogmatic objectivism
and psychological sensationalism of their own arguments as real
and essential. However, at this crucial and ironic point, Husserl
falls into the same dilemma that he attributes to Descartes and
Locke. He does not examine the implications of his own idea
that it is the scientific method which creates reality and being in
order to perfect scientific predictions. He does not fully appreciate the radicalism of his own phenomenology by developing the

philosophical implications of his epistemological constructivism or the sociological implications of the meaning of the domination of nature and scientific predictions. Instead, Husserl's focus is on a broader project of the history and evolution of human consciousness from the Greek and medieval world through the Renaissance and the Enlightenment to present contradictions between science and universal philosophy, and between predictive knowledge and knowledge of values and ideals. What are the epistemological implications of the new nature of objectivity of method and empirical reality and its implicit critique of naturalism? Why has this view of nature become so successful? What are the adjacent sociological and political implications of the relationship between science and predictive improvements? If objective reality is a construct, what are the epistemological and sociological implications of this thesis? This would have taken Husserl into the realm of epistemological constructivism and sociological materialism, which he did not enter. Husserl kept his analysis of the mathematization of nature within the limits of phenomenological philosophy and psychology, whereas Scheler would attempt to deal with some of these social issues with his theory of science and the domination of nature.

Both Husserl and Scheler made important contributions to the study of positive science and phenomenology. While Husserl placed science within the evolution and history of Western consciousness and the existential crisis that resulted from positivism and the crisis of reason, Scheler would examine the historical origins and a priori technological and mechanistic structure of science. The latter was unable to make the causal and historical connection between science and the rise of capitalism since, in his sociology of knowledge, they were merely parallel events. And Husserl, while connecting science and existentialism, was unable to see its a priori political and technological nature or its relationship to the rise of modern industry, work, and capitalist social relations of production. His main focus was on examining the implications of the two entirely contradictory views of science and human life that

had resulted in a crisis of Western civilization. The phenomenologists were never able to develop a true historical, sociological, or
economic foundation for the study of modern science because of
their emphasis on the history of experiential phenomena and the
idealist structure of human consciousness. For them, the development of modern science was more a transformation of human
consciousness and understanding of experience and phenomena,
a mental process rather than a social and economic issue. They
were never truly able to see beyond and transcend the limits of
German Idealism in Kant, Schelling, and Hegel.

For the phenomenologists, the central problem is either the loss
of meaning in modern science produced by the loss of universal philosophy and metaphysics—resulting in epistemological skepticism
and existentialism, as is the case for Husserl—or the methodological, theoretical, and technological imperative to dominate and
control nature, as it is for Scheler. Husserl's major philosophical
error was his inability to see beyond phenomenology, the history
of human consciousness, and the method of scientific inquiry. He
thought his major accomplishment was to move beyond science
back to universal philosophy, but failed to recognize that both science and philosophy were, in fact, grounded in history and the
underlying social institutions and structures of modern society.
For this reason, we will continue to examine these issues in chapter
4, but from the perspective of Marx and his theory of historical
materialism as he connects scientific rationality and industrial production; in chapter 6 we will continue this analysis by examining
the Frankfurt School and the profound contributions to this discussion by Max Horkheimer, Herbert Marcuse, and Jürgen Habermas,
who recognized the importance of phenomenology for its analysis
of the problem of scientific domination, technological and formal
rationality, and the existential crisis of naturalism and nominalism.
However, the phenomenologists failed to see the deep structural
relationships between phenomenology and the economic and
political institutions of modern society. They did not inquire into
the central and critical importance of the underlying structures

of political economy, work, and technology, and the shared contradictions within positive science and industrial capitalism.[28] Instead, they focused more on the philosophical and existential crisis caused by positive science, which had resulted in a profound crisis of reason, human existence, and the meaning of cultural life. The members of the Frankfurt School saw the problem of modern science from an entirely different perspective: as product of the relationship between the rise of positive science (and technology) and modern capitalism (and political economy). They, like Scheler, recognized the a priori structure and logic of positive science, but moved beyond him by historically and sociologically connecting positive science to the structure and logic of capitalist production and the internal relations of power and authority within work. It is in this manner that individuals become commodities and things producing surplus value in industry and commerce; they become commercial objects of alienation, market exchange, and work exploitation. The logic of objectivism, mechanization, mathematical quantification, and technology come to form the conceptual foundation of both science and human labor. The social imperative of alienation occurs at the level of phenomenal experience and consciousness, but also at the level of work and industrial relations. The critical theorists view the crisis as a product of modern technology, capitalism, and liberalism. Horkheimer and Habermas would develop the insights uncovered and initiated within social and transcendental phenomenology with their own concepts of the "eclipse of reason" and "the silencing of reason," respectively.

Social Phenomenology and the Domination of Nature: Max Scheler

In his important work on the sociology of knowledge and science, Scheler took the broad philosophy of knowledge and the corresponding analysis of subjectivity and consciousness into a new area of investigation. He moved beyond the idealism of the transcendental subject and history of phenomenal self-consciousness and culture to examine the three main stages of cognition and developmental psychology: forms of Western consciousness and cultural ideals from religion (revelation and awe); metaphysics-philosophy (wonder, existential meaning and erudition, and the essence and being of reality and absolute values); and natural science (practical knowledge and the quantitative laws and mastery of nature). Scheler is aware that he is expanding Hegel's notion of the Objective Spirit and connecting it with cultural sociology as he moves from the mathematization of nature in Husserl to his theory of the domination of nature. His analysis of the sociology of knowledge gives special attention to phenomenology, positivism, and the positive sciences. According to Scheler, the development of perception and thought are rooted in valuation and social life, thereby integrating epistemology and sociology. Each form of consciousness has a different style, language, emotion, and worldview that takes us beyond the concepts of Kant's theory of pure reason and transcendental subjectivity.

This section will emphasize Scheler's theory of positive science. He focuses his study on the history of consciousness and the discovery of the hidden values underlying the foundations of modern science and technology. These values help "select" the objects of homogeneous empirical experience, scientific observation and laws, and natural science. Here, Scheler places a different emphasis on the formation of the mathematical objects and laws of positive science. Unlike the neo-Kantians, he uses the term *select*, rather than *create* or *construct*, since it is only one form of knowledge that establishes its objects and laws from the valuation process of consciousness and the desire to dominate the external world of nature. Science, in its origins and development, becomes a central object of sociological inquiry. Scheler writes: "This very origin of science would lead us to an assumption which the history of science has already confirmed: the forms of *productive techniques* and human *work* (in the technical sense) are parallel to forms of *productive-scientific thought*."[29] He is drawing a clear but under-developed connection from the Enlightenment and the rise of

Western science to the conceptual logic and social organization of modern technology and work. Positivist science is the "ideology of recent Western industrialism."[30] As mentioned above, much of the critical theory of knowledge after Scheler would attempt in more sociological detail to historically and socially expose these connections between consciousness and reason on one hand and industrial production and technology on the other.

According to Scheler, the distinctive aspect of modern positive science is its ability to develop a purely "theoretical mode of cognition" based on logical and mathematical methods, quantifiable laws, and experimental procedures that have a technical and practical application in the real world. It is capable of creating objects or phenomena within a temporal and spatial setting that are reducible to universal and mechanical laws of spatial relationships, physical causality, and motion. This is a different worldview, with a different emotional and cognitive form, from that of the ancient Greeks and medieval Christians, with their emphasis on being, substance, accidents, quality, form, essence, and force. The moderns see human beings as pragmatic and functional tool- and machine-makers and technicians, not as rational and contemplative beings. This transformation required a profound cognitive, emotive, and psychological revolution in human consciousness, ethos, and valuation system. The origins of science are to be found in the economy of work and commerce, along with these other psychological and cognitive changes. Due to his social phenomenology and residual idealism, Scheler is clear in his rejection of a strictly Marxist interpretation of the origins of Western science, since for him there are also philosophical, theoretical, and emotional interests involved in its creation. There is a strong desire for freedom from scarcity and dependence on nature, which limits its theoretical framework to only those elements and laws of nature that are measurable and quantifiable and thus capable of prediction and calculation. Both the theoretical/philosophical and practical/technical elements of positive science are reflections of the need to dominate and control nature.

The notion of *Herrschaftswissen* (knowledge or science of domination) was first introduced to sociology by Scheler in his work "Probleme einer Soziologie des Wissens" (1924), later revised and expanded by the inclusion of his essay "Erkenntnis und Arbeit," in *Die Wissensformen und die Gesellschaft* (1926). This concept reflects his theory that science is a particular form of knowledge that has an a priori imperative built into its concepts and method, which are directed at the utilitarian domination and control over nature. Against Marx, Scheler argues that the relation between science and philosophy is dialectical, as the economic foundations of industry play a central role in the formation of science, but are not its only cause. He views Bacon, Saint-Simon, Comte, and Marx as crude materialists and reductionists, while arguing for a developmental psychology which would include the biological drive of society's entrepreneurs and bourgeois leaders, with their ethos of work and individualism, to explain the origins of positive science. The cognitive and intellectual values of philosophy, biological drives of leaders, and the technical interests of industry interact and parallel one another to create a new form of scientific cognition and psychology. They do not directly or mechanically cause each other; instead, they complement and parallel one another, since there are multiple psychological and cognitive reasons behind the rise of science. However, the importance of Scheler's phenomenology (forms of cognition and consciousness) is that he does see economics as central to the creation of science: "The sociological origins of positive science are always *economic communities of work and commerce*."[31] He maintains that the desire to control external nature and material production does not exist in Buddhist metaphysics and religion, since this tradition directs cognition and actions to the control of humanity's inner psychic nature. Nor does it exist in Greek science, philosophy, or religion, which affirm the value and dignity of the world through ethics and contemplation. These different forms of cognition and psychology help explain the distinctive patterns of human behavior in modern European society.

Critically reacting against his contemporaries, Scheler began to undertake a comprehensive cultural phenomenology in his theory of the main forms and stages of human consciousness. Not limiting himself to a materialist or deterministic interpretation of history, he outlined the historical preconditions for the evolution of Western positive science, with emphasis on work, contemplative and Hellenistic philosophy, and positive science. His more detailed and comprehensive overview and explanation of the rise of modern science of Copernicus, Kepler, Galileo, Leonardo, and Newton included the following: an inner desire for personal freedom and control over nature coming from modern work and crafts in patriarchal societies and pure philosophical and metaphysical contemplation and independent thinking; freedom from the biomorphic metaphysics and religion of the medieval Catholic Church; a return to the Platonic and Pythagorean mathematics and science of nature, as well as a rejection of medieval Scholasticism and anti-mathematical Aristotelianism; the Protestant Reformation with its dogmatic principles of the centrality of grace, work, and calling, and the dismantling of the hierarchical power of the Catholic Church and its view of Pelagianism, along with its elimination of the order of estates and classes; the rise of nominalism, Cartesian analytic geometry, and dualism between the rationalist mind and the mechanical body, and rejection of speculative and abstract religious metaphysics and the organic view of nature; the separation of church and state resulting in the lessening of the secular and religious power of Catholicism; and the rise in state sponsored secular universities, large commercial cities and trade, and the importance of the Renaissance and its romantic naturalism with a new perception of nature. Unfortunately, Scheler did not get into the specifics necessary to expand these references or detail their connections to the rise of positive science. There was no mention of social priorities or historical or structural causation.

Scheler's goal was less to develop a historical sociology or critical theory of Western science than to introduce the reader to a new sociology of knowledge and cultural phenomenology. In the end, he was unable to move beyond cultural philosophy and its linear time frame of the development of consciousness from religion, art, economics, philosophy, and science toward a more critical and materialist social theory. Nor was he able to make the theoretical and historical connections between science and political economy, between idealism and materialism, and between consciousness and ideas and the total social system. Scheler was, however, able to raise important questions about the social uniqueness and the broad historical and phenomenal context of positive science and its relationship to European society in general, but not to develop a comprehensive social theory of modern science. He was unable to organize the cognitive and psychological material in an historically and sociologically coherent fashion that could provide the reader with an understanding of the central, interrelated causal features of the rise of Western science. He concluded that scientific knowledge was only parallel to the technical nature of production and work, but did not delve any deeper into the nature of modern science and technology and their relationship to modern industrial production. Because of Scheler's own criticisms of an economic and materialist interpretation of history, the historical and logical relationship between science and work would remain relatively static and undeveloped until a more dialectical and critical rethinking of Marx's theory of historical materialism evolved along with the debates within the Frankfurt School. Scheler is clear in his arguments that neither science nor work is the causal origin of the other; instead their origins are interdependent. However, their exact relationship is never clarified. To explain their relationship, Scheler retreats into a phenomenology and history of the mind, cultural ethos, and a corresponding psychology of "drive-structure" of society's leaders.

In spite of these limitations within philosophy and sociology, Scheler does make an important contribution to the study of science by maintaining that technology is not a later or subsequent application of scientific theory to the study of and integration with nature. Rather, the drive to dominate nature is inherent and embedded in the method and theory of science. *Herrschaftswissen* already exists in the concepts and structure of scientific inquiry— its very objects, observations, measurements, logic, mathematics, and causal and scientific laws—prior to its application in the natural world, since science and technology, knowledge and the will to dominate, "co-determine" each other. The need to organize commerce, industrial production, and work along a highly efficient and technical order capable of pragmatic quantification, technical measurement, prediction, and economic laws of behavior is intimately connected to the inner mechanistic and functional workings of the scientific method, observation, and discovery. They are part of a common spirit and emotional drive to dominate both the economy and nature. The scientific categories are already assimilated with technical knowledge and application.

Scheler emphasizes that the technological and mathematical dimension in science is not a product of its application, but is embedded in its very concepts and theories about the natural world and physical environment itself. Science is by nature in its method and theory a form of technical knowledge; its concepts and ideas are a priori technological.[32] Arguing against pragmatists and Marxists, he contends that these transformations occurred within science's own methods, logic, and theories. It was not caused by the needs, values, and objectives of industry, but by the "will to methods" or expansion of industry's own quantitative and formal values and ideas, which turned all of nature into various forms of capital, commercial exchange, and profit through its "will to endless acquiring."[33] The quantification and predictability of all experience, as well as a new spirit and consciousness of theoretical and market competition, undermines the medieval search for qualitative concepts, traditional order, and teleology in favor of the laws of nature and the market. "Everywhere production aims at *inexhaustible* stocks of merchandise or goods of knowledge."[34] This is a major contribution to the discussion between philosophy and sociology about the origins of modern science and its underlying metaphysics or a priori technical and mechanical imperatives.

Scheler makes two important contributions in his study of a sociology of knowledge of science and the domination of nature: he raises the central questions of the historical origins and relationships between, on the one hand, the rise of the modern industrial economy and work and modern natural science, and, on the other, the underlying and embedded technological and mechanistic foundations of both modern work and positive science. However, it would remain to later philosophers and social theorists to unpack the meaning of these relationships in more social and historical detail over the next century.

RADICALIZING KANT, EXISTENTIALISM, AND THE NOTHINGNESS OF REASON: ARTHUR SCHOPENHAUER

The theory of knowledge and critique of reason developed by Kant gave rise to many different intellectual and philosophical traditions, including idealism, phenomenology, existentialism, and critical social theory. They all responded positively, but in different ways, to his critique of empiricism and rationalism and their correspondence theory of truth; his theory of subjectivity, representations, and the constitution theory of knowledge; the primacy of human creativity in knowledge and ethics; and the rejection of the passivity of knowing. According to Kant, we can never know external objects in their substance and objectivity; we can only know their representations and impressions. We can never know objects directly through perception, causality, or primary or secondary qualities. Experience and knowledge are representations or constructs of the a priori forms of intuitions (time and space) in perception and the a priori categories of the understanding (substance and causality) in experience.[35] The ability to say a simple sentence such as, "the chair on the other side of the room was moved in front of the table by the instructor twenty minutes ago," presupposes ideas encased in the forms of intuition of a spatial and temporal continuum and within the categories of the understanding of substance (physical objects) and causality (movement of the table). These Newtonian categories of the mind (subjectivity) framed and organized the chaos of indeterminate intuitions and formless sensations—blind and unarticulated impressions—into a coherent form of experience and knowledge, i.e., objectivity. All knowledge is subjective in origin but objective in form and structure (universal or transcendental nature of the human mind). This led later to the famous Hegelian saying, "subjectivity creates objectivity": consciousness (mind) creates the objective world of perception and experience, sensation and thought, impressions and ideas.

Unlike in the other epistemological traditions of empiricism and rationalism, there is no access to an objective reality of empirical facts (inductive logic and passive mind) or rational ideas (deductive logic and active mind). Kant rejected the notion that we have access to an external, objective reality (thing-in-itself) through the empirical facts of perception or the ideas of the mind. There is no knowledge of objective truth or objective reality beyond and behind the power of human reason. We can never know before we know; we can never know what we do not know; and we can never know what is behind our knowledge of representations and appearances. That is, we know only the constructs of the mind (Newtonian forms of time and space and categories of substance and causality), not the reality behind the constructs. Although not an existentialist himself since he was a key figure in German idealism, Kant could be referred to as the father of existentialism because of his constructivist theory of knowledge, theory of representations, and implicit critique of realism. The idea of perception and ideas as representations and his theory of the thing-in-itself (external or objective reality) would provide the foundation stones for Schopenhauer's own theory of representations as dreams and illusions. His goal is to outline the universal and necessary logical conditions for the possibility of knowledge of that world (transcendental subjectivity) in terms of the sensations, forms of intuition, categories of the mind, and creative imagination.[36]

Epistemology rests on the Kantian notion that we only know

appearances through the transcendental subject and never the objective, external thing-in-itself. At the very beginning of *The World as Will and Representation* (1818 and 1844), Schopenhauer argues that we do not see the sun or the reality of the sun, but only our idea of the sun. Within the traditions of both rationalism and empiricism, the idea of the sun reflected or mirrored the essence or reality of the sun. But with the Copernican Revolution in Kantian philosophy, with its constitution theory of truth, the idea and the reality become distinct; this is the dilemma of double affection. The perceiver cannot get behind the perception (impression) or understanding (idea) of the sun to its original and foundational cause or formal reality. With the constitution theory of knowledge, subjectivity is always an intricate and invaluable part of objectivity and the two cannot be separated. Thus, there is no pure objectivity of ideas or empirical facts without the transformation and constitution of human consciousness. We cannot get from the idea of the sun (phenomenon) back to the reality of the sun (noumenon); this is an impossible epistemological task. There is no sun in itself.

Kantian philosophy, as is interpreted by Schopenhauer, maintains that knowledge is a transformation and construction of the external or noumenal world based on the a priori categories of the mind of time, space, causality, distance, and motion. The underlying innate forms of knowledge are a product of human reason and not our immediate perception of the real world. The latter is never knowable because it is a construct of these a priori categories which change it in the act of sensation and understanding, perception and experience, everyday knowledge and science. Therefore, we do know the real world, but only our perception and ideas of it. It is this insight of Kant's Copernican Revolution in philosophy which provides Schopenhauer with the intellectual foundations of his existentialism and later turn to Hinduism. For Schopenhauer, there were two forms of cognition: (1) sufficient reason of perception, understanding, and science that gives us access to the representations, appearances, and nothingness of Kant and the illusions and veil of Maja of Hinduism; and (2) art and philosophy and their access to the pure forms of Plato and the contemplation of true being of Hinduism.

The first sentence of the book represents an interesting and provocative anticipatory summary of the entire work: "The world is my representation." What does this mean? Schopenhauer is revealing the broad framework through which his writing should be interpreted by beginning with the concept of representation, which is the centerpiece of Kant's epistemology and critique of pure reason, understood as a criticism of the traditional theories of knowledge in empiricism and rationalism and the building of the a priori and universal foundations of knowledge of the sensible impressions and intellectual world. The term *representation* (*Vorstellung*) here refers to a number of Kantian terms, in which the world is *phenomena, appearance, subjectivity, construct* or *creation, mind, consciousness, objectivity, perception* and *experience, sensation* and *understanding, constructed experience, senses,* and *ideas,* as well as to ideas from Hinduism, where the world is *illusions, dreams, veil of Maya,* and *nothingness.* "The whole world of objects is and remains representations."[37] Schopenhauer pushes Kantian epistemology beyond Kant into a radical existentialism with his idea that the world of representations of substances and matter in time, space, duration, and causality is only a creation of human consciousness and thus represents only a veil of illusions and dreams produced by the human mind. The forms of sensibility and understanding—the principles of sufficient reason—that create the natural objects of the world are cognitive inventions of our perception and experience. There is no objective reality to be seen or known, but only the constructions and representations of the mind. "This world as representation exists only through the understanding, and also only for the understanding."[38] There is an external world of forces, objects, gravitation, heat, light, etc., but these are mere phenomena. The world of the sensibility and perception is a world of meaningless sensations, unarticulated impressions, formless empirical information, and incomprehensible intuitions, while the world of the understanding or forms and concepts of the mind organize this meaningless universe into what appears as a comprehensive picture of empirical reality. But there is no way that we can get beyond these conceptual constructs to see nature as it truly is; we know only the constructs of our ideas and understanding. We cannot see the construct and reality at the same time; we only know the representations, which are products of a "ghost of our own nothingness."[39] These representations are a product of our will-to-live which, according to Schopenhauer, is the "essence of life" in our knowledge and actions.[40] We only know what the mind has constructed—we only know the mind; we only know our representations of sensations and experience—we only know nothingness. This is the central epistemological foundation for the evolution of existentialism and also provides insight in a world of our will and desires and the world of our knowledge and representations as a world constructed by the human will-to-live in a world of egoism (*principium individuationis*), doubt, and suffering in search of the creative and beautiful.[41] Schopenhauer's critique of reason and representations, as well as his theory of the will-to-life, seem to provide Nietzsche with the initial insights and foundation for his own theory of human suffering and pain, spiritual and intellectual decadence, and the will to power toward dignity, beauty, and freedom.

According to Schopenhauer's interpretation of Kant's critique of pure reason, we cannot know the sensations of objects and the objects of sensation at the same time; we only know the sensations and experiences of objects—representations. We cannot know both the objects of external reality and the sensations of objects, objects and the impressions of objects, and objects and the ideas of objects. The latter are mental constructs of perception and experience, sensations and ideas, and sensibility and the understanding. This theory of knowledge is a direct rejection of Western realism, rationality, and materialism. The thing-in-itself is the world of perception, without the organizational principles of the forms and categories of the mind—perception without time and space, without substance and causality. It would be a formless mass of meaningless information. All knowledge is a representational construction or re-construction of subjectivity integrating the mind and body, form and matter, understanding and perception; the world is a constructed experience; all knowledge—perceptions and experience—is mediated by the mind. The world as will and representation is a world constructed by action and the mind (forms of intuition and categories of the mind); objectivity is a construct of subjectivity or consciousness and appears in the form of the objectivity of perception, experience, and knowledge (representations and consciousness) and the objectivity of the will (body and desires)—all of which is simply an illusion or dream of nothingness and meaninglessness. We have access only to the phenomenal world of the appearances and not to the noumenal reality, since our ideas are only re-presentations of our perception and experience.

There is no access to the reality of an objective, natural world independent of our perception and experience of it. What would this thing-in-itself or noumenal reality look like, how could we know it, and how could we know that we knew it? To know this world, we would have to experience it before we experienced and changed it. Without the categories and forms transforming and restructuring the objective world, there would be no way of knowing the universe independent of the structure of the human mind: forms of intuition of time and space and the categories of the understanding of substance, accidents, and causality. This is the famous Copernican Revolution in Kantian philosophy. Kant's theory of knowledge is summarized in his statement: "Thoughts without content are empty, intuitions without concepts are blind." This theory of knowledge represents a rejection of objectivism, realism, and a copy theory of knowledge. These insights were then expanded by later thinkers. The German existentialism of Schopenhauer and Nietzsche is grounded in a radicalized form of German Idealism and Kantian theory of knowledge as representations (sensations and ideas). They will push Kant's theory of the transcendental construction of reality in epistemology and moral philosophy to its extreme: objective reality and moral universals are subjective constructions of the mind. Similarly, does a photograph simply reflect, or create and transform, the reality we see? Or is it the only reality we have? The theory of representation runs from Hume's skepticism to Kant's transcendental idealism to Schopenhauer's existentialism. The intellectual irony of Schopenhauer's critique of reason and the understanding is that it is grounded in Kantian subjectivity (transcendental consciousness) and theory of representations, but ends in existential subjectivity (relativism and nothingness). Existentialism evolves out of the problems of traditional epistemology and the subjectivity of German idealism.[42]

Moving from the idea that the natural and moral worlds are constituted by the mind and representations, Schopenhauer evolves to the position that the world is only consciousness, ideational illusions, and solipsistic nothingness. In the end the only thing an individual knows is the structure of their own mind in the form of ideas and perceptions; reality has been reduced to pure consciousness. In the history of Western thought, theories evolved that the senses reflect objective reality (Hume), the mind reflects ideational reality (Descartes), the mind interprets and constitutes reality (Kant), and the mind creates and is the only reality (Schopenhauer). This last position is a form of existential captivity: the world is nothing but projections of the human mind, a collection and experience of phenomena, appearances, illusions, and dream—nothingness. Nietzsche would begin with these philosophical ideas from Kant (representations) and Schopenhauer (nothingness, illusions, and dreams) and push them even further into existential nihilism and moral relativism in classical sociology. Existentialism has been reviewed as a product of social change, with the loss of natural law and species being (alienation), ethics, values, and substantive reason (disenchantment), immanent presence, telos, and meaning of God in the world (rationalization), and the loss of guiding cultural norms and social values (anomie). The logic, reason, and values of the lifeworld have been replaced by the liberalism and market rationality of capital and the last man.

According to Schopenhauer, representations are appearances, illusions, and distortions of reality. All the world is a representation and construction of the perceptions and ideas of the human mind. Since I experience only the sensations of the sun or know only the idea of the sun, I never know the sun itself; this is the dilemma of double affection which is transformed into the veil of Maya. I never know the natural reality of the external world or the "thing-in-itself." I only know the creations of sensibility (time and space) and mind (causality and substance) as projected onto the external world, that is—I only know the representations of the world in human consciousness, never the immediate presentations of the external world themselves. The subject only knows the forms of objectivity that exist a priori in the transcendental structure of the mind. Reality prior to conceptual transformation is inaccessible to me and thus all knowledge is only a meaningless construct. Schopenhauer takes this Kantian insight into the nature of perception and experience and turns it into an existential crisis. Since we only know the representations of the senses and understanding, perceptions and ideas, we are limited to knowledge projected and created by our own minds. And since this knowledge does not permit us access to objective reality or the thing-in-itself, we know only subjectivity or nothingness.

Schopenhauer next turns to the world as will, which is the body in motion searching for the realization of its physical desires, emotions, and passions. But like the mind, the body ends in the nothingness of suffering and pain, because every passion realized is another passion sought but unfulfilled. His theory of the will is a theory of human suffering, as philosophy is turned into a search for the path to salvation and escape from nothingness: escape from the veil of Maya and the pain, suffering, and meaninglessness of the world. The search for meaning of the will-to-live in the world of materialism, utilitarianism, and egoism offers no solution to the unremitting and unrelenting desire for more and more; the will-to-live is a world experienced as a will to egoism, pleasure, happiness, desires, wants, etc. Instead of turning to a social and political understanding of this concept of will, and a possible solution to it in the rejection of liberalism (as seen in Camus), Schopenhauer views the will-to-live in metaphysical terms of the distortions and illusions of the "veil of Maya." The world of knowledge and truth (the world of representations) and the world of striving and wants (the world of will and action) provide us with illusions and distortions of reality; desires are never completed or satiated. In the last line of the book Schopenhauer writes, "this very real world of ours with all its suns and galaxies, is nothing."[43] In the end, there is only "the terrible pain . . . the most frightful desolation and emptiness . . . and an excessive inner torment, an eternal unrest, and an incurable pain" that represents the modern hell of nothingness—the private existential hell of torture, torment, and terror without Christian metaphysics.[44] Neither Western Enlightenment nor liberalism provides solutions to the existential dilemma of the veil of Maya and the nothingness of the world. For Schopenhauer, the answer lies in the paths to salvation heralded by Hinduism, Platonic philosophy, and medieval monastic life.

Salvation can be achieved through the will-less self, pure resignation and contemplation, asceticism and self-mortification, and the creation of the beautiful soul. That is, salvation can only be achieved through the rejection of representations, human desires, the will-to-live, and egoism. One must turn to resignation and pessimism, asceticism and self-mortification, as exemplified by the lives of the Christian saints and monks in medieval monasteries, the contemplation of the beautiful in the virtuous life of the saint, ascetic, and the artist, and by following the ideals of Hinduism, the beautiful soul, and eventual union with *Brahman*, the supreme spirit, and the philosophical contemplation of the eternal forms or ideas in Plato's philosophy. Through resignation, asceticism, rejecting the will-to-live and modern individualism, and the momentary pleasures of life, each person is able to achieve a level of serenity and knowledge of the cosmos and beauty of art.

Schopenhauer is searching for the truth (thing-in-itself) and meaning of human existence amid the existential crisis of cognitive illusions, the dreams of representation, and the universal suffering and pain of the will-to-live in the Western world. He finds truth among the ancient Greeks and Hindus in the contemplation of beauty and Being. Plato's theory of beauty and forms and Hinduism's theory of *atman, Brahman*, and *samsara* (cycle of birth and rebirth) replace the void left by Schopenhauer's critique of materialism, utilitarianism, individualism (egoism), and the Enlightenment. In the end, *atman* is *Brahman*—the self is will and life itself. Neither the mind nor the body can lead to truth and wisdom or happiness and pleasure, since they are merely illusions and dreams of the mind and body—there is only nothingness. The mind realizes itself in the phenomena and dreams of the appearances, but never in objective reality or scientific truth. The body only reproduces the samsara of eternal suffering and pain, life and death. All reality produced by the mind and body is an illusion; the concrete and objective world of Galileo and Newton and the materialist and egoistic world of Hobbes and Locke are all dreams created by humanity to give the appearance of reality, happiness, and purpose. They mean nothing. In the end, there is no meaning or purpose to human existence, only existential despair, torment, and suffering. The only solution for Schopenhauer is to escape from the will-to-live (body) and the will-to-truth (mind) through asceticism, resignation, and aesthetic contemplation in the life of the saint, ascetic, or the artist; the only solution is to lose oneself in the contemplation of beauty (Plato) and the oneness of Being (*Brahman*). This integration of Greek philosophy and Hinduism offers Schopenhauer the only means of escaping the nothingness and pain of the mind and body. There are no answers provided by Enlightenment science and liberalism—the values and institutions of modern Western society only produce and reproduce the existential dilemma. Existentialism arose out of the dilemma of Kantian epistemology, the thing-in-itself, and the theory of double affection. Nietzsche would begin his analysis of the human condition with the absurdity of the nothingness of the every-day world of human experience and knowledge. Schopenhauer's theory of phenomena, representations, appearances, dreams, objectivity, and nothingness of all forms of everyday and scientific knowledge provides the existential introduction to Nietzsche's theory of the tragic vision and cultural decadence of Western reason and science. For Schopenhauer, the path to salvation out of the nothingness and torment of the constantly changing world is through the ascetic denial, resignation, and rejection of the will-to-live and a resigned contemplation of art and philosophy by the beautiful soul, whereas for Nietzsche the path out of the existential anxiety and fear was the exact opposite, involving an unrelenting resistance to human suffering by means of the overwhelming aesthetic creativity of the will to power in art.[45]

THE CRISIS OF REASON AND SCIENCE IN EXISTENTIALISM: FRIEDRICH NIETZSCHE

The skepticism and existentialism implicit in Husserl's writings push beyond Kant's critique of reason and the later phenomenological critique of science to the very foundations of Western science and rationality. Phenomenology develops the thesis of the epistemological skepticism of realism and the methodological crisis of reason that expands into Weber's theory of the iron cage and social rationalization. What began as cracks in the edifice of the universal axiomatic laws of mathematics and physics and the unquestioned objective reality and truth of science has turned into a questioning of the application and organization of social institutions, which are in turn based on the narrow and oppressive principles of the rationalization of Western society. This chapter has moved from Husserl's critical phenomenology, skepticism, loss of spirit, and the crisis of European science and reason and Scheler's theory of science as the domination of nature into the further and logical devolution and deterioration of Western reason manifested in Schopenhauer's inner despair, unceasing torment, and resigned asceticism, and in Nietzsche's philosophy of existentialism. This evolution of the crisis of modernity culminated in Weber's socio-logical theory of rationalization, the iron cage of formal reason, and spiritual and ethical disenchantment.

Both Arthur Schopenhauer and Friedrich Nietzsche radical-ized Kant's critique of pure and practical reason in ways that gave rise to German existentialism.[46] They pushed the initial insights of Kant about epistemology and moral philosophy well beyond their limits to argue for the underlying subjectivity and relativism of all scientific knowledge. In addition, they added a profound and dis-turbing existential content to Kant's theory of consciousness and will. While Schopenhauer had developed the pessimism and exis-tential anxiety deeply embedded in Kantian philosophy, Nietzsche expands upon his work by explaining the crisis of modern exis-tence in terms of Greek mythology and tragedy. According to Nietzsche, Greek drama, the dialectic between the Apollonian and Dionysian drives, and the decadence of Socratic rationalism provided key insights into the full implications of Kant's thought and the underlying tragedy of modernity. Weber then borrowed the ideas of the two radical Kantians to develop his own theory of rationalization and disenchantment. For Weber as for Nietzsche, the solution to the dilemma of modernity lies in ancient Greece. An important result of these ideas was Weber's methodological and theoretical discourses on modernity.

Decadence is a central category in Nietzsche's thought and holds his whole philosophical system together. He radicalizes the critical elements in German idealism to reject the reification and rationalization of the Enlightenment in particular and Western civilization in general. That is, he holds the ancient Greeks as his standard of rationality, rejecting the loss of the dialectic between reason and the senses, intellect and instincts, and the Apollonian and the Dionysian drives. He bemoans the loss of moral praxis and the will to power, the reification of false consciousness and the artificial standards of cognitive universality, as strongly as he announces the precipitous moral and intellectual decline of the

West into the mentality of the herd, and its fall into nothingness in the final stage of nihilism of the ascetic individual and last man. This is a world of bended knees, broken minds, and the adoration of idols and false gods. This is the world of utilitarianism and liberalism—the cornerstones of modernity. It is only a short step from here to a critique of the world of the utilitarian specialist, the technical bureaucrat, and consuming narcissist—the realm characterized by Weber as inhabited by "specialists without spirit, sensualists without heart." They are the crowning achievement of a decadent society engulfed in narrow egoism and consumed by the fate of formal rationality in which everything has lost all meaning and purpose.

Nietzsche received a chair in classical studies at the University of Basel, Switzerland, in 1869 and began a ten-year teaching career in Greek literature and philosophy. Some of his earliest, unpublished writings examined Greek philosophy in terms of the epistemological debates of the nineteenth century. Nietzsche's major insights were borrowed from Kant, Hegel, and Schopenhauer. As he confronts the epistemology of German idealism he undertakes a radical critique of the Enlightenment and the foundations of Western rationality and science. Behind the Platonic images on the cave wall, behind empirical facts or the veil of Maya, there is no truth. The world of immediate experience is only a reflection of the illusions and deceptions of consciousness. Very early in his writing he articulates this anthropomorphic view of nature and reality and connects it with the deeper pessimism and moral resignation of Schopenhauer. He conjoins the epistemological insights of Kant and Hegel—that all objectivity is ultimately subjectivity—with the existential anxiety and metaphysical fears of Schopenhauer. Behind the objective appearances of phenomena there is only nothingness. Appearances become illusions and constructs of human consciousness as they change over time in history. In his earliest examination of the pre-Socratic philosophy of nature, Nietzsche treats Greek physics and metaphysics as the beginnings of a rumination about Kantian epistemology. Classical humanism offers Nietzsche the philosophical opportunity to work through and expand his ideas about German idealism. The works of Thales, Anaximander, Heraclitus, Parmenides, and Anaxagoras are interpreted as the projection of human qualities or ideas upon nature. From Nietzsche's perspective they are the earliest philosophical expressions of Kant's transcendental subjectivity and categories of the understanding. Nature is viewed as a human construct. "The Greeks, among whom Thales stood out so suddenly, were the opposite of realists, in that they believed only in the reality of men and gods, looking upon all of nature as but a disguise, a masquerade, or a metamorphosis of these god-men. Man for them was the truth and the core of all things; everything else was but semblance and the play of illusion."[47] Human beings were not passive reflectors of reality, but true creators, as they became the measure of all things. Being and becoming are explained through anthropomorphic metaphors which reflect the values and ideals of the polis.

The Copernican Revolution in philosophy occurred when Kant argued that the sensations of perception are meaningless without the systematic organization of consciousness in time and space. Subjectivity is involved in the very creation of objectivity. The conscious mind helps form the objects of experience. Kant had made the distinction between the phenomenal appearances and the thing-in-itself. The appearances are what we know, while the thing-in-itself is external to the perceiving individual, beyond all knowing and consciousness. Nietzsche rejects the empiricist implications of the thing-in-itself—that there is an underlying metaphysical basis for knowledge—and instead maintains, with Schopenhauer, that what the human mind knows is only itself, the self-images of its own impressions and reflections. There is no correct perception or reflection of external reality in the mind. What stands before the individual are not objects or immediate impressions, but forms of consciousness. This is a world of linguistic metaphors, poetic images, and products of the imagination, creating an unbridgeable chasm between reality (thing-in-itself) and knowledge. Nietzsche offers the insight: "But in any case it seems to me that the 'correct perception'—which would mean 'the adequate expression of an object in the subject'—is a contradictory impossibility. For between two absolutely different spheres, as between subject and object, there is no causality, no correctness, and no expression: there is, at most, an *aesthetic* relation."[48] He is aware that over time philosophers have taken these metaphors and fetishized them into external objects existing in a real empirical world. They become a disenchanted prison of the "residue of metaphors" and "graveyards of perception." Nietzsche takes Kant's critique of reason and theory of objectivity and, in the process of transforming them, challenges the very foundations and assumptions of Western science and truth. Skepticism and relativism give birth to science, as knowledge dissolves into appearances, science into illusions, and objectivity into art.

These ideas began to germinate in two of Nietzsche's earliest unpublished essays, "The Philosopher" and "On Truth and Lies in a Nonmoral Sense." They come together in his first published work, *The Birth of Tragedy* (1872). It is here that Nietzsche leaves his remarkable imprint on modern thought. Rejecting traditional neoclassicism and the aesthetic theories of Lessing, Klopstock, Schlegel, Goethe, and Schiller, he offers an entirely new perspective on the origins of Greek tragedy. Nietzsche rejects the neoclassical view of the underlying beauty, nobility, catharsis, reconciliation, and final justice of the world. He maintains instead that there is no inherent teleology, no final goal, no ultimate meaning, and no absolute truth to be found in the world. The ontological foundations of the Greek worldview are shattered as mere subjective illusions. It is in this context that Nietzsche introduces his ideas of the Apollonian and Dionysian drives in Greek tragedy. This approach allows him to integrate his theory of Greek aesthetics and drama with Schopenhauer's metaphysics and epistemology.

But just as one thinks Nietzsche is about to fall victim to a fit of resigned disgust or existential pessimism before the relativity and meaninglessness of science, art raises humanity to the highest levels of human dignity, joy, and nobility. Once the universalist claims to science and truth, metaphysics and epistemology, are rejected, a panorama of the world opens before us as a playground of human creativity and self-actualization. Meaning is not to be found in the world, but is to be aesthetically created in art, literature, philosophy, and politics. Thus, Nietzsche's early assault on Enlightenment science and the Kantian theory of knowledge is only an introduction to his theory of Greek art and tragedy. This relationship between science and art will be the cornerstone of his critique of rationalism and the Enlightenment.

The publication of *The Birth of Tragedy* marks the high point of Nietzsche's relationship with Schopenhauer. For Nietzsche, the key to understanding the origins of Greek tragedy lay in Schopenhauer's philosophy of the world as both representation and will. The world we know and act upon, according to Schopenhauer, is a product of our own perceived appearances and phenomenal illusions, as well as our own wants and desires. We are always caught in the understanding and will of our own egoism. The world is a product of the subject from which we can escape only by resignation, asceticism, and philosophical contemplation. The human mind transforms the meaningless sensations and organizes them within a coherent framework of time, space, and causality to produce perceptions. "This world as representation exists only through the understanding, and also only for the understanding," Schopenhauer writes.[49] The world we see in our perception is like that of Plato's cave, our dreams, and the Hindu veil of Maya. It is a false impression and illusion that reflects forms of consciousness and not external reality. The objectivity and reality of the material world is called into question by a reconstruction of the process of knowing. There is an external world, but it is unknowable as it is in itself. Physics and science never know the reality of nature, only the consciousness and impressions of it.

Schopenhauer has taken Kant's epistemology and radicalized it. He pushes it to its logical extreme by emphasizing the centrality of the subjective. We experience the world as a constructed entity or representation of consciousness not only through our concepts and understanding, but also through our actions and will. The objectivity we experience as both external reality and the movement of our own bodies is the product of our will. It is not the Cartesian ego which is the most knowable thing, but one's own body, with its drives, instincts, needs, and strivings. The will produces a world of constant striving after pleasure and satisfaction without limits. There is a never-ending quest for satisfaction and a never-ending fight with our passions and fears. The result is a world "without peace and calm," in which "true well-being is absolutely impossible." It is a world of suffering and pain which has no meaning or purpose. Schopenhauer interprets this experience of the world through Greek mythology. "Thus the subject of willing is constantly lying on the revolving wheel of Ixion, is always drawing water in the sieve of the Danaids, and is the eternally thirsting Tantalus."[50] The world is a place of "excessive inner torment, eternal unrest, and incurable pain"; a world of immeasurable suffering, injustice, and cruelty.[51] We can only escape the pain by leaving behind our individuality, our will, and our physical needs in order to reach a state beyond all happiness and pain—a state of will-less contemplation of the Idea or pure form of beauty. Here we become one with being and our own nothingness. Schopenhauer attempts to solve the problem of reality by an unusual integration of Hindu mysticism and Platonic rationalism.

Nietzsche relies heavily on Schopenhauer by accepting his general interpretation of Kant and the existential misery and suffering of the world. However, he deals with this everyday pain not by retreating into a transcendent experience beyond the world into pure Being and form, but rather by engaging the world directly through art. This is what the Greeks were able to do in their tragedies and mythology, in the process creating a world of nobility and beauty beyond anything else ever attempted in Western culture. Nietzsche substituted the Greek tragic experience for Schopenhauer's existentialism of fear and anxiety; and for Schopenhauer's theory of representations and will, he substituted the ideas of Apollo and Dionysus. Schopenhauer is transformed into Silenus, as there is a metamorphosis of German existentialism into Greek tragedy. Nietzsche poetically and masterfully portrays the mythical unfolding of the Greek stories of the conquest and odyssey of the Trojan War; the loss of friends and families to years of unremitting warfare and palace intrigue; the patricide, incest, and exile of Oedipus; the curse on the house of Atreus, the death of Agamemnon, the matricide of Orestes, and the unrelenting vengeance of the Furies; and the eternal punishment of Prometheus. But underlying all the dramatic suffering exhibited in these plays is a quest for truth, reconciliation, forgiveness, community, and moral harmony. It is a search for universal standards of justice and beauty. In a world of becoming, without meaning or values, the Greeks forged a moral community, cosmic order, and physical beauty out of nothingness and despair. Martha Nussbaum has eloquently summarized the power of Nietzsche's view of ancient Greek tragedy.

> But then, by showing how life beautifully asserts itself in the face of a meaningless universe, by showing the joy and splendor of human making in a world of becoming—and by being, itself, an example of joyful making—it gives its spectator a way of confronting not only the painful events of the drama, but also the pains and uncertainty of life, personal and communal—a way that involves human self-respect and self-reliance, rather than guilt or resignation. Instead of giving up his will to live, the spectator, intoxicated by Dionysus, becomes a work of art, and an artist.[52]

Greek tragedy is a story of pride, arrogance, and hubris; murder, incest, retribution, and indescribable pain and suffering. The existential condition, outlined initially by Schopenhauer, was presented openly in the mythology and artistic creations of classical Greece. This is a world described by Silenus, a follower of Dionysus, as so hateful that it is better not to have been born, but if born, to die early.

With all the suffering portrayed in Greek drama, there was also individual moral struggle, courage, nobility, and honor in the efforts and personality of the tragic characters themselves. And Nietzsche sees in these individual strivings the underlying secret to humanity. "The Greeks were keenly aware of the terrors and horrors of existence; in order to be able to live at all they had to place before them the shining fantasy of the Olympians."[53] Art could provide mythology and drama, that is, an aesthetic form and cultural experience in which existence became meaningful and the individual protected. Art acted as a "metaphysical solace" and "pretentious lie." It was used to explain being; to offer a theodicy to give meaning to human suffering and death; and to provide a purpose to human life under the most horrible circumstances. Finally, through art both pain and suffering were sublimated into happiness and beauty.

Nietzsche develops his own aesthetic theory of Apollonian and Dionysian drives. Apollo, who takes his place in the Greek pantheon as the god of enlightenment, moderation, and dreams, is the form-giver in art, politics, law, and science. He symbolizes the inner drive or human need to create artistic form, political order, and metaphysical meaning in the world. Natural law, Olympian mythologies, social ethics, and political constitutions are created through the Apollonian desire to give meaning and purpose to human existence. The Dionysian element, on the other hand, represents the irrational, communal, and destructive dynamic, which undermines old traditions and creates new values. Art is the "completion and consummation of existence and [its] guarantee of further existence."[54] Underlying this dialectic between form and will, teleology and chaos is the ultimate truth and tragic vision of the ancients. Dionysian wisdom provides the creative impulse to aesthetic change, as it recognizes that reality is a world of becoming and chaos producing only suffering and pain. Much later, in 1887, Nietzsche would express the same idea in *The Genealogy of Morals*: "Whoever, at any time, has undertaken to build a new heaven has found the strength for it in his own hell."[55] But it is from the cry of unbearable agony that artistic constructions of unparalleled beauty and nobility of soul arise. Terror results in joy and sublime serenity. Beneath the Apollonian forms of civilization lie the unrealized dreams and falsifying ideals that deny and repress the misery of human existence. Life demands both meaning and illusions in order to continue.

Dionysus strips the Apollonian veil of its facade and appearances and reveals a hypostatized reality. But remarkably, the Greeks were able to balance this knowledge of the absurdity and nothingness of the world with the corresponding drive to create an illusory cosmos of order, purpose, beauty, and justice. They created a world in which "Apollo found it impossible to live without Dionysus."[56] Nietzsche was able to integrate the beliefs of Winckelmann, Schiller, and Goethe in the nobility, beauty, and simplicity of ancient Greece with Schopenhauer's dire pessimism of the plight of humanity in the modern abyss. "Apollo overcomes individual suffering by the glorious apotheosis of what is eternal in appearance: here beauty vanquishes the suffering that inheres in all existence, and pain is, in a certain sense, glossed away from nature's countenance."[57] Apollonian culture represents a victory of the human spirit and will over existence and becoming; the joy and beauty of culture have subdued the reality of suffering and misery. Nietzsche believes that "life is at bottom indestructibly joyful and powerful" even in the face of human misery and tragic suffering—and quite possibly because of it. This perspective represents a radicalization of the Kantian and Hegelian insight that the truth of objectivity is subjectivity. The Apollonian forms and Dionysian creativity set the framework for Nietzsche's later theory of the will to power (*Wille zur Macht*) of the *Übermensch* as a will to constructive form and self-realization. It is this tragic wisdom of the Greeks that will provide Weber with the critical foundations for his theory of science, culture, and rationalization.[58] Although this analysis of Nietzsche's understanding of classical Greek mythology may appear to be merely an interesting digression, it is nevertheless central to his understanding of modern reason and science.

For Nietzsche, all knowledge systems which make claims to universality and truth of being, including Socratic rationalism, Western Christianity, modern science, political liberalism, and Kantian morality, are simply forms of decadence and idolatry, because they make us passive recipients of received truths. The aesthetic dynamic of Dionysian creativity and destructiveness is lost and only the traditional and orthodox forms of knowledge are passed on to a passive and conformist herd of people. Illusions are treated as real; becoming reifies into being, particularity into universality; and modish fashion becomes mistaken for originality. Nietzsche is aware that, with an acceptance of a radical Kantian theory of knowledge, there is a real danger of skepticism. This is the very thing he wishes to avoid. For Nietzsche, reality is constituted through art, as the human spirit "would sooner have the void for [its] purpose than be void of purpose."[59] The collapse of the illusions of objectivity, epistemology, and foundationalism—rejection of the first principles of being, truth, and God—does not lead to skepticism, despair, pessimism, or negative nihilism. It only spurs Nietzsche on to a view of humanity as continually striving and creating ever new Apollonian forms of culture and social institutions.

Through a self-conscious revaluation of traditional values found in religion, politics, and morality; through an acceptance of the decisions and actions of the moment (theory of eternal return of the present); and through a reliance on the practical will to power, the self-overcoming individual as *Übermensch* constructs a moral and political universe that has meaning and purpose. Aesthetics has replaced metaphysics, and active nihilism and moral autonomy have replaced a subservient adaptation to a culture of death and revenge, as art transcends science and truth. Kantian epistemology and moral philosophy are transformed into Nietzschean aesthetics. We can only be creative, free, and wise in a world we ourselves have made; nobility and human dignity are grounded in self-determination. To live in a culture which denies existence in favor of an afterlife, heaven, political revolution, etc. only brings humiliation, slavery, and moral tyranny. Individuals have throughout history sought peace and knowledge in different forms of decadence, including happiness (Aristotelianism), God and salvation (Christianity), duty and moral universals (Kantianism), pleasure and hedonism (utilitarianism), truth (scientism), and equality and liberty (liberalism). Nietzsche characterizes these cultures as the "metaphysics of the hangman," which ultimately destroys any vestiges of Dionysian creativity. In *The Will to Power* he writes: "Man, imprisoned in an iron cage of errors, became a caricature of man, sick, wretched, ill-disposed toward himself, full of hatred for the impulses of life, full of mistrust of all that is beautiful and happy in life, a walking picture of misery."[60]

Morality and truth are not discovered through contemplation, but lie in the character and courage of those willing to create their own moral values and truths beyond good and evil, beyond universal categories and the moral imperatives of religion, theology, and philosophy. The ultimate justification for morality lies in life-affirming praxis or action. "Everyone [must] invent *his own* virtue, *his own* categorical imperative."[61] Nietzsche, relying on Aristotle and Kant, argues that self-determination and self-realization are the only principles of pure and practical reason that can resist the modern forms of tyranny. However, this is not easy, as only the rarest of individuals are willing to challenge traditional authority and Enlightenment rationality as forms of idolatry. Those capable of accomplishing it will be able to recreate the lost heritage of Dionysus.

This chapter has traced the startling and exciting development of various modern theories of knowledge from the Cartesian ego, empiricist psychology, transcendental subjectivity, and phenomenological subjectivity to the existential will-to-live and will to power. These various schools of thought, with their growing emphasis on the role of subjectivity and the a priori forms of sensibility and the understanding—especially in idealism, phenomenology, and existentialism—have called into question the traditional views of the foundation of Western science and knowledge and have provided the basis for incisive critiques of dogmatic objectivism, realism, and naturalism. The introduction of the notions of subjectivity and human consciousness to the process of experiencing and knowing has profoundly weakened the traditional defense of the philosophical claims to objective truth and objective reality. With the evolution of the various competing theories of subjectivity and the corresponding attempts to justify objectivity and mathematical science, it eventually ends with subjectivity as the only existential reality and truth. With a growing emphasis on subjectivity and the role of human consciousness in knowing, there has been a decline in objectivism. This split between the subjectivism and objectivism has resulted in a growing inability to define and justify the traditional basis of science in Western reason and philosophy. It has unconsciously undermined the rational foundations of a science grounded in the existence of a knowable and objective world of objects, data, and facts. This decline has been followed historically by the rise of existentialism and classical social theory. As possible explanations for an understanding of Western rationality and science, these two traditions have traced the evolution of science from a reflection of reality in innate or empirical ideas toward a reflection of the imperative of formal reason and industrial technology.

Here the question begins to move away from philosophy into sociology. This is important for our study since it opens up the possibility of further epistemological criticisms, as voiced in chapter 1, and the necessity to clarify and explain the various competing claims to objectivity, whether in the form of epistemology or ontology, by introducing sociological, economic, and political categories. Scientific phenomena and categories, which at first were thought to be products of human subjectivity, were never really independent of the historical and social process; the latter were just ignored. Husserl vaguely hinted at this insight of the social foundations of knowledge in his very brief analysis of the domination of nature, Scheler opened the door with more extensive writing on the topic, and Marx and Weber addressed the discussion directly. The evolution of the notion of subjectivity, as constructing objectivity, began initially with Kant, was historicized by Hegel, sociologized by Scheler and Marx, and then proceeded slowly thereafter. The difficulty with this insight is that the meaning of subjectivity shifted from consciousness and scientific knowledge in the eighteenth century to the social relations of production in the nineteenth century to the cultural values and economic structures of the total social system in the twentieth century. What began with epistemological subjectivity ends with sociological subjectivity. This leads us to an introduction to one of the important classical social theorists of the early twentieth century, Max Weber, who, influenced by German existentialism, continued this critique of reason and science into sociology.

Rationalization and Disenchantment in Modern Society: Max Weber

Echoes of Nietzsche's critique of Western science and Greek rationalism, as well as his critique of epistemology and foundationalism, are incorporated by Weber into his analysis of the disenchantment of traditional myths and ideologies in the process of rationalization.[62] In his important work on Weber, Wilhelm Hennis summarizes the connection between Weber and Nietzsche: "Weber accepted without any reservation Nietzsche's diagnosis of the time: God is dead. He treated it as the 'basic fact' that we are fated to live in a 'godless time, without prophets.' All objective order of values deriving from the Christian conception of God breaks down. Weber is the first to have drawn the most radical scientific conclusions from Nietzsche's diagnosis of nihilism."[63] In his famous but relatively unexplored essay "Science as a Vocation" (1917), Weber accepts the idea that science has certain presuppositions or a priori practical values that account for its limits and problems. After first examining science as a social institution undergoing a process of bureaucratization and specialization in the United States and Germany, Weber turns to an analysis of the ethos and meaning of modern science. He moves into a critical social phenomenology and history of Western experience and consciousness, thereby expanding Husserl's goal of searching for the meaning of science.

With his tantalizingly brief and suggestive outline of the history of Western thought, Weber offers the reader an alternative to the normative imperatives of natural science. In his search for the meaning of *science*, he outlines a genealogy of the major periods of Western reason and science (*Wissenschaft*) from the Greeks to the present. He describes the historical process of rationalization as the development of the formal logic and methods of science over time from Greek philosophy to early twentieth-century natural science. His purpose is to outline this transformation of scientific knowledge from philosophy, politics, art, theology, and morality to its more limited and contemporary form in natural science and neoclassical economics. Concomitant with this, there is a slow erosion in the search for values or substantive rationality in Western thought. Weber starts with the classical Greek view of knowledge as *episteme* (universal knowledge). Plato perfected the Greek inventions of the technical tools of concepts, logical method, and clear analytical thinking. He was able in the *Republic* to transform the search for universals and absolutes into questions about virtue and right action (ethics) and citizenship and the good life (political philosophy). This classical form of science focused on the movement out of the cave toward sunlight and self-enlightenment through the philosophical contemplation of the eternal questions of beauty, truth, and justice. It was a search for universal knowledge of physics, mathematics, and nature, along with the quest for the good life and virtuous activity in the *polis*.

Science for the ancients meant philosophical contemplation of universal forms and eternal truths in the face of changing illusions and shadows. Weber refers specifically to the beginning of the seventh book of Plato's *Republic*, in which individuals are chained before a wall on which images are projected by a fire behind them. Blinded by the darkness and limited in movement by the chains, they mistook the images and illusions on the wall for reality. In time, they begIn slowly to free themselves from their chains, turn around, and leave the cave for the sunlight where they see objects more clearly and no longer as distorted images. Enlightenment was the search for light and life itself as manifested in the knowledge of true being. Science was a political philosophy which sought answers to questions about social justice, the good life, and the ideal state. It was Socrates and his followers who discovered the revolutionary dialectical method and formal concepts capable of attaining universal knowledge. "And from this it seemed to follow that if one only found the right concept of the beautiful, the good, or, for instance, of bravery, of the soul—or whatever—that then one could also grasp its true being."[64] With them began the search for the eternal knowledge of objective reality contained in the ideal concepts of politics, aesthetics, and morality. According to Weber, Platonic science sought practical knowledge about how to act rightly in Athenian life as a good citizen and friend. It helped instruct the Athenians about the nature of courage, moderation, wisdom, and justice. The distinguishing thing about Greek science is that it offered knowledge about the meaning of life and ultimate reality.

The next great period of scientific inquiry occurred during the fifteenth century with the Renaissance and its return to the Greek spirit after being mired in the scholasticism and mysticism of medieval Catholicism. With individuals such as Leonardo da Vinci, science now expressed itself in an art form of rational experimentation and the controlling of experience. It was the precursor to modern natural science, as experiments were undertaken to enhance theoretical knowledge about nature, as expressed in exquisite works of art by the Italian masters. Experiments in physiology and biology were designed to help in drawing the human body. This was also the period of technical experimentation in art and music which was thought to help clarify the meaning of life through the study of biological science and true nature. In the seventeenth century, Galileo and Bacon continued this form of empirical research based on careful observation and analytical thinking into astronomy and physics as they developed a mathematical and deterministic view of the natural world.

With the Protestant Reformation, science was closely attached to pietist theology since it was viewed as an expression of both the laws of nature and the laws of God. Weber tells us that the biologist Jan Swammerdam declared that the proof for God's existence was contained in the anatomy of a louse. From classical Greece to pietist theology, science was a tool for the search for meaning and truth whether in eternal forms, art, nature, or God. It represented a search for the significance and purpose of human action within the world—some standard by which to measure the end and goal of human life. But with the development of positivism in the nineteenth and twentieth centuries, everything changed. Science was transformed into a quantitative and mathematical calculation for achieving personal happiness and economic utility. Weber does not privilege any particular historical form of science over the others in his historical and phenomenological overview of the development of Western rationality. There is no teleological philosophy of history leading to the final form of natural science.

The older forms of science as ways to true being, art, God, and nature are viewed by positivists as illusory folly, and replaced by natural science. But modern science cannot teach us anything about what is meaningful in the world. To emphasize his point, Weber reiterates Tolstoy's statement: "Science is meaningless because it gives no answer to our question, the only question important for us: What shall we do and how shall we live?"[65] The world is constituted by mathematical and quantitative relationships expressing a blind and purposeless nature where everything is dead and void. Formal rationality is meaningless, since it cannot speak to the fundamental cosmological and ethical questions about human life. It cannot tell us anything about reality, teleology, or metaphysics, since its only purpose is to master life and dominate nature. It is only a useful technology for controlling our natural and social environment in more efficient and productive ways. It appears that Weber has taken Nietzsche's *Twilight of the Idols* and integrated it with German phenomenology as the foundation for his reading of the genealogy of Western rationalism from Platonic philosophy to modern physics and economics. But this process also represents the narrowing of human reason to the most technical and formal questions about the external and disenchanted world.

Weber refers to Nietzsche's "last man," who applies science as a technique and calculus for mastering utilitarian happiness. He is the most contemptible of modern individuals, seen as a replacement for the overman (*Übermensch*). In *Thus Spoke Zarathustra* (1883), Nietzsche recounts the tale of Zarathustra the hermit and prophet, who comes down the mountain after ten years of solitude to teach the people in the marketplace about the new man—the overman—who strives to improve himself through knowledge, hard work, spiritual development, and virtuous activity. One must still have "chaos in oneself to be able to give birth to a dancing star." But Zarathustra is laughed and jeered at by those who do not understand his words. He then warns them of the coming of the last man who seeks only personal happiness and is "unable to despise himself." There is no reflection, no dreaming, no seeking something beyond humanity itself; there is no longing for something other. There is only a bombastic arrogance and stultifying satisfaction with the present moment. The Faustian agreement with Mephistopheles has been lost. Community and friendship have been replaced by the need for security and protection; creativity and work by entertainment; exertion and effort by pleasure and satisfaction; and difference by equality and sameness. Exasperated by modernity, Nietzsche explodes: "Everybody wants the same, everybody is the same: whoever feels different goes voluntarily into a madhouse."[66] This is the world of the utilitarians, who not only seek immediate enjoyment and happiness, but who are incapable of reaching beyond themselves to something greater and more noble, beautiful, and divine. These are the true believers of a herd religion who accept the common belief in good and evil. Zarathustra challenges them to reach beyond themselves to something greater and question their accepted views of life. Weber continues the story, but is no more optimistic of its ending. He recognizes that the scientific search for the mastery of life and pursuit of happiness is illusory since science is ethically meaningless. In the end, there is only the conformity and emptiness of the marketplace.

With the Protestant Reformation, scientific revolution, and the Enlightenment, there was a growing demystification and rationalization of society. Here Weber provides Husserl's theory of the meaning and crisis of science with a sociological and structural framework. Science was slowly replacing all forms of traditional knowledge about a world of meaning, enchantment, and mystery. Nature was being reduced to scientific principles and natural laws. The Protestants rejected what they viewed as Catholic idolatry and mysticism, magical rites and enchanted sacraments, in favor of asceticism, professional vocation, specialized labor, and methodical, systematic work. But with the rise of modern science and the Enlightenment, religion came under closer scrutiny and disappeared as a significant public institution. This led to a situation where the institutions and values of capitalism generated by Protestantism continued after the decline of religion. With the advent of secular society, capitalism continued without its cultural supports and ethical foundations. In the famous lines at the end of *The Protestant Ethic and the Spirit of Capitalism* (1904), Weber surveys the human condition with a remarkable pessimism and apparent fatalism:

> The Puritan wanted to work in a calling; we are forced to do so. For when asceticism was carried out of monastic cells into everyday life, and began to dominate worldly morality, it did its part in building the tremendous cosmos of the modern economic order. This order is now bound to the technical and economic conditions of machine production which today determine the lives of all the individuals who are born into this mechanism, not only those directly concerned with economic acquisition, with irresistible force. Perhaps it will so determine them until the last ton of fossilized coal is burnt.[67]

The result was a society that became an iron cage, locking those inside into a social machine that they neither understood nor controlled. Individuals became cogs in a specialized economy and bureaucratic state. Technical civilization overwhelmed traditional culture and its capacity for self-reflection in philosophy, art, and theology. As they became more efficient expressions of formal rationality, societies were created that were shallow and empty of broader economic and political purpose. Individuals were lost in the quest to satisfy the functional and administrative needs of the social system. Only the emptiness and the silence of nothingness could be heard.

Capitalism no longer needed religion to legitimate its activities, resulting in a society which had fallen ever deeper into an abyss of mundane passions and repetitive activities. Rationalization produces the last man, a technician without reason and self-consciousness, a sensualist without compassion and virtue, a person who no longer seeks the truth or searches for meaning in life. The result is a highly educated and specialized individual without direction or purpose, bound to the material world of pleasure, but without feelings, passions, or desires. Even today with the development of cyber-capitalism in Silicon Valley, the machine, which goes faster and is more technically efficient and productive, does not change its fundamental nature or its formal rationality.

The Greek view of science as *episteme* or knowledge of universal truth, essence, and form has disappeared as modern knowledge has simply become a particular form of reasoning to accomplish particular ends. Science has become a formal rationality (*Zweckrationalität*) of technical means. The substantive rationality (*Wertrationalität*), or practical ends, of pre-modern science toward equality, fraternity, and justice has been lost in a society in which means have become ends in themselves. The formal rationality of Enlightenment science, which has been embedded in social institutions, is now an independent force of nature. This is what Weber refers to as the tragic process of rationalization and the fate of public disenchantment—it is a world without myth, meaning, or hope. Practical reason has been exiled into the iron cage. Weber continues his earlier argument that modern science contains its own hidden assumptions about reality when he states: "Science contributes to the technology of controlling life by calculating external objects as well as man's activities."[68] It already contains a priori values that influence the type of knowledge and objects of experience that it seeks to explain. By excluding ethical and political values, science represses self-reflection on its own moral imperatives and hidden assumptions at the same time that it becomes useless in the face of questions about the purpose of life and the meaning of human existence. It replaces one set of ethical values with another set of technical values. Science cannot respond to Schopenhauer's or Nietzsche's existentialism and nihilism, but begins to make more sense with Weber's expansion of the ideas of Husserl and Scheler.

Weber's historical account of the rationalization of society begins with modern industry, with its calls for greater formal efficiency, capital accounting, division of labor, factory discipline, and productivity, and develops into the rationalization of the state through the formal impersonality of its routinized bureaucracy, organizational hierarchy, technical expertise, and efficient decision-making. This mentality pervades all aspects of social life and institutions. Rogers Brubaker summarizes the extent of rationalization as it permeates the economy, law, state administration, and religious ethics: "In each of these institutional spheres, rationalization has involved the depersonalization of social relations, the refinement of techniques of calculation, the enhancement of the social importance of specialized knowledge, and the extension of technically rational control over both natural and social processes."[69] Material well-being coincides with administrative domination and the loss of individual freedom; technical control over nature with the growth of the iron cage; scientific and technological progress with disenchantment and nihilism; and formal rationality with depersonalization and alienation. As society becomes more formally rational, there is a decline in traditional liberalism, democracy, and the public sphere. There are two elements of the tragic fate of humankind running concurrently through modernity: the loss of freedom in bureaucratic and formal organizations and the loss of meaning in disenchantment and science. Disenchantment occurs with the reduction of knowledge to calculation and control where "the ultimate and most sublime values have retreated from public life either into the transcendental realm of mystic life or into the brotherliness of direct and personal human relations."[70] Rationalization, on the other hand, appears with the rise of impersonal and technical forces that determine human action from above in the form of economic markets, industrial factories, political bureaucracies, and governmental administration. In a rationalized society, the intentions and meaning of human action are more and more reduced to the language and values of neoclassical economics and marginal utility theory, that is, to the imperatives of work and power. This tension between substantive and formal rationality that characterizes the whole of Weber's theory of modernity Horkheimer will refer to later as the "eclipse of reason," while Habermas uses the term "the silencing of reason."

Husserl emphasized the crisis of science and the skepticism of modern reason in the face of the philosophical and epistemological collapse of its traditional meaning and truth claims to objectivity and reality; Scheler emphasized a sociology of knowledge, the technical and mathematical form of scientific knowledge, and the domination of nature; Schopenhauer the nothingness and meaninglessness of representations and reality; Nietzsche the decadence and emptiness of all objective and universal meaning in the world; and Weber the evolution of phenomenology and existentialism into the formal reason of the iron cage and the rationalization of bureaucracy and society. With the epistemological and existential undermining of the traditional meaning and normative objectivity (method and being) of science, phenomenology had reached its limits. The remaining chapters will detail the expansion of the crisis of Western science beyond philosophy, epistemology, and the forms of consciousness into the realms of history, sociology, and political economy. The next two chapters further expand our understanding of knowledge, science, and objectivism. We will examine how these abstract and speculative philosophical issues are turned into questions about metaphysics, history, and political economy.

PART II

Natural Science, Political Economy, and the Domination of Humanity

The Metaphysics and Method of Natural Science: The Politics of the Ghost in the Machine

THIS CHAPTER WILL CONTINUE the analysis of the previous chapter by deepening the investigation into the nature and foundations of modern natural science, with an emphasis on its history and materialist metaphysics: that is, from within its internal logic, concept formation, theoretical evolution, and practical applicability. It will examine its usually unarticulated values and principles, assumptions and secular theology, worldview and theory of nature, which are not the result of empirical analysis and evidentiary verification. These values make science possible because they provide a picture of nature as a mechanical, deterministic, and quantitative machine. Without these metaphysical principles, science would not have the view of physical reality that would permit the application of the scientific method and theories to the study of the physical world; without these principles, science would lack the foundations upon which to ground its logic, methods, and legitimacy; and without these initial assumptions, scientific theory and methods would be impossible. The logic and structure of modern scientific inquiry are constructed on these very foundations, which are beyond the parameters of science itself. They provide the philosophical and non-scientific foundations of the physical laws of nature and are referred to as the "metaphysical foundations of natural science." Although these metaphysical principles guide the construction of science—idea formation, theory construction, empirical testing, etc.—the principles are not themselves products of scientific investigation, but of ontological abstraction and theoretical speculation. They represent a revolutionary change in the modern *Weltanschauung* from the earlier classical view of nature as a living and dynamic being. According to historical materialism, however, they are the product of deeper historical and social changes that are part of the development of modern capitalism that forms a newer vision of nature than that created in classical Greek philosophy and medieval Christianity.

The apparent origins of these metaphysical principles lie in the laws of Euclidean geometry, physics, and astronomy, classical mechanics, and, later, the celestial mechanics of Francis Bacon, Galileo Galilei, René Descartes, and Isaac Newton. The three simple natures of figure, extension, and motion provided the basis for these later discoveries. Descartes' writings in the seventeenth century on method and metaphysics provided the philosophical justification for this new worldview, based on his functional theory that all of physical nature was open to mathematical and quantitative analysis and laws. The metaphysics of science was a doctrine about the natural world that assumed certain fundamental principles and conceptions about constant matter, space, and time as true, without any empirical or theoretical analysis or testing. These physical principles of the material world, along with the corresponding relationship between ontology (being) and epistemology (truth), had the epistemological status of a theology of nature and "uncritically accepted ideas about the world."[1] These assumptions were in turn based on other metaphysical principles, such as the ultimate reality of mathematical explanations and laws, mind/body dualism, *res cogitans* and *res extensa*, primary and secondary qualities, the analytic/synthetic method of reductionism, the quantification and mathematization of experience and logic, intuition of mathematics and first principles, and the view of the world as a functioning and predictive machine that could be known, controlled, and dominated for utilitarian purposes.

This mechanization and mathematization of the natural world became an extension of the social organization of industrial production: nature was seen as useable and disposable parts of a machine, not a living or moral entity to be respected. Natural science reflected less the reality and laws of nature than the logic of capital and abstract labor. Raw materials could be extracted and used in production in the same way that labor and surplus value were extracted from living human labor in the industrial factories. Later, the abstract theories of natural science would be reconceptualized into an epistemology of realism, objectivism, and naturalism that could then be operationalized with its systematic observations, explanatory laws, theoretical experiments, and quantitative predictions, for technical and formal use in both the academy and production. The same logic and metaphysics that underlay capitalist production became the basis for scientific inquiry. Their metaphysical foundations were based on the same historical and economic institutions. Newton's advances in the mechanical laws of the universe in the areas of motion, gravity, and differential calculus only furthered these metaphysical and physical principles of the Cartesian paradigm. Metaphysics deals with the nature of being and reality: the existence of God and the human soul, the existence of nature as an objective, external reality, and the knowledge of truth derived from pure reason based on geometric intuition, logical deduction, and the distinctions between mind and matter, essence and attributes. Metaphysics deals with the nature of substances: the divine substance of God, the thinking substance of the human soul, and the extended substance of matter in motion. Descartes seeks a synthesis of divine and natural ontology and epistemology as he tries to show how physics, method, and science are derived from these fundamental metaphysical postulates of God, soul, and matter.

Toward the end of the seventeenth century, John Locke sought to integrate medieval Christian theology with modern political liberalism by integrating the state of nature, natural rights, private property, and market freedoms with medieval ideas of natural law, God, ethics, and the social responsibility of a moral community. In the same century, Descartes attempted a similar project, only this time integrating natural law with natural science, and Christian scriptures and theological traditions with the laws of physics. With the full development of Enlightenment rationality in politics, science, and epistemology, medieval metaphysics and natural law became unnecessary and redundant.

Descartes tried to establish the metaphysical foundations of nature and science in his major works *Discourse on Method of Rightly Conducting the Reason and Seeking Truth in the Field of Science* (1637) and the *Meditations Concerning First Philosophy* (1641). In the *Meditations,* Descartes tried to justify the method and logic of natural science by applying the three fundamental principles of Cartesian metaphysics of the self, pure universal ideas, and God. Metaphysics is the real foundation of natural science. Belief in the method of science and the existence of objective reality is ultimately based on the prior metaphysical arguments validating the existence of human consciousness and God in pure thought. The existence of God and nature had to be philosophically established before the method and logic of science could also be grounded in the nature of God. In the end, according to Descartes, what we know is only the existence of the innate ideas of our mind and God. This had to be accomplished before the method of science could be legitimately applied to the study of nature. And by rationally and deductively proving the existence of an external, objective, and physical reality, as well as the legitimacy and rationality of human consciousness and science, the foundations for natural science could be firmly established in Christian theology and the accepted values of seventeenth-century European metaphysics. The laws of God were reflected in the form of human reason, reflection, and perception—that is, the universal principles of natural law were reflected in the laws of natural science. Metaphysics became the foundation for the logic and method of science. The validity and applicability of the method and logic of science had to be justified through the existence of God and the creation of the universe, and through the recognition of the validity of human consciousness and formal reason in the human ability to know that physical reality. For Descartes, the early attempt to prove the existence and nature of objective reality, the validity and objectivity of human perception and understanding, and the laws of science rested on medieval theology. His goal was to justify modern science and reason by logically connecting metaphysics, epistemology, and the scientific method, thereby grounding perception and natural science in natural law. It is in this attempt to justify natural science that the metaphysical foundations of science are found, and with them the depiction of nature upon which scientific research, method, and theories develop. With the evolution of the Enlightenment, however, natural law, religious reasoning, and theology became increasingly irrelevant. Yet the metaphysics of nature and natural science remained, providing the stable and rational basis for science's research method and logic of inquiry.

THE METAPHYSICS OF CHRISTIAN COSMOLOGY AND THE METAPHYSICS OF NATURE

In his attempt to justify the ontological existence of the objective reality that we see and the epistemological reality of science that reflects that reality, Descartes undertook an epic journey through human consciousness, the existence of God, the existence of perceptual objectivity and nature, and the validity of natural science. Christian cosmology and belief in the existence of God were central to the metaphysics and method of modern science. In fact, Christian metaphysics became the foundation for the metaphysics of nature and for belief in an objective reality independent of the knowing subject. In *The Logic of Modernity*, Gerald Galgan quotes S. V. Keeling, who reaffirms the necessity and connection between Descartes' metaphysics and method:

> Science . . . cannot establish for itself the legitimacy of its own procedure; methodology cannot of itself demonstrate that the character, connection, and order of our thoughts exactly represent, correspond point for point, with the character, connection, and order of independent fact. So if certain knowledge about the ultimate character of parts of reality is to be attained by science, science must be guaranteed by something more radical than can be supplied by inference from its own procedure. . . . Without a supporting Metaphysics the Method would be no more than an elaborate speculative hypothesis. Again, without a supporting metaphysics we should have no right to believe that the Physics . . . really is a body of certain knowledge about *this actually existing natural world.*[2]

"Science . . . cannot establish itself" as its own underlying foundation and justification. Method without metaphysics would be merely a speculative belief system, based on faith alone. However, the dilemma arises with this recognition that the scientific method of observation, hypothesis formation, testing, and validation cannot itself be the basis for accepting the proposition that method gives us access to empirical reality. How are objective reality and scientific method to be integrated so that the latter truly reflects the former? Descartes was aware that this could only be accomplished by a metaphysics grounded in Christian cosmology. Only something other than nature could give us access to the reality of the laws of nature. Toward that end, Descartes begins his search for the grounding of science by rejecting empiricism and starting with a form of radical skepticism, by which he rejected all knowledge of the senses as a dream, illusion, or deception of God. In this manner, he could begin with a clean slate in order to raise the question about whether there was one thing that could be clearly and distinctly known and could not be doubted. This knowledge beyond doubt would be the Archimedean point that would provide Descartes with the beginning of his deductive reasoning and ultimate justification of modern science. He concluded with his famous line: "I will suppose that the sky, the air, the earth, colors, shapes, sounds, and all other objective things (that we see) are nothing but illusions and dreams that he [God] has used to trick my credulity."[3] The question raised is whether the objective reality provided by human senses, perception, physics, and astronomy is a constructed world of a deceiving and evil God. By beginning anew epistemologically, such radical doubt allows Descartes to establish firmly that particular knowledge which will be the basis and justification for the existence of nature and the validity of science. He concludes that even if he is deceived, there must be something to be deceived; therefore, he, as pure consciousness, must exist. Although his famous phrase does not appear in this work, having appeared four years earlier in the *Discourse on Method*, it does nicely summarize his thinking at this stage: "*Cogito ergo sum*" (I think, therefore I am).[4] Even if my consciousness is deceived in thinking that the world, my body, and all sensation is an illusion, I must exist, because deception implies the existence of that which is deceived.

From this premise of the primacy of individual consciousness, Descartes would soon argue that consciousness had an idea of an infinite and all-knowing being, and that this idea could not be caused by a finite, limited, and mortal mind. So from the idea of consciousness as the thinking substance (cogito), as pure thought, Descartes derived the idea of God in three distinct proofs of the existence of God: the idea of God, cause of the idea of God, and the ontological argument or deduction of the existence of God from the essence of God. And it is from the idea and existence of God as a divine, all-wise being, that perception and science are justified in claiming that human knowledge of the world is an actual reflection of external reality and physical nature. Science is true because it has been justified by the existence of a God who by his characteristics could not and would not falsify our access to the natural world in the form of experience and science. The belief in numbers, shapes, positions, movements, and other traits of the physical universe found in mathematics and geometry is not a product of human invention or the imagination. Descartes thus proved to his satisfaction, based on various medieval justifications, that God exists and is infinite, perfect, and all-knowing, and most important of all, "he is not a deceiver, I can infer as a consequence that everything I conceive clearly and distinctly is necessarily true."[5] The validity of natural science and the mathematical laws of physics rested on the perfection and benevolence of God.

At the end of the Fifth Meditation, Descartes tries to define clear and distinct ideas and their relationship to an acceptance of corporeal reality. This, too, is based on a proof of God's existence which was reaffirmed as a restatement of St. Anselm's ontological argument: "And now that I know him, I have the means of acquiring clear and certain [and perfect] knowledge about an infinity of things, not only about God himself," but also about corporeal nature, mathematics, and geometry.[6] With the proof of God's being and existence, Descartes attempts to justify the intellectual perception and properties of the world of natural objects that are independent of human imagination and perception but can be thought clearly and distinctly. "When we turn to physics, we find Descartes speaking as though physics could be deduced from metaphysics."[7] God has created a world that can be known with certainty and clarity through the intuitions of the mind and deductions of the natural laws of physics (order of being). Even if God had created other worlds, the laws of physics would still apply, as they are deduced from the pure intuitions and innate ideas (a priori forms) of human consciousness.[8] These a priori forms of thought are innate in the human mind and are derived through deduction from Christian metaphysics as the foundations for the universal laws of physics.

Perhaps the most interesting and revealing statement in Descartes' work is a sentence near the start of the Fifth Meditation:

"I [come to] recognize an infinity of details concerning numbers, shapes, movements, and other similar things … it does not seem [to me] as though I were learning anything new, but rather as though I were remembering what I had previously known—that is, that I am perceiving things which were already in my mind."[9] Descartes does not return to the First and Second Meditation, where the emphasis was on the possible deception of the concrete, empirical world of immediate physical perception. With the recognition of the thinking substance and the existence of a non-deceiving God, he now begins to associate knowledge about the world and knowledge about the self as both are mediated by God. Science from this perspective is grounded not in empirical perception (empiricism) but in pure thought of mathematics and geometry (rationalism), since it is only in pure thought that ideas can be thought clearly and distinctly. The example used here is that of the description of a triangle—its three angles are equal to two right angles, and the square of the hypotenuse is equal to the squares of the other two sides. These descriptions are neither invented nor imagined by consciousness, but are the true essence of being. Descartes summarizes this thought with the idea that "it follows that all that I clearly and distinctly recognize as characters of this thing [triangle] does in reality characterize it."[10]

Whether it is his examination of the nature and existence of God or the triangle, Descartes contends that the mind reflects the essence of an objective and external reality. These ideas are innate to human consciousness or the thinking substance and, therefore, are not themselves constructs of consciousness. Nor can they be derived from sense experience. The very foundations of natural science are wedded to the proofs for the existence of God, since the latter ultimately justifies clear and distinct ideas, particularly those about nature and physical reality. Clear and distinct ideas express the ontological reality of the thinking self, God, nature, and being. Descartes concludes the Fifth Meditation with the words that "all knowledge depends solely on the knowledge of the true God."[11] And just as important for our understanding of the nature of the physical sciences is that our knowledge of nature depends on the same type of innate, reflective knowledge of God; that is, it depends on the pure ideas of universal human reason because this is the ultimate understanding and human justification of God. By integrating the knowledge of self and God, existence and thought, being and thought, and reality and mathematics, "the self knows only its own mind" as innate ideas, which certainly limits our understanding of nature.[12] Knowledge of the metaphysics of divine cosmology defines and determines human knowledge of the natural world in terms of clear and distinct ideas of reason. "And thus I recognize very clearly that the certainty and truth of all knowledge depends solely on the knowledge of the true God."[13] In its understanding of the essence of nature, its principles, rules, and logic, the human mind knows only itself and its own structure and logic. Descartes is here anticipating the Kantian problem of the "thing-in-itself."

A central question is whether the Cartesian proofs for the existence of God and nature limit our understanding of objective reality to these innate ideas of medieval and classical metaphysics, theology and physics. Does applying the method of Christian metaphysics to the study of nature reflect the principles of physical reality and the laws of nature, or does it instead construct nature according to the propositions and properties of medieval theology? How does the metaphysics of Christian cosmology affect our knowledge of nature? Descartes argues that metaphysics determines the innate content and formal structure of human reason, which provide the deductive basis for our understanding of our intuition of the geometric laws of our immediate physical environment. These laws are based on extension, figure, and motion, whose essence is the general mathematical laws of physics and pure thought. From this perspective, our knowledge of nature is only a reflection of our knowledge of ourselves as pure thought (cogito). From another perspective our knowledge of phenomena never moves beyond our own consciousness, "a world fabricated by pure finite, human intelligence."[14]

Epistemology is ultimately grounded in metaphysics, since it shares the same core principles of clear and distinct ideas or pure theoretical intuition and mathematical understanding. The innate or a priori ideas of the cogito (I think) form the basis and constitution of the human mind by which our understanding of corporeal substances or nature is achieved. The physical accidents or qualities of the self and nature, which exist in sense perception of the subject only and not in external objects, are particular and changing, and thus do not reflect the essence of nature as pure thought. The latter delineates and defines how we think about the natural phenomena; we think in a certain prescribed and ordered way because of the a priori structure of the mind. The pure ideas of consciousness and the eternal truths of nature are the product of the perfection of God and are innate to human reason; they are part of the "innate constitution of the mind" implanted in us by God and projected onto nature as its universal principles.[15] Nature consists of the objects of pure reason, which in turn are projections of the substance of God's essence and being. We access these principles through deductive intuition. This relationship between metaphysics and method reflected in the innate ideas of human consciousness, theoretical principles of nature, and universal laws of geometry have profound implications for the individual's perception and understanding of objective reality. Although Descartes argues that these principles and laws are inherent in the mind since they are given to us by God, the central question remains as to the distinction between the method of science as an act of discovery of these laws, on one side, and the method of science as an act of construction of these laws, on the other. Galgan in *The Logic of Modernity* writes:

> What I really know in knowing this object or any other thing in the world is the nature of my mind—the nature of myself as "res cogitans.". . . Scientific methodology has no access to the essence of things independent of itself. Modern scientific knowledge, in sum, discloses not the essence of natural things but the essence

of finite thought—the essence of human thinking. . . . Modern
science is fated to deal, not with nature as given or pregiven, but
with nature as assimilable to the thinking of the finite human
subject—nature as quantifiable or mechanical.[16]

This crucial and profound insight surrounds the justification of
modern natural science by medieval metaphysics (God as infinite
and perfect non-deceiver) or the justification of mathematical science by the universal form of knowledge and consciousness of the
cogito (pure thought). Both metaphysics and method—as expressions of God and consciousness—share the same type of innate
and universal categories, creating an interesting and unresolved
problem about our knowledge of the natural world around us.
Descartes sees the line of connection evolving from the consciousness of the self, method of clear and distinct ideas, proof of the
existence of God, and the ultimate validity of our knowledge about
nature and the physical reality as the logical development of the
idea of "I think, therefore, I am." But it is the problematic connection between the form of knowledge of the cogito and God—since
both are clear, distinct, and innate ideas—which gives rise to the
dilemma connecting metaphysics and science.[17] Science thus
appears as the external manifestation of these innate ideas as it
justifies nature, but also constructs nature through a certain form
of consciousness. The essence and logic of science comes from
within the self; the reality of nature is an expression of the essence
of consciousness and innate ideas. The question Galgan raises is
central to the later development of the relationship between the
constructivism of Marx's social epistemology and theory of historical materialism: What is the epistemological and ontological
status of Western science, and does it reflect the essence of nature,
the innate ideas of God, or the consciousness of the cogito? Do we
have access to empirical reality, or is the latter merely a metaphysical construct?

METAPHYSICS AND PHYSICS AS THE FOUNDATION OF MODERN SCIENCE

In the *Meditations*, Descartes justifies the existence of an objective world and the legitimacy of natural science and its distinctive universal method on the basis of the existence of God and clear and distinct ideas. The close connection between the medieval theory of Christian cosmology and the modern form of human consciousness provides Descartes with the basis for his connection between metaphysics and method. However, as we look closer into the characteristics of mathematical science and its systematic method in his earlier work, *Discourse on Method,* the method, procedure, and theory of pure reason is justified on the basis of a new, secular, and more modern metaphysics of science constructed from the ideas of pure reason. To develop a more detailed analysis of this second form of metaphysics in Descartes' writings, and the possible limitations of their application to and justification of natural science, it is necessary to investigate the relationship within science itself between the new historical metaphysics and method of natural science. The medieval metaphysics of divine cosmology of the *Meditations* justifies the existence of individual consciousness and God, as well as the validity of the universal knowledge derived from the clarity, sharpness, and distinctiveness of pure ideas, and ultimately the legitimacy of the new method of science found in the *Discourse on Method*.[18] The metaphysics of science contains Descartes' theory of mathematical science and extended substance or matter. He originally incorporated this aspect of his metaphysics within his analysis of clear and distinct ideas and the existence of physical reality, under the belief that the natural world was an integral part of his metaphysics of self, reason, and God. Physics was integrated with the metaphysics of pure consciousness and ideas. However, with later developments in the history and philosophy of science, as we have already seen, another metaphysics hidden within Descartes' philosophy would become evident, which creates a new view of nature that he sees as the mathematical and universal essence of physics and nature. Today this metaphysics is seen as particular, historical, and social and thus must be investigated on its own.

The new secular metaphysics of science found in the *Discourse* has different implications than that articulated in his *Meditations*. Its purpose is to expand our understanding of the propositions, procedures, and principles of his theory of substance, knowledge, and nature as it attempts to justify the universal characteristics of science; its underlying theory of being and knowledge, existence and thought; the specific and formal operations of the scientific mind and method; and the presumed primary and universal characteristics of nature as a pure idea. Thus, the modern metaphysics of science grounds the method, ontology, epistemology, and technology of natural science (that is, physics) while the traditional and medieval metaphysics of cosmology justified the existence of nature as a valid object of perception and knowledge, along with its status as an objective, universal, and non-illusory explanation of nature.

Descartes' theory of epistemology and the metaphysics of nature focuses on the distinction between thought and being, method and reality, and epistemology and ontology. It represents a philosophy of nature and knowledge (method) that is grounded not in reality, but in the interests and values of human consciousness. The metaphysics of mathematics and science precedes actual scientific inquiry, but makes this form of knowledge possible, since nature now conforms to the fundamental categories of scientific consciousness. Here the whole new modern world of nature opens up for our review. Metaphysics creates both nature (objectivity) and method (theory), and thus science (truth) itself. Metaphysics is the foundation of method, because it has theoretically constructed the empirical reality of the objective world which underlies and makes possible the method itself; metaphysics creates the reality within which the scientific method and theory operates. In turn, metaphysics not only makes science possible, but legitimates its application and use. This is why Descartes' philosophy of metaphysics is central to our appreciation of his contribution to the understanding of science and method. Descartes never explicitly distinguished between metaphysics based on the existence and character of God and metaphysics based on the principles of natural science. The purpose of the former is to justify the existence of objective reality and the theoretical validity of science, whereas the purpose of the latter is to articulate the foundations of the substance and character of nature as extension, figure, time, and motion, and the validity of its distinctive method.

Within this modern metaphysics, nature appears as an objective and external phenomenon with the characteristics of a functional machine organized around the principles of a non-living mechanism. The purpose of human consciousness and science is to explain the internal structure, materialist dynamics, and reductionistic functioning of its intersecting parts within the whole assembly of nature. To understand this complicated process, the method appropriate to this second form of metaphysics describes a certain kind of knowledge in which the mind is perceived to be separated from the physical world in a mind/body dualism, whose goal is to know the primary (mental) and not secondary (sense perception) qualities of this world. The fundamental purpose of human knowledge is not only to know the essence or true forms of reality as pure mathematical ideas, but to achieve knowledge that is useful for the control and domination of nature itself.[19] For Descartes, the metaphysics and method were integrated into a single comprehensive science, while later theorists would separate the two fields into ontology and utility, materialism and domination. However, as early as the seventeenth century, it was clear that the true purpose of theoretical and mathematical knowledge was its usefulness in the domination and power over nature. And this required the development of a special type of mind and method, which Gilbert Ryle described as "the ghost in the machine."

CARTESIAN THEORY OF SUBSTANCE, METHOD OF DISCOVERY, AND SCIENCE

Descartes did not follow Aristotle's theory of substance, causality, and teleology, but instead articulated a new theory of substance and knowledge, based on the distinctions between, on the one hand, *res cogitans* and *res extensa*, the mind and body, and primary and secondary qualities of human knowledge; and on the other, the analytic/constitutive and synthetic/deductive method. To clarify these distinctions within his theory of substance or physical matter, he provides in the Second Meditation the example of beeswax, which has rather distinctive secondary or sensible qualities of sweetness, odor, color, hardness, sound, and shape. But these very accidental and provisional characteristics change over time, especially when brought close to a fire. Its physical appearances derived by the senses radically change; the initial secondary qualities of the wax have been altered. Descartes asks the question of whether the same wax remains after the changes have occurred, since all its secondary appearances have been altered by the fire but what remains is still considered wax. At this key point he undertakes a critique of empiricism and contends that the perceived wax was not a reflection of its essential qualities: "Certainly it cannot be anything that I observed by means of the senses, since everything in the field of taste, smell, sight, touch, and hearing are changed, and since the same wax nevertheless remains."[20] Descartes is raising the key question of what objective reality is, and how we know it. Is it the secondary or particular characteristics of wax that are perceived through the senses and change over time, or is it the primary and universal characteristics of the object that are known through the mind?

Descartes begins to take a position of epistemological skepticism, since the senses do not give us reliable knowledge of the objects of immediate experience. Knowledge of the secondary qualities of perception constantly changes and does not give us access to an object's primary or universal characteristics. Descartes even doubts that these sensations justify or confirm the existence of an objective reality outside the human mind or validate a resemblance between objects and our ideas. They appear only as inclinations to believe in the existence of an external reality. After abstracting from our knowledge of the senses and the imagination, he arrives at the conclusion that the true knowledge of the wax lies in its simple nature or ultimate elements of physical size or extension or figure (length, width, and depth), location (spatial relationship with other objects), flexibility, movement (speed and size), and duration (time). These characteristics or fundamental attributes of the natural phenomena provide the natural world with a determinate nature or form that is "immutable and eternal." Wax is thus an extended and quantifiable substance in time and space measured by the human mind. This substance and its relationships are expressed in the form of primary qualities of external bodies or objective substances, since they are expressed in mathematical propositions and calculation of clear and distinct ideas. The natural world has thus been reduced to a materialist, quantitative, and mathematical world of experience within Descartes' theory of knowledge. These principles of shapes, numbers, and movements are the eternal and universal "essence of material things . . . (that have) a certain determinate nature, or form, or essence, which is immutable and eternal which I have not invented and which does not in any way depend upon my mind."[21] These characteristics of objects are not the product of the authority of traditions, observations, sense perception, human invention, or creative imagination, but are accessible only to the understanding of pure reason as innate ideas; they are the product of the "light of nature" and are the fundamental principles of natural law. That is, the defining characteristics of physics and nature exist innately in the structure of the mind, but are not the products of reason itself. The essence of nature as an extended substance is expressed in the clear and distinct ideas of mathematics and coordinate geometry which comprehend nature in terms of its physical extension, causal relationships, curvilinear and rectilinear motion, and changes in time.

This position provides the foundations for epistemological rationalism and the metaphysical foundation of modern physics. The
secondary qualities of objects are not the product of distinctive
ideas and reason, but subjective and accidental forms of perceptions, and therefore not the basis for scientific inquiry; they do not
express the universal characteristics or essence of nature.

Descartes has created a metaphysics of science whereby nature
is defined as having specific characteristics. He divides knowledge into primary and secondary qualities, perception and the
understanding, and mental and physical characteristics. It is clear
from his writings that the metaphysics of science is based on the
metaphysics of cosmology, as his theory of objective reality and
science is contingent on the prior existence and perfection of God,
as articulated in the Third Meditation. According to Descartes,
the truth of the physical reality of physical substances can only be
known through human reason and clear and distinct ideas, and
not through the "superficial appearances" of the constantly changing qualities of human perception of the senses. Clear and distinct
ideas exist in each human mind, whereas appearances are qualities
produced by the senses. Descartes continues to expand these ideas
about substance, objective reality, and nature in the Fifth and Sixth
Meditations. At this point in his analysis he offers the example of
the triangle and its various descriptions arising from clear and
distinct ideas, such as the nature of its lines, angles, figures, and
measurements.

Descartes argues that because he has theoretically and logically justified the existence of the consciousness, ideas, and God,
he has proven the validity of clear and distinct ideas. "And thus I
recognize very clearly that the certainty and truth of all knowledge depends solely on the knowledge of the true God. . . . And
now that I know him, I have the means of acquiring clear and certain and perfect knowledge about an infinity of things . . . also
about that which pertains to corporeal nature, in so far as it can
be the object of pure mathematics."[22] Divine metaphysics has justified knowledge and existence of the physical world (sensations)

and objective substances (thought and ideas), mathematics, and the metaphysical principles of theoretical science and corporeal nature. Metaphysics has helped us to move beyond the radical doubt and epistemological skepticism of all forms of knowledge and opinions in the First Meditation. Descartes writes that "truth is the same as being" and that "everything, generally speaking, which is discussed in pure mathematics or analytic geometry does in truth occur in them [sensible objects]."[23] Thus mathematics is the essence of the natural order created by God and known by humans through the power and authority of clear and distinct ideas and a non-deceiving God.

To delve deeper into the metaphysical form of nature and its picture of the corporeal world as a mathematical system and structured order, we must turn to Descartes' discussion of the particular method of modern physics that he outlines in the *Discourse on Method* as the analytic and synthetic method. In this work he examines the precepts of logic and the order of scientific discovery based on the chain of reasoning and mind in geometry and algebra. In the second part of the *Discourse,* he summarizes the method of physics as a mechanical procedure that (1) begins with a suspicion and doubt of traditional knowledge (skepticism); (2) undertakes a detailed study (analysis) of a particular problem (materialism) based on its simplest constitutive parts (atomism); (3) moves to self-evident and pure ideas (intuition); (4) proceeds to examine their interrelationship with other component elements, issues, and ideas (functionalism and deduction); (5) continues to a systematic and logical integration of the main issues and demonstrates how its interrelated parts form a comprehensive and integrated whole expressed as a scientific theory of the universal laws of prediction and regulation of nature (synthesis); and (6) ends with a general restatement of the whole process from initial propositions to general conclusions in mathematical categories (summary).[24] The Cartesian method, which reflects the mechanical arts of modern technology, proceeds from radical skepticism, analysis of the distinctive parts of the problem under consideration, the synthesis of the component parts into a comprehensive physical theory of matter and motion, and final summary of the formal method of its mathematical logic and essential conclusions about the geometric laws of nature. That is, the method of science begins with radical doubt and refusal to accept as true any claim that is not certain and evident. It avoids all prejudices and prejudgments and limits true knowledge to the immediate and overwhelming intuition of clear and distinct ideas. The scientific method is grounded in the immediate certainty of mathematical truths and the undeniable self-evidence of its logical proofs and reasoning. Herein lies its truth, utility, noble character, and logical foundations.

After an introductory remark about methodical doubt, Descartes argues that this approach—the order of discovery— must analytically divide the scientific problem under investigation into its simplest component parts in order to find those principles that are the simplest and easiest to know and cannot be doubted or questioned. He then gradually incorporates this knowledge into a synthetic mode of composition that contains the more comprehensive and universal laws of nature and physics based on these initial principles of clear and distinct ideas.[25] Following the method of geometric reasoning from initial principles, he reaches his conclusion that true knowledge is a mathematical science based on the analysis of certain initial intuitive propositions and analytic first principles of science; a general theory that synthe- sizes and integrates its various component parts into a universal and comprehensive theory of physics; and a final summary and review of all aspects of the theory itself.[26] According to Descartes, this method is the foundation of modern science. The generation of scientific and synthetic propositions results from their deduc- tion from the intuition and analysis of first principles.

Throughout his work, Descartes illustrates his philosophy and methodology with examples from geometry, often referring to tri- angles to show the actual logic and chain of reasoning from pure intuition to theoretical conclusions that underlie this distinctive analytic and synthetic method. The general method of geometry and algebra forms the basis for physics and "all things knowable to men," because it provides examples to explain his notion of clear and distinct ideas. Ideas that are clear, intuitive, immediately certain, evident, direct, and beyond doubt, and that are distinct, different, independent, and separate from other ideas—ideas like the knowledge of the existence of the rational soul and a perfect Being—are the basis for all other knowledge of the nature of material substance, that is, extension and its different modes or accidental properties.[27] Descartes argues that it is quite clear that a triangle contains three angles that are equal to two right angles, or that all the parts of a circle are equidistant from the center of a sphere; and we know these geometrical truths with the same clarity and certainty as we know the existence and perfection of God. These are self-evident truths of cosmology and mathematics resulting from the "light of reason," which are independent of human knowledge and exist innately in the human mind. Mathematics and physics are simply following these same principles of natural law "which God has so established in nature and the notion of which he has so fixed in our minds."[28] These same principles and laws apply equally to the method and logic of mathematics, as well as to the study of the matter, motion, and situation of the celestial objects such as the earth, planets, stars, water, tides, plants, metals, fire, light, etc.

Descartes then proceeds to apply his distinctive analytic method beyond mathematics to more concrete areas of scientific research, as he begins a brief summary of the laws and structure of human anatomy and physiology developed by David Harvey. Human biology is broken down into its distinctive parts, functions, and motion. Descartes then makes the judgment that the movement of the human body is similar to the motions of a clock with its distinctive weight, location, and functioning of its weights, gears, and wheels. The laws of nature and physical matter and the rules of mechanics created by God become the laws of mathematics, celestial astronomy, biology, human anatomy, medicine, organic nature, and terrestrial physics. This is possible because the human body and its internal organs, and animal anatomy in general, are perceived as a machine and thus the world of planetary and human motion, the anatomy of its parts and functions, and the prediction of its movement and actions are possible because all are based on the rational structure and inner logic of the industrial machine. This also reflects Descartes' belief that this method is applicable to all areas of philosophical, metaphysical, and scientific inquiry and discovery; it was an expression of the overall unity of knowledge that he summarized with the metaphor of the "tree of knowledge." The distinctive aspects of his mechanistic natural philosophy, three laws of bodily motion and dynamics, and mathematical theory of physics were derived from the integration of a number of different intellectual and philosophical traditions, including the neo-Platonic theology of Augustine, the neo-Aristotelian Scholasticism of Thomas Aquinas, the Greek mathematics of Euclid, and the modern mechanical science of Isaac Beeckman, Francis Bacon, Galileo Galilei, Marin Mersenne, and Pierre Gassendi.

In the Sixth Part of the *Discourse*, Descartes makes perhaps his most interesting and insightful comments about natural science and its relationship to the physical world. As we get deeper into the natural order and laws of physics, it seems that the distance between metaphysics and physics grows more and more pronounced. Descartes recognizes that his understanding of science is different from the traditional view, as he states that science reflects both truth and utility. Rejecting the speculative and contemplative philosophy of medieval scholasticism, he briefly outlines the practical and technical importance of modern physics and its knowledge of terrestrial and celestial nature. He then proceeds to relate this new formal knowledge of the nature and behavior of our physical environment to the different technical skills of industrial workers in agriculture. "We can employ these entities [fire, water, air, stars, the heavens, and other bodies] for all the purposes for which they are suited, and so make ourselves masters and possessors of nature."[29] Descartes has moved from an initial metaphysics of being and nature as the basis for truth about natural phenomena to the foundation of knowledge in our ability to dominate and control nature in agricultural production. Metaphysics has changed into a new form of technical and instrumental rationality based on the mechanical arts and specialized training in the workplace where there is also a distinction between analytic (simple division of labor) and synthetic (complex managerial control) knowledge.

This new form of knowledge is now useful "in bringing about the invention of an infinity of devices to enable us to enjoy the fruits of agriculture and the wealth of the earth without labor," and in bringing about human health, wellbeing, and happiness.[30] This new view of industrial work and science is reaffirmed in the previous part of the *Discourse*, where Descartes contends that the human body, the rules of nature, and the modern physical sciences are best understood "as a machine created by the hand of God."[31] This disenchanted view of nature represents a rejection of both the ancient Greek philosophy of Aristotle and the medieval scholastic view of nature as a living organism. The study of the body of a human being and of nature as a whole along with its various parts—found in the wide variety of natural sciences from physics to medicine—reflects the internal dynamics and deterministic functioning of a machine. The metaphysical postulates of Christian theology, modern ontology, and natural science have now been incorporated into this new reflection on the industrial design of nature and physics. All issues in science can now be broken down into their simplest component parts, their internal functioning, and their technical manipulation of nature.

Descartes' two main concerns in the writings considered in this chapter are the grounding of physics in metaphysics and the development of his rationalist theory of knowledge. As the Enlightenment and modern physics developed in the eighteenth and nineteenth centuries, there was less and less need to maintain the dependent relationship between science and metaphysics. The medieval dimension was no longer considered necessary, since the natural postulates and first principles of science were viewed as standing on their own without the assistance of a divine cosmology needed to justify the validity of pure reason, analytic mathematics, and physical science. And with the writings of post-modernism, especially in the works of W. V. O. Quine, Thomas Kuhn, and Richard Rorty, the underlying validity of physics came to no longer rest in metaphysics, but in utilitarianism. The tension between metaphysics and utilitarianism subtly existed in the seventeenth century, but expanded to an unbridgeable divide by the twentieth century. These primary and universal metaphysical postulates of nature have been replaced by the metaphysics of science since the first principles, laws of nature, and corporeal phenomena are no longer grounded in the existence of God and nature, but rather in the a priori categories of the human mind—whether these are transcendental and universal (Kant) or historical and social (Marx). The understanding of Descartes' philosophy as the "ghost in the machine" has been displaced by notion of the "ghost in the factory."

Metaphysics of the Domination of Nature and Machine Production

Contemporary social and political theorists have studied these same questions of the metaphysical foundations of modern science, not from the perspective of theology and cosmology, but from that of the history and political economy of science. They are more interested in examining the formal rationalization, technical interests, and cultural disenchantment (*Entzauberung*) of science with its methodological imperatives of domination and control. From this perspective, science no longer reflects natural law, universal truth, or the essence of natural reality, but is instead understood as a social and political construct whose underlying principles and methodological impulses are driven not by an attempt to mirror the essence or structure of reality, but by the necessity to technically control nature for industrial production and market profit. Science is now connected to the structures and logic of capitalism and not the natural law of a perfect Being.

As previously discussed, Descartes' thesis of the "ghost in the machine" focused on three main issues: (1) the nature of the thinking substance is pure consciousness (*res cogitans*) separated from the body and physical world; (2) knowledge of this world is through pure reason and the clarity and immediacy of ideas; and (3) the primary qualities of the physical phenomena are extension, figure, and motion that are reducible to mathematical principles and geometric propositions.

> To Descartes the material universe was a machine and nothing but a machine. There was no purpose, life, or spirituality in nature. Nature worked according to mechanical laws, and everything in the material world could be explained in terms of the arrangement and movement of its parts. This mechanical picture of nature became the dominant paradigm of science in the period following Descartes . . . Descartes gave scientific thought its general framework—the view of nature as a perfect machine, governed by exact mathematical laws.[32]

These fundamental principles would later be amended by many issues—including the theory of energy, relativity, subatomic physics, and quantum physics—but the basic model of nature remained intact. It is this quantification and mathematization of the physical environment that permits Descartes to develop a theory of knowledge (epistemology) and philosophy of science (methodology) that treats the natural world as a technical, quantifiable, and predictive device with the general characteristics of materialism, mechanism, determinism, functionalism, and utilitarianism. Nature is a machine or clock that runs according to methodical and orderly rules and quantifiable measurements, thereby providing predictable results generated by its own natural laws. Underlying this view of nature is a science whose goal is the creation of causal relationships, hypotheses, predictions, and universal laws[33] that can be used to aid in the production of material wealth in agriculture and industry by dominating the immediate organic and inorganic environment. Gone are the ancient and medieval views of nature as alive with meaning and purpose, potentiality and final causes, beauty and spirituality, passions and perception, emotions and feelings, and coherence and finitude. Science and industry are integrated in a comprehensive metaphysical and economic system. "In turn, the mechanical structure of reality (1) is made up of atomic parts, (2) consists of discrete information bits extracted from the world, (3) is assumed to operate according to laws and rules, (4) is based on context-free abstraction from the changing complex world of appearance, and (5) is defined so as to give maximum capability for manipulation and control over nature."[34] With the revolution in seventeenth-century consciousness, science turned into a form for the measurement and management of nature, in a clear example of "the colonization of the lifeworld" by machines, technology, and science. Morris Berman maintains that the creation of a mechanistic science was Descartes' greatest historical legacy.[35]

With all the changes in modern physics from Descartes to the present, the central epistemological issue remains the same: What is the relationship between our scientific knowledge of the world and the underlying normative assumptions, speculative presuppositions, and axiomatic postulates? That is, what is the relationship between objectivity and science? Before science can begin to develop its theories of nature with its initial self-evident truths (Descartes) or with initial observations and experiments (Newton), it must have an innate understanding of the physical reality it is investigating. Without this knowledge, which is rarely articulated or recognized, science is impossible. E. A. Burtt has written that "the precise nature and assumptions of modern scientific thinking itself have not as yet been made the object of really disinterested, critical research.... Surely here is need for a critical, historical study of the rise of the fundamental assumptions characteristic of modern thinking."[36] To undertake scientific inquiry, there must first be a set of metaphysical principles about the reality of the objective world. This world evolves as a set of theoretical speculations about the reality of the external world. It is this metaphysics of extension, figure, and motion which makes science possible for Descartes. Thus ontology and epistemology—the nature of being and knowledge—are essential ingredients in the development of the metatheory which forms the foundation of natural science.

F. S. C. Northrop has written about this issue. Although he was writing about Einsteinian mechanics and Heisenberg's theory of quantum physics and indeterminacy, the main philosophical issue clearly relates to the earlier science of Descartes.

Hence, physics is neither epistemologically nor ontologically neutral. Deny any one of the epistemological assumptions of the physicist's theory and there is no scientific method for testing whether what the theory says about the physical object is true, in the sense of being empirically confirmed. Deny any one of the ontological assumptions and there is not enough content in the axiomatically constructed mathematical postulates of the physicist's theory to permit the deduction of the experimental facts which it is introduced to predict, co-ordinate consistently and explain.[37]

Substance or objectivity is a construct of metaphysics—ontology and epistemology—and without this set of assumptions and postulates about nature, science has no basis on which to develop its distinctive method and theories, whether they are grounded in rationalism or empiricism or both. The access of science to the external world is predicated on these nonscientific assumptions about the ontological dualism between the mind and body, primary and secondary qualities, and natural assumptions of matter and extension and the first principles of geometry. The a priori categories of time, space, magnitude, figure, and motion are essential just to perceive the external world, no less to explain it in scientific theory. Objectivity is created through these categories. The metaphysical problem arises when we see that these essential categories are themselves not open to empirical validation or scientific proof; we cannot know them through observation or intuition. Yet without them, experience and knowledge are impossible. Northrop summarizes his argument: "we know the object of scientific knowledge only by the speculative means of axiomatic theoretic construction or postulation. . . . It follows that there is no *a priori* or empirical meaning for affirming the object of scientific knowledge."[38] There are no intuitive first principles or immediately observable scientific data, there is no neutral and privileged access to objective reality though pure reason or sense perception, theory or observation. The world that we see and know, especially in the context of modern physics, is a construct built upon a priori metaphysical and mathematical principles of ontology and epistemology, which are the product of philosophical assumptions of a mechanical and causal system. Within this framework, science accumulates the observations, facts, and empirical evidence to justify its hypotheses and theories, not directly but through its deduced consequences. However, without the metaphysical presuppositions and prior foundations, science would be impossible.

The recognition and validation of natural science is not based on its ability to reflect a defined and phenomenal reality; it is based on the internal logic of its method to produce observations and ideas that reflect its explanatory concepts and predictive conclusions. That is, it is based on its ability to conceptually reproduce the internal workings of its metaphysical assumptions and mathematical mechanisms about parts, functions, and a comprehensive and integrative theory. Science reproduces and represents the initial corporeal assumptions about nature, as well as its projected hypotheses and theoretical conclusions. Science is true only within the historically constructed framework of its own internal ontological values, scientific method, and mechanistic logic. And its ultimate justification rests on the unconscious assumptions of these very principles and values.

The traditional search for the foundations of science in rationalism and empiricism ends with the recognition that there are no true mathematical principles and empirical facts that can be found or discovered in nature. Rather, they are invented only after the scientific revolution and perhaps more importantly after "the death of nature" through its mechanistic and deterministic laws. Neither observation nor reason can justify facts, since the latter are the product of a particular method, theory, and deductive inferences. Facts are validated neither through experience (empiricism) nor through reason (rationalism) but by means of utility—internal operational utility of science in terms of its categories, causes, consequences, and deduction and external utility of its success in sustaining machine technology and industrial production. These different forms of utility in terms of prediction and production require a certain view of nature, grounded in philosophical dualism of the mind and body and metaphysical realism of extended substance, by which nature is viewed as a dead machine that can be controlled for human purposes. Nature has no independent life, purpose, or ethical basis for existence other than serving the technical and formal interests of human beings. Modern issues of matter, extension, figure, and motion have replaced the medieval focus on matter, essence, form, quality, and potentiality, along with the finite coherence, harmony, and perfection of the cosmos. This has resulted in the devaluation and secularization of nature. When this model of nature would be applied in the twentieth century to the study of society, economy, and human psychology (examined in chapter 5), there resulted a corresponding abuse of humanity for the purposes of domination and control over labor, industry, production, and the academy. In the process of explaining nature, the independence, teleology, and ethics of nature were replaced by the human desires and goals of the mathematization and quantification of experience and knowledge replaced. The irony of all this is that in the finite medieval view of nature, human beings were seen as central, whereas in the modern view, humans became insignificant and hapless creatures in a world where they had no profound purpose or existential meaning.[39] The naturalistic and infinite world became disenchanted and dehumanized, without a

final cause, as humans were reduced to pleasure-seeking specta-
tors in a lifeless social machine and atomistic market economy.
Alexandre Koyré has referred to these radical changes as "the
crisis of European consciousness."[40] All aspects of plant, animal,
and human nature were reduced to mechanical laws of motion
and causality. "All the processes of nature, moral and political no
less than physical, were reducible to matter and motion and com-
pletely accounted for in mechanical terms."[41] In the modern world
the reasoning and purpose of God was replaced by the logic of the
machine and modern technology.

Modern science needs a passive, mechanical, and deterministic
world, and there is no science that can prove that modern metaphysics is superior to the ancient and medieval universe. In fact,
a case could probably be made that these earlier worldviews, with
their respect for a living environment and ethical attitude toward
nature, are far superior to modern mechanistic laws of the machine.
And it is the technical method of natural science that mediates
between this unconscious and speculative worldview and observational and mathematical experience. The traditional separation
of ontology and epistemology, metaphysics and science, have kept
secret the need to reflect rationally on these underlying assumptions about nature and human reason. The irony of Western science
is that metaphysics cannot be justified empirically or scientifically and the science cannot be rationally accepted without these
philosophical assumptions about the universe. F. S. C. Northrop
continues by writing that "any theory of physics makes more physical and philosophical assumptions than the facts alone give or
imply."[42] Access to objective facts can only be achieved by returning to the metaphysical foundations, theoretical assumptions, and
scientific results of the deductive consequences.[43] These deductive
consequences, resulting from hypothesis construction and observation, are grounded in initial assumptions about a mechanistic
nature. Nature is a construct of these unconscious and historical
principles and hidden assumptions; science, with its distinctive
method, first principles, and accumulated evidence, is grounded

in them also. Knowledge of nature is the result of knowledge of human consciousness and its metaphysical and constructed realism and mechanism of *res extensa*.[44]

David Hume pushes the argument further in sections 4 and 12 of *An Inquiry Concerning Human Understanding* (1748), where he argues that the very foundations of science in the ideas of substance (external objects), causality, and self could not be proven by either deductive reason or inductive experience. He ended his work with the conclusion that science, objectivity, and representations are a product of the human imagination—they are created constructions. We never experience objective reality, only our representations of it in the mind.[45] Thus, the foundations of science rested no longer on a belief in the existence of God, but upon a natural and projected belief in the underlying structure and reality of nature itself. Following this metaphysics, the categories and principles of science were grounded. Hume's skepticism potentially undermines the foundations of the Western Enlightenment and modern science by calling into question the key principles of science—the existence of a knowable external world and physical causality between objects and events.

Hume in sections 4 and 12 of his work is unable to justify either through the senses (empiricism) or reason (rationalism) the nature of external objects (substances) because (1) perception never sees the objects themselves, just their impressions (the dilemma of double affection and critique of naive realism); (2) the cause of our representations of the world are only representations; and (3) they are only secondary and subjective qualities and impressions of the objects (the collapse of the distinction between primary and secondary qualities). In section 14 Hume develops his theory of perception and experience, cause of representations, and primary/secondary qualities, to show that we never have experience and knowledge of an external reality, but only of our own sensations and representation. On the other hand, in section 4 he argues that we cannot justify causal relationships among objects, because pure reason and deductive logic cannot discern causality through pure reflection (the billiard ball theory). Nor can experience and inductive reasoning (the idea that the future will be like the past) justify causality, because induction requires the acceptance of inductive reasoning to justify its own argument. With these points, the Enlightenment begins to shake before Hume's skepticism. There will be further discussion of Hume's empiricism and skepticism and their importance for the social sciences in chapter 5.

Immanuel Kant's goal in the *Critique of Pure Reason* and the *Prolegomena to any Future Metaphysics* is to save Hume from himself and science from Hume's skepticism. These philosophers never asked from where these concepts were derived. After Descartes, the debate increased as to the origins of these metaphysical foundations of natural science—God (Descartes), nature (Newton), imagination (Hume), consciousness (Kant), spirit (Hegel), or society (Marx). These speculative assumptions about the natural world began as innate ideas of mechanical science in Cartesian philosophy and evolved into the a priori categories of the understanding in Kant's critique of pure reason,

COLONIZATION OF SCIENCE AND THE LIFEWORLD BY THE LOGIC OF CAPITAL

With the rise of contemporary history and philosophy of science and the separation of the medieval metaphysics of scholasticism from science itself, science loses its direct connection to God, perfection, and absolute truth. Its initial metaphysical postulates about matter and nature, its first principles of mathematical and geometric origins and simplicity, and its theoretical breadth of causality and explanation in nature are now based on other epistemological groundings within the history of modern philosophy, including transcendental subjectivity, paradigm construction, social consensus of utility and pragmatism, and historical and materialist consciousness. With the dismemberment of the metaphysics of the soul, God, and nature, what remained the same from the seventeenth until the twenty-first century was the foundational principles and metaphysics of natural science, whose validity no longer lies in God and being, theology and ontology, but in the economy and industrial utility; that is, it is no longer based on the ontological "why" question but the technical art of the "how" question. The technical *Weltanschauung* and rules of nature in modern science have lost their justification in God and being, and must rely instead on the logic of its internal machinery of measurement, management, and manipulation, as well as its explanatory and predictive success. With the loss of an epistemology tied to theology, how is the validity of science maintained; what justifies the metaphysics of science today and the necessary connection between science and reality, between thought and being? Are its first principles about a mechanistic and mathematical universe just another form of speculative abstraction or unjustified rumination, or are they connected to the proven success of technological rationality in scientific experiments, industry, and the market?

The metaphysics underlying ontology and epistemology have been replaced by the logic and structure of capital. Carolyn Merchant in *The Death of Nature* writes: "The idea of scientific progress has been associated with the rise of technology and the 'requirements of early capitalist economy.'" [46] Merchant outlines the historical unfolding of capitalist agriculture from the medieval communes, with their common land and cooperative economy, local governance and self-regulation, and village concern for the ecological system. This system began to decline throughout Europe in the sixteenth century due to increased population; division of labor; land enclosures by wealthy landlords; dismantling of craft guilds in urban areas; the decline of the peasants and their village economies; increasing tensions between wage labor and capital; and the rise of merchants, commerce, and small industries. These transformations provided the conditions for the later Scientific Revolution. "Because nature was now viewed as a system of dead, inert particles moved by external, rather than inherent forces, the mechanical framework itself could legitimate the manipulation of nature. Moreover, as a conceptual framework, the mechanical order had associated with it a framework of values based on power, fully compatible with the directions taken by commercial capitalism."[47] Berman in *The Reenchantment of the World* views the relationship between science and capitalism as a dialectical congruence and an informal interplay within the historical totality. There is no clear and direct causal relationship between consciousness and capitalism, but "it will be necessary, therefore, to look at science as a system of thought adequate to a certain historical epoch."[48] He rejects the view that science is "an absolute, transcultural truth" independent of the norms, values, and institutions of the social system from which it evolved.

Capitalism, the market economy, and industrial machinery are the necessary prerequisites for the Scientific Revolution and the development of the metaphysics and method that form the basis for natural science. Berman writes about this connection between science and capitalism:

> The equating of truth with utility, or cognition with technology, was an important part of this general process. Experiment, quantification, prediction, and control formed the parameters of a world view that made no sense within the framework of the medieval social and economic order. . . . Modern science, in short, is the mental framework for a world defined by capital accumulation, and ultimately, to quote Ernest Gellner, it became the "mode of cognition" of industrial society.[49]

The main issue here is of the technical and mechanistic reductionism of science: the reduction of modern science to unproven and unconscious metaphysical assumptions about the essence and being of the natural world; the reduction of science's distinctive internal method—based on atomism, mechanical functionalism, and theoretical synthesis—to the rhythm and logic of formal technology and industrial machinery; the reduction of its epistemology and ontology to the social imperatives to dominate and control nature; and the reduction of its technical specialization and formal division of its parts, ideas, and theories to a reflection of the social organization of capitalist production lead to a conclusion that natural science itself is an historical form of cultural consciousness and political ideology. Science is the result of the colonization of consciousness and the lifeworld by the economic system. It constructs a particular mechanical and deterministic reality of nature (and of society)—behind the appearances of logic and method, epistemology and ontology, matter and causality, and explanation and prediction—that conforms to the underlying values of capitalist society in its materialism, atomism, specialization, mechanism, and manipulation of nature.

Science does not examine an objectivity independent of and external to consciousness and ideas; its perceptions, understanding, and knowledge of nature are a social construct based on the logic of capital and not the logic of reality. As Kant once said, integrating subjectivity and objectivity, there is no access to essential, objective reality as a "thing-in-itself." Moving beyond Kant, all knowledge, consciousness, and perception of reality is a form or *Gestalt* created under the conditions established by the historical and social system at a particular moment in time. With the social parameters set by the political and economic conditions of ancient Greece and medieval Europe, the science and technology of modern society could not have evolved; the substructure, preconditions, and assumptions simply did not exist. This leads us to one of the most interesting and profound questions of our times: what would science as a socially and historically distinct metaphysics, method, and consciousness look like under a different social system, one framed by the principles of equality, worker control, democracy, and ecological justice—that is, a socialist society? More succinctly, what is the relationship among science, nature, and social justice? If modern science and capitalism share a common logic and consciousness, would a transformation of the latter logically require a transformation of the former?[50] These questions will be examined in more detail in the following chapters.

Implications of this view of science and nature develop in the writings of Jürgen Habermas, who adapted Talcott Parsons's structural/functionalist theory of the social system to reflect the social pathologies endemic to modern society.[51] The distinct elements of modernity are divided into two main areas: the *System* and the *Lebenswelt*. These in turn reflect the main ideas and structural points of classical social theory. Society is viewed as a comprehensive and integrated *System* of the state and economy and the *Lebenswelt* of culture, socialization, and psychology. Political economy is expressed in the alienation of work and the structural contradictions of capitalism (Marx) and the rationalization of the modern bureaucratic state (Weber), while the *Lebenswelt* is manifested in the culture and values of modern technology, disenchantment, and loss of cultural and personal meaning in life (Weber); anomie, cultural dérèglement, loss of collective conscience and values, and the rise of individual madness (Durkheim); and the psychology of serious depression and unconscious repression (Freud) and the homelessness and anxiety of the individual (R. D. Laing and C. Lasch). As each structural element of society becomes more atomistic, mechanical, and culturally vacuous, there is a corresponding effect on the individuals in this social totality who become more alienated, disenchanted, anomic, and mentally and intellectually lost in a meaningless universe. Science historically evolved in a world without human creativity and dignity and without a moral economy and true democracy (Marx), without substantive reason and purpose (Weber), without collective ideals and social values (Durkheim), and without a strong and integrated sense of self and personal well-being (Freud). And science, with its view of the world as a lifeless and mindless machine, was an essential part of this world and integrated itself into it without much effort.

According to Floyd Matson in *The Broken Image*, science is not the cause of the problem, but is certainly part of the overall social pathology. "The central tradition of Western thought which has cherished the essential dignity and liberty of the individual, is, quite simply, no longer tenable in the face of more scientific knowledge of man."[52] As science and positivism move beyond the physical environment to the study of humanity and social interaction, the metaphysics of natural science become embedded in the logic and method of the new social sciences (scientism). The result is the rise of humanity as a biological organism and social mechanism, as found in the categories of the behavioral and positivistic social sciences, with their own mechanical rules and laws. One glaring result of these changes is the loss of critical reflection on the traditional political and economic ideals of social and democratic justice (nominalism) and the development of a science which cannot delve beyond the surface phenomena (realism) to understand or change history. The study of humanity itself is examined within the rules and regulations of the inert form of matter in motion. This aspect of the social sciences, as we move from the alienation and disenchantment of nature to the domination and alienation of humanity, will be examined more closely in chapter 5.

In recent years there has been a lively debate in the philosophy of science between the analytic tradition (Carnap, Hegel, Nagel, Braitwaite, and Popper) and the historical tradition (Burtt, Koyré, Duhem, Kuhn, Feyerabend, and Quine). The former school of thought stresses the definition and logic of scientific enquiry; analysis of its methodological presuppositions; the verification, falsification, or validation of scientific theories; and some metaphysical claim as to the empirical reality which underlies the conceptual and scientific framework (the correspondence theory of truth).[53] The latter school stresses the historical, cultural, and relative social context of the theories; the *Weltanschauung* underlying the structures and problems to be solved; the political and ideological claims of modern science; and the irrationality (transscientific foundations) that grounds its methodological approach.[54] The debate has called into question the rationality, objectivity, and progressiveness of modern science (and indirectly modern technology and society) and, in turn, has led to a re-evaluation of the epistemology and metatheory of science itself. It has problematized the ocular metaphor which since the seventeenth century has dominated epistemological and theoretical thinking: the notion that the human mind acted as the *mirror of nature* reflecting its intricacies, complexities, and laws.[55]

In the context of a social epistemology and theory of science, this chapter's purpose is to inquire more deeply into some of the following questions: What is rationality, and what is science? What is the relation between scientific knowledge and its empirical referent? Does science investigate the real world, or only the metaphysical components of that world? Finally, if science is one symbolic representational system among others, what is its objective status and claim to universal knowledge?

Though these are important questions, traditional philosophy of science has been hampered by its inability to incorporate material from both the sociology of knowledge and social theory into its framework, thereby resulting in what Larry Laudan has described as the increasing insularity of academic philosophers from social science. The same claim could easily be made against traditional social scientists. Though both Kuhn and Feyerabend recognize that the creation of paradigms does not necessarily lie in rational, progressive, and scientific criteria, the reasons for these shifts have only been vaguely analyzed. Why and how does science develop and progress if the criteria for its development has been shifts in conceptual frameworks, belief systems, and cultural configurations of the world? The answer to these problems has been conceived of in terms of the methodological quest for instrumental progress (Mary Hesse), science's problem-solving effectiveness (Larry Laudan), science's technical interests and instrumental control (Jürgen Habermas), and its manageability and pragmatism (Willard Quine).[56] It is the social practice underlying the methodological and scientific imperatives which must be more clearly analyzed before the philosophy of science can be synthesized with the sociology of science. That is, the technical underpinnings of modern science—which will help explain its metaphysical foundations, quantitative and mathematical data, explanatory and predictive models, self-corrective learning processes, and the goal of the domination of nature—will then be joined to the perspectives of the Critical

Theorists, who hold that an approach to nature whose presuppositions are in the domination of nature (scientific objectivity) entails the domination of man (social and technological objectification). These seem to form the crucial link between philosophy of science and social theory, philosophy and sociology.

If the "mirror of nature" is inadequate as an epistemological metaphor, as the historical tradition seems to indicate within the philosophy of science, so too is the metaphor used to describe humanity's relation to objectivity and rationality in terms of simple productive labor (Marx). Nature is not simply the reflection and mirroring of the labor process and the economic and political institutions, which structure the parameters within which work is performed. Human beings are not simply "economic animals," nor are they simply the mirror of production. It is the rethinking of these two metaphors, one philosophical and the other sociological, that will help in the process by which we rethink our ideas of social practice, social ethics, and our relation to nature.

THE DUHEM-QUINE THESES AND THE CRITIQUE OF THE MIRROR OF NATURE

Both physicist and historian Pierre Duhem and the epistemologist Willard Van Quine have developed a neo-Kantian analysis of modern science which transforms the metaphysical categories of Kant's Transcendental Analytic into a logical conceptual system—a symbolic form. However, the transition of Kantian categories from the realm of metaphysics to logic maintains the fundamental Kantian structure of a priori synthetic judgments, the distinction between the phenomena and noumena, and the inability to know reality as it is in itself distinct from our conceptual framework of the understanding. Neo-Kantian philosophy of science is, as Henry Veatch has recognized, a critique of the principles of the verifiability and falsification theories, inductive and deductive models of scientific methodology.[57] It is this same Kantianism, radicalized by Paul Feyerabend, which leads to methodological and theoretical anarchism, the breakdown of a philosophy of science, and the call for the democratization of science itself.[58] It is this Kantian foundation, running throughout the historical tradition of the philosophy of science, which continues to stress our inability to confront the reality of the physical world independent of the conceptual and theoretical (linguistic and logical) frameworks which we bring to an interpretation of the natural world. Our inability to know nature in itself and to know only our relation to it has resulted in a renewed interest in the methodology, principles, and procedures of natural science; it is a rebirth of epistemology. What we know then is our own conceptual structures overlain in a synthetic unity upon nature. What are these conceptual grids; where do they come from; what are the assumptions that ground them; and what is their relationship to nature and to social interrelationships?

Duhem views science as a logical, symbolic representation which is neither true nor false, but a system of mathematical propositions.

> The observation of physical phenomena does not put us into relation with the hidden reality under the sensible appearances, but enables us to apprehend the sensible appearances themselves in a particular and concrete form. Besides, experimental laws do not have the material reality for their object, but deal with these sensible appearances taken, it is true, in an abstract and general form. Removing or tearing away the veil from these sensible appearances, theory proceeds into and underneath them, and seeks what is really in bodies.[59]

The mathematical symbols, hypotheses, and experimental laws are, for Duhem, arbitrary in that they do not depend on the real state of the physical bodies they represent. The only criteria for being scientific are adherence to the laws of non-contradiction, valid syllogism, and accurate calculation. The scientific theories represent not the hidden realities, but the rules and procedures of mathematical analysis. "Thus, a true theory is not a theory which gives an explanation of physical appearances in conformity with reality; it is a theory which represents in a satisfactory manner a group of experimental laws."[60] The categories of the experimental laws organize the appearances so they may be systematized, classified, and organized to permit "intellectual economy." It aids in the process of recollection and communication to have reduced the complexity of the sensible world to a manageable proportion of deductive laws. What makes for a good theory? Duhem holds that it is a question of usefulness, convenience, and beauty, but also predictability. He developed his philosophy of science reflecting his Kantian preoccupation with the separation of science and metaphysics, appearances and reality; it represented his break with the copy theory of truth ("the mirror of nature") in order to develop a symbolic theory of truth.

Ernst Cassirer in *The Problem of Knowledge* (1906) believes that Duhem's thought is the final product in a symbolic theory of science which goes back to Heinrich Hertz and Henri Poincaré.[61] It was Duhem's critique of the modern positivist tradition and the separation of fact and theory which so excited Cassirer. Because the physical fact is so intimately connected with the theoretical orientation of the scientific investigation, no physical fact could be used as the basis for the verification or falsification of any particular theory. According to Cassirer, only another theory could perform such a function. "A physical fact implies a whole set of theoretical statements and is significant only in relation to this whole."[62] The traditional positivistic objectivity of method and theory rested ultimately on the object(ivity) of the physical world. However, now, that objectivity is viewed as a synthesis of experimental calculation and symbolic representation, objectivity and subjectivity.

Willard Quine in "Two Dogmas of Empiricism" (1953) takes up similar ideas when he critiques the notion that science could be a "mirror of nature"; rather, he asks the question of the relation between reality and language by which we grasp that reality. However, that reality is already pre-formed by the conceptual and linguistic structures.

The fundamental-seeming philosophical question, How much of our science is merely contributed by language and how much is genuine reflection of reality is perhaps a spurious question which itself arises from a certain particular type of language. Certainly we are in a predicament if we try to answer the question; for to answer the question we must talk about the world as well as about language and to talk about the world we must already impose upon the world some conceptual scheme particular to our own language.[63]

Since we cannot get outside our conceptual scheme in order to compare it to the objective reality, we cannot answer the question of the correctness of the conceptual system. According to Quine, it is the "efficiency of communication and prediction," plus elegance and conceptual economy, which become the measurements of the adequacy of the conceptual framework. Therefore, the mirroring of nature, the correspondence of theory to fact, of concept to reality, is undermined by Quine, who accepts the fundamental Kantian restrictions on metaphysical knowledge. Recognizing his debt to Duhem, Quine likewise is critical of radical reductionism, which holds that every meaningful statement must be translatable into statements about the immediate physical world. He recognizes that the physical world of objective experience is a social construct having the same ontological status and objective reality as the gods of Homer. Both are mythical and religious creations where one is necessary for individual worship and the other for scientific investigation. They are both artificial and unreal since they are historical and cultural posits. The only difference between the Greek gods and scientific theories is that the myth of physical reality provides us with more predictable experiences necessary for modern science. They provide us with a greater utility and manageability of our organization of experience and scientific experiments and knowledge.[64]

The objectivity which is a "conceptually imported" tool for the management of the complexity of the external world is bounded by the symbolic forms, structures, and the cultural values of manageability. As in the Kantian tradition, objects are posited, but now no longer on the basis of the transcendental subjectivity, with its static and universal categories of the understanding and intuition. They are now the mythological posits which are neither true or false, but better or worse in explanation and prediction. Neither Pierre Duhem nor Quine were able to make the transition to a broader conceptualization of the underlying foundations of these myths of physical objects other than vague and abstract reference to the technical uses that could be made of modern science. These orientations were viewed within the context of the cultural significance and meaning attached to the physical world on the basis of their technical interests. No wider connections were to be made to connect the philosophy of science and epistemology to social theory—no examination of the relation between technical interest, rationalization, industrialization, modern technology, and the fundamental changes in the structures of work organization and social subsystems.

For Quine, the conceptual form underdetermined by experience impinges on experience "only at the boundaries." Like Duhem, he believes that at the interior of any theory there are no direct links between empirical experience and statements of fact. This point thus has two important implications: the first is the idea that there are no factual statements which are immediately verifiable through experience, since it is only the total science which can be measured against experience, and a conflict at any interior point in the scheme would involve a reexamination of the logical connections that exist within the system. The second point is that there is always the possibility that more than one conceptual representation could apply in any particular case because there is an underdetermination of experience. It is because of these two mentioned points that Quine is led to make the argument that the traditional Kantian distinction between logical and experimental additions to our knowledge, between logically and empirically true statements, is no longer tenable, due to the integrated system of logical laws that make up the total science and the empirical underdetermination of nature in science.

> Furthermore it becomes folly to seek a boundary between syn-
> thetic statements, which hold contingently on experience, and
> analytic statements, which hold come what may. Any statement
> can be held true come what may, if we make drastic enough
> adjustments elsewhere in the system.[65]

A recalcitrant experience can be incorporated into the total language form by the proper adjustments and reevaluations in other
parts of the system. Quine does not explain what is the basis for
such shifts and adjustments in the symbolic code, or the possibility
of a total reevaluation of the adequacy of the conceptual representation. This would involve an historical and sociological view of
science, and the transition from a theory of knowledge to a theory
of society (sociological epistemology).

In his *Philosophy and the Mirror of Nature*, Rorty has recognized
that Quine's holistic approach to science is a critique of the epistemological foundations and the visual metaphor that lie at the basis
of modern theories of knowledge, and the notions of objective
certitude and rationality. Knowledge and science can no longer
be based on the adequacy of the correspondence between the
scientist's theory and the empirical reality to which the theory corresponds. "I shall be arguing that their [Quine and Sellars] holism
is a product of their commitment to the thesis that justification
is not a matter of a special relation between ideas (or words) and
objects, but of conversation, of social practice."[66] When correspondence is replaced by communication and intersubjective practice,
privileged representations—either in terms of epistemological and
methodological structures (subjectivity) or in terms of the structures of the corresponding external world (objectivity)—are no
longer relevant. Thus the quest for accurate representation, certitude, and truth as the mirroring of nature is reconceptualized into
a metapractice. It is at this point that philosophy has reached its

own undetermined boundaries of analysis. The analysis of social practice and conversation lies in the historical and social contexts in which they take place. If knowledge is not grounded in nature or transcendental conditions of subjectivity but in the forms and structures of social interaction, then the latter becomes the real conditions which ground scientific development and the real basis for a philosophy of science. But what are the legitimate sociological boundaries for social interaction and communication?

The Metaphysical and Social Assumptions of Natural Science

It has been recognized by the conventionalists, instrumentalists, neo-positivists, and neo-Kantians that science is not a reflection of nature, but a symbolic and linguistic construct created by the community of scientists working under a variety of social expectations and intentions. Exactly what these normative assumptions are, which ground and justify science, will be the subject of this section of the chapter. The hidden assumptions which guide and direct scientific inquiry can be cosmological or sociological. On the one hand, they involve the underlying epistemological and ontological presuppositions and assumptions entailed by the acceptance of the scientific theories themselves. Later, theorists moved from these initial metaphysical assumptions and values about nature to examine the historical influence of the logic and structure of political economy and society on the perception, method, and explanatory laws of science itself. With the help of the philosophy of science, we have recognized that the meaning of rationality, objectivity, and truth in the natural sciences has been affected by custom and tradition along with the acceptance of a particular symbolic form. It was Duhem who traced the transition of the essential properties of reality from one cosmological school of thought to the next. He began with the Aristotelian notion that substances were formed by the unity of matter and form, then developed to the Newtonian view of the mass, shape, and hardness of the atomic structure, and, finally, evolved to the Cartesian notion of the distinction between thinking substance and extended substance. Duhem saw occultism and scholasticism in these attempts to explain the underlying structures of the physical reality.[67] But it was really Burtt and Koyré who began to examine the more fruitful aspects of the question in their analyses of the mathematization of nature and experience.

It is the conceptual and theoretical transformation of nature from a dynamic cosmos (where mind and rationality are part of the process in which substance is in constant transition from actuality to potentiality) to a mechanized and formalized structure capable of quantitative and mathematical analysis. Copernicus and Kepler mark the beginning of the process of turning humanity from the center of the cosmological stage into an irrelevant spectator of its doings (almost an alien intruder in its domain). The teleology of Aristotle and medieval causality is replaced by the classical mechanics of Galileo and Newton. This represented the development of modern consciousness in terms of the metaphysics of modern science. But what is this metaphysics which lies at the heart of the foundation of the scientific *Weltanschauung*? As we have seen, it is the quantification of human experience and the application to the multiplicity and complexity of nature of mathematical formula. The key scientific categories of mass, force, motion, time, and space are now defined in terms of mathematics. The world began to be seen as a dead, mechanically interrelated, causally determined, and mathematically definable reality. Galileo, drawing on the Platonic tradition, made the distinction between primary and secondary qualities of matter. The former represented what is real, immutable, and universal in nature—that which can be mathematically examined and tested. The latter represented the sensible qualities of human beings—sight, sense, taste, color, etc.—which are subject to change and therefore of no interest to science.

It was inevitable that in these circumstances man should now appear to be outside of the real world: man is hardly more than a bundle of secondary qualities. Observe that the stage is fully set for the Cartesian dualism—on the one side the primary, the mathematical realm; on the other the realm of man. And the premium of importance and value as well as of independent existence all goes with the former. Man begins to appear for the first time in the history of thought as an irrelevant spectator and insignificant effect of the great mathematical system which is the substance of reality.[68]

The scientific metaphysics and the mathematical a priorism of classical mechanics represented a new way of systemizing and conceptualizing the natural world, which also included the implications for a new philosophical anthropology—later made more explicit by Hobbes—where the political and ethical worlds would come under the growing domination of scientific materialism. The transformation from the medieval world of purpose, rationality, and hierarchy to the modern one of formalistic mechanics has resulted in the gradual ascendancy of man's control over nature. As opposed to Greek stress on philosophical contemplation and political discussion, the modern consciousness is attuned to the quest for knowledge as the furtherance of man's domination over nature (*homo faber*). It is this desire to master and control which lies at the heart of modern physics. This spiritual revolution of the seventeenth century was described by Alexander Koyré as having the following characteristics.

They are: (1) the destruction of the Cosmos, and therefore the disappearance from science of all considerations based on that notion; (2) the geometrization of space—that is, the substitution of the homogenous and abstract space of Euclidian geometry for the qualitative differentiated and concrete world-space conception of the pre-Galilean physics. These two characteristics may be summed up and expressed as follows: the mathematization (geometrization) of nature and therefore, the mathematization (geometrization) of science.[69]

THE QUEST FOR A NEW OBJECTIVITY AND ETHICS— NATURE, TELEOLOGY, AND DEMOCRACY

What had begun as an investigation into the questions of objectivity and rationality has developed into the broader concerns of social theory and social ethics. Hans Jonas raised the issue in its most general form.

> It is at least not senseless anymore to ask whether the condition of extra-human nature, the biosphere as a whole and in its parts, now subject to our power, has become a human trust and has something of a moral claim on us not only for our ulterior sake but for its own and in its own right. If this were the case it would require quite some rethinking in basic principles of ethics. It would mean to seek not only the human good, but also the good of things extra-human, that is, to extend the recognition of "ends in themselves" beyond the sphere of man and make the human good include the care for them. For such a role of stewardship no previous ethics has prepared us—and the dominant, scientific view of Nature even less.[70]

The purpose of this chapter was not to formulate an articulate answer to Jonas but to develop the parameters within which a response could be forthcoming. How do we deal sociologically with the concept that nature has a moral claim "for its own and in its own right"? Would this involve the creation of a "new science" or a return to a spiritual and dynamic physical world within one of the older cosmologies? How do we free nature to permit it to assume its own internal dynamic unencumbered by our scientific representations, whose only purpose is to dominate and control? Jonas discusses the symbiotic relationship between man and nature in the modern technological world. "Their irreversibility conjoined to their aggregate magnitude injects another novel factor into the moral equation."

Is this another form of the Kantian dilemma of the thing-in-itself?

What is the essential reality of nature, divorced from the subjective categories of the scientific understanding which have distorted its own movement and resulted in an ecological and ethical crisis? Quine would have responded that it is meaningless to deal with this idea, since the notion of a pure and absolute objectivity lying behind our conceptual schemes is to fall victim to the "mirror of nature" perspective.

> Hence it is meaningless, I suggest, to inquire into the absolute correctness of a conceptual scheme as a mirror of reality. Our standard for appraising basic changes of conceptual scheme must be, not a realistic standard of correspondence to reality, but a pragmatic standard. Concepts are language and the purpose of concepts and of language is efficacy in communication and prediction. Such is the ultimate duty of language, science, and philosophy.[71]

Another approach, which has been taken, is to reject the possibility of developing a "new science" and recognize the instrumental nature of science and restrict its application along the imperatives of democratic action. Habermas sees transcendental anthropology as indicating the universal and unsurpassable boundaries of science in terms of the objects of possible experience and the biological necessity for dominance over nature. They are anthropological imperatives built into our psychological and biological structures. Joel Whitebook is critical of Habermas's surrender of both nature and science to the authority and influence of instrumental reason.[72]

With Descartes and Galileo the teleological view of nature was replaced by the mechanical view. Whether it is the conformity of an event to a concept (idealism) or the conformity of a concept to an event (empiricism), both the teleological and mechanical perspectives represent fundamental difficulties when dealing with the concept of nature. The former does not consider the materialist foundations of conceptual forms, and the latter does not consider the metaphysical and technological assumptions that ground science. Nature is reduced to either a speculative occultism or to a formalistic machine-like mechanism. Maurice Merleau-Ponty has recognized in his Paris lectures on the concept of nature that there have been two fundamental orderings of nature by human consciousness—the order of causal explanation and the order of totality.[73] Sociology is beginning to offer a new possibility: for with the development of the sociology of religion (Durkheim, Mauss, and Lévi-Strauss); American pragmatism (Peirce and Dewey); phenomenology (Schutz, Berger, and Luckmann); social interactionism (Mead and Freire); neo-Hegelian sociology (Frankfurt School); and neo-Kantian sociology (Gadamer and Habermas), there has developed the recognition of the structural and institutional foundations of modern consciousness and thus the foundations of a new social epistemology. Reality is a social process, and the conceptualizations of the physical and social worlds are in terms of social categories and not simply in terms of subjective consciousness.

> This concealment is made possible by the fact that in capitalist society man's environment, and especially the categories of economics, appear to him immediately and necessarily in forms of objectivity which conceal the fact that they are the categories of the relations of men with each other. Therefore, when the dialectical method destroys the fiction of the immortality of the categories it also destroys their reified character and clears the way to a knowledge of reality.[74]

Thus the forms of natural objectivity and the categories of symbolic representations are forms of social objectivity and social reflection. The categorical structures are reflections of the social imperatives for domination within the historically specific structures, as nature becomes simply a formal, abstract reflection of society (mirror of society), with society determining its basic meanings and goals. The notion that humanity is the measure of all things has its origins in Greek sophistry, but its realization in terms of total rationalization and social administration is seen by some as being the real cause of the political and ecological crises of modern society.

Merleau-Ponty has indirectly offered us a way out of the Kantian antinomies of either causality or totality, brutalized nature or "demonology," in his analysis of the victory of anthropological philosophy over nineteenth-century Romantic philosophy of nature. Though it begins from within the Kantian framework, it can then be re-translated within the new developments of social epistemology.

> It is in the "concept of freedom" only and consequently in consciousness and man that the conformity of the elements to a concept takes on a real sense, so that the teleology of nature is a reflection of "noumenal man." The truth of teleology is the consciousness of freedom. Man is the only goal of nature, not because Nature prepares him and creates him, but because man retroactively confers upon nature an air of finality by positing its autonomy.[75]

The truth of teleology or the independent movement of nature—unconstrained by technological, capitalist, or management imperatives—is the social consciousness of rationality and freedom. Only in a free and democratic society, where the consensus can be defined and articulated within a non-distorted public realm (which also attempts to free consciousness from cultural and physical poverty, maldistribution of income and wealth, and the organization of social priorities and institutions around the "economic man") can the internal dynamic of nature itself be freed from the categories and symbolic forms which try to dominate rather than cooperate. This would entail a rethinking of the relationships between nature and democracy within the framework of Jonas's ecological ethics, Feyerabend's democratic science, Habermas's communicative ethics, Lukacs's concrete totality, and Rorty's knowledge as edification. The choices of return to an organic metaphysics or an anthropological reductionism can be overcome if we see that the truth of teleology and organic totality of nature becomes possible in modern society only where there is a social consciousness and social ethics of freedom. Marx had already thought through, in a seminal form, the social implications of a constitution theory of truth whose origins lay in Kant's critique. Alfred Schmidt had recognized the strong Kantian element in Marx's thought in the epistemological content of social praxis, Marx's critique of the "mirror of nature," and the constitution theory of truth. For Schmidt, "there does exist between Marx and Kant a relationship which has not yet been sufficiently noticed."[76] Schmidt translates Kant's transcendental affinity into Marx's social formedness in an attempt to show that objectivity is always a social constitutive process within history. Marx held in the *Theses on Feuerbach* that, unlike in scholasticism, the truth of his theories must be proved in practice.

> In fact, practice in general can only be the criterion of truth because—as a historical whole—it constitutes the objects of normal human experience, i.e., plays an essential part in their internal composition.[77]

Because domination of nature has been so closely tied to the domination of man, it is only by freeing the latter that the former can realize its own possibilities. Philosophy of nature is thus not reduced to a phenomenology of consciousness but to a critical ethical theory of society, which challenges the conventional wisdom regarding growth, productivity, technological centralization; the division between concept and execution; and the centralization of knowledge in the hands of the technocratic elite.

For Rorty the goal is a "philosophy without mirror," which eliminates the traditional concern for an epistemology of grounds and strives toward self-cultivation (*Bildung*) and sees objectivity as "a conformity to the norms of justification (for assertions and for actions)." It attempts to break down the distinctions between fact and value, subject and object. Rorty relies on Gadamer's notion of the *"wirkungsgeschichtliches Bewusstsein"*: a consciousness which in the process of knowing history reinterprets both itself and history.[78] The being of the historian is already involved in the process of making and knowing history. Objectivity is an artificial creation which reflects the ontological status of the individual in the world as a Dasein. *Hermeneutics*, then, is a step forward from *Phenomenology*, for the truth behind the pure things is always the intentional life of human consciousness engaged within the world. However, the concept of objectivity is replaced by history which still leaves intact the distinctions between nature and the individual, not to mention that the process of education is still perceived to be a movement within the growth of the individual. This critique of objectivity is replaced by history which still leaves intact the distinctions between nature and the individual, not to mention that the process of education is still perceived to be a movement within the growth of the individual. This critique of objectivity, with its roots in Kantian and Hegelian thought, has evolved into the ideas of American pragmatism and German cultural hermeneutics. In the process the notion of society has become another idealist abstraction, which sets up the dualism between another form of objectivity (society) and subjectivity (individual), rather than that between humanity and nature.

Jonas, Feyerabend, and Habermas have attempted to synthesize epistemology and ethics back into the broader sociological context of the structures of society. For them the critique of objectivity becomes a sociological critique of science and technology and the social praxis which underlies moral action within society. Though philosophy of science was crucial in the examination of the rationality of science, it was so from the perspective of a logical and linguistic study. However, the definition and delineation of objectivity within the community through language and intentionality is in itself not a sufficient enough basis upon which to build an analysis of science; for language is only a part of the constitutive foundation of reality. Work, power, and ideology (political economy and critical theory), along with language, make up a more comprehensive field for a social epistemology.[79] It is the concrete social totality, which is the constitutive basis for knowledge, along with the possibility of conscious moral action, that turns both epistemology and ethics into social theory. Science and technology thus have become caught up in a more concrete analysis of society's relation to nature and its ethical implication. To develop these important insights, it is necessary to integrate them with Marx's theory of political economy and historical materialism in the next chapter.

CHAPTER 4

From Epistemology to Historical Materialism: Nature, Science, and Society from Kant to Marx

THE LAST CHAPTER ENDED with the recognition of the importance of the metaphysical and political foundations of the natural sciences, because they allow for the technical application and economic utility of science itself. If reality and truth are no longer understood as the ultimate arbiters of scientific research and methods, then the question naturally arises as to the origins and nature of formal reason and the social elements within science itself. That is, questions arise as to what the social content of science truly is and how it developed. The goal of this chapter is to expand postmodern theory of social epistemology, phenomenology of consciousness, and the metaphysics of science by connecting Immanuel Kant's theory of consciousness and experience with the critical social theory of Karl Marx—connecting Kantian epistemology to Marxian historical materialism and theory of political consciousness—in order to determine the exact extent of the historical and social nature of modern science. In this manner, the theories of science, objectivity, and truth move

beyond a philosophy of knowledge into the areas of critical sociology and political economy.

If science is not a reflection of ontology or reality, then what are
its actual historical and social origins? If the truth of the technical experimentation, research methods, and philosophy of science
lies in a socially constructed reality, then why is one view of reality
superior to another? Why is one theoretical paradigm accepted as
true and not another? The answer seems to lie in its utility, technical
application, and utilitarian success, but this answer, as interesting
as it is, only leads systematically and logically to another question: What is the historical and structural nature of the "society"
that underlies and grounds the rise of natural science? Is it just a
question of social consensus within a limited community of technical experts, or is the question even more complex and daunting?
The nature of the social dimension of science leads us to question
the institutions and values of modern commercial and industrial
capitalism at the heart of modernity. The central question then
becomes: Is there a clear and profound connection between consciousness and history and the critique of pure reason and the
critique of political economy?

If subjectivity defines and creates objectivity; if the human
mind is constitutive of objective experience and knowledge; and
if there is no access to objective reality or the thing-in-itself, then
how and why did modern science develop in the seventeenth and
eighteenth centuries? If there is a break between knowledge and
objective reality, what links the two elements into a coherent claim
of truth? Kant, even if unknowingly and unintentionally, undermined the absolute and universal status of knowledge and science,
and by doing so created the conditions for these later historical
and social questions.[1] Kuhn in his writings helps to expand Kant's
theory of knowledge as it evolves into a broader social epistemology. By turning to Marx at this stage in our analysis, we will be able
to move beyond a critical epistemology to a more comprehensive
social theory of natural science. This is the point where neo-Kantian philosophy of science transforms into a critical sociology, with

its discussion about the historical and social origins of modern science; this is the point where Kant and Marx meet in a central and profound dialogue.

As we have already seen in chapter 1, Kant produced a Copernican revolution in Western epistemology with his thesis in the *Critique of Pure Reason* (1781 and 1787) that the human mind or transcendental subjectivity creates the world of perception, experience, and knowledge as a representation (*Vorstellung*), or reconfiguration and reformation, of intuitions and perceptions within the categories of the mind. Consciousness is not a passive recipient of intuitions or ideas; it does not mirror or reflect an external reality or truth in acquired pure facts or empirical data. Rather, it is itself the cause or creator of the world we experience as external, objective, and real. Kant proceeded to philosophically reconstruct the universal and necessary conditions for this form of knowledge in his analysis of the "a priori forms of intuition" of time and space and the "a priori categories of the understanding" of substance and causality. The human mind constructs a world of concrete objects as mental representations moving and interacting with each other in a Newtonian spatial and temporal universe. As Kant famously said in the *Critique of Pure Reason*: "Thoughts without content are empty, intuitions without concepts are blind."[2] There must be an integration of the mind and body, as well as the traditions of rationalism and empiricism; there must be an integration of both rational concepts and ideas that give form, order, and structure to the material content of the intuitions and impressions of our senses. The world we inhabit is a world of representations that have been constructed by the a priori forms of human thought, and not reduced to innate ideas given to us by God or specific empirical facts discovered and accumulated by science. As we have seen in previous chapters, this radical idea formed the foundation of much of modern philosophy and social theory from Hegelian philosophy, classical social theory, existentialism, phenomenology, Marxism, neo-Kantian philosophy of science, pragmatism, the Frankfurt School, and so on.

Moving beyond Kant's theory of consciousness and representations and Kuhn's neo-Kantian theory of paradigms, normal
science, and social consensus, it is Georg Friedrich Hegel who helps
expand our understanding of the relationship between knowledge and society, in his masterpiece *The Phenomenology of Spirit*
(1807). He begins with a brief exploration of Kant's critique of pure
reason and the latter's theory of human consciousness, discussing
the dialectical characteristics of sense certainty, perception, and
the understanding. Hegel then moves beyond consciousness and
knowledge of the natural world to examine the evolution of the
social dimension of the enlightened forms of self-consciousness
and the community in Western culture, from classical Greece to
the French Revolution. The phenomenal world of the mind has
changed from a focus on knowledge and nature to the social and
cultural values and ideals of society, as Hegel undertakes an analysis of the master-slave relationship in ancient Greece, the slave
morality and stoicism of imperial Rome, and the religion and
unhappy consciousness of medieval Christianity.[3]

The final historical period examined is modernity, with the rise
of the hedonism and utilitarianism of Jeremy Bentham and James
Mill, the romanticism of Goethe, Schiller, and Cervantes, the individualism and liberalism of Hobbes and Locke, and, finally, the
practical reason and moral philosophy of Kant. At this point in the
Phenomenology Hegel takes an unanticipated and unusual turn,
with the creation of the objective spirit in his analysis of Aristotle
and Rousseau. Here reason should be made into a social object,
that is, into a concrete set of social institutions—the family, civil
society, and the state—which would enhance and make real the
ethical community, moral economy, and classical polity articulated
by the ancient Greeks. However, what actually occurs historically
in the evolution of modern times is an Enlightenment culture of
distance, distorted and oppressive objectivity, alienation, the logical inflexibility and distance of Kantian morality and reason, and
the political terror of Robespierre and the French Revolution.

Instead of the concrete realization in modern society of the classical ideals, community, and the spirit of the Athenian polity in the modern context, the objective spirit and its corresponding social institutions are crushed and replaced by the abstract idealism of the absolute spirit (religion, art, and philosophy). Self-consciousness cannot be achieved as a historical and social phenomenon in an alien world of moral and political oppression, of imposed empiricism and political ideology. In this modern world of the absolute spirit, ethics, beauty, harmony, and truth can be realized only in the illusions and abstractions of pure thought. According to Hegel, this modern form of unhappy consciousness is finally overcome with the return to the objective spirit and political community in the *Philosophy of Right* (1820). The modern state offers a way to integrate the Greek polity and liberalism, natural law and natural rights, and *Sittlichkeit* and *Moralität*. In this manner the moral, aesthetic, and political ideals of the absolute spirit are actualized and made real as the objective spirit, in the cultural, economic, and political institutions of modern society.

Marx recognizes the attempt by the creative spirit of humanity to transform both nature and society, but only at the level of Hegel's critical idealism.[4] This is the point at which Marx begins to reflect on the various elements of historical materialism and a grand synthesis of German epistemology, phenomenology, and aesthetics, British political economy, and Greek political theory. Economics and thought are integrated into a grand synthesis revealing the origins of modern consciousness and reflective intellectual thought in the capitalist mode of production (*Produktionsweise*). The central ideas of human creativity and subjectivity in Kant's theory of knowledge and moral philosophy will be expanded during Marx's lifetime to include a broader understanding of the role of human consciousness in experience and science, ethics and politics, and culture and the economy. Hegel moved beyond Kant in order to introduce a broader understanding of natural and social consciousness, as well as the social framework in which to examine issues of freedom, human dignity, and self-determination. Hegel placed consciousness within a phenomenology of a cultural self-understanding and evolution of the social institutions and political ideals of rights, equality, and reason. Hegel's theory of objective spirit was an attempt to make historical and socially concrete the individual and abstract Kantian ideals of practical reason and moral philosophy, by integrating the ancients and the moderns. Marx would further this development in German philosophy by attempting to integrate these epistemological and phenomenological traditions with the critique of political economy (*Horizontverschmelzung*).[5]

According to Kant, subjectivity creates the rational objectivity of perception, experience, and the categorical imperative; for Hegel, the subjectivity of the self-conscious mind or spirit creates objectivity in the form of self-conscious cultural values and social institutions; on the other hand, for Marx, subjectivity is transformed into the economic structure and social relations of production, to create the objectivity of nature and science, as well as the objectivity of political economy and the superstructure of social institutions, ideas, ways of thinking, and consciousness. Within the history of philosophy and social theory, there are various forms of subjectivity and objectivity, consciousness and objective reality, in idealism and materialism. Kant grounds his epistemological theory of objective reality and the Newtonian laws of mathematics and nature in the transcendental subject and its transcendental unity of apperception. Hegel grounds his phenomenological theory in the historical idealism of subjectivity and social consciousness, in the history of the objective spirit of social institutions and culture. And Marx grounds his theory of nature and objective reality in social labor, the law of value production, and historical materialism.[6] Marx is also aware of how reason and self-consciousness have been used negatively to create ideological illusions and distortions in order to hide and obscure the physical, social, and political reality from critical review, in order to protect and ensure economic stability, security of private property, and class power. The relationship between the superstructure and base, the natural sciences and modern political economy, will be the focus of this chapter. Although the relationship between natural science and society will remain at the relative periphery of Marx's writings, he does introduce important dimensions of this relationship that will become a central focus in later twentieth-century critical writers on the physical environment and the ecological crisis. In this chapter on nature, science, and society, we will explore in more detail the relationship between Marx's theory of historical materialism as it is applied to Kant's theory of the forms, categories, imagination, and knowledge of the human mind in perception and understanding. Toward this end, the beginnings of Marx's theory of consciousness and ideas will be examined.

MARX'S THEORY OF HISTORICAL MATERIALISM AS A CRITICAL AND SOCIAL EPISTEMOLOGY

Marx outlines his theory of historical materialism throughout his major works, including *The German Ideology* (written in 1845–46, published in 1932), *The Communist Manifesto* (1848), *A Contribution to the Critique of Political Economy* (1859), and *Capital* (1867). In the preface to *A Contribution to the Critique of Political Economy*, he summarizes his theory of historical materialism with the following words:

> In the social production of their existence, men inevitably enter into definite relations, which are independent of their will, namely relations of production appropriate to a given stage in the development of their material forces of production. The totality of these relations of production constitutes the economic structure of society, the real foundation on which arises a legal and political superstructure and to which correspond definite forms of social consciousness. The mode of production of material life conditions the general process of social, political, and intellectual life. It is not the consciousness of men that determines [*bestimmt*: conditions] their existence, but their social existence that determines their consciousness.[7]

In this passage Marx articulates the central notion that it is the mode of production—the economic structure of society, consisting of the social relations and class system of production and the productive and technical forces of production—that constitutes the true foundation of both sensuous and intellectual consciousness. The notion of social consciousness constitutes all the cultural forms of consciousness, including our awareness of self, the other, community, and nature. It includes the legal, political, religious, artistic, and intellectual consciousness of humanity, as well as our immediate perception of physical reality and our scientific understanding of the mechanical laws of nature. They are all historically defined products of the economic conditions of production. "Consciousness must be explained from the contradictions of material life, from the conflict existing between the social forces of production and the relations of production."[8] According to this perspective, science acts as both a force and ideology of production as it both affirms the necessity of expanded production and confirms the necessity of its cultural legitimation. From his other writings, it is clear that science itself is part of this general ideology and social superstructure. It is the "mode of production of material life which conditions" the general foundations of social and conscious life; it is the economic structure of society that constitutes the foundations of pure reason, the phenomenology of spirit, and the history of Western consciousness at the social, cultural, and intellectual levels.

Earlier in *The German Ideology*, Marx and Friedrich Engels write that "the production of ideas, of conceptions, of consciousness, is at first directly interwoven with the material activity and the material intercourse of men, the language of real life."[9] The superstructure is constituted by the sensuous consciousness and language of the physical environment (Kant); the intellectual consciousness or self-consciousness of the human and cultural environment of ethics, politics, and philosophy (Hegel); and theoretical consciousness of natural science (Descartes and Newton). The perception, knowledge, and science of nature is an intimate and inextricable part of our broader understanding and meaning of the human world, defined by the historical mode of production and social form of intercourse.[10] Even later, in the *Dialectics of Nature* (1883), Engels wrote: "From the very beginning the origin and development of the sciences has been determined by production."[11] Placing the theory of historical materialism within the context of a Kantian epistemology, we see a picture emerging of the various foundations of knowledge, from Kant's forms of intuition and the understanding based upon the Galilean mathematical and experimental method, Cartesian logic, utility, and metaphysics, and the Newtonian laws of motion and physics; to Hegel's evolution of social consciousness, based upon the self-understanding of the ancients and the moderns; and to Marx's theory of consciousness, knowledge, and ideology based on the categories of political economy and capitalism.

New forms of knowledge—based on hypothesis and thesis construction, empirical testing, mathematical formulation, experimental confirmation, and theory validation—are simply forms of abstraction that lie hidden in the abstract forms of labor and value production. The categories, methods, and theories of scientific thought are products of the abstract relations of economic production. The laws of nature are, in reality, the laws of capital retranslated to explain nature and its laws in terms of the relations of production. The categories of classical economic theory focus on the immediate empirical world of economic exchange and abstract their ideas and theories from the underlying forms of economic exploitation and worker oppression that exist in a critical theory of labor value—wage labor, necessary labor time, surplus labor time, surplus value, unpaid labor, etc. Classical economics abstracts and mystifies the reality of labor exploitation by not recognizing the alienation and slavery of the purchase of labor power.[12] The theory of science, as conceptual and methodological abstractions, attempts to connect scientific abstraction and economic abstraction. As epistemology develops from idealism to materialism, the concepts that provide the formal basis for our intellectual view of the world, including natural science, are found to reside in the economic structure of society. German philosophy of knowledge has evolved from a critical epistemology and idealist phenomenology to Marx's social theory of materialism and consciousness. In the latter, science and capitalism are intimately and dialectically embedded in the totality of the modern social system. The intellectual origins of natural science lie deep within the origins of commercial and industrial capitalism, and not deep within the reality of ontological laws of nature. Science is a political discipline, based on the reality of political economy, and not on an independent reality of mechanics.

Unfortunately, Marx never fully develops or expands the implications of his theory of historical materialism, but he leaves tantalizing traces of his argument throughout his later writings.[13] Nor does he include science within the framework of this general materialist theory since he does not connect scientific epistemology with historical materialism; and, finally, he leaves open for discussion the exact historical and social meaning of "the economic structure of society" in the above quotation from his 1859 work. These oversights have led to deep divisions and debates as to the overall meaning of his theory of historical materialism on the one hand, and its relevance to an analysis of science and nature on the other. The debate about historical materialism and the internal dynamic of the mode of production has focused on the dialectical relationship between the productive forces (*Produktivkräfte*, technical foundation of industry: science, technology, instruments, factories, raw materials, land, capital, etc.) and the social relations of production (*Produktionsverhältnisse*, social foundation of industry: class organization and division of labor within factories) in the workplace. Which component has historical and economic priority, which component defines and "determines" the fate of history, and, finally, which component has the most important and lasting effect on the creation of science and technology?

There are two major schools of thought involved in this debate: Instrumental or orthodox Marxists and Structural or critical

Marxists.[14] The former school emphasizes a perspective within historical materialism that is based on a particular understanding of the nature of social science, whose foundation lies in naturalism, reductionism, determinism, crude materialism, and predictivism, that is, positivism. The second school stresses a different understanding of Marx that is more critical, interpretive, historical, and dialectical.

The Instrumental School views the productive forces as the driving and determinative force of history, with the rationality and productivity of the natural sciences and technology leading the way.[15] Natural science from this perspective is seen as a universal and absolute reflection of an immutable external reality, based on empirical evidence and pure facts, that determines the movement of history. In this view, science shares the ontological and epistemological foundations of modern positivism in its empiricist (empirical facts and evidence) and rationalist (mathematics) forms, which are independent of the social system as they reflect both thought and being. Science is used by and is subservient to capitalism for the production of property and profits, but does not reflect the latter's underlying values or laws, institutions, or class structure.

The Structural School takes a quite different approach, interpreting science as having the characteristics of both the economic base and the cultural superstructure. That is, science is part of the economic mode of production, and is also a concrete manifestation of its underlying political and ideological structure. Science has a dialectical relationship with the economic base, as it reflects the values of the capitalist economy and is a product of that economy. Science is a priori technological and political, with its concepts, methods, and theories reflecting the priorities, logic, and institutions of capitalism. Without these institutions and structures of liberal modernity there is no natural or bourgeois science. Traditionally, science either mirrors the physical reality of nature, as in analytical Marxism, or mirrors the underlying reality of capital in critical Marxism. In *Marxism and Domination* (1982), Isaac Balbus has summarized this debate succinctly:

The basic assumption of the structural theory is that the form of technology that develops under capitalism is repressive because this form is determined by capitalist relations of production. The basic assumption of the instrumental theory is that the form of technology that develops under capitalism is not repressive because this form escapes determination by capitalist relations of production.[16]

Balbus details the analytical elements in Marx's writings, which are mainly contained in the notebooks IV and VII of the *Grundrisse*, whereas the structural view is mainly articulated in volume 1 of *Capital*. There is no need to enter this interesting but extremely complex debate at this time, since the key idea here is the relationship between science and society. This relationship has already been captured by the general concept of the economic structure of capital.

In *The German Ideology*, Marx and Engels articulate for the first time the initial outlines of historical materialism:

> The production of ideas, of conceptions, of consciousness, is at first directly interwoven with the material activity and the material intercourse of men, the language of real life....The same applies to mental production as expressed in the language of politics, laws, morality, religion, metaphysics of a people. Men are the producers of their concepts, ideas, etc.—real, active men, as they are conditioned by a definite development of their productive forces and the intercourse corresponding to these, up to its furthest development.[17]

The fundamental categories of consciousness by which we explain external reality in all its natural and social forms and, in turn, organize our most fundamental ideas and ideals—from ethics and politics to metaphysics—are constructs of the human mind, grounded in the material forces and social and historical relationships of civil society. The economic structure frames the basic categories of human consciousness and cannot be divorced from them. Kant simply assumed that the fundamental categories by which we access the external world were the universal and transcendental forms of Newtonian physics, which were embedded in subjectivity from the start. Marx now turns to a historical and materialist interpretation of human consciousness and the categories of experience by revealing that "consciousness is, therefore, from the very beginning a social product."[18] Interestingly, he does not mention science and nature in this work.[19] However, when *The German Ideology* is joined with his early philosophical writings on science and nature in *The Economic and Philosophical Writings of 1844*, science and nature, too, must be viewed as a historical and social product.

From Marx's writings, there are a number of different approaches by which a reader could connect the categories of science to the structures of economics, including (1) science as an a priori technological and productive force; (2) science as an expression of the cultural values and social ideals of the class structure and social relation of production; (3) science as a metaphysical worldview; (4) science as a form of alienated consciousness; and (5) science as a form of abstractionism—theoretical and conceptual abstractions of thought and reality—reflecting not the apparent empirical evidence and facts about nature and the external world, but rather reflecting the historical abstractions and hidden relationships of exchange value and commodity production.[20] As a productive force, science is similar to modern culture, metaphysics, and alienated consciousness, since it is a physical reflection of the abstract relationships of production projected onto the physical reality. Each of these different dimensions or interpretive forms of science makes a connection with the economic foundations of capitalism, but with particular emphases on different aspects of the general mode of production, whether it is the relationship between science and formal reason and technology, the economy, consciousness, culture and politics, metaphysics, or the abstract and underlying relationships within industrial production between labor and capital. By dividing science into these various political and social dimensions, we begin to better appreciate the complexity and weakness of Marx's own theory of historical materialism, as we get a more complete understanding of how to deal with the difficult question of relating science to history, economics, utility, and capitalism.

This connection between science and society helps articulate the various and complex relationships between science and nature within historical materialism. These involve science as technology and formal application; empirical research and pure theory; epistemology and materialism; alienation of mind and body; and the highly conceptual and intellectual abstractions of modern science in its concepts, methods, and theories. At each level of development in the formation of its accumulation of empirical data, concepts, theories, research methods, metaphysics, and technology, science contains hidden elements and assumptions derived from the economic and social system from which it evolved and by which it continues to maintain the hegemony of both its ideas and social reality. Science represents a particular historical and social form of political economy and political ideology.

There are thus five distinct forms of social epistemology and historical materialism in Marx's and Engels's writings. The first is science as formal knowledge and economic technology—in its various forms of mechanical, industrial, military, and optical technology—as it reflects the broader needs of capital: science is a projection of the operational and technological needs of the economy, by which science itself became a productive force. This is known as the "industrialization of science."[21] Investigations into the following areas connect science, technology, and capital: scientific inquiry into the telescope was related to the particular needs of the military; into the nature of heat and thermodynamics related to issues of the steam engine; into Galileo's mathematical science and theory of inertial moment and terrestrial mechanics as a response to the military need for an accurate ballistic theory; into the understanding by Newton of moving bodies, acceleration, and velocity related to the trajectory of military weapons, cannonballs, and navigation; and into the stars and heavens related to maritime navigation and commerce. Richard Clarke has written that the laws of motion discovered by Isaac Newton "were a response to specific technical problems of early capitalism."[22] The origins of modern science lie in the scientific and technical response to the productive requirements and needs of capital. Marx states that the very aim of science is provided by the economy: "But where would natural science be without industry and commerce? Even this 'pure' natural science is provided with an aim, as with its material, only through trade and industry, through the sensuous activity of men. So much is this activity, this unceasing sensuous labour and creation, this production, the basis of the whole sensuous world as it now exists."[23]

The second form is science as a sociology of knowledge and historical anthropology (human nature at a particular historical moment). From this perspective, science is a theoretical reflection of the economic and social relations of production and the conditions of human life under capitalist production. This does not represent a theory of knowledge in which the human mind reflects an objective, external world, but rather reflects the inner human dynamic and social relations of capital itself. In a letter to Engels on June 18, 1862, Marx makes the clear and direct connection between biology and Charles Darwin's theory of evolution, on the one hand, and anthropology and the nature of English society on the other:

It is remarkable how Darwin rediscovers, among the beasts and plants, the society of England with its division of labor, competition, opening up of new markets, "inventions" and Malthusian "struggle for existence." It is Hobbes' bellum omnium contra omnes and is reminiscent of Hegel's *Phenomenology*, in which civil society figures as an "intellectual animal kingdom," whereas, in Darwin, the animal kingdom figures as civil society.[24]

Marx's understanding of Darwin's biology, with its theory of the competition and struggle within the animal kingdom, is a reflection of the self-interest, competition, and aggression of a market economy projected onto the natural sphere. Science reflects the structures of society in the content of its concepts and theories about nature.

The third form is science as metaphysics. This approach to science is metaphysical because it examines the very assumptions and concepts of science, which are never articulated but make science possible and are the unconscious products of the capitalist social system. Since the seventeenth century, the human mind—in perception, experience, and knowledge—had organized the world into a coherent and systematic entity and abstract thought by means of fundamental categories based on concepts of matter and motion, time and space, substance and accidents, cause and effects, and motion and velocity. These categories were integrated into a reductionistic and mechanical view of the physical world, and their concepts were integrated into a phenomenal world of appearances created by the synthetic unity of apperception of subjective consciousness; they provided the basis for viewing science as another form of political economy. The metaphysical values of science reflect the underlying assumptions and presuppositions of the scientific method and the logic of capital.

The fourth form is science as sensuous and alienated consciousness and objective labor. A more critical understanding of science is found in his early *Economic and Philosophical Manuscripts* (1844), where Marx argues that perception, experience, and scientific knowledge are forms of alienated consciousness because a social and epistemological reality is created by production that distorts social relationships, undermines human dignity and freedom, and constructs a view of nature that is an alien and exploited product of capitalist social relations in the workplace. In addition to the traditional forms of industrial alienation—such as the alienation of the product of private property; the process of fragmentation and class division of labor; a loss of a sense of personal identity and the beauty, meaning, and purpose of work; and a disappearance of the moral community and our species identity and relations with others—workers are alienated from nature itself, at the level of perception, science, and ecology. The alienation of labor becomes embedded in the alienation of consciousness from the external world of perception and nature.

The fifth form is science as social epistemology, in its intellectual and conceptual abstraction and the integration of epistemology and materialism, thought and being, at the level of abstract theory. This final approach to the relations between science and the economy is based on the abstractions of commodity production and exchange as the foundation for the abstractions of scientific inquiry, methods, and theories. As the basis for and a result of production and the exchange of commodities that are bought and sold on the market, knowledge of nature produces a distinctive Western pattern or form of abstract thought in philosophy and science, which is reflected in its experimental and mathematical research methods and theory construction. This level of scientific abstraction in concepts, ideas, and formal reason is an expression of the abstractionism and technical rationality of the production, sale, purchase, and profit calculation of commodities in a market economy—that is, the abstraction of the immediate appearances of commodity exchange; market interaction; and the concrete buying and selling of products from the deeper and unconscious social relations of wage labor, abstract labor, labor time, and capital formation within the production process. These abstract and theoretical categories must be redefined and recalibrated into quantitative and mathematical terms of business expenses, labor and utility costs, consumer prices, and yearly profits. These abstractions and underlying social relations of production are rarely understood and never reflected upon, because economists are more concerned with immediate, empirical issues of supply and demand, profits, and consumer tastes within a market economy. The abstract and theoretical laws of nature reflect these abstract relationships in capitalist production. The latter are never investigated, and the connection between the two forms of abstraction is thus lost.

In *The German Ideology*, Marx and Engels criticize the crude materialism of Ludwig Feuerbach's distinction between sensuous perception and the true essence of things: "the sensuous world around him is, not a thing given direct from all eternity, ever the same, but the product of industry and the state of society. . . . Even the objects of the simplest 'sensuous certainty' are only given him through social development, industry, and commercial intercourse."[25] The world we see and experience changes over time and is transformed by the human activity of labor. In a capitalist society the form that labor and production assume—as capital and private property—also changes the objects that are perceived through sense certainty. The act of everyday perception, along with the accumulation of theoretical and mathematical knowledge and science, changes over time, just as the object of perception changes in a capitalist society according to the laws of value and capital accumulation. Subjective consciousness does not see or know reality, but only the reality created by capitalist production in terms of the roads, bridges, houses, agriculture, industry, and commerce. Even something as simple as the perception of a cherry tree is a historical and social product that has come about by the industrial transformation of profit making and agriculture. Perception and knowledge, experience and science are social products. One can also see that the philosophies of Aristotle (substance) and Hegel (self-consciousness) are expressions of this unity of nature and human beings.

HISTORICAL MATERIALISM IN THE TWENTIETH CENTURY

The goal now is to return to Marx and reconnect his more comprehensive economic concept of historical materialism with both social epistemology and structural economics, in order to see science in its various forms as a productive force and operational and formal technology, as a value-laden metaphysics and political ideology, as a historical and materialist reflection of social reality, and as a theory of knowledge based on the relationship between thought and being, as well as ontology (philosophy) and utility (science). Following closely on Hegel's social phenomenology and idealism, Marx recognizes that, in history, consciousness of the immediate physical environment is at first an alien social product. This consciousness does not evolve out of the abstract categories of the human mind, by which the order and meaning of nature and society are created, but out of material and historical social relationships that form the basis of those ideas. The categories of both modern science and self-conscious reflection in ancient philosophy are the result of "the sum of productive forces, forms of capital, and social forms of intercourse."[26] "Consciousness is therefore from the very beginning a social product, and remains so as long as men exist at all."[27]

However insightful Marx is in his writings, he never explains in depth how consciousness and ideas are directly connected to material production; how the categories, methods, and theories of natural science are actually related to capitalism. Nor does he ask about the following substantive issues regarding science, technology, and society: What are the politics and ideology of science, especially regarding its liberal epistemology, metaphysics, and technology? Is natural science a reflection of capitalism and, therefore, locked into a particular historical and economic social system? Is modern science and technology inappropriate for use in a socialist society? How would the ideas and theories of science and technology change in a socialist society—that is, what would science and technology look like under democratic socialism? Finally, what are the implications of these relationships for our understanding of nature and the ecological crisis? These questions form the heart of a deeper understanding of the social epistemology of science.

Understandably but unfortunately, Marx left these issues unexamined. He had other priorities, such as connecting historical materialism to alienation in the *Paris Manuscripts*; undertaking a critique of idealism (Hegel), crude materialism (Feuerbach), and French socialism (Fourier, Saint-Simon, and Proudhon) and civil society (Ricardo and Smith), in *The German Ideology*; critiquing capitalism by understanding the history, inner dynamic, and class organization of industrial production—universal abstract labor, economic exploitation, and the creation of surplus value; and studying the inner structural, logical, and ethical contradictions of the laws of value and capitalist production toward developing a classical theory of social justice, in *Capital*. These were his priorities, which twentieth-century scholars understood and tried to expand into new areas of analysis. However, the goal of this chapter is to help reconstruct a more comprehensive social epistemology and historical materialism that is implicit in Marx's writings but made more explicit in the writings of twentieth-century authors.

One key question left unanswered by Marx is whether human emancipation in a truly democratic society entails the transformation of natural science and machine and human technology. That is, would science and technology have to change to reflect the ethical and political priorities of the new social system? This is a major point of contention between Instrumental and Structural Marxists. The former school of thought views science as a reflection of ontology or natural reality, having the characteristics of realism and nominalism. Science is an objective, neutral, and independent expression of intellectual curiosity and theoretical enlightenment about our immediate physical environment, whose knowledge may be used effectively and productively in either a capitalist or a socialist economy. From this perspective science is an objective mirror of reality and is indifferent to the manner in which it is used by opposing types of societies and for entirely different purposes. Under a capitalist system, the use of science can be exploitative and dominating, whereas its use under socialism would be liberating. Under capitalism science and technology continue the exploitation of surplus value (living labor) without limit, whereas in a socialist society, productive efficiency and industrial expansion free workers from dehumanizing and alienating work, at the same time that they expand the material wealth and social surplus for all members of society. Human emancipation requires a revolution of thought and action whereby society is transformed, and science and technology are turned into economic forces for the good of the whole.

By contrast, structural Marxists stress that science and technology are productive forces of a particular type of economic system, thereby reflecting the underlying values, politics, and imperatives of that system. This means that science, as stated by Friedrich Tomberg, is a "bourgeois science" or political ideology, reflecting the distinctive social relations of production of capitalism. When applied to production in an entirely different social system, it only reproduces those same exploitative social relationships of capitalism.[28] Science becomes the Trojan horse of capital. The values of capitalist production, labor exploitation, class division of labor, and surplus value extraction in capital continue to be the effective driving forces even beyond capitalism, into a socialist and democratic society, thereby undermining and destroying the society's publicly stated values, ideals, and institutions. Even with the best intentions, the productive forces contain the social relations of production of capitalist industry, which remain the dominant forces in society. The social relations of production are unconsciously reintroduced and reproduced into production by the hidden values of bourgeois science and capitalist production, of which the citizens are totally unaware. In this way, the social system is undermined by the very relationships that a new socialist society thought it had escaped and left behind.

One way to access these questions, since Marx does not deal with them directly, is to examine the relationship between the productive forces and the social relations of production. Examining the role of natural science in the mode of production and in the rise of industrial consciousness and the ideology of the cultural superstructure will help in understanding the deeper meaning of natural science in industrial production. The relationship between the productive forces and social relations of production is complex, because here again Marx does not lay out the historical and social details of his social epistemology and historical materialism.

However, when he makes explicit reference to this relationship, his description of their intersection is mainly dialectical and not deterministic. Therefore, there is no historical priority given to the scientific and technological features of society or to the class relations of production in understanding history or explaining social change. Again, in *The German Ideology,* he argues that they are so closely intermingled in history because they "determine" or "condition" each other in a dialectical fashion.[29] "Industry and commerce, production and the exchange of the necessities of life, themselves determine distribution, the structure of the different social classes and are, in turn, determined by these as to the mode in which they are carried on."[30] Dialectics in history and production is essential for understanding the role of science and technology in production—the role of mental and technical production on one side and the class structure, private property, and law of value (abstract universal labor, surplus value, and exchange value) on the other. It is the inseparable characteristics of capital within the mode of production that gives us a better understanding of the utility and role of science in relation to machine technology and industrial production. Science and technology are necessary for each other's maintenance and expansion and, in turn, for each other's rationalization and legitimation, and for their mutual expansion and acceptance as essential and indivisible elements of the capitalist mode of production. This dialectical relationship will help us mediate between the instrumental and emancipatory approach to science and the structural and repressive interpretation of science.

Natural science or mental production is necessary for further economic development within modern society. It expresses an aim or need of capital for further expansion in production and commerce. It also represents an abstraction of its concepts and theories from empirical reality and an abstraction from the internal and structural logic of capital. Thus, science's connection to nature and the economy sometimes becomes difficult to understand. In its search for natural reality and truth, science appears distant from the practical economic needs of society in the same way that exchange value or congealed alienated labor (abstract, simple, and general labor time contained in production of marketable substances or commodities) appears as an abstraction from everyday use value, commodity exchange, and utilitarian consumption.[31] Marx views these forms of abstraction as intimately interrelated and a common product of modern machine production. The abstractions of both science and commodity production are the results of the same historical social system and class structure, one at the level of thought production and the other at the level of material production. And in both cases, science and production appear to be relations between things—empirical reality and use values. But in reality, they are abstract relations between scientists and nature (concepts and theories) and human beings alienated from nature in exploitative social relations of production (universal labor contained in exchange value). A key conclusion of this theory of abstraction is that if both science and production are abstractions that are dialectically related to each other, it makes it impossible to remove science from the logic of capital; it makes it impossible for science to become the basis for a new emancipatory technology that frees human beings from an alien and exploitative production process. The science and technology of capitalism is necessarily quite different from the science and technology of democratic socialism. The latter would require natural science to be integrated into a new theory and method of science, with a critical and emancipatory theory of ethics, politics, and social justice.

HISTORICAL MATERIALISM, CAPITAL OVERPRODUCTION, AND ECONOMIC CRISES

Since they are dialectically interconnected, the productive forces and social relations of production become the barrier to further economic reproduction and surplus expansion, leading to a serious economic crisis. The barrier to production is social labor and capital. In classical economics the underlying cause of economic problems lies in the slowing economy and declining demand, which only increases the crisis, thereby necessitating some form of state intervention. In book IV of the *Grundrisse*—on capital, overproduction, and the economic barriers to production—Marx refers to the writings of both John Stuart Mill and Jean-Baptiste Say, who argued that there is an inherent balance between supply and demand in a capitalist economy, and that crises arise as a result of overproduction and realization of use value or commodities. Marx takes issue with their accounts and contends that the crisis and breakdown of the economy are caused by the rational production of capital itself, the increasing exploitation of surplus value, and the strong scientific and technological advancement. This is the result of the structural problems created by the interdependent and reciprocal relationship within the economy between the massive technical and machine advances on one side of production and surplus extraction from labor on the other—the logical contradictions within capital between the productive forces and social relations of production, and between the production of use value and commodities and the production of value and abstract labor. The barrier to production and the carrier of crisis lies in capital itself.

Overproduction is a crisis of the overproduction of exchange value (abstract labor and surplus value), not the overproduction of use values (commodities). The logical imperative of capital is to produce as much as possible (surplus labor), while at the same time restricting the worker's ability to consume (exchange value). When capital cannot create more value, it begins to halt production. Demand exists under conditions of expansion and crisis; the underlying cause of the crisis is the inability of the workplace to realize surplus value production. The result is that within a competitive, expanding, and international economy, and with further economic and scientific development and advances in the productive forces, there is a decrease in the necessary labor time (working time necessary to maintain the costs of labor power). This decrease, in turn, results in an initial and relative decline in the production of surplus value in a particular commodity; at the same time there is an increase in the absolute mass of surplus value produced.[32] "One part of capital on hand is constantly devalued owing to a decrease in the costs of production at which it can be reproduced."[33] This contradiction of capital and the law of value is already contained in the concept of capital itself.

First of all, there is a limit, not inherent to production generally, but to production founded on capital. . . . It is enough here to demonstrate that capital contains a *particular* restriction of production—which contradicts its general tendency to drive beyond every barrier to production—in order to have uncovered the foundation of overproduction, the fundamental contradiction of developed capital.[34]

According to Marx, economic expansion could result in increasing production for the individual well-being of workers, human emancipation, and social wealth of the community. But, because of the structural limits and contradictions of the class system—class production for surplus value and profits, and not for the welfare of the citizens in general—there is an alternative path followed with the increasing advancement of science and technology. That path includes the expansion of industrial production, the intensification of workplace exploitation, structural contradictions, and serious economic problems. It is not that lower market demand results in the overproduction of commodities, cutback in production and use values, decline in labor consumption, and rise in unemployment. Rather, it is because of the overproduction of capital or the overproduction of the technical means of production, the diminishing labor necessary to produce various commodities as exchange value, and declining surplus value production and capital (profit) realization. This is what Marx calls the *Verwertungsprozess*: the contradiction between the production and realization of surplus value, capital, and profit.[35] Capital's increase in scientific rationality and technical application to production thereby reduces the necessary labor time for workers to reproduce themselves—increasing surplus value—at the same time that they reduce the numbers of workers needed in production, creating a problem of realization in market exchange and consumption. This is the fundamental contradiction within the sphere of capital production: scientific rationality and increased production combined with decreasing need for workers and the realization or transformation of labor value in commodities into money and profit or objectified labor. Workers are redundant and reduced, as is the necessary cost of their labor and production (necessary labor time), which in theory produces more surplus value. However, it also produces less labor in the exchange value of workers' products, since the amount of living labor in each product decreases. Marx refers to this as the devaluation (*Entwertung*) of capital, and it is the structural and logical basis for functional stagnation and economic crises. "As soon as it cannot posit value, it does not posit necessary labor. . . . It therefore restricts labor and the creation of value—by an artificial check. . . . By its nature, therefore, it posits a *barrier* to labor and value creation, in contradiction to its tendency to expand them boundlessly."[36]

With the advancement of science and technology, this historical barrier and logical contradiction is centered in the production process, following the decrease in the amount of the necessary labor time (time necessary to reproduce worker and family) and a decrease in wages, while also decreasing the number of necessary workers as a result of their replacement by the forces of production. This reduction in the workforce results in the decline in the production of surplus value and future consumption of exchange value. This overproduction takes places at the same time as the rationalization and expansion of the productive forces and the enormous advances in the productivity of workers. This gives the false appearance in the economic realm of an overproduction of goods, overpopulation, higher unemployment, and significantly decreasing consumer demand. Marx views these as a problem of the underlying structural contradictions and realization of capital (surplus value) and exchange value (money), and not an over-production of use value or commodities.[37] The crisis of capital is expressed as changing relationships within the various component parts of capital.[38] And with the production and realization crises, there is a corresponding destruction in the value of labor and capital (raw materials, machines, labor capacity, etc.).

The crisis results from the structural dynamics and internal contradiction of production and the creation of surplus value. Wage labor is the foundation of capital or social wealth, as it creates a surplus through the production process. That surplus, in turn, becomes exchange value, which assumes the concrete form of money in actual exchange. In his analysis of Pierre Proudhon's economic theory, Marx recognizes that Proudhon's crisis theory is grounded in the realization of profit, which is measured in terms of production costs and capital investment based on the means of production (labor, raw materials, utilities, factories, etc.), plus profits, equals the final market price of each commodity (initial cost of labor and materials + profits = price). The profit is added to the general costs of production. For Proudhon, economic crises are related to the realization of profits and prices, whereas for Marx, surplus value and potential profits are already incorporated into each commodity. The general increase in the productive forces of science and technology, and in the corresponding productivity of labor, tends to devalue commodities, since each product contains less labor time, and therefore less value in its production, while at the same time increasing the production of surplus labor time (unpaid labor) and the mass of surplus value. With the decline in value of each product, due to increased productivity and labor time necessary to produce each object, there is increased pressure to realize the value in each product through increased surplus production. With the rise of the centrality of science and technology in industrial production, consumer goods are produced more cheaply, with a reduction in the necessary labor time required to produce each product to a minimum, accompanied by a corresponding decline in the surplus value in each product, while the total mass of goods and surplus value increases. These contradictions within the production process itself between the devaluation and realization of commodities increases the capitalist's need to further increase production and realize more of the declining surplus value. This problem is further aggravated by increased competition, on one hand, and the need to increase consumption due to declining surplus value and profits on the other.[39] Over time this leads to economic stagnation, underconsumption, and the destruction of capital.

The historical irony here for Marx is that it is the very rationality and efficiency of the total mode of production that limit labor and value creation, which is the basis for capitalist production. Simply increasing consumption does not get to the heart of the problem. More and more goods are produced, and more and more total mass of surplus value is created at the very same time that there is correspondingly less labor and less surplus value in each commodity. The mass of surplus value increases with the dramatic increase in mass production, while the percentage of surplus value and profits realized in each commodity decreases. With an expanding economy and growth in technology and productivity, less labor is necessary in production, and wages correspondingly decline. The necessary labor time required to produce each product is reduced; each commodity costs less and each commodity contains less surplus value. Thus, these crises result from the inner contradiction and realization problem between surplus value and necessary labor time. The production of surplus value does not increase at the same rate as the increase in the productive forces, creating a barrier to further production. The source of all capital, profits, and wealth has been reduced—the labor time to produce a commodity. The barrier to continued economic growth lies in capital and value production.

According to Proudhon, the solution to the problem would be to increase consumer demand, while for Marx, it is to increase new avenues of economic exploitation by expanding surplus production, labor exploitation, and the realization of surplus value by

increasing the relative surplus by diminishing the absolute necessary labor time to a minimum. The realization of capital becomes
more difficult the more necessary labor time and wages are dimin-
ished. This is what creates the contradiction between commodity
production and surplus realization. In order to compensate for this
loss, the mass of commodity production must increase in order to
keep up with the decrease in the rate of surplus value extraction
as workers have been replaced by machinery and technology. The
answer to these problems is to restrict the use of productive forces,
which is impossible in a competitive market economy, or increase
its application and intensity, resulting in more commodities, but
less surplus value in each.

In time, overproduction of capital based on scientific advancement, technological innovation, machine production, wage labor,
and capital accumulation results in the overproduction of capital, not the overproduction or underconsumption of consumer
goods. The problem is not an oversupply of consumer goods and
the need to increase workers' wages in order to increase consumption, but an overproduction of capital that infringes on the
creation of surplus value. Overproduction is defined by Marx
as "production which cannot be transformed into money, into
value."[40] It is a situation in which the production of commodities is out of sync with the realization of capital as money and
exchange value, which represents the realization of the exploitation of human labor in the workplace. Marx is aware that at
first the sale of commodities in the market appears to be tied
to the production process without limits. That is, realization is
intimately bound to the production of surplus value, just as surplus value in production is intimately bound to the circulation of
exchange value.[41] Capital exists in the form of wage labor in industry and money in circulation, and is realized only in exchange
and consumption, where it is then reinvested in production as
objectified labor. The logic of capital is expressed as the imperative to expand production and increase absolute surplus labor
(lengthening the workday or week) and relative surplus value

(increasing productivity, efficiency, and intensity of work through the productive forces), but also to widen circulation and the sale of commodities through expanding the world market. The realization problem is not reflected in the circulation and sale of use value and consumer goods, but is reflected in the exchange and realization of value. Capital must balance the needs of production and circulation, and it is this balance that is historically and logically problematic. This distinction between the overproduction of capital and the overproduction of commodities is essential for Marx, because the latter problem may be resolved within the circulation, exchange, and consumption of consumer goods by increasing workers' wages and individual consumption, whereas the overproduction of capital requires the intensification and increase of labor exploitation, alienation, and the appropriation of surplus value within capitalist production. The overproduction of capital entails the overconsumption of labor. This is the central distinction between the realization of commodity exchange and the realization of commodity production, the rationalization of the market and the rationalization of production.

The traditional method for the expansion of circulation had been accomplished by expanding consumption, creating new needs, advertising, creating new products and use values, revolutionizing ways of life, etc. One method of accomplishing the increase in relative surplus value is the development of natural science, whose "theoretical discovery of its autonomous laws appears merely as a ruse so as to subjugate it [nature] under human needs, whether as an object of consumption or as a means of production."[42] When interest in a particular commodity is lost, then the commodity no longer has a use value. The intricate and essential balance between production and circulation is broken, resulting in a serious crisis. In the beginning of industrial development, there is a close correlation and structural balance between production in the industrial factory and exchange in the market. Over time, modern science creates enormous social wealth in production, requiring less labor time. Labor power is replaced by science and technology, resulting in enormous economic output and growth, which under capitalism becomes a class barrier to further production.

The productive forces and rational scientific development lead to a barrier to further production and ultimately to economic crises. As already seen, the productive forces lead to economic expansion with the potential for increasing the social wealth, equality, and a better life for all, but this is ultimately a hindrance to the further development of capital, property, wage labor, and private wealth. Since the newly created wealth cannot be reproduced or redistributed based on an alternative social system, the capitalist system begins to fall into a serious production crisis. There is a potential increase in the social wealth produced by the rationalization of production, but there is a real decline in value production based on the institutional priorities of capitalist production. As the system expands through scientific technology applied to production, the actual production of surplus value, capital, and profits decreases. One can argue that classical economics deals with this economic crisis at the level of phenomenal appearances of market demand and underconsumption, and not at the level of production and surplus value creation. The problem lies in the law of value, the production of surplus value, and the logic of capital, and not in the law of the market, supply and demand, or the logic of consumption.

> But to the degree that large industry develops, the creation of real wealth comes to depend less on labor time and on the amount of labor employed than on the power of the agencies [productive forces] set in motion during labor time . . . whose "powerful effectiveness" . . . depends rather on the general state of science and on the progress of technology, or the application of this science to production. (The development of this science, especially natural science, and all others with the latter, is itself in turn, related to the development of material production.)[43]

The underlying cause of the economic crisis lies in the nature of capital and the contradictions between the productive forces and social relations of production. However, in the *Grundrisse*, Marx never clarifies these two distinct issues: What is the dialectical or interconnected relationship between science and technology, and what is the relationship between the productive forces and social relations of production? These questions are central to this issue. Is the cause of the problem the totality of the mode of production of capital, or does the problem lie in the class structure itself and its limits to production? If the latter, then science could potentially provide an emancipatory function in society; it could be used for the health and wellbeing of society as a whole. If the former, then science is an inextricable and essential form of capital and class. The discussion of whether science and technology have emancipatory or repressive potential comes down to the meaning of the concept of "dialectical." Does *dialectical* refer to class restraints or limits on the rational and efficient production, due to the class system and commodity production? Or is science a central and necessary part of the evolution of capitalism and its social relations? Does the term *dialectical* simply refer to a historically transient and temporary interconnectedness that limits its productive potential, or does it refer to an intrinsic historical and permanent social interconnectedness? Is science restrained by the class system, but potentially able to free itself from it, or is science an intimate part of that system, sharing its underlying values, assumptions, and laws; that is, are the laws of nature a reflection of the laws of value and capital?

The key point for our understanding of the nature of science and technology in Marx's writings is that science and technology, theory and practical application, cannot be separated from the class structure and primacy of the production of surplus value. The two spheres of productive forces and social relations of production are intimately linked in a capitalist economy. Thus, neither science nor technology is neutral and independent of the class divisions and social organization of production; the productive forces are dialectically related to the values and institutions of social labor and industrial production. This means that scientific and technical advancements cannot be the basis for human emancipation from the economic scarcity and the physical necessities of life. Surplus production cannot be used to satisfy human needs, overcome poverty and human misery, or be the basis for future equality and true democracy; it cannot be used to overcome value and capital production. Science is not independent of the law of value or the logic of capital. With increased production in a capitalist society, there is an overproduction of capital, increase in surplus value (relationship between necessary labor and surplus labor), and decline in the rate of profit (measured in terms of both constant and variable capital), leading to economic crisis and breakdown.[44] This occurs because the economic system becomes more productive and efficient, not less. "The gradual growth of constant capital [productive forces] in relation to variable capital [labor] must necessarily lead *to a gradual fall of the general rate of profit*, so long as the rate of surplus value or the intensity of exploitation of labor by capital, remains the same."[45] A point in production is reached when the reduction in necessary labor time, which is absolutely necessary to increase the amount of surplus value, is reduced to such a point that labor is no longer able to maintain or enlarge the total mass of capital—that is, the expansion of the productive forces cannot keep up with the structural requirement to expand surplus value. Stagnation and crisis ensue. In economic growth lies the clue to the mystery of the decline in profitability; in expansion of material production lies the clue to the declining surplus value; and in capitalist production lie the barriers to future production in social labor and value production within a class system.

The underlying cause of the economic crisis lies in the initial rise in the rate of surplus value production or rise in labor exploitation (essence), even in an economy characterized by an overproduction of commodities (appearance). The reality is that there is a relative scarcity of surplus labor or surplus value. Capitalism does not produce to satisfy human needs, but only to create surplus value and profits by ever increasing means of labor exploitation.

Marx measures profit as the relation between necessary labor time
to pay the costs of production and surplus value and capital formation above these initial costs—that is, production costs and profit
formation. Profits increase with the increase of surplus labor over
necessary labor, increasing exploitation of labor over the necessary
costs of labor. Looking closely at these issues from Marx's later
writings, the role and logic of modern science and technology in
his theory of historical materialism begins to look more analytically clear and theoretically precise.

The overarching framework of Marx's labor theory of value
and corresponding economic crisis theory is outlined in the
Grundrisse. In the third volume of *Capital* he develops a more precise and theoretically clearer analysis with his theory of the rising
organic composition of capital, the declining rate of profit, and his
broader economic crisis theory. Marx expands his analysis, found
in the rough drafts of his extensive earlier work, with the much
fuller development in *Capital* of the problem of capital production
and realization. This theory of the organic composition of capital
consists of the ratio between constant or dead capital of machinery, factories, and raw material (value of the means of production)
and variable or living capital consisting of the value of labor
power (wages). With the increase in constant capital of the productive forces as a percentage of the total capital compared to the
declining amount of labor input in production—that is, with the
increase in constant capital over variable capital—there is a logical
and structural crisis forming in capital production. On this issue,
Paul Mattick in *Marx and Keynes* (1969) writes: "By assuming a
constant rate of surplus-value, the rising organic composition of
capital leads to a gradual fall of the rate of profit, since it is only
the variable part of capital which yields surplus-value, while the
rate of profit is 'measured' on total investments, i.e. constant and
variable combined."[46] Marx is much clearer in the third volume of
Capital regarding the exact nature of the economic crisis, which
includes the following: (1) an increase in the productive forces of
science and technology; (2) an increase in labor productivity; (3)

a decline in the amount of labor and value in each commodity; (4) the creation of more commodities, use value, and exchange value; (5) an increase in the mass of surplus labor; (6) an increase in the total mass of capital; and (7) a tendential fall in the rate of profit with the rising organic composition of capital. These logical and structural contradictions of capital could potentially lead to economic stagnation and a realization crisis.

As Mattick has recognized, Marx's law of the tendential fall in the rate of profit is derived from a combination of his labor theory of value with his theory of capital production and accumulation.[47] This rise in constant capital relative to variable capital has concrete negative economic results. There is "an artificial overpopulation," higher variable capital or labor unemployment, along with a depreciation of constant capital and a falling rate of value and profit resulting in economic stagnation.[48] Mattick writes that "the contradiction of the capitalist mode of production, however, lies precisely in its tendency towards an absolute development of the productive forces, which continually come into conflict with the specific conditions of production in which capital moves, and alone can move."[49] Corresponding to this overproduction of capital, there is also an overproduction of commodities and a disproportionality of consumption, further adding to the crisis conditions of the economy. But Marx is quick to remind us in *Capital*, reiterating his comments from the *Grundrisse*, that the goal of production is not the satisfaction of human needs or the balancing of production and consumption, but the creation and expansion of value and capital.

According to Marx, there are historical counteracting tendencies which compensate for and temporarily overcome these contradictions of social labor. These include the increasing growth of constant capital with the expansion of scientific and technological advances; increased exploitation of absolute and relative labor time and surplus value in the workplace; an increase in state interventionism, tax reductions, and deficit spending, international trade, imperialism and colonization; increased industry monopolization and price fixing, etc. With these actual economic changes in the production process the workplace population is expanded, along with the intensity and extension of work and labor exploitation, resulting in a potential increase in production and consumption, and an absolute increase in the mass of surplus value and accumulation of profits, thereby avoiding the apparent contradictions of the rising organic composition of capital and the declining rate of profits.

Because of the complexity and expanse of the modern crisis theory of capital production, modern science and machine technology cannot be the basis for the elimination of alienated labor or resolution of the problem. In fact, science and technology as productive forces are intimately connected with the problems of production and capital formation. The values, rationality, concepts, theories, and methods of natural science are intimately bound—historically, socially, and logically—to the logic of production, capital accumulation, and the realization of surplus value. Any social consensus reached within the scientific community (Kuhn's thesis) is locked into these underlying and hidden metaphysical, political, and ideological values of capital accumulation and scientific inquiry. The separation of epistemology from historical materialism is a serious hindrance to adequately answering these questions. This same dialectical relationship between science and technology on one side and the class system on the other produces the very conditions for the economic crisis of overproduction. The inner logic of liberalism, initially expressed in the political theory of John Locke, shows a deep, unbridgeable divide and inner logical contradiction between individual freedom and communal responsibility, natural rights and natural law, and a market economy (*chrematistike*) and household and moral economy (*oikonomike*).[50] Marx takes these unresolvable contradictions in political theory and articulates them further in the form of political economy, as the contradictory relations between use value and exchange value, necessary labor and surplus labor, and capital production and surplus realization. In both cases, liberalism—as a political

and economic entity, as a projection of individual rights and freedom, and as sphere of production and distribution—is inherently
contradictory at the levels of both reason and logic and of ethics
and social justice. That liberalism has been able to survive as a
viable social system for so long is a monument less to its ideals and
institutions and more to the transformation of the workplace, the
evolution of monopoly capital, the creation of the welfare/warfare
state, and the ideological power and political naivety of possessive
individualism and the perceived rationality of economic competition, market self-interest, individual merit and accomplishments,
and the centrality of a materialist and utilitarian view of self-worth
and happiness. It has also been unfortunately aided in its unusual
historical viability in contemporary society by the idolatrous
enshrinement of these political and economic values in the dimin-
ished ethical ideals and "pelvic morality" of Western religions.

As an essential part of the productive forces, science and
technology are structurally embedded in the capitalist mode of
production. This is key, since a central question being considered throughout this chapter is whether the embeddedness and
essential connection of science to the capitalist production is a
temporary, and perhaps unfortunate, historical moment in its evolution, or whether science continues to express the ideology and
values of capitalism in every social system in which it is applied.
Does science unconsciously reproduce the hidden values, social
relationships, and organizational principles of capital even in non-
capitalist socialist and democratic societies? Are the productive
forces forever tied to the social relations of production of capital or
do they form an independent force of production to be later used
for emancipatory purposes after capitalism in a viable economic
and political system?

From this perspective, science is firmly grounded and justified
in capitalist production and in its economic crises. It also constitutes an essential and intricate part of the various forms of social
epistemology and historical materialism. Looking clearly at these
issues, the role of natural science and technology in Marx's social

theory begins to look a little clearer. Whether natural science is viewed as an expression of the technical forces of production; the class relations of industrial production; the historical, structural, and dialectical interface between these two features of the mode of production; the basis for capital accumulation and the realization of surplus value; the theoretical and mechanistic reflection of abstract labor and value exchange; the concepts and theories of the superstructure reflecting the inner logic of the economic base; or the representative of the technical and production needs of machine industry and economic expansion, science is intimately tied to the world of material production. From these perspectives, science is woven into the very sinews of the modern economy. It is not a neutral observer of the objective laws of nature that can be applied in any historical moment, in any historical economy, but rather reflects the inner logic and natural laws of the value production of capital.

HISTORICAL MATERIALISM AS ABSTRACT THOUGHT IN SCIENCE AND LABOR

This section will connect Kant's epistemology with Marx's historical materialism, by expanding the theory of abstractionism in mind and body, thought and labor. This integration of Kant and Marx is achieved by relating the latter's historical theory of science to the former's notion of transcendental subjectivity, a priori concepts of the understanding, and the synthetic unity of apperception. This is the thesis developed by Alfred Sohn-Rethel about the historical and social connection between the evolution of abstract thought in philosophy and science, in economics and physics, in manual and intellectual labor, and in exchange value and scientific theory, in his major work *Intellectual and Manual Labor* (1970). According to Sohn-Rethel—who tried to follow Marx closely on the subject of historical materialism and the origins of modern science, but who was also aware of Marx's ambiguity on these issues—these abstract concepts were only a derivation and reflection of the equally abstract nature of commodity exchange or commodity abstraction. Sohn-Rethel adheres to Marx's principle that the social existence of human beings conditions and defines the nature of human consciousness. Their ideas, values, ideals, and ideologies are a product of the forms of social labor and the organization and technology of the manufacturing process, whose ultimate goal is the production of surplus value and its realization in money. At the beginning of the book, Sohn-Rethel combines these elements of commodity production and commodity exchange into the idea of money, since the latter acts as the concrete and phenomenal form of capital as exchange and profits in a market economy. Thus, abstract thought in philosophy and natural science is not the result of the synthetic creativity of the imagination of consciousness, but rather "the social-synthetic function of money," which abstracts from and obscures its true origins in the process of production.[51] "Money abstraction" emerges out of "exchange abstraction" or the exchange of commodities as forms of abstract labor in a market economy. The idea of abstraction emerges out of the appearances of capitalism since the abstraction of exchange value lies at the heart of the new social system.

According to Sohn-Rethel, modern abstractions in thought, ideas, and science ultimately arise out of the exchange of social labor as a historically specific form of market exchange of abstract labor, which is the general, homogeneous, and universal labor in commodities that becomes the basis for the exchange of market commodities. This abstraction in labor, production, and the market becomes the basis for the determination of wages, commodity prices, and factory profits in the economy. As a particular historical and social form of labor, it is the substance of value and exchange value in capitalism, and the foundation of capital and commercial profit. Crucial to Sohn-Rethel's argument is that the social nature of abstraction does not arise out of labor or production directly, but only becomes real in the commodity exchange.[52] Abstraction originates in the production process and the creation of commodities and exchange value, but is only given its concrete manifestation as money in the exchange process, in which the commodity is abstracted from its physical properties of use, time, location, consumption, etc. Sohn-Rethel focuses on the form and process of commodity exchange. Although he recognizes the connection between commodity production and commodity exchange, he clearly places the causal and practical emphasis for the rise of intellectual thought, using abstract concepts, ideas, and theories in the exchange process and the abstraction of money from use value. The substance of commodities lies in abstract labor extracted through the wage contract, and thus is a distinct product of the social relations of production. However, it becomes an object of reflection in the actual exchange, which is the more important form of abstraction for understanding the creation of a priori categories of experience and thought. "The knowledge of nature necessary in commodity producing societies is based on the pattern of the exchange abstraction. It is knowledge of nature in commodity form."[53] This is the basis for his interpretation of historical materialism and the transformation of Kantian idealism and epistemology into political economy and historical materialism; it is the foundation upon which Sohn-Rethel constructs the basis for his understanding of the nature of human consciousness and knowledge about the world. This is his remarkable contribution to the general discussion of the origins of human self-reflection and conceptual thought.

Sohn-Rethel has strengthened our understanding of the relationship between abstract thought and manual labor, science and exchange abstraction; at the same time, however, he weakens the relationships between thought and production, the productive forces and social relations of production. Sohn-Rethel sees the relationship between the two economic spheres of production and consumption, but his emphasis is clearly on the exchange value (exchange of labor) of production, because it is the embodiment and appearance of abstraction. Production is the origin of abstraction, but it is in exchange that it develops into a historical form of economic and theoretical consciousness.

In Sohn-Rethel's theory of historical materialism, abstraction or reflective abstract thought is ultimately tied to abstract money and exchange. However, a stronger argument would be that although abstraction is made real in the exchange process (the abstract labor of production becomes real through the exchange of commodities and money in the market), it is in the production process that abstract labor is created by alienated workers. The Kantian categories of the understanding that inform our perception and knowledge of the world— by which we perceive and experience the everyday objects and their causal relations, and by which the ideas and theories of Galilean laws of motion and Newtonian physics are created—are a product of a distinct form of capital, social labor, value production, and money exchange: abstract universal labor and money as the homogeneous universal equivalent. Science is a result of the abstraction of the commodity in its production and exchange, and money is its concrete historical appearance. Sohn-Rethel asks the central questions of epistemology, but now in the context of social theory:

How is pure mathematics possible? How is pure natural science possible? How are synthetic a priori judgments possible? . . . That the "pure natural science" is possible is not disputable; it is a fact. Accordingly, we must be able to show how it is possible. This was Kant's approach, and this remains the postulate of historical materialism.[54]

The process of abstraction from empirical reality occurs in both concept and thought formation in modern science and in industrial production, distribution, exchange, and consumption in the modern economy. The foundations of empirical and mathematical science (intellectual labor), along with the foundation of commodity production as abstract value and commodity exchange as money (exchange value), have their common basis in economic activity and the creation of exchange value. In both cases, abstraction is expressed as the abstract value of labor and money. Human labor under capitalism—which is characterized by the mechanical division of labor, class system, general abstract labor, private property, factory production, etc.—is the substance and measure of the worth and value of both production and exchange. But commodity production and commodity exchange are understood as complex conceptual and theoretical abstractions from the actual historical and social conditions of industrial capitalism. The former creates abstract labor and the latter creates abstract value. Production and exchange form the essential formal structure and logic of capitalism, and are quite different from the actual utility (use value) and consumption of commodities. According to Marx, money as the basis for actual exchange is the physical embodiment and phenomenal appearance of the abstraction of human labor. Underlying the institutions of political economy, production, and exchange are the forms of labor specific to a capitalist society. Sohn-Rethel argues that "the birth of modern science in European society [is] based on wage-labor," because commodity exchange is the "original source of abstraction" and that "this abstraction contains the formal elements for the cognitive faculty of conceptual thinking."[55] It is this historical connection between forms of thought and forms of commodities that is the basis for Sohn-Rethel's argument. Its external expression is in the form of money, but its abstract expression is in the form of alienation and exploitation of human labor. This is the historical origin and social basis for the distinction between intellectual labor of concept and theory formation and manual labor of production and exchange in the workplace and market.

Sohn-Rethel maintains that it is the very nature of commodity exchange that forms the world of abstract ideas and thoughts. They are concrete social expressions of universal thought. The actual economic process is engaged with concrete situations, empirical wants, particular needs, consumer tastes, and market calculations. Money is a concrete object of use in market exchanges, but it also reflects the deeper, underlying abstract forms of production and exchange; it is a universal equivalent and abstract form of exchange based on human labor. It has physical characteristics of gold, silver, coins, etc., existing in uniform time and space; it also has characteristics of being "abstract substances" which are "homogeneous and uniform, indivisible, and incapable of becoming or of perishing."[56] Commodity production and exchange manifest the characteristics of reason and thought, while actual commodities and money exchange express the more concrete and empirical characteristics of sense perception and phenomena. The movement and exchange of commodities in commercial markets became the basis for the study of movement in the physical world.[57] The categories and theories of modern science evolve out of the abstract forms of the social relations of capitalist production.

In a later essay, "Historical Materialist Theory of Knowledge," Sohn-Rethel closely follows Engels's writings on natural science and materialism, building upon the latter's theory of commodity production. Sohn-Rethel states that the basic categories of modern thought are derived from commodity production, which includes a money economy, commerce and trade, merchants, private property, class system, division of labor, and slave labor.[58] In this statement on the subject of historical materialism, he makes a clear connection between Marx and Kant, integrating economic and social theory with modern epistemology or the "commodity form" (*Warenform*), and money exchange with the "thought form" (*Denkform*) and abstract concepts. Science is just another intellectual manifestation of the superstructure that evolves out of the economic foundations of modern society. Commodities are material objects produced by an abstract relationship between labor and capital in industrial factories built upon abstract labor, exchange value, and surplus value; commodities represent the underlying abstraction of the social relations that form the core of the use and abuse of human labor in modern production.

This complex and abstract relationship of production and exchange, which is also an abstraction from use value and the physical properties of commodities, forms the basis for the abstract creation of the categories of thought and being in

Western science. The true relationship and value of an object as abstract labor, exchange value, and capital disappears among the phenomenal appearances of a market economy and international commerce. The ideas and relationships of "commodity abstraction," "value abstraction," and "commodity production"—which refer to the labor in the social creation and market realization of abstract human labor—are lost among the classical economists, with their emphasis on concrete and quantitative commodity prices, market exchange, consumer demands, market competition, individual consumption, and private profits. With the "fetishism of commodities," the underlying structure of labor exploitation and alienation in the production and exchange of abstract human labor and surplus value are transformed into an idealized view of the market purchase of use value, market exchange, and consumer goods.

The abstract and mathematical categories of natural science are thus grounded in the abstraction of social labor, value exchange, and surplus value that underlie the concrete production and market relations of capital. In turn, there are other forms of correspondence between science and production, such as the centrality of scientific inquiry, data accumulation, and mathematical calculation, which is a theoretical expression of the abstract forms of economic rational bookkeeping and empirical profit calculation; hypothesis creation, designed to test scientific laws and profit calculations and business and market projections based on economic laws; empirical verification of hypotheses and confirmation of natural laws and the rational determination of business supply of material and consumer demand for finished products; and the end products of science and production, which are truth and profits, respectively. In *Zur gesellschaftlichen Funktion der Naturwissenschaften* (1973), Peter Bulthaup continues this line of thought, writing that the "transcendental conditions for the possibility of science with its unambiguous fixation on isolated natural relationships are at the same time that of social labor, which is determined through the combination of clear, fixated natural relationships in the machinery and the integration of individual labor in the industrial production."[59]

REINTEGRATION OF PRODUCTION AND EXCHANGE AS FOUNDATION OF MODERN SCIENCE

By helping to develop the unarticulated and underdeveloped ideas in Marx's writings, Sohn-Rethel has expanded the connection between epistemology and materialism, thought and being, knowledge about nature and its connection to the social reality. However, he has also narrowed the understanding of commodity production to the very limited concept of the "commodity form," or money and abstract exchange value. In order to clarify Marx's and Engels's theory of historical materialism, Sohn-Rethel moves the foundation of their theory from industrial production to market exchange and coined money. In so doing, he unfortunately misses their key points about historical materialism's origins in the foundations of the mode of production and commodity production. In his analysis of Marx's theory of abstract labor and commodity exchange, Sohn-Rethel reduces historical materialism to a misplaced emphasis on commodity exchange at the expense of commodity production, thereby reducing historical materialism to market exchange and commodity circulation.[60] Historical materialism is rendered critically ineffective, because the underlying economic foundations of abstract value and exchange value have been separated from the broader process of production with its social relations of production, class organization of production, private property, wage labor, value production, division of labor, universal abstract labor, alienation, etc. By limiting abstract thought and science to the abstraction of market exchange, Sohn-Rethel's social epistemology and economic theory lose the heart of Marx's economic theory, and perhaps more importantly, the connection between science as a productive force (economic base) and science as a political ideology (superstructure). That is, by separating commodity production from commodity exchange, the productive forces from the social relations of production, the form of production from the form of exchange and money, and thought and science from the actual production of abstract and exchange value, Sohn-Rethel makes it even more difficult to understand the nature of modern science and its relationship to capitalist society as a whole. Nevertheless, with his theory of abstractionism in the modern economy and natural science, Sohn-Rethel certainly makes a substantive contribution to and expansion of Marx's theory of historical materialism.

Building upon Sohn-Rethel's contribution, it is important to recognize that the concepts of abstract labor and value creation in Marx's writings are central parts of both commodity production and commodity exchange. Value is created in production, but realized in exchange. The secret to modern science rested in the nature of modern capitalism, and not some inherent access to an ontological reality, an inherent metaphysical principle, or an epistemological truth. Science does not reflect an external being or objective reality, but is itself the reconstruction or representation of the underlying economic system of commodity or value production at the level of abstract thought. Just as an understanding of the formal aspects of the nature of abstract labor in commodities and exchange is an abstraction from the concrete and material conditions of factory work, division of labor, industrial production, and market exchange, so too are the formal elements and a priori categories of experience abstracted from the structures and logic of social production and commodity exchange. Economic abstraction occurs in the process of production and exchange, whereby the underlying value of commodities is measured by the abstract labor of production and the universal or abstract value/labor in commodity exchange. The abstraction of production and exchange is based on a historically and socially specific kind of labor, which is the product of wage labor and surplus value.

Franz Borkenau in his work *Der Übergang von feudalen zum bürgerlichen Weltbild* (1971) has summarized this nicely: "The mechanics, that is, the science of the manufacturing period is the scientific adaptation of the process of production in manufacturing. . . . Mechanics is actually an exact science in comparison to workers' rate of work. So is manufacturing the requirement of modern mechanics."[61] According to Borkenau, the Newtonian mechanics of the laws of motion, force, and gravitation are based on the quantifiable, mathematical, and predictable laws of production in the workplace. The rationalization and mechanization of the workplace produces commodities, which are defined and measured by the labor time in each commercial object. The abstractions of both forms of cognition and the forms of value production interface with each other, thereby creating an intimate connection between science and labor, intellectual and manual labor. Borkenau describes this rationalization process of work and the mechanical worldview as a product of both the productive forces and social relations of production.[62] The abstract concepts and theories of philosophy and science—the mathematizing of nature (*die Mathematisierung der Natur*)—are the products of the abstractions of manual labor and machine production.[63] Knowledge of objective reality is, in part, a "self-consciousness of humanity" based on the mode of production by which humanity creates its own material and intellectual world.[64] The abstract nature of commodity production—with its underlying law of value in this new economic system of production, exchange, commerce, banking, etc.—created the ideals, values, and concepts by which we understand our relationship to other human beings and organize our relationship to nature and external reality.[65] Science is grounded in political economy and wage labor, and not in an existential or objective physical reality.

Natural science manifests all aspects of machine industry and the production and exchange of human labor value. It is an intricate part of the logic and dynamic of a historical and social form of production, and cannot be mechanically or artificially abstracted from its social foundations and summarily placed into an alternative social system with the ethics and politics of a moral economy and egalitarian, participatory democracy. The relationship between science and technology and the forms of social labor and class structure are not one-dimensional but dialectical, because they affect and condition (*bestimmen*) each other in the evolution of society. Any transformation of society based on the principles of human dignity, emancipation, and social justice occurs not because of a technological revolution (crude instrumental materialism), but because of class consciousness and a demand for social change (historical idealism). Political domination is present in both science and technology and in the class system of production and distribution; both would have to be radically changed for the realization of true human emancipation and democracy.

SOCIAL EPISTEMOLOGY, HISTORICAL MATERIALISM, AND SOCIAL JUSTICE

Just as the political theories of Hobbes and Locke and the economic theories of Smith and Ricardo are reflections of the transformations of civil society in its early stages into abstract concepts and superstructural theories, so, too, do Galileo's and Newton's classical mechanics and laws of motion, inertia, and gravity reflect the broader laws of social labor and value exchange. As noted above, Marx and Engels write in the *The German Ideology* that "this 'pure' natural science is provided with an aim, as with its material . . . only through trade and industry."[66] That is, the economy provides science with a particular purpose (in expanding production) and a substance or material content (in technical control and the domination of nature). For science to become the neutral and objective theory of the laws of physics, chemistry, and biology, or to become the technical basis of capital accumulation and production in an alternative social system, would require a complete rethinking of the nature and logic of science, and a complete break with the values and logic of commodity and capital production. Isaac Balbus summarized this position succinctly and powerfully with the following:

It is the capitalist effort to maximize surplus-value in the face of the workers' resistance to this effort that determines the process of technological development. The industrial revolution does not bring about capitalism; capitalism helps bring about the industrial revolution. Like the factory itself, modern machinery is introduced into the labor process not because it is per se more efficient, but because, according to Marx, it is the most efficient "means of creating surplus-value."[67]

According to Marx, science helps define our relationship with nature and society as it supports and maintains the existing class structure; it also helps create the world we experience every day in mind and body. Science is a product of humanity's sensuous activity and theoretical creations, but it also creates the very objects of sensuous perception and experience, just as it creates the laws of the physical world. The world we inhabit, perceive, understand, and scientifically investigate is a historically and socially created product, of which science is the most abstract and theoretically sophisticated form. To place science in an alternative universe or social system would require a transformation of its intellectual concepts, theoretical ideas, and social aims.

Marx remained decidedly unclear about the full implications of his theories of natural science and historical materialism in the *Grundrisse* and *Capital*. He began to develop the idea of historical materialism early in his writings in *The German Ideology*, but he never used the term. Throughout his writings, he also never clarified the relationships among the economic mode of production, human consciousness, and social institutions, that is, between the economic base and social/cultural superstructure or between consciousness and social existence. This is not unusual for him, since he also never developed a comprehensive theory of social justice, which was implicit throughout his writings.[68] Such a theory would perhaps have been too philosophical and idealistic. But despite these two limitations, these areas represent the key to unpacking the complexity of his later writings. What appears to be is not the essence of what is. Although Marx's purpose was not to develop a full materialist theory of social epistemology and historical materialism as a rejoinder to the idealism of Kant's critique of pure reason and Hegel's phenomenology of the spirit, he attempted to undertake just that—a materialist theory of knowledge that complements his critical theory of social justice. Marx was not an academician, and thus did not develop the theories of social knowledge or social justice, but he did outline the social and historical foundations of these types of reflection. That is, he wrote about historical materialism and social justice, but did not develop the metatheory, theory, and methodology behind these approaches. Nevertheless, it seems clear from his work that natural science was so embedded and framed in the logic and structure of capitalist production that science could not be conceived of as an objective and neutral search for the truth. In the same way, the mode of production in capitalism could not be the basis for the realization of the equality, freedom, and dignity of humanity beyond economic exploitation and wage slavery.

Epistemology, moral philosophy, and phenomenology were negated as forms of philosophy with the rise of Marx's materialist theory of knowledge and ethics. Capitalism abused both logic and reason with the invention of natural science and, in turn, abused ethics and justice with reduction of human productivity to surplus value. Marx has sometimes been compared to the classical economists who were interested in defining the empirical laws of economic behavior in terms of price, profit, and production and then were rejected for not accomplishing this task successfully. Both knowledge (natural science) and ethics (social justice) should be examined with an emphasis on the knowledge of the productive forces of science and technology, their underlying consciousness and ideology, as well as their role in the formation of the rising organic composition of capital and fall in the rate of profit, economic stagnation, and economic crises. These were the two central subjects of Marx's famous economic writings. The aim was not to justify the naturalism of science or the nominalism of ethics, that is, positivism. It was rather to show that both positivism in epistemology (science reflects reality) and positivism in economics (capitalism as rational, free, and good) are illusions and ideologies of science and liberalism. Marx's theory of historical materialism is an attempt to mediate and integrate epistemology and economics, science and justice, but he never truly developed in a comprehensive social theory the connections between them.

The purpose in writing the *Grundrisse* and *Capital* was not to develop an economic theory based on the empirical data of supply and demand, competition, price determination, profit calculation, consumption patterns, or even a theory of economic crisis based on the overproduction and underconsumption of commodities. Nor was it to develop a science of the labor theory of value and falling rate of profit that would be open to hypothesis creation, empirical testing, economic prediction, and scientific verification. Rather, Marx's main purpose was to demonstrate the essential and internal logic and dynamic of the structures of capitalism in the exploitation and degradation of wage slavery and the iron cage of industrial factories. Just as his theory of historical materialism was a continuation of Kant's and Hegel's critique of pure and phenomenal reason, his theory of capital production of surplus value was a continuation of the ethics and politics of Aristotle. One of Marx's major contributions to Western thought was the melding of the two areas of epistemology and political economy into a general theory of historical consciousness and social institutions. Similarly, he attempted to provide in *Capital* the skeletal framework for a new theory of social justice and a new theory of science and technology. Toward these purposes, he outlined a labor theory of, on the one hand, value extortion and the concomitant economic crises that followed; and on the other, the centrality of science and technology as productive forces in creating the conditions for the tendency toward economic crises of stagnation, declining profit rates, unemployment, recession, economic concentration, and so on. In both cases Marx dealt with the logical and structural impact of science and technology and economic alienation. Here too, he did not provide a developed social theory of these areas, nor did he attempt to integrate them into a comprehensive social theory. Today, they stand isolated and undeveloped.

Nor was the purpose of the *Grundrisse* and *Capital* to develop a theory of science and technology and historical materialism. A philosophy of sensuous consciousness and science already exists in an underdeveloped form in the early philosophical manuscripts. The later writings articulate these ideas as they evolved into the productive forces and as they affect the structural foundations of capital production. The two crucial elements in human emancipation—knowledge and ethics—have usually been separated into the early philosophical writings and the later scientific ones. Now we begin to see their connections, since the early writings provide the preparatory outline for the technical and economic analysis of their essential role in the economy. This is the missing link for Marx's theory of historical materialism and social justice. Science can now be seen in its form as (1) sensuous consciousness and perception of the natural world; (2) phenomenology of self-consciousness in the culture and ideology of superstructure; (3) alienation of false consciousness and science; (4) theory of social justice with the numerous references to Aristotle's politics and ethics in *Capital*; and (5) critical methodology of historical materialism with its origins in both idealism (epistemology) and materialism (social epistemology).

These two intersecting themes, which run throughout his writings and constitute the essence of capital, are expressed as the use and abuse of human labor in the economic base (social justice) and the science and technology of the capitalist mode of production (historical materialism). Without the exploitation and domination of labor, the scientific and technological domination of nature, and the expansion of class production, there is no surplus value or profits. Although there is no developed theory of historical materialism or theory of social justice in Marx's writings, they are both essential for the development of Western society. In the future, the two prerequisites of a free society will be a moral economy based on the inherent dignity, freedom, and creativity of human labor; and a moral science based on the symbiotic and harmonious application of science and technology to the realization of fundamental human needs (physical, spiritual, and political needs) and the continuous health of the organic environment, which are central components of social justice in both Aristotle and Marx. Social justice and alternative forms of science and technology could free humanity from political, economic, and physical bondage to capital and nature by freeing the productive forces and social relations of production from their historical and social ties to capital.

As mentioned above, many secondary interpreters of Marx maintain that he did not fully develop a theory of historical materialism, and rarely mentioned the idea of natural science. However, on closer look, his overall studies on economics and exploitation are themselves crucial statements in these two areas. The more Marx delves into his labor theory of value and economic crisis theory, the more he develops the implications of his theory of materialism and science. The same may be said of his theory of social justice, which frames the totality of his writings but is never articulated concretely into a fully formed philosophy. Although the references to historical materialism and natural science are few and tantalizing, there is no comprehensive theory of either area. However, the argument made in this chapter is that Marx's general social theory is, in fact, about historical materialism and natural science. From the perspective of the productive forces; superstructure of false consciousness and political ideology; economic interests and material requirements of production; operational and technological application of science; and exploitation of labor leading to the overproduction and stagnation of capital and the production of formal logic, theoretical reason, and conceptual abstractionism, science cannot be divorced from the particular historical mode of capitalist production. Science cannot be arbitrarily and ahistorically removed from these social relations and structures. Rather, its historical categories and theories are so enshrined in the logic of capital that science is an a priori form

of pure ideology and bourgeois science; it is the basis for alienation and exploitation of nature and humanity, production of class
inequality and surplus value, and the economic crises and structural breakdown of the capitalist economy. Science ingrained with
the class consciousness and market imperatives of capital cannot
be the foundation for theoretical truth (epistemology) or human
liberation (social justice). It reflects the structural imperatives and
logic of capitalist production. A radical transformation of a society based on wage slavery and political oppression would require
a total transformation of the modern state, cultural superstructure, and economic mode of production, and by definition the
productive forces. This would require a transformation of human
consciousness and science itself.

PART III

Social Science, Positivism,

and the Domination

of Reason and Society

CHAPTER 5

The Rise of Positivism and the Decline of Critical Reason in the Social Sciences: The Positivist Dispute in German Sociology

BY THE END OF THE TWENTIETH CENTURY, classical and contemporary social theory in the American academy had been replaced by the scientific methods of natural science (*Naturwissenschaft*) and formal rationality (*Zweckrationalität*). Theory became a convenient and conventional afterthought and a utilitarian research tool. It now serves the process of rationalization as a technical utility and validation for the questions and problems to be resolved in the following areas: research designs and techniques, controlled experiments and hypothesis creation, deductive and causal analysis, and the formation of intervening variables and predictive inferences in empirical research, as it supports a particular naturalistic logic, theory, and methodology of science, with its narrow and specialized questions and its limited conclusions. This is the method of quantitative research and experiments, measurement, standardized observation, and deductive logic, which specializes in mathematics, data collection, social surveys, questionnaires, statistics, and formal patterns of behavior for the creation or confirmation of predictive, explanatory, and universal laws of human

276 SHADOWS OF THE ENLIGHTENMENT

behavior. The second method utilized by the social sciences applies qualitative or interpretive methods and inductive logic to undertake research designs that focus on issues of participatory observation, interviews, field research, focus groups, content analysis, ethnography, history, etc.[1] Although qualitative sociology appears to be quite different from quantitative analysis, it contains many of the same epistemological and methodological assumptions. Qualitative analysis, like quantitative, can reduce its truth claims to positivist, objective, observable, and explanatory features. Both traditions, in different ways, have fallen under the spell of analytic philosophy and Anglo-American positivism.

It was the classical social theory of Marx, Weber, and Durkheim that argued against this narrow and positivist approach to social science and its attempt to universalize its epistemology and methodology to the exclusion of other intellectual and philosophical traditions. In positivist social science, knowledge and theory are reduced to empirical evidence and verification; objectivity; distance and detachment; nominalism and neutrality; and reflection based on observation and social facts, mathematical and logical proofs, causal hypotheses and explanations, and the creation of general laws of human behavior. This has been referred to by members of the Frankfurt School as the "eclipse of reason," the "silence and liquidation of reason," "contempt of theory," "poverty of philosophy," and the "death of philosophy," in that it undermines the critical German, French, and Italian social theories in favor of the methodology of the natural sciences. The result is a loss of critical idealism and materialism; dialectical and historical reflection; integration of ethics with politics and morality with political economy; critical political economy; the study of the historical origins, institutions, and structures of Western capitalism; and the ideals of social justice. Historical sociology has turned to critical realism, rational choice theory, social explanations, and a search for unobservable mechanical and causal laws of historical development; positivist ethnography has dropped naturalism, but turned to nominalism and realism.

As a result of this "new barbarism," theory of the classical horizons has been lost in American sociology, along with the integration of philosophy, history, and political economy into a critical sociology, and has been replaced by unreflective, uncritical, and cursory empirical observations and research. Theory has been replaced by a formal and mechanical sociology based on an ahistorical and atheoretical history of ideas, literature review, content analysis, and summary of the findings of empirical research; theory has become part of a culture industry for academic consumption and methods justification. Both quantitative and qualitative research methods are central to the formation of critical social theory. However, when connected with specific and narrow positivist methodologies and epistemologies, they are very limited in their particular research questions, methods, and conclusions. In American sociology, there are three primary social theories or paradigms: structural functionalism, symbolic interactionism, and conflict theory. Unfortunately, they simply do not capture the enormous complexity of continental sociology, as the latter is usually made to conform or fit into the three paradigms of the American tradition. In the process, the classical traditions of Marx, Weber, Durkheim, and Freud are distorted and lost, since they do not conform to these particular designations or paradigms.

In the American tradition, theory has been used to frame a particular problem or issue under scientific investigation; it can confirm and legitimate the problem; it can provide an overview of similar investigations within the history of sociological thought; it can expand the variables and our understanding of the constructed hypothesis; it can actually help create, articulate, and validate the objects of investigation; and it can make the history of social concepts and traditions operational and functional in order to explain contemporary issues and problems. Theory is used to justify and validate a particular research question or problem. But this is deceptive because, in the final analysis, the central questions and issues in utilitarian sociology and research design are ultimately framed by the applied technical method. According to

Jürgen Habermas and C. Wright Mills, methods define theory in contemporary American sociology; theory has become reflexive rather than reflective in both quantitative and qualitative research. Methods, in both forms of positivism—abstract or atheoretical empiricism of qualitative methods, and critical rationalism of quantitative methods—define the nature of objectivity, research design, logic of inquiry, verification, truth, and science. By so defining the methodology of inquiry, it also defines the issues, problems, objects, and ultimately the theory of inquiry. A key result of this approach is that quantitative and qualitative methods in American sociology define out of existence questions of history, political economy, structure, functions, ethics, and critique (immanent and dialectical); it defines out of existence classical and contemporary European social theory, as it never challenges the underlying assumptions of scientific positivism, political liberalism, or economic capitalism. Nor is it capable of challenging its own nominalist assumptions about distinguishing between fact and values, science and ethics.

David Hume and the Epistemology of Empiricism and Skepticism

This chapter will trace the evolution of the critique of positivism and its epistemological and methodological relevance for the social sciences from the early writings of David Hume to the positivism debate between the critical theory of Max Horkheimer, Theodor Adorno, and Jürgen Habermas, and the critical rationalism of Karl Popper and Hans Albert. An outline of this evolution of positivism is an important discussion within the social sciences, and sociology in particular, because it defines the parameters of the discipline that have a crucial role in defining the legitimate aims of social science and its corresponding ability to articulate the acceptable range of methods, questions, issues, and theories that can be discussed within the discipline. It was Hume, in the first four chapters of his major work *An Enquiry Concerning*

Human Understanding (1748), who laid out the basic epistemo-logical features of positivist and empiricist philosophy.[2] He begins by outlining the mental geography of the structure and operations of the human mind in the sensations, reason, and the imagination. He then proceeds to analytically break down the various compo-nents and functions of the mind in order to detail the foundations of experience; the origins of ideas in sensuous impressions and perceptions; the association and causal relations between ideas; and the rational foundations and justification of modern science in causality, induction, and reason. All knowledge of the everyday world from immediate perception and experience to the causality and science of reason is ultimately grounded in the information provided by empirical sensations. The origins of the perceptions and ideas lie in our impressions of the world around us, which are themselves reflections of the immediate objects of experience. Perceptions of hearing, seeing, feeling, etc., and ideas are both impressions of the world differing only in their immediacy and intensity. Our impressions and thoughts are "faithful mirrors and copies" of the objects of our senses.[3] Using examples of the "golden mountain" and the "virtuous horse," Hume continues to stress that ideas themselves are products of our perception; they are just less lively and immediate. All knowledge is ultimately a product of our senses and experience, even our most lofty and abstract ideas. "All ideas were copies of our impressions."[4]

Hume then moves beyond immediate sense experience and directs his attention to the foundations of science and the issue of epistemological realism. He asks: How can we be sure of the existence of a world of our experience as "matters of fact" beyond our immediate experience and memory? This form of knowledge assumes the existence of an external and objective reality beyond our experience, which is reflected in our senses and mind. Offering the examples of a letter from a friend, a discovered watch in a desert, and the hearing of an articulate voice in the dark, Hume reaches for the conclusion that rational inference is a product of cause and effect, which is the basis for all human reasoning and ultimately all rational knowledge, and is itself ultimately grounded in experience. Hume is aware that he is directly rejecting the form of reason developed by rationalist philosophers like René Descartes. Knowledge of the physical world cannot be obtained by a priori reasoning independent of experience, since all knowledge of objects (senses) and cause and effect (reason) are "discoverable not by reason, but experience."[5] Knowledge of cause and effect cannot be derived either directly from the senses or from human reason. Rather, it is a product of accumulated experience of the past and present and inferential reasoning. Causality arises from inference, but is justified only by experience. Hume concludes that "all the laws of nature, and all the operations of the bodies without exceptions, are known only by experience."[6] He uses his famous billiard ball example to make his argument rejecting rationalism as the basis for a logical connection between cause and effect. Rationalism or a priori reasoning cannot achieve any knowledge of the actual direction of the second billiard ball struck by the first ball. Upon careful consideration and examination of a particular billiard ball, it would still be impossible to determine or infer the original motion of the first ball no less than its effect on the second ball struck on the billiard table. The second ball could go right, left, or remain in place. The causal relationship between striking the ball and its effects could not be predetermined before the experience itself simply by reflecting on the nature of a billiard ball. It is the experience which ultimately justifies and validates the causal connection between the two events since "the mind can never possibly find the effect in the supposed cause"[7] and "all our reasoning a priori will never be able to show us any foundation for this preference."[8] This example represents a continuation of Hume's critique of rationalism. The effect of an action cannot be determined beforehand by a simply prior reflection on the action itself. This type of reasoning eliminates all forms of rationalist and a priori reasoning in metaphysics, mathematics, and physics, since all knowledge is ultimately reducible to experience and observation.

It is at this point that Hume switches to a critical examination of empiricism and inductive reasoning as the possible basis for our knowledge and reasoning about cause and effect. He is quite aware that he is involved in a dangerous dilemma that will lead eventually to his epistemological skepticism, which becomes fully visible in chapters 5 and 12. By offering the example of bread—with its sensible qualities of color, weight, taste, etc., and its secret powers of nourishment—he is stymied by the logical difficulty of relating the causal relationship between the sensible qualities of the bread and its secret powers of sustenance. Hume is asking for clarification about the nature of logical inference and causal reasoning. For him, it is not clear how to justify inductive inferences based on accumulated experience. It is at this point that he has turned his critical insights upon his apparently recently justified philosophical arguments in favor of experience and causality. That is, he is now calling into question the very nature of empiricism itself, since the logic of induction based on experience is itself based on previous examples of the question. Hume is aware that making a statement based on past experience and causal relationships implies the acceptance of the logical assumptions of inductive reason. However, he quickly recognizes that this type of reason is based on an acceptance without proof or justification of the logic of induction itself. To say that all swans are white is based on our previous experience and inductive logic. But what justifies the actual use of inductive logic itself? The acceptance of inductive reasoning has not been logically proven and requires a deeper examination, which eventually leads Hume to his famous epistemological skepticism about empiricism and science. What is the philosophical justification for arriving at rational conclusions about effects based on our knowledge of causes from previous experiences? He maintains: "It is impossible, therefore, that any argument from experience can prove this resemblance of the past to the future; since all the arguments are founded on the supposition of that resemblance."[9] The logical justification of the relationship of causes to the effects or the past to the future are ultimately based on an initial acceptance and justification of the unproven validity of the logic of inductive reasoning prior to its application in explaining a specific event, experience, or object. Thus, Hume ends chapter 4 of his work with the beginning of his skepticism that neither a priori rationalism or a posteriori empiricism can justify the logical links between cause and effects in scientific inquiry.

Throughout these initial chapters, Hume outlines the basic features of positivism and his theory of perception, ideas, causality, and science. This theory of knowledge holds that there is an external, autonomous, and objective world of empirical facts (objectivism) that can be known and copied through impressions and ideas (realism) using the methodology of the natural sciences (naturalism) as the only legitimate and universal form of knowledge (scientism), which must be kept separate from normative, ethical, and evaluative judgments (nominalism) that could distort its objectivity, neutrality, and empirical evidence.[10] Hume's ideas for most of the first four chapters became the accepted foundation and justification for a belief in empiricism: that sense experience and scientific observation are the only legitimate forms of knowledge. However, even in Hume's own writing, this thesis began to fall apart quickly, due to his unusually perceptive logical mind. By his dogged inquiry into the foundations of inferential and inductive reasoning based on past sense experience and empirical evidence, Hume could not conclude that inferences from past experiences provided the logical justification for making statements about the present and future, since the argument itself rests on the unproved logical assumption that all future experiences will and do resemble the past. It is at this point in his analysis that the foundations of empiricism are called into question with this critique of logical inference based on experience. He concludes with the argument: "It is not reasoning which engages us to suppose the past resembling the future, and to expect similar effects from causes which are, to appearance, similar."[11]

Hume maintains that neither the senses nor reason can justify the relationship between cause and effect or between past and future. This is an important issue, since the very foundations of empirical knowledge and science are at stake. He addresses it at the beginning of the next chapter with his argument that to accept the notion that the future will resemble the past is the result not of philosophical logic, but of custom or habit. That is, the causal relationship is the result not of reason, but of a psychological pre-disposition or instinct of the human imagination to view reality in terms of connections and associations such as contiguity in space, resemblance in time, and causation in relationships. It is at this point that the very foundations of empiricism as a legitimate theory of knowledge—with its ideas of perception, objectivity, substance, causality, and science—begin to be seriously questioned. Frederick Copleston writes: "The idea of substances is derived, therefore, neither from impressions of sensation nor from impressions of reflection. It follows that there is properly speaking, no idea of sub-stance at all. The word 'substance' connotes a collection of 'simple ideas.'" [12] Objectivity is not a product of the senses, but a system-atic collection of simple ideas into a coherent picture or image of an external object created by the human imagination. Nor can objects of perception be the product of human reason by means of a causal inference, since the objects of perception can never be compared to the original objects. We only have our perceptions, with no access to the original object. The world that we see and construct is thus a world of human imagination. [13] Knowledge of the external world is based on sensations, ideas, and the causal relations of ideas that are ultimately a product of the imagination. As we have already seen with Immanuel Kant's critique of pure and practical reason and Georg F. Hegel's phenomenology of the spirit, Hume's notion that the physical reality is a construct of the imagination will be transformed into the transcendental subjec-tivity and phenomenological subject, respectively. And with the rise of sociology in the nineteenth century, the idea will develop that it is society which forms the basis for the construction of our physical and social reality.

Having undermined the law of causality, Hume in chapter 12 undertakes a more detailed analysis and critique of physical

objects and substances, causality and representations, and primary
and secondary qualities of physical objects. This chapter is thus the
key to his entire work, since it contains three skeptical arguments
concerning the existence of an external and independent world of
empirical objects and substances upon which empiricism and later
rationalism exist. Hume begins chapter 12 with three logical arguments critical of the existence of an objective reality prior to and
independent of human perception; these are based on his epistemological critique of naive reality and representations, the cause
of representations, and his theory of primary and secondary qualities of the objective world. The ontological belief in realism that
there is an objective, external universe that exists independently of
all human knowing and existence is a "blind and powerful instinct
of nature."[14] He uses the simple example of a hard, white table.
However, a closer consideration of this issue reveals that when
we perceive the table with our senses, what we see are representations of the table and not the actual table itself; our perceptions of
the table are a result of our impressions and sensations, and these
representations are believed to exist independently of our perception of it. We can never get back to the original object, perception,
or cause of the impression. We only have access to our copies or
representations of the original objects in the external world. This
epistemological dilemma between perceptions and objects has
been called the problem of double affection. We can never know
the object and our perception of the object at the same time. We
only have access to the latter. We know only the perceptions of
objects and not the objects themselves, and there are no perceptions of the objects in themselves, or causes of the perception, or
causes of the idea of objects. According to Hume, we cannot get
outside of perception. We cannot see a pen, table, or classroom,
only the sensuous impressions of these objects. The implications
for Hume are profound, since he concludes that experience and
observation cannot be the true basis for knowledge and science.

With his dogged logical analysis, Hume concludes that we can
never know anything except the images present to the human

mind, and not any objective reality behind it. Our knowledge of the house or tree is nothing but a perception or image of these objects, which are assumed to exist independently of our knowledge of them. According to him, there is no logical argument which can make the connection between our representations and objective existence of physical objects. It is simply an assumption made by our natural instincts to believe that our representations are objectively real. He is stuck in the logical conclusion that there is absolutely no way to logically prove the existence of an external world from the representations themselves; that is, to prove that objects cause perception. The second argument of skepticism is based on the relation between cause and effect. It appears that objects cause our perceptions, but a closer look at the nature of experience reveals that there is no logical connection between representations and objectivity. Hume thus rejects both naive realism and the causal relationship between objectivity and representations to conclude that we have no access to anything behind our representations and perceptions. "The mind has never anything present to it but the perceptions and cannot possibly reach any experience of their connection with objects."[15] The idea that there is a connection between perceptions and objects is without any foundation in human reason or experience.

Hume's third and final argument rejecting the existence of an objective, external world lies in perception and his analysis of the primary and secondary qualities of objects. Most philosophers have traditionally argued that the secondary characteristics of physical objects derived from the senses—such as the color, sound, smell, feel, and texture of an object—are the result of the perceiver and not the object itself. They are perceptions and products of the human mind and are, thus, secondary to the object itself. On the other hand, the primary qualities and characteristics of extension and solidarity that can be measured mathematically are generally understood as coming from the object and not the mind. Here again, Hume turns the argument upside down as he continues to argue that even the primary qualities are products of the senses and not the objects themselves. Hume concludes that our knowledge of the world is a product of our own experience and provides us with representations, primary and secondary qualities of objects, and the appearance of an objective reality, which are all the result of the representations of the human mind. The conclusion Hume draws from his arguments is that the existence, causality, and characteristics of an apparent objective world are the result of our perceptions, which cannot justify any knowledge of objectivity. We are the cause of both the primary and secondary qualities of objects. Since we have no knowledge of an objective world, we cannot make judgments or evaluations about that world in itself.

Pulling all this material together in a comprehensive and skeptical theory of epistemology, Hume argues that our knowledge of the world is a product of our perceptions and mind; it is knowledge of copies and not originals leaving humanity without any real knowledge of the cause of those perceptions. Hume has undermined the foundations of empiricism and inductive and causal reasoning with his rejection of realism and objectivism, since we have no knowledge of or access to the objects in themselves. This makes it impossible to base knowledge and science on empiricism, because it is a psychological construct of the interaction between subjectivity and objectivity. From this perspective, it is clear that Hume's skepticism is a forerunner of Kant's critique of pure reason. This critique of objectivity and substance also translates into a critique of causality and knowledge construction through reason. That is, neither the senses, perception, or reason can justify the objects of perception through induction—"the sun will rise tomorrow" or through the cause and effects of action through deduction—the billiard ball theory.[16] The knower can only see the impressions or representations of objects and their subjective qualities; they cannot see the objects or substances themselves. Induction cannot justify itself by its own logic; and it cannot use inductive reasoning to logically justify induction, since this is circular reasoning. This involves assuming the validity of induction in the very attempt to justify and prove the validity of induction. And one cannot justify knowledge of the objective world through the senses. We do not have access to objective reality through perception or through cause and effects. The conclusion that Hume reaches is that science cannot justify itself through the senses, causality, or reason of induction or deduction. A close reading of the early chapters of this work shows that Hume is the father of modern positivism. It could also be said that after chapter 4, he had become the father of postmodernism.[17] Since we know only the perceptions of objects and not the objects themselves, there are no perceptions of the objects in themselves, or causes of the perception, or causes of the idea of objects.

The various subsections of this chapter examine the rise of positivism in the form of abstracted empiricism and critical rationalism, inductive and deductive reasoning, in the social sciences; and their implications for the development of a holistic and integrative critical social theory. We will examine the relationship between positivism and sociology, science and methods, within a broader framework of the critique of reason. Within the framework of quantitative and qualitative sociology, there is a general recognition of a fundamental split between methods and theory which leads to a critique of positivism in sociology in the form of the metaphysics of science as propaganda, ideology, and dehumanization (Mills); the alienation of reason and social theory (Alvin Gouldner); the eclipse of reason (Horkheimer); and the commodification, fetishism, and loss of reason, memory, and experience (Adorno).

C. WRIGHT MILLS, CRITIQUE OF ABSTRACTED EMPIRICISM, AND THE METAPHYSICS OF SOCIAL SCIENCE

Hume's writings introduced us to the problems associated with empiricism as a philosophical theory of knowledge of objective reality. With the writings of C. Wright Mills and Max Horkheimer, we are engaged with empiricism as it has been applied to the social sciences, and sociology in particular, and the resulting difficulties and weaknesses. According to Mills in *The Sociological Imagination* (1959), traditional sociology is viewed as the scientific study of society, with emphasis on its social institutions, values, culture, and social and interpersonal relationships, which may be divided between quantitative research methods—interviews, sampling, statistics, opinion polls, surveys, questionnaires, and mathematical modeling—and qualitative methods, which focus on observation, ethnography, fieldwork, individual experiences, participatory observation, content and textual analysis, and personal interviews.[18] Mills's major contribution to this issue lies in his analysis of the examination of the underlying metaphysical assumptions and philosophical presuppositions of this understanding of sociology and its research methods. The metaphysics of social science include the hidden and undisclosed values and normative assumptions found in its epistemology, methodology, and politics.[19] These hidden assumptions and values reflect deep and repressed political ideologies within the inner framework of sociological methods, which impart these assumptions about the nature of social reality and objectivity during their empirical applications. Mills's main argument is that there is a close relationship between methods and politics within sociology that is rarely if ever discussed, because they are hidden within the underlying metaphysics of science and built into the research methods themselves, even before they are applied in concrete empirical studies. The conclusions are to some extent already contained in the premises and procedures of the research methods themselves before their actual application. Although Mills focuses on the examination of abstracted empiricism, his criticisms are equally valid for the quantitative research method of critical rationalism, as will be seen later in this chapter.

According to Mills, the main principles of the metaphysics of science lie in (1) epistemology and its theory of knowledge and science based on the belief in objectivism, realism, and naturalism; (2) the methodology and application of social science which rest upon a philosophy of science of positivism, psychologism, and

pluralism; and (3) politics or the underlying, but hidden, ideological values of science itself. It is the epistemology and method
of natural science that define the discipline of sociology and the
social reality it investigates. This is similar to Hume's argument
above. The epistemological foundations of natural and social
science rest upon the following: There is an external reality (objectivism) that is knowable (realism) using the objective, neutral,
non-value-laden method of the natural sciences (naturalism) as
it examines individual attitudes, public opinions, contemporary
events, and statistical social behavior (psychologism). He uses the
term "the metaphysics of science" to denote that area of epistemology, philosophy of science, and methodology which assumes the
existence of a knowable natural and social reality, but which itself
is grounded in abstract assumptions, presuppositions, and normative values of empiricism. The latter are not knowable through
science and thus form a metaphysics beyond the physical world.
From Mills's perspective, these dogmatic and speculative assumptions about the nature and characteristics of social reality, which
make the study of society into a scientific inquiry possible, are not
themselves open to scientific inquiry. Science does not objectively
and impartially study the social reality, he argues, but rather predefines, delineates, and determines that reality through its method
of inquiry. It creates its own metaphysical world, which is given the
appearance of an actual social reality. Mills writes: "Yet because of
epistemological dogma, abstracted empiricists are systematically
a-historical and non-comparative; they deal with small-scale areas
and they incline to psychologism. Neither in defining their problems nor in explaining their own microscopic findings do they
make any real use of the basic idea of historical social structure."[20]
The epistemological presuppositions of abstracted empiricism
make the method of positivism possible but contain, according to
Mills, highly questionable political assumptions that distort and
repress our knowledge about the nature of society itself.

   In his analysis of the method of inquiry used by sociology, he
turns to the scientific method of the natural sciences. Positivism, as

it is used in quantitative and qualitative research, forms the philosophical justification for the application of scientific method used in sociology, which views the social world as similar to the world investigated by the natural sciences. The application of this method in turn constructs a social reality amenable to the application of the method of the natural sciences, with its reduction to quantifiable, calculable, and mathematical rules and laws that can be used for economic, government, bureaucratic, and academic purposes. Its focus is more on everyday consciousness and social interactions, not on the social relations of production, hierarchy, and class; it isolates and quantifies human experience in terms of personal relationships and psychological experiences, while losing issues of depth psychology, social pathology, and the structures of power. Without the ability to raise these types of questions, sociology turns into a conformist ideology interested in piecemeal reform, scattered analysis, mechanical facts, and thin theory. The method of the natural sciences creates the social world and its basic concepts, ideas, theories, and reality. Method precedes, predefines, and pre-creates its own objectivity, and then studies the social reality it has in effect constructed. "The kinds of problems that will be taken up and the way in which they are formulated are quite severely limited by the scientific method. Methodology, in short, seems to determine the problems…[and] it has been largely drawn, with expedient modification, from one philosophy of natural science."[21]

Mills refers to this aspect of the metaphysics of science as an "arbitrary epistemology," "a methodological inhibition," and the "substantive thinness" of sociological research.[22] Borrowing the methodology of the natural sciences in order to study the complexities and structures of the social reality distorts and simplifies that reality, as it turns social science into a conformist ideology which is incapable of challenging the institutions, structures, and values of modern society. And worst of all, it reduces theory to a simple summary of the empirical data collection process. By this means, access to social reality is through the "scientific method" and the various forms and measurements of sociological analysis.

The second methodological principle of abstract empiricism is pluralism, which emphasizes the importance of particularly narrow, specific, and diffuse areas of specialization and intellectual concentration within sociological research and empirical investigation, leaving unquestioned and unexamined the broader picture and total structure of society. These narrow areas of research are compatible with the focus on the psychological and individual opinions developed in surveys, opinion polls, statistical research and analysis, and quantitative and qualitative research. Much of the focus of sociology has been on public opinion polls, voting behavior, interviews, political consciousness, etc. This approach is characterized by Mills as "psychologism" because "the questions asked in these studies are put in terms of the psychological reaction of individuals," even when the questions are directed at a knowledge of the "institutional structures of society."[23] Mills juxtaposes the different sociological approaches of psychologism and structuralism to emphasize his main point. A weakness of the psychological approach is that "abstract empiricism is not characterized by any substantive propositions or theories. It is not based upon any new concepts of the nature of society or of man or upon any particular facts about them. It is more interested in statistical and technical knowledge."[24] Theory is reduced to a collection of empirical data representing individual reactions to issues of rising consumer costs, crime, suicide, voting preferences, and so on. "Social theory as a whole becomes a systematic collection of such concepts, that is, of variables useful in interpretations of statistical findings."[25] Theory is reduced to statistics-gathering and analysis of results, as well as discovering and measuring common ground and causal relationships in order to uncover the relationship between individual personalities and collective similarities. Theory has lost all its traditional content and substance, as it is reduced to a collection of statistical evidence, causal relationships, and explanatory theories of social and individual behavior. The classical structural insights of alienation, rationalization, anomie, and repression have disappeared. A major weakness of the former approach, based on the natural sciences, is that the key questions surrounding the nature of modern society and its macro social institutions and structures go unrecognized and remain unconnected to the psychological opinions and values of those actually studied in statistical surveys.

This leads to the third principle within the metaphysics of science: the hidden politics of science. Because of its very limited view of science and methods, sociology is unable to develop a comprehensive, integrative, and critical theory of modern society. "It is evident that an empiricism as cautious and rigid as abstracted empiricism eliminates the great social problems and human issues of our times from inquiry."[26] This particular method depoliticizes the social sciences by its method of positivism and pluralism; in the examination of particular issues, it isolates itself from the issues of history and structure of capitalist society as an interrelated and integrated whole. The broad structures, functions, and principles of modern society are lost, and with them, macro social theory itself. These questions, in turn, would require a complex set of new methods, insights, and research tools beyond naturalism—such as those found in historical, hermeneutical, phenomenological, and critical sociology, with their emphases on political economy, human consciousness, and the evolution of modern industrial society. But compared to the natural sciences and even to other social sciences, the theories and methods generated by these branches of sociology are not considered science, because they are not grounded in the metaphysics of science and in the epistemology and methodology of physics and chemistry. In the process, sociology has become a scientific discipline without theory, without reflection, and without critique. By taking these other views of science out of consideration, the discipline has become de-politicized because it is no longer able to reflect upon or question the social system as a whole. The classical questions of social alienation and economic exploitation, bureaucratic rationalization and scientific disenchantment, cultural anomie and personal dérèglement, and psychological rationalization and unconscious repression are methodologically eliminated and theoretically forgotten.

The reduction of science and abstract empiricism to forms of psychology with its focus on individual opinions, statistical surveys, interviews, and participatory observation represses any possibility of understanding the history, structures, and culture of modern capitalism as it eliminates historical sociology, political economy, hermeneutics, and critical social theory, along with their distinctive non-positivist methods, from consideration. By applying the method of natural science; by emphasizing a practice of accumulating scientific information based on psychological beliefs, opinions, and behavior through quantitative and qualitative methods; and by reducing sociology to a very narrow range of methods and theories, Mills argues, American sociology is no longer capable of asking profound and insightful questions about the nature of society. Because it cannot question the ideological foundations of society itself, it has become a form of political propaganda and ideology.[27] By stressing a particular and exclusive method based on the natural sciences, sociology has effectively eliminated theory itself from its consideration. The scientific method defines the parameters and content of social theory. Within the Anglo-American tradition of sociology, method creates theory and, in the process, theory is reduced to a summary of statistical evidence and empirical data based on the psychological orientations of those observed. The scientific method determines, deflects, and ultimately de-politicizes theory by not being able to construct a social theory grounded in structure and history. Thus, by reducing sociology to the method of natural science, it has lost theory, history, and critique. It becomes a conformist defense of liberal society, because it no longer has the theoretical or conceptual framework to challenge the assumptions, values, and institutions of the society it is scientifically studying.

From Mills's perspective, the idea that it is method which creates theory helps explain the disappearance of social theory from the American academy. "By distracting attention from issues of power and authority, they distract attention from the structural realities of the society itself."[28] There is no longer any knowledge of the different traditions, epistemologies, and methodologies that helped create social theory throughout the nineteenth and twentieth centuries in European sociology. Everything has been reduced to the method of the natural sciences. Because of nominalism and objectivity, sociology is no longer an ethical or human science. In this way, methodology and epistemology become a political and ideological issue, since they confine sociology to a limited range of fragmented questions and problems that may be raised within the contours of positivism, which create the very objects and facts of analysis and repress others that do not conform to the universal method of the natural sciences. Method creates the theory, questions, and issues under consideration, which leave aside a whole range of issues that do not conform to its particular positivist methodology, and ends in a "propaganda for conformity."[29] In the end, psychology replaces structure, economy of facts replaces political economy, content analysis replaces hermeneutics, biography replaces history, and personal dissatisfaction and psychological disorientation replace alienation and disenchantment. Mills closes his analysis of abstracted empiricism and positivism with the pessimistic recognition that positivism in the social sciences creates forms of intellectual dehumanization and political ideology.

MAX HORKHEIMER, CRITIQUE OF POSITIVISM, AND THE ECLIPSE OF REASON AND THEORY

Although Max Horkheimer presented his lectures and published his finding in the mid-1940s, a few years before Mills's critique of abstracted empiricism, Horkheimer offered a complete and more systematic picture of the rise of empiricism and positivism from within the critical history of German idealism, existentialism, and classical social theory, which would continue to frame the positivism debate later in the twentieth century. Horkheimer developed the idea that the positivist method of the natural sciences applied

to the social sciences leads not only to the scattered metaphysics of liberalism, but to disenchanted existentialism, the death
of democracy and the public sphere, and ultimately to the terror
of fascism. He begins *The Eclipse of Reason* (1947) with an overview of Max Weber's theory of rationalization and its distinction
between substantive and formal reason.[30] In chapter 2, Weber's
theory of existential phenomenology and science as the domination of nature is examined. This section will focus on his theory of
the rationalization of science and its impact on the social sciences,
the iron cage, and the loss of reflective reason and substantive
social theory.

Weber's theory of rationalization is a structural outline of the
impact of the decline and breakdown of medieval feudalism; the
rise of the nation state; commercial capitalism; large independent
cities with their own military; the Enlightenment; the Industrial
Revolution; and the main organizational, bureaucratic, cultural,
and intellectual trends within the economic, political, and social
institutions of modern capitalist society.[31] The institutional logic
and organizational imperatives of these new institutions are also
reflected in the transformation of the purpose and goals of human
reason, from substantive rationality to the technical science and
formal rationality of the natural sciences. Science is both an
expression and model for social techniques and the rationalization of social life, as its specific form of rationality finds expression
in the logical foundation of Western social institutions, based on
the principles of scientific calculation, theoretical predictions,
technical control, disciplinary specialization, and political and
instrumental mastery of both knowledge and institutions. That
is, the same form of rationality that permeates Enlightenment
rationality permeates all aspects of society, including rational
bookkeeping; capital accounting; mechanization and coordination of production; rational technology; the specialized division of
labor; the modern bureaucratic state; and formal rational law and
legal administration based on hierarchy, abstract legal procedures,
precedent, and rational decision-making. This rationalization of

industry, politics, and the law also precipitates the rationalization of the cultural and social life of rational and systematic consumption, art, music, medicine, and the academy.[32]

As already mentioned in dealing with his essay, "Science as a Vocation" (1917), Weber distinguishes between the traditional view of substantive reason (*Wertrationalität*) and formal reason (*Zweckrationalität*) in order to highlight his understanding of the historical development of Western consciousness and thought, especially as it is distinguished from non-capitalist societies. Substantive rationality is that form of intellectual and theoretical inquiry which focuses on substantive ethical, political, aesthetic, religious, and scientific concepts and issues— from the ancient Greeks to early modern thinkers—and which seeks access to universal knowledge, essence, and truth about the nature of our universe and the objective meaning of human life. In his brief phenomenological survey of the Western mind and the evolution of human consciousness, Weber summarizes the essential and universal search for substantive reason from Platonic philosophy to modern physics and biology: (1) the nature of Platonic and Socratic philosophy of science, politics, and art searching for the form and reality of the concept, true being, essential reality, the good life and justice, and aesthetic beauty; (2) the importance of Leonardo da Vinci and Renaissance art and his concern with art and beauty in the fifteenth and sixteenth centuries; (3) the early science of Roger Bacon and Galileo Galilei with their experimentation and search for the truth of science, nature and the universe in the sixteenth and seventeenth centuries; and, finally, (4) with Jan Swammerdam's search for theology and God through biology and the anatomy of a louse in the sixteenth and seventeenth centuries. Throughout this historical period, reason was used in philosophy, politics, art, early science, and theology, searching for objective truth and the essence of reality and being in numerous fields of study. However, Weber stresses that this ended in the eighteenth and nineteenth centuries with the rise of the Enlightenment and the coming of formal reason, liberalism, individualism, and utilitarianism.[33]

With the Enlightenment there arose a search for a new kind of knowledge based on the formal and technical rationality of the natural sciences, whose goal was also distinct from the search for absolute and essential truths of substantive reason. This new form of rationality and its relation to the social and physical environment focuses on the technical and instrumental control over nature and society. Weber writes that the only goal of the natural sciences is to master life technically by means of scientific technology, theoretical calculation, and measurable prediction.[34] It is incapable of finding meaning, purpose, or the essence of reality. The search for knowledge and truth no longer rests in the areas of philosophy, politics, art, and theology, but in the study of the immediate physical environment, using the method of domination and control over nature for practical utility, utilitarian happiness, and material wellbeing and pleasure. The traditional search for the ends or being of reality in truth, beauty, justice, the good, and God are viewed as irrelevant and unknowable to formal reason and modern science. "Natural science gives us an answer to the question of what we must do if we wish to master life technically. It leaves quite aside, or assumes for its purposes, whether we should and do wish to master life technically and whether it ultimately makes sense to do so."[35] We can only know the practical tools and technical means of accomplishing particular ends, but never the truth of the ends themselves. At this point in his analysis, Weber quotes a powerful line from Leo Tolstoy: "Science is meaningless because it gives no answer to our questions, the only question important for us: 'What shall we do and how shall we live?'"[36]

The world of the Enlightenment is an existential void and spiritual desert. In Friedrich Nietzsche's *Thus Spoke Zarathustra* (1883), Zarathustra enters into this void to voice his concerns about the apparent meaninglessness of the world to the local town citizens after twenty years of monastic life searching for the truth. His conclusion is that "one must still have chaos in oneself to be able to give birth to a dancing star."[37] But the enlightened townspeople no longer understand or care about the meaning of life or substantive concepts, such as "love," "creation," "longing," and "star," which have long since disappeared with the ancient and medieval traditions, as they "go voluntarily into a madhouse" searching for herd conformity and utilitarian happiness. According to Nietzsche, this is the time of the most despicable man, "the last man who invented happiness," who has lost all substantive reasoning and spiritual hopes. This last man lives isolated and imprisoned in an iron cage of disenchantment, because all the ultimate values, ideals, and meaning found in classical and traditional societies have been replaced by the necessity to calculate and master life for material happiness. In this lonely and rationalized society, there is no longer any mystery or intellectual concepts or discussions about the meaning of human life; there are only an existential emptiness and loss of ethical, political, and theological concepts. Humanity can no longer reason, reflect, or critically evaluate the course of human existence or the purpose of human life. There is only a profound and pervasive nothingness in the air expressed in the systematic and progressive manipulation of nature and the increasing degradation of humanity through formal reason and natural science.

With its emphasis on the natural sciences, the Enlightenment has created a view of humanity without imagination, vision, or hope for a better life of beauty, wisdom, understanding, and justice. Science can master this universe, but cannot truly know it or cultivate its ideas or its better angels. The iron cage of bureaucracy imprisons the human soul and spirit as it lives a mechanical and meaningless life of liberal pleasures and temporary distractions. And it is an iron cage that is a product of its own enlightenment. What is left, Weber writes, is a "mechanical petrification" led by "specialists without spirit, sensualists without heart; this nullity imagines that it has attained a level of civilization never before achieved."[38] The specialists without the objective and absolute spirit are the scientists, technicians, and bureaucrats, whose formal and technical skills have replaced both substantive reason and objective social institutions based on a moral community and the ideals of justice, while the sensualists and utilitarians without heart are the liberals and economists who lack virtue, passion, moral sentiment, and wisdom. The iron cage of rationalization, positivism, and disenchantment without reason or virtue is a market economy and bureaucratic society, which have lost the ability to reflect upon the basic concepts of beauty, truth, freedom, community, and justice. It is an empty, lonely world of technicians, machines, industry, and bureaucracies. At the same time that he rejects rationalization and disenchantment, Weber in his essay "'Objectivity' in Social Science and Social Policy" (1904) is adamant about ensuring that politics, ideologies, and values do not enter the academic classroom in the form of the projected and distorted values of the teacher as a prophet or demagogue. "It is said, and I agree, that politics is out of place in the lecture room" because the "prophet and demagogue do not belong on the academic platform."[39] He is aware of the dangers of abusing and exploiting the stature, prejudice, and power of the academic platform and the authority of the professors to enforce political ideologies; students in this situation are unable to resist because of their precarious and vulnerable positions.

At first, it appears that Weber is calling for academic objectivity and neutrality, as he rejects all forms of political imposition and ideology. However, upon a closer evaluation, he seems to be rejecting not substantive or political reason, but the hidden shadows and unconscious values of positivism and formal science. That is, he appears to be rejecting the values of the scientific prophets of technical calculation and experimental prediction and the authoritarian and rhetorical power of the demagogic preacher behind the natural sciences, which produce a metaphysics and a vocation of science because: (1) their method is valid for the purpose of the technical mastery and domination of the world, without any relevance or relationship to questions of the meaning of human life; (2) their method is a form of technical or formal reason, characterized by mathematical and quantitative experimentation, measurability, calculation, and prediction; (3) the world is a mechanical and non-living machine whose every movement can be methodologically calibrated and structurally predefined; (4) it is a universal method, because it is the only scientifically appropriate method for the study of nature and society; (5) science is meaningless, but not valueless; it is disenchanted, but not without values, because of its main directive of universalism, utilitarianism, control and mastery over nature and humanity, and nominalism or the scientific elimination of distorting values, concepts, and substantive reason; (6) science can offer us no course of action, sense of purpose, sense of the direction or meaning in the world, or reflective criticism of its own method and actions or of the social world from which it comes; and, finally, (7) the logic and method of science and the technical laws of the universe are valid and worth knowing, as are the historical and cultural sciences, but they cannot answer the substantive and existential question of why they are worth knowing. This is the present situation of the iron cage, wherein stands a lonely and isolated "last man" who is the prophet and demagogue of this lost and unreflective world without reason, ideas, and theory. Toward the end of the essay, Weber compares the university professor who sells his knowledge and methods to that of a greengrocer in a food store selling cabbage to the local townspeople. The university professor is acting as a prophet and demagogue while selling his valuable tools, training, and mechanical techniques for university position, power, and money.[40] The last man is, in fact, the university professor without substantive reason and a purposeful goal in life, who teaches formal reason and the scientific mastery of nature.

While Weber's theory of rationalization focused on Enlightenment rationality, the natural and technical sciences, and moral and political disenchantment, Horkheimer now applies the concept of rationalization to the study and methods of the social sciences, and sociology in particular. Mills stressed the loss of substantive social theory; structure and history; the reduction of sociology to psychologism, statistical behavior, and quantitative methods; and the overriding concern with technical science and formal methods in the application of positivism and empiricism in contemporary sociology. Horkheimer instead focuses on the subjective rationality of science and its eclipse of substantive reason, its contempt for theory, and its inability to recognize the decline of democracy or the rise of fascism in American society. He adjusts and expands Weber's distinction between substantive and formal reason by redefining that crucial distinction with the new vocabulary of objective and subjective rationality, in order to emphasize the impact that rationalization and the method and logic of the natural sciences have on the social sciences.[41] To do so, Horkheimer outlines the history of objective reason starting from the ancient philosophy of Plato and Aristotle and continuing with the medieval scholasticism of Augustine and Aquinas; the French philosophy of Montaigne, Bodin, and l'Hospital in the sixteenth century; the natural rights theory of Locke and Rousseau; the rationalism of Spinoza; and the German idealism of Kant, Hegel, and Fichte. As with Weber, this summary provides a broad outline of the possibilities of the theories and concepts of objective reason in Western thought, now undermined and repressed by the rise of subjective reason in liberalism, positivism, nominalism, naturalism, and fascism.

Horkheimer begins his analysis of subjective or technical reason by stating that this form of limited reason is only interested in the statistical calculation, mathematical probabilities and classification, logical inference, and explanatory deduction of operational categories for the purposes of specific subjective or individual goals and self-preservation and the technical means of achieving these advantages. At the same time, objective reason revolves around the universal standards for individual moral and social action—the ethics and virtue of individuals and the objective social and cultural institutions within society. The goals of subjective reason are technical mastery and the coordination and primacy of means over ends, whereas the goals of objective reason are ethics and justice. "The theory of objective reason did not focus on the coordination of behavior and aim, but on concepts . . . on the idea of the greatest good, on the problem of human destiny, and on the way of realization of ultimate goals."[42] It searched for the ultimate social and political ends of human life in the principles of objective truth, structure of being, and natural law, and in the objective institutions within which these values could be realized in the political, economic, and cultural life of the community. This is a restatement of Aristotle's integration of ethics and politics, of moral philosophy and social institutions. But with the rise of formal reason during the Enlightenment, reason itself has been reduced to the coordination of conflicting individual, normative, and calculable interests in the form of market justice. There are no longer higher standards or concepts for the evaluation of human behavior than the existential nihilism and economic tyranny of market pluralism, material self-interest, and technical irrationality. However, from the Renaissance to the Enlightenment, the rationalist theory of humanity in European philosophy still believed in the "light of reason," and held to the doctrine "revealing the content of reason as reflecting the true nature of things and the correct pattern of living" and was capable of "harmonizing human life with nature both in the external world and within man's own being."[43]

This search for true being and true meaning in theology and philosophy ended with the rise of subjective reason during and after the Enlightenment, with its emphasis on nominalism (Berkeley), empiricism (Hume), relativism and nihilism (Nietzsche), and the perspectivism of knowledge (Weber). Horkheimer, in turn, connected these intellectual and philosophical turns of the rise of science, neutrality, false objectivity, and pragmatism, and the rise of existentialism and moral nihilism with the political transformations that were occurring in Europe, including liberalism, tolerance, and democracy. These changes resulted in the loss of concepts, meaning, and reason—loss of social justice—in a devolving world of science, liberalism, and fascism. In the process, substantive reason was displaced and repressed in the social unconscious of the iron cage. The decline in objective reason starts with the split between philosophy and theology as the basis for the search for objective truth and reality. According to Horkheimer, a dramatic change to the classical and scholastic worlds occurred with the rise of Calvinism and the British Enlightenment. With the rise of Calvinism and its doctrine of *Deus absconditus*, which argued for the absolute distance, remoteness, and indifference of God to the meaningless world he created—coupled with the Protestant variation of the Pauline Indifference, which accepted unquestioningly the material world as it is—the traditional foundations of the search for objectivity in ethics and politics in ancient classical humanism and medieval scholasticism began to falter.

There was no longer the stronger desire to search for the speculative, metaphysical, and theological essence or being of the world. The world as a place of sin and moral transgressions required a strong ascetic life to control passions and desires, as well as thoughts and philosophies that called the world into question. Adjustment, control, and asceticism were the necessary and required responses to a world without inherent or divine meaning. The traditional power of Catholicism, religion, and metaphysics was neutralized, and the foundations of scientific and moral knowledge were reduced to the empirical world. The search for objective truth and reality was called into question, since transcendent knowledge was perceived as a metaphysical superstition and cultural mythology. From this faltering of traditional scholasticism, Horkheimer argues, came the rise of science, empiricism, nominalism, and positivism in the British Enlightenment, as a further indication of the decline of the traditional view of substantive reason. Empiricism reduced all knowledge to the empirically given world of objective perception and rejected all knowledge based on universal concepts, principles, and ideas as the essence of truth and reality. The Calvinist rejected the world as having any inherent meaning or purpose which must be controlled by an ascetic calling in the workplace, whereas empiricism rejected any knowledge that was not based on the empirically given world of immediate experience. The traditional search for truth in metaphysics and theology, ontology and philosophy, or ethics and politics was rejected as false because there were no real universal truths. Knowledge and reality were being reduced to the empirical world of immediate experience. As knowledge and science were changing, so too was the political universe. The belief in the universal truth of natural law, natural rights, and democracy was being undermined by the tolerance of pluralistic and competing political interests, which resulted for Horkheimer in a dangerous neutrality, relativism, and passivity. It also produced the need for social control and stability to mediate self-interests and competing political goals. Horkheimer writes that "this explains the tendency of liberalism to tilt over into fascism and of the intellectual and political representatives of liberalism to make their peace with its opposites."[44] Just as in epistemology and science, the universal ideals of politics in liberalism and democracy are lost in the historical moment of scientific rationality of data collection, coordination, and theory construction and the market rationality of conflicting self-interests. In both cases of knowledge and politics, the search for the universal concepts and ideals in scientific and political truth is lost.

Horkheimer does not stop here, but then takes a darker turn— and, unfortunately, a historically and sociologically accurate one. Concepts, ideas, and theories no longer have any transcending ethical and social value, since they are simply the results of factual data collection and summaries of empirical surveys and experimental studies. "Concepts have become 'streamlined,' rationalized, labor-saving devices. It is as if thinking itself had been reduced to the level of industrial processes . . . in short, made part and parcel of production."[45] The academy and its social science disciplines are been integrated into the capitalist economy: economics has become the academic study of efficiency and productivity; political science is the study of stability and order; and sociology has become the examination of functional equilibrium. The logic of formal and subjective reason, described as the mechanization and mathematization of reason, represents the application of the logic and method of industrial production within advanced capitalism into new areas of society—academic production, cultural production, political technology, etc. Even when these disciplines occasionally break from their assigned roles of conformity and ideology and begin to challenge the assumptions and institutions of the social system, they lack the concepts, methods, and theories that could provide the framework for a truly critical perspective. Theory and justice have been displaced, repressed, and replaced by utility, material happiness, and cultural ideology.

Mills stressed in his writings the political and ideological conformity implicit in positivist sociology and the broader liberal arts tradition in the United States because of its inability to critically question society in terms of its power structure and historical evolution. Horkheimer turns to the darker side of Weber's theory of rationalization, and the epistemological, methodological, and political implications of the rise of positivism and the silence of reason in the social sciences. Horkheimer's description of the results of these Enlightenment transformations is mind-numbing and intellectually shattering. "Reason has liquidated itself as an agency of ethical, moral, and religious insight," beginning with the empiricist writings of Bishop Berkeley.[46] The overt reference in this sentence goes back to the beginning of the British Enlightenment and the foundations of positivism in the empiricism of Locke, Berkeley, and Hume. With its emphasis on the concrete empirical world, it suppressed the desire and need to develop metaphysical, philosophical, and theoretical concepts which could raise questions about the meaning of life, happiness, the good, and justice. More important than the immediate loss of concepts and reason is the meaning of the term "liquidate," which in the context of this work seems to refer to the Holocaust and the systematic and horrifying liquidation of the Jewish people throughout Europe during the Second World War. First, the Nazis ban and burn books, concepts, and ideas, and then exterminate human beings in the gas chambers of the concentration camps throughout Europe. The liquidation of substantive reason and social theory preceded the extermination of human beings; the end of reason and theory leads to the rise of fascism, since there are no thoughts of resistance and no ideas about social alternatives upon which to base them. The holocaust of the mind precedes the holocaust of the body.

The Eclipse of Reason was originally a series of lectures presented at Columbia University in 1944. Horkheimer's presentations are important not only for their substantive arguments, but also for their historical timing, just before the invasion of Normandy in northern France. He fears that at this key historical moment, the American academy of liberal arts has been transformed into a defense of the given institutions and values of liberalism, resulting in an unfortunate and unavoidable continuation of classical disenchantment, moral nihilism, alienation, and the eclipse of reason, logic, and science. Without these critical traditions, ideas, and concepts, and without our moral, ethical, social, and political values, reason is silenced, thought is lost, and reflection remains mechanically and causally reflexive in the measurement and calculations of the empirical world. Horkheimer has insightfully proposed that the rise of positivism and the displacement of the humanities has removed any opening for rational dialogue and debate in the academy and the public sphere, since the ideas and traditions that would support that creative and self-defining activity are no longer available. Heinrich Heine presciently wrote in 1820–21: "Dort, wo man Bücher verbrennt, verbrennt man am Ende auch Menschen"; "where they burn books, they will also ultimately burn people." This is true today, even when the idea of "burning of books" is replaced by the repression of books and a "woke" culture and academy—a more subtle, easier, and metatheoretical way of eliminating inconvenient and substantive ideas, which are then forgotten and transformed by an eclipse of reason and an exile of thoughts, theories, and traditions from consciousness. With the loss of these principles and ideals, we lose our heart, spirit, and intellect, along with our ability to recognize the instrumental and technical world of the last man and to change history and society for the better. This liquidation of reason has produced both the iron cage and the holocaust of the mind and the body; and today it has produced a proclivity in the United States toward the end of democracy and the rise of fascism. In the end, silence is an ethical and political betrayal of humanity, our inherent dignity, our ultimate purpose and meaning in life, and, finally, our dreams and future. There is only existential nothingness and the end of our hopes for true enlightenment, justice, and democracy, as we descend deeper and deeper into the morass and confusion of authoritarianism and plutocracy.

Sociology must begin to redefine itself and recover its creative imagination, lost intellectual traditions, and future possibilities. This includes reconstructing classical and scholastic natural law, Enlightenment natural law and natural rights, neo-Kantian and neo-Hegelian classical social theory, critical theory, interpretive social theory, dialectical and immanent critique, ethnological anthropology, phenomenology, ethnomethodology, existentialism, hermeneutics, history, critical epistemology and pragmatism, ethnology, social psychology, and more recently to recover intersectional social theory, queer theory, and feminist theory.

After these introductory remarks about the decline of Western reason, Horkheimer turns to an analysis of democracy, tolerance, and fascism. He does so to highlight and stress his thesis that positivism leads to methodological and theoretical problems in sociology; but more importantly, that it leads to serious political, economic, and structural problems, since reason based on the principles of natural reason and natural law is no longer capable of being a guide in the search for ethical and political meaning in human life. As reason loses its moorings and ancient traditions in the concepts of reason, objective truth, ethics, and politics, it easily adjusts to its new functional role in aiding tyranny and political oppression. Thus, Horkheimer begins with the philosophy of positivism in the social sciences, and then connects this to the politics of positivism and the confrontation between liberalism and Nazism. Without spirit and heart, without reason and virtue, and without community and social ideals, the last man, who created the technical rationality and liberal unhappiness of the iron cage, is slowly transformed into the last technician of the barbed wire cage surrounding the concentration camps and our minds. This is the iron cage, redesigned and recalibrated for the extermination of humanity. There is no one to resist because the concepts and ideas capable of substantive reflection, evaluation, and critique have been replaced by a technological and formal reason of explanation, measurement, and calculation. The mechanized technicians know the mathematical rules, theoretical projections, anticipated technical problems, and statistical results, but cannot answer the one question of importance: what are they doing and why are they doing it? They are simply concerned with train and time schedules, numbers of incoming prisoners, organizational supplies, movement within the camp, and the mathematical calculation of the flow of numbers in and out of the crematorium.[47]

And this terror occurs because of the "eclipse of reason" and the inability of society to sustain reflective wisdom and social virtue within a true moral community and working democracy, which have been historically supplanted and suppressed in science by positivism and nominalism, and in politics by public tolerance, democratic pluralism, and moral relativism. Horkheimer summarizes this process of technical rationalization and theoretical alienation as he reintegrates Weber, Marx, and Freud when he writes: "What are the consequences of this formalization of reason? Justice, equality, happiness, tolerance, all the concepts that, as mentioned, were in preceding centuries supposed to be inherent in or sanctioned by reason, have lost their intellectual roots."[48] Today the iron cage and the barbed wire fences are no longer necessary, since the scientific imperatives for the domination of humanity and nature are repressed and carried within us in our everyday unconscious memory. We no longer are able to see the cage of the last man or the last technician, because the cage lies buried deep within our own spirit and hearts which are no longer able to see or feel, to judge or evaluate, or to think or reason. Social theory in the American academy has been rationalized and repressed, and with it, so too, has ethical reason. All aspects of the cultural reality—including truth, politics, religion, and justice—have been turned into fetishized objects to be bought and sold in the market-place of ideas like the greengrocer's commodities.[49] All we can do is measure, experiment, calculate, and plan. Today, we can create enormous technological wonders and send these machines voyaging to the far reaches of another interstellar galaxy, but, as Weber pondered, we cannot ask the question: Why and for what purpose?

Objective reason cannot be sustained in a capitalist society, where everything is reduced to formal reason and technical facts. Even the quest for truth within philosophy is transformed from the search for truth into the clarification of the scientific method. "The positivists reduce science to the procedures employed in physics and its branches; they deny the name of science to all theoretical efforts not in accord with what they abstract from physics as its legitimate methods."[50] The search for truth has been reduced to the search for methods, using physics as its objective, formal model. The older tradition of objective reason is now viewed as speculative metaphysics or cultural ideology. However, when asked for the justification of natural science itself, the usual response of the positivists is that the verification itself is based on the application of the scientific method. Method justifies science. Horkheimer recognizes the circular reasoning in this response and writes: "But their eyes are closed." Ironically, this is very close to the response that Zarathustra remembers when he revealed the most despicable last man in the marketplace, who asked: What is love, what is a star? Not knowing how to respond to his own question, he simply blinked. When questions were raised by the listeners in the town square regarding equality, knowledge, pleasure, and happiness, they all blinked.[51] These are the last men who, furthering the Nietzsche reference, worship the scientific method as a form of decadent idolatry. The truth of science lies in its formal reason of experimental success, practical utility, instrumental logic, and quantitative methods—the logic and methods of natural science—but not in a search for objective reason or existential, political, or structural meaning. The scientific facts "ascertained by quantitative methods, which the positivists are inclined to regard as the only scientific ones, are often surface phenomena that obscure rather than disclose the underlying reality."[52]

Horkheimer argues that social theory becomes just another form of speculative metaphysics, because it lies outside of the method-ological and epistemological parameters of physics and science, while a theory grounded in positivism reflects objective reality and its functional organization within the existing social system. There are no longer legitimate concepts, ideas, and theories which could possibly question the legitimacy of this social system using the technical methods of the natural sciences. Horkheimer argues that positivists and technicians have only contempt for the use-lessness of social theory. Social theory and its analysis of the deep structures of society are contemptuous and frivolous. Moving beyond Nietzsche, Horkheimer appears to make another classical reference, returning to the New Testament, when he writes that with the abandonment of objective reason and classical philoso-phy, "positivism hands science over to the hazards of historical development."[53] The phrase "hands over" is used in Matthew 26 to describe how Jesus was betrayed and "handed over" by the trai-tor Judas in the Garden of Gethsemane to the police force of the Sanhedrin and then eventually to the Roman governor Pontius Pilate, and ultimately to his death. Horkheimer seems to be making the analogy as a means of dramatically stressing the idea that posi-tivism is guilty of the contempt and betrayal of human reason, as it has "handed over" substantive reason to the local townspeople. Positivism itself is a traitor to the search for truth that will lead to death—but not just to the death of one Jewish person, as in the biblical story, but to the death of millions of Jews in the Holocaust.

KARL POPPER, CRITICAL RATIONALISM, AND THE CRITIQUE OF EMPIRICISM IN NATURAL SCIENCE

Karl Popper wrote his famous work *The Logic of Scientific Discovery* (German original: 1934) that appeared in English in the late 1950s in which he developed his theory of critical rationalism as a response to the epistemology and philosophy of science of empiricism and its general principles of scientific induction, reliance on sense experience, and the requirement for empirical verification. Popper begins with a restatement of Hume's self-criticism and skepticism of an empiricism grounded in experience and inductive reasoning. The epistemology of empiricism argues that knowledge is based on the systematic accumulation of sense experience and observable facts through induction; while rationalism contends that knowledge is grounded in reason, hypotheses, experiments, and the formal application of the scientific method through deduction. Following Hume's skepticism, Popper reaffirms the notion that experience alone cannot justify or validate the correctness of a particular theory.

Popper begins with an analysis of the method or logic of empirical science with a restatement and reconsideration of Hume's dilemma that the inductive method requires the principle of induction as the basis for its own justification, resulting in a problem of circular reasoning: to validate induction, one needs to apply induction. This means that as one begins with a singular statement, based on observation that a particular swan is white, it is necessary to use induction to arrive at a universal theory or hypothesis that "all swans are white." Popper argues that to make a universal statement or law from a particular observation is problematic, however, because "no matter how numerous" the observations, the conclusion is not logically justified. There may still be non-white swans; the conclusion itself is based on induction. This is "the problem of induction" as one moves from singular to universal statements, from experience to universal hypotheses and laws. The logical difficulty of this approach is that the justification of induction or moving from particulars to universals lies in the logical fact that this very method requires the acceptance of the validity of inductive reason. The justification of the use of induction in the process of establishing the validity of universal laws or hypotheses from singular statements is based on the principle of moving from observation and experience to hypotheses and laws using inductive inferences. That which is to be proven is used in the very process of validation. For Popper, this logical inconsistency makes empiricism and induction problematic. "To justify it we should have to employ inductive inferences; and to justify these we should have to assume an inductive principle of a higher order; and so on. Thus the attempt to base the principle of induction on experience breaks down, since it must lead to an infinite regress."[54] Perhaps even more interesting than undermining the logic of induction as the basis for scientific inquiry is the idea that hypotheses are theories. That is, theory is uniquely and logically tied to the scientific method and hypothesis creation. This will later have profound implications, when this scientific method and "logic of knowledge" approach is applied to the social sciences during the famous positivism debate in Germany.

This critique of empiricism was simply a tool for the introduction to Popper's theory of critical rationalism and his analysis of the method of natural science based on the procedures of contemporary physics. From this perspective he outlines the appropriate method based on predictions, deduction from theory, experimental testing, and "verification" of the experiment. Popper states that in the end theories are accepted through some form of conventionalism and rational agreement about the rules of the logic (deductive reasoning) and the method (explanatory causality) in modern science. Science thus begins with (1) an accepted universal law or scientific hypothesis about the physical reality; (2) singular statements or initial conditions about an event that form the basis for an experiment; (3) joining the universal law to the singular conditions or physical event; and, finally, (4) predictions that are deduced from theory and, thereby, testable, or the deduction of an occurrence causally predicted by the law in relation to the initial conditions to form a singular prediction. To clarify his main points, Popper offers the simple example of the tensile strength of a piece of thread. The scientific method begins with (1) the universal statement, law, or hypothesis of the tensile strength of a piece of thread, which when overloaded with heavy weights will break; (2) the limit of holding or lifting the weight of a particular thread is one pound; (3) the object being lifted on the thread is two pounds; and (4) the conclusion is that thread will not be able to hold the weight and will ultimately break. Causality is defined by the universal law or theory, the initial conditions, the singular prediction, and, finally, the explanation and confirmation of the results.[55] Popper is aware of the a priori technological, predictive, and explanatory interests in his definition of the logic of scientific discovery.

Popper concludes his analysis with the recognition that it is the scientific method based on causality, experimentation, testing, and prediction that defines the provisional and utilitarian validity of a scientific theory. Although the "principle of causality" guides his explanation of events, he refuses for logical reasons to turn it into a metaphysical or universal principle. It is, however, an important element in his explanation of the scientific method. "It is a simple rule that we are not to abandon the search for universal laws and for a coherent theoretical system, nor ever give up our attempts to explain causally any kind of event we can describe. This rule guides the scientific investigator in his work."[56] All objects and events in the natural world can be explained using the method and universal laws of natural science, thereby reducing philosophy and epistemology to a theory of science and method. Popper proposes reducing empirical science to the study of its logical method, rules, and technical procedures. He rejects the empiricist/positivist view, since he considers it a pseudo-problem and methodological dogma, which refuses to look beyond questions of method to engage in issues of the actual origins, historical development, and its underlying philosophical and epistemological theories of knowledge. The focus of positivism is on the behavior of scientists, naturalism, experience, and the inductive and empirical method. Positivism remains uncritical and dogmatic because it views science as reflective of objective reality and truth rather than an expression of scientific, theoretical, and inter-subjectively testable conventions. The empirical method is the technical procedures and logical rules, but not the reflections of absolute reality. As we move from universal laws, singular statements, and deduction to particular predictions, the scientist is following a conventional or logical method of scientific analysis that is analogous to the conventional rules of the game and the logic of chess. Popper rejects the focus of empiricism on immediate experience, while he concentrates on the broader issues of theories of knowledge, method, and science. His major concern is for the technical utility and application of the theory for temporary explanations and predictions; he is less concerned with the truth claims of the scientific inquiry itself. It is the logic of science, technically and formally imposed on the experimental object, that ultimately defines the truth of science and the accumulated experience of this method over time, and that produces the applicable universal law or theory.[57]

Popper's theory of critical rationalism and scientific discovery also rejects some central epistemological elements and traditional principles of positivism as he replaces realism, foundationalism, empiricism, psychologism, and empirical verification with critical rationalism, conventionalism, social consensus, and methodological falsification. Even with these changes, his overall theory of knowledge and science remains firmly embedded within the positivist tradition, with its emphasis on technical and formal reason and its reduction of theory to method and empirical science to the logic and method of physics. Empirical science is "intended to represent only *one* world: the 'real world' or the 'world of our experience.'"[58] Popper calls this the criterion of demarcation that distinguishes between an objective real world and the metaphysical universe of speculative thought. Empirical science is based on the logic or theory of reflection upon the method or procedure of scientific discovery, using experience, deduction, causation, and explanation. He revisits the issue of experience and induction again from the first few pages of chapter 1, restating the logical fallacy that the truth or falsity of a statement is decided by experience alone and thus can never be the absolute basis for truth claims. Theories are not experientially or inductively verifiable, because the possibility always exists that the opposite could be true. Thus he turns to the method of natural science, in which the truth of a statement or theory is its ability to be falsified. He replaces the method of verification with the method of the falsification and provisional acceptance. "But I shall certainly admit a system as empirical or scientific only if it is capable of being *tested* by experience. These considerations suggest that not the verifiability but the falsifiability of a system is taken as a criterion of demarcation."[59] Experience cannot be used to verify logically the truth or falsity of scientific statements or universal laws, but only to provisionally validate them as not having been falsified or refuted as untrue. Experience is thus the basis for the falsification and not the verification of science, since universal laws "are never derivable from singular statements, but can be contradicted by singular statements. Consequently, it is possible by means of purely deductive inference . . . to argue from the truth of singular statements to the falsity of universal statements."[60] According to Popper, this is the only legitimate basis for scientific statements. At this point in his analysis of the method of science, Popper rejects an argument later used by Thomas Kuhn and Willard Quine, that deductive statements can never be falsified because science is always able to create *ad hoc* arguments capable of avoiding falsification. Popper rejects this as an inappropriate behavior by scientists. Popper believes he has solved "Hume's problem of induction" since universal laws cannot be validated by the method of induction and experience alone.

Perhaps Popper's most interesting and most revealing claim is that "the act of conceiving or inventing a theory seems to me neither to call for logical analysis nor to be susceptible to it . . . it may be of great interest to empirical psychology; but it is irrelevant to the logical analysis of scientific knowledge."[61] This is certainly an important statement for his analysis of the discovery of natural science, but of even greater importance to the development or lack of development of a social theory. According to Popper, theory is irrelevant if it is not testable and justifiable. Through his work, he seems to equate theory with method. The intellectual origins, rational reconstruction, and intuitive inspiration of a theoretical discovery in experience as "the sole source of knowledge" involve issues of psychologism, perceptual experience, and sensationalism and are therefore not relevant to the questions of the logic, method, and validation of a statement using the scientific method. This theory of knowledge contends that science is simply the systematic and organized collection of perceptual knowledge.[62] Only the conclusions or predictions that can be tested by means of logical deduction are testable, have technological applicability, or have any scientific justification or falsifiability. Besides rejecting empiricism and positivism as a legitimate philosophy of science, Popper also rejects the conventionalism of Henri Poincaré and Pierre Duhem, who argue that hypotheses cannot be refuted by experiments, because science does not study the laws of nature, but the laws of the human mind. Popper summarizes this Kantian epistemology and critique of pure reason by saying "that it is our own intellect which imposes its laws upon nature."[63] The product of scientific inquiry from this neo-Kantian interpretation is that the laws of nature defined by physics are therefore "inventions, arbitrary decisions, conventions, and logical constructions." There is no relation between methodology and ontology. Although they contend that theoretical systems are not verifiable, they are also at the same time not falsifiable. The implication of the conventionalist perspective is that science investigates the constructs of the human mind, not the properties of nature itself, and thus these constructs "are not falsifiable by observation." Popper rejects this form of conventionalism because it is not empirically falsifiable, due to its creative ability to always find ad hoc or auxiliary hypotheses and justifications for its own laws and theories to help explain away any apparent inconsistencies or irregularities.[64] Perceptual experience is the foundation of empiricism, as science organizes these perceptions into a coherent confirmation of the initial theoretical framework based on the accumulation of empirical facts. Theories are based

on universal laws that, like "water" and "glass," cannot be empirically confirmed and justified.

Popper is also critical of the logical positivist view of science,
which begins with an initial theoretical problem or protocol sentence based on conventions that can only be tested against other
statements or sentences. These initial protocol sentences are viewed
by the logical positivists as similar to the given facts of immediate
phenomena of experience. Quoting Rudolf Carnap of the Vienna
Circle, Popper says that they are "the simplest known facts." This
is just another form of psychologism and classical positivism,
translated into the logical language of formal speech, since protocol sentences are linguistic records of "immediate observation, or
perceptions."[65] These sentences, although based on experience, can
only be confirmed by a logical comparison to other sentences and
statements. In the end, the central question reemerges: How do we
establish the truth of any scientific statement, or more accurately,
how do we establish the truth of any scientific statement through
formal testing using deductive reasoning, since this is the only
valid and objective scientific approach? In the end, the two forms
of positivism are relatively equal as theories of knowledge. Instead,
Popper argues that science begins with a theoretical problem that
is reached by a general agreement among scientists that then leads
to experimentation, prediction, and provisional validation. In the
end, it is utility that provides a clear indicator as to the validity of
scientific statements. Throughout Popper's writings, the logic of
deduction and the technical rules of the method end with a confirmation based not on ontology and experience, but utility and
technical practicality.[66]

The Positivism Dispute between Critical Theory and Critical Rationalism in German Sociology

In 1961, a series of symposiums were held at the German
Sociological Association in Tübingen, West Germany. Popper
began a methodological dispute with members of the Frankfurt

School over the nature of natural science and its relationship to the method of the social sciences. At the conference, he and Adorno gave lectures on the theme of the logic of the social sciences. Two years later, Habermas initiated a critical response to Popper which, in turn, received an equally important response from Hans Albert.[67] The debate continued for a number of years and resulted in the publication in 1969 of the famous work *Die Positivismusstreit in der Deutschen Soziologie*. This debate allowed Popper to expand his theory of the logic of scientific discovery in natural science to its relevancy and application to the logic and methods of the social sciences. At the conference, the epistemological and philosophical clash between critical theory and its view of dialectical science and critical rationalism and its neo-positivist science was firmly established. Very interesting now is the transformation and adjustments of Popper's logic of discovery, and its relevance for the social sciences and sociology in particular.

Popper's presentation on "The Logic of the Social Sciences" was the first contribution to the conference, followed by critical responses by Adorno and Habermas. Both Popper and Adorno begin their analyses with dialectical reasoning. Popper emphasizes the Socratic dialectic between knowledge and ignorance, while Adorno stresses the dialectic between concept and reality. This is probably as close as they would ever get to an agreement on the path of sociological research. Popper begins his general critique of empiricism with the argument that science does not start from observation or perception, but from a problem with the accepted knowledge of the social reality, or "from the discovery of an inner contradiction between our supposed knowledge and the supposed facts."[68] These problems eventually lead to problems in social theory. Thus, science begins with an observation and problem that is translated into a problem within our accepted knowledge or theory about the social world. He summarizes succinctly his position in the sentence stating that sociology as a science begins "with an observation which creates a problem."[69] The method of the social sciences, closely paralleling the critical rationalism of the natural sciences, begins with a particular problem, as attempted solutions or conjectures are proposed and publicly considered within the scientific community to support or refute the solution offered. Public criticism is the only means of scientifically testing and validating a tentative solution to the problem raised. "The so-called objectivity of sciences lies in the objectivity of the method," Popper states. "This means, above all, that no theory is beyond attack or criticism."[70]

Popper's emphasis is on the nature of objectivity as a product of the particular scientific method, not the personal objectivity of the scientists themselves. This form of objectivity of critical rationalism rests on a method and tradition of mutual criticism, cooperation, tolerance, and competition in a free society. This sentence is central to his theory of the logic and methods of the social sciences, and is the basis for the key critical responses by both Adorno and Habermas in their public presentations. There are four main issues deeply embedded in the sentences and following material, each of which calls for an interesting and provocative response by the critical theorists: (1) the foundation of sociology and the other social sciences lies in naturalism or the deductive logic and method of the natural sciences; (2) the nature of objectivity is narrowed to include both method and science, but fails to consider the social objectivity and history of social reality, which will eventually call the very notion of objectivity itself into question or undermine it entirely; (3) the method begins with an accepted theory and social problem, but there is no discussion of where and how the theory originates, i.e., no discussion of the method, logic, and actual origins of the social theory, which is the foundation stone of Popper's whole analysis of the social sciences; and (4) Popper begins with an accepted theory that produces a problem, conjecture, and test-able solution that appears in the end to undermine his own view of knowledge, science, and objectivity and the very concept of theory itself.[71] These four positions are for the most part simply accepted by Popper as epistemologically given aspects of the logic of the social sciences, but in fact come to frame the inter-esting debate with his colleagues in Tübingen.

At this point, Popper returns to the argument of *The Logic of Scientific Discovery*, that science does not verify truth claims since it can only test and potentially falsify them. Thus scientific justifi-cation in sociology is always provisional and temporary, based on deductive logic and public criticism. As in that book, Popper also seems to reject empiricism, scientism, inductivism, nominalism, and neutralism in the social sciences as forms of "misguided natu-ralism." However, he does not appear to reject naturalism itself, but only a particular variation of it, in empiricism and psycholo-gism. Popper's argument becomes more complex at the end of his presentation, when he states: "We term a proposition 'true' if it corresponds to the facts or if things are as described by the propo-sition. This is what is called the absolute or objective concept of truth which each of us constantly uses."[72] Observation is crucial for testing the results of a deduction from the initial theoretical premises of an argument. He continues to develop his theory of causal explanation: "Thus the basic logical schema of every expla-nation consists of a (logical) deductive inference whose premises consist of a theory and some initial conditions, and whose con-clusion is the explicandum."[73] Popper ends his presentation by arguing that "we can never justify our theories rationally," but that we can rationally examine and publicly criticize our theories and thus distinguish between good and better theories. Popper began his presentation with a problem of theory and ends with the criti-cal evaluation of a theory, but never truly examines the nature of social theory itself, since it is the scientific method and not social critique that occupies his complete attention.

Adorno responds to Popper with the second essay of the con-ference, "On the Logic of the Social Sciences," and later in an introductory essay to the book on the positivism debate, "Sociology and Empirical Research" (1957). These essays focus on Adorno's critique of the epistemology of rationalism and the methodology of positivism, as well as his theory of consciousness, dialectics, social objectivity, structuralism, and the eclipse of social theory in analytical sociology. He begins his essay by saying that he examines the logic of sociology and the social system, whereas Popper limits himself to the logic of thought and analytical methods that are then applied to the examination of society itself. Adorno objects to the idea that the study of society "passes through a series of stages from observation to the ordering, processing, and systematization of its material."[74] For him, this is a mechanical and distorting procedure by which the assumed method of the natural sciences is simply superimposed upon the study of society, reflecting not the reality of society, but the accepted reality of the traditional interpretation of the appropriate scientific method. He refers to this as an absurd and ignorant cliché of science, which undermines any serious attempt to study the complexity and diversity of society. The central point throughout Adorno's two critical essays is that Popper, along with the neo-positivists and analytic philosophers, confuses two entirely different views of the object of study: the objectivity of society and the objectivity of the scientific method. The problem with this confusion surfaces quickly when one realizes that the method borrowed from the natural sciences, whether it is based on inductive or deductive reasoning, empiricism or rationalism, is incapable of viewing or examining the integrative and reciprocal complexity and totality of society—that is, the "social objectivity" or total social system. The "concept" of modern industrial society is simply too complex—in its structures, social institutions, cultural values, political economy, forms of consciousness, and history—to be deduced from simply empirical observations or logical principles. Method and society are complex and contradictory ideas within sociology. For Adorno, the object of study for sociology is the concept of society, which will require an entirely different and dialectical method of scientific discovery than the study of nature. The traditional beginning of a positivist interpretation of sociology lies in the contradiction between observation and knowledge (theory), object and subject, while, according to Adorno, the contradiction lies deeper, in the structural and institutional totality of a capitalist social system itself. This occurs because of the internal and antagonistic oppositions and social imperatives brought about by a class society.

The contradictions are therefore not logical and methodological, but concrete, structural, and historical contradictions of the social system itself, seen by both Hegel and Marx. Again, Adorno distinguishes between the problem of methods and the problems of the social objectivity or social reality. The contradiction lies not in the logic and method of study between knowledge and observation, between hypothesis creation and observational confirmation or falsification; rather, it lies in the nature of class production, the organization of alienated labor, and class distribution of social wealth. Production for workers' satisfaction and distribution to meet human needs are in contradiction with the owner's control over production and profit accumulation.[75] Industrial production and wealth distribution based on the social ideals of human dignity and human needs, social ethics and political and human rights, are in contrast to an actual historical form of production and distribution based on class power, economic exploitation, private property, and alienated labor. The contradiction lies in the very concept of industrial society. The reality of the social system contains its own inner structural and logical contradictions, found in economic production, distribution, social ethics, and political ideals versus the historical and social reality of class inequality, power, property, and alienation.

Adorno's concern is less with an abstract and formal sociological method than with a sociology that could examine and explain these complexities of the total social reality of capitalist production and distribution. He recognizes that the traditional method of social reach could not extend to the social complexities and structural contradictions of objective society; method is incapable of explaining the social totality and, in fact, represses and hides it from theoretical consideration. Method represses both the concept and the theory of society. In the end, the traditional analytical method results in the loss of a critical theory of social objectivity along with its structures, functions, and history; and its replacement by a technological and formal rationality, based on a method of mechanical calculation, problem solving, formal predictions, and technical solutions. The objectivity and dialectic of method make an objectivity and dialectic of society impossible. The danger of placing sociology on a par with the natural sciences is to lose questions of the social objectivity or social totality, which examines the nature and mechanism of society, with its institutions, culture, traditions, and ideals. Ironically, science actually represses and distorts knowledge, and leads to a silence of reason and abandonment of social theory, in which the researcher is unable to voice a concept of society, the structures of society, a dialectic of society (immanent critique of values and ideals and structural contradictions of production for capital and profit or for needs and humanity), or a history of society.[76] Science produces silence because its method of discovery is unable to raise these questions. And its theory is not a product of comprehensive social research of the full range of social structures and interaction, but of limited, methodologically framed questions. The method frames the problems, questions, observation, data collection, and conclusion. As a result, method undermines true objectivity and logic, because the conclusions are in some measure baked into the formal definitions of the initial theory and problems. From the perspective of analytical science, method creates theory. Yet from a critical perspective, the social totality should frame the real issues and questions and be the foundation for social theory.

The final question is how many concepts, ideas, and theories are lost because the traditional method based on natural science is so limited and restrained. Method preconditions and predetermines the social problems, logic, and conclusions of scientific research, resulting in a very limited understanding of social theory. To some extent, the problems raised in the analytical science of neo-positivism are formal, epistemological, and artificial questions, because they are defined, delineated, and derived from the primacy and directives of the method and not from reality. The objectivity of both method and its constructed reality is a product of the analytical method, and thus is far removed from the real world in both theory and method. Objects of study are created by the method and not by a critical insight into the real problems within society. "One would fetishize science if one radically separated its immanent problems from the real ones, which are weakly reflected in its formalism," Adorno writes.[77] The theories, facts, and conclusions are already part of the immanent logic and method of positivism, but not the logic and structure of advanced industrial society, resulting in "an irrelevance to which countless sociological investigations are condemned in that they follow the primacy of the method and not that of the object."[78] The conclusions are to a great extent already contained in the type of method, logic, and problems raised, which have a built-in political imperative toward social control and domination. The questions and problems are formal and mechanical and ultimately designed to resolve technical and administrative issues for more bureaucratic and economic efficiency—or, even under the best conditions, to examine real social problems, but without questioning the underlying social system and structures that cause them.

According to Adorno, in critical social theory, "methods do not rest upon methodological ideals but rather upon reality."[79] Social objectivity should be examined by a variety of methods, to accommodate the complexity and density of society. With positivism, however, objectivity is a product of the method, and not detailed, comprehensive historical research. It results in the accumulation of particular reified and formal social data, producing both fetishism and ideology, which is useful for business and government administration, commercial research, statistical data, positive career development, and other technical purposes. Science is operationally useful for the measurement of the status quo, but not useful for delving into the depth and breadth of the structural and social reality—not for social critique. It produces subjective meaning of public surveys and interviews that collect the expressed opinions, attitudes, and behavior of individuals, but not the social objectivity of "the conditions, institutions, and forces within which human beings act."[80] Positivism results in the abandoning of oneself to the authoritarian world of purely factual information and formal observation, without the protection of the critical and dialectical knowledge of the potentialities and possibilities, concept and reality of society. This is accomplished by an immanent comparison of the social reality to its own social ideals. To make his point more directly, Adorno explores the contradiction between the concept of liberalism, with its ideals of freedom and equality, to the reality of liberal society based on inequality and power. "There are sociological theorems which, as insights into the mechanisms of society which operate behind the facade, in principle, even for societal reasons, contradict appearances to such an extent that they cannot be adequately criticized through the latter."[81] Formal scientific reason cannot perform this critical function of concept formation, structural analysis, and comparative social contradictions. Social theory is the final goal of sociology as a distinct discipline, not the accumulation of facts, figures, functional hypotheses, and formal procedures. "An empirical research devoid of theory which gets by with mere hypotheses is blind to society as a system, its authentic object, since its object does not coincide with the sum of all the parts."[82] Positivists want to reduce theory and the total structure or essence of society to a classification system of facts and hypotheses, knowledge to observation, science to *techne*, criticism to protocol sentences, wisdom and imagination to social appearances, and social research to methodological discipline.

A number of important questions arise from Adorno's critique of critical rationalism and his analysis of the nature and method of social theory: How is theory or the concept of society created, and from what methods are macro social theories formed? How do these theories develop problems from which hypotheses, predictions, criticism, and technical solutions are applied? How can positivism and the analytical method develop criticism and find solutions that are compatible and integrated into traditional social theory when their method and logic of analysis are antithetical to each other? What happens to those aspects or elements of theory that do not conform to the techniques of analytical scientific analysis? Popper focuses on the logic, consistency, and internal integrity of the sociological argument, but does not consider the formative nature or origins of social theory itself. Method and theory are contradictory in the manner of Popper's argument—an issue he does not consider, especially since social theory cannot be sustained using the positivist method. These are all crucial questions, since the logic and method of theory creation in classical and contemporary social theory are quite different and even contradictory to the quantitative and qualitative methods and techniques of neopositivism. These questions are implicit in Adorno's presentation of critical theory because he clearly makes a central distinction between method and concept, method and object of inquiry.

Many social theorists use quantitative and qualitative findings, but the theory construction goes well beyond anything that Popper offers or considers. Popper's exclusive focus is on hypothesis creation, method of criticism, and the falsification of theory, but he never discusses the actual creation of theory, or if theory is even possible, given his analytical assumptions about the nature of social science. There is a real divide if not a contradiction between Popper's view of theory and methods, since the method of inquiry for quantitative and qualitative information rests upon entirely different philosophical and epistemological premises than the broad, holistic, and integrative social theories, which focus on the nature of society and not on subjective consciousness and the opinions, attitudes, and behavior of its inhabitants. Adorno believes the Popper's view of sociology borders on metaphysical speculation and logical fetishism, if not outright political ideology, since it does not question the underlying assumptions and values of the existing society. Adorno stresses that the focus of analysis should be on the internal structural contradictions of the concept and object of liberal society—that is, the dialectics of immanent and structural critique—and not on the inner contradictions of the formulation, consistency, and logic of scientific inquiry.

Adorno insists that the main goal of sociology is not self-reflective logic, or the desire to develop the internal logical consistency of method or to restructure a theory to avoid internal logical problems, inconsistencies, and contradictions. Its goal instead is to develop a critique of the "structural constitution of society," to reject the actual irrationalities and abuses of the rationalization, disenchantment, exploitation, and alienation of modern capitalism. Popper's approach to sociology endangers the discipline, as it rests on the precipice of the empty abstractionism of psychologism, fetishism, and commodification of individual attitudes, as well as the logic and methods of analytical positivism. Popper's approach has become the main focus of sociology today. The abstraction of commodity exchange and social relationships has filtered down into the very logic of social science as it distances itself from the real problems of social objectivity—the contradictions of the structural totality of society—and turns instead to the contradictions of abstract problems in logic and method. Adorno raises an important issue when he states that the ultimate aim of sociology should be social justice and an alternative view of society, but unfortunately the idea is merely a whisper in the night, which is not mentioned again.[83]

Adorno continues his critique of positivism in his later essay "Sociology and Empirical Research." Following upon his presentation, he argues that theory goes beyond the accumulation of empirical facts and the natural science model of discipline. Rather, theory compares what is to what could be; it compares the social reality to its own ideals, reality to its own concept of itself. "It must dissolve the rigidity of the temporally and spatially fixed object into a field of tension of the possible and the real."[84] Neo-positivism may see contradictions within the logic of its own argument between theory and hypotheses, but not between theory and reality. It is unable to see the contradiction between the potentiality of society's material production and the ultimate satisfaction of human needs, and the reality of commodity production and exchange value; it is unable to see the emancipatory potential of human and political rights and the alienated economic rights to private property and class privilege. Positivism measures what is, through statistical continuity and the laws of probability, but cannot imagine what could be, even when the latter lies within the very essence of the empirical. It is only when theory sees the contradictions between thought and reality that it becomes the basis for a critical social science.

For Adorno, theory reproduces the epiphenomenal world of the appearance or the summary of the statistical and mathematical evidence from surveys, questionnaires, and interviews, but does not reflect the essential reality of the structures of society.[85] It can quantitatively and qualitatively measure what is, but not what could be (concept, essence, and potentialities) or what should be (ethics and politics). Theory represents the summary of statistical relationships and subjective opinions, which can then be the basis of a contradiction with a particular problem raised by observation. Theory is then open to skepticism and criticism by the problem raised and whose only technical solution is by means of deductive reasoning, which calls the original theory into question by forming a hypothesis to be tested. As Popper writes: "A theory or a deductive system is an attempt at explanation, and consequently an attempt to solve a scientific problem—a problem of explanation."[86] For him, theories are synonymous with deductive systems, but not with social systems. There is no imagination or creativity, only technical and administrative measurement, calculation, and computation. Sociological methods become the limited and contingent philosophical justification in predefining the problems, issues, and objects of analysis, just as theory is reduced to the lowest level of measuring the appearances of reality. Sociology "sanctions the primacy of the method over the object" as the method creates the objects of study; predefines its basic formal logic and categories; predetermines its conclusions; and mystifies its theory as mathematical science.[87] In the process, what began as an empirical and scientific study of social reality turns into a distortion and rationalization of that reality for administrative and economic reasons. Theory and substantive reason disappear from the academy as they become part of the simple dogmatic ceremony of statistical summarization and measurement, as well as the academic celebration of the obvious. This is the metatheory of political ideology as it leads to continued administrative and technical control and the domination of humanity. And in the process, objectivity has lost all objective meaning and purpose in human life, leading to an ideological and existential crisis; it also leads to the alienation of consciousness and reason, as humans are reduced to statistical objects and mathematical residue in a calculated formula for administrative and commercial control. Science has evolved from the technical control of production and the workplace to the technological manipulation of consciousness for social control, profit maximization, and property accumulation. Adorno contends that even at the remaining edges of traditional sociology, the general areas of cultural science and interpretive sociology are also reduced to the study of reflexive and reactive consciousness of the culture industry. Science is incapable of examining the issue of the objective meaning of literature, art, and culture as social expressions of deeper and expressive meaning when integrated into a critical social theory. Science is now part of the culture industry itself.

Adorno reinforces his case for the discrepancy between the appearance and essence of the social world with the example of the many attempts to give life to the statistical evidence that workers are no longer alienated in advanced capitalist society. This is confirmed by a number of statistical surveys conveying the social appearances or subjective consciousness of average workers. Since this empirical method of science is incapable of penetrating into the underlying essence or structure of society, it does not recognize the discrepancy between its statistical studies of subjective consciousness and the actual social objectivity or mechanism of the class and power structure over private property and the means of production in the industrial workplace. "Appearance is always also an appearance of essence and not mere illusion. Its changes are not indifferent to essence."[88] In spite of his criticism of empirical science, Adorno also recognizes the importance of integrating this approach with critical theory—integrating appearance and essence, the subjective and objective, opinions and concept, and facts and structure—in order to gain a more critical and total picture of the complexity of the social reality, as well as the depth of alienated and exploited labor. Adorno is here simply expanding the creative insights of German idealism and materialism for the social sciences with their view of the integration of external phenomena with the transcendental subject (Kant), cultural appearances with the dialectical spirit (Hegel), and alienated and social labor with the structures of political economy and the social relations of production (Marx). Subjectivity and consciousness must always be understood as an intimate and critical part of objectivity as nature, spirit, and society, respectively.

Jürgen Habermas and the Positivism Dispute

Habermas joins the positivism debate with an initial response to Popper and Adorno, and later adds another essay in response to Hans Albert's defense of analytic philosophy and critical rationalism. Habermas reinforces and expands Adorno's contribution to the philosophical discussion about the nature of science with his two contributions, placing special emphasis on the following aspects of critical rationalism: (1) analysis of its logical and methodological inconsistencies in the interpretation of the social sciences; (2) its inadequate understanding and repression of the importance of the concepts of social objectivity, social totality, social system, and structuralism for social theory; (3) its inability to appreciate the Hegelian and Marxian traditions and their ideas of dialectics, hermeneutics, and immanent critique; (4) the political and ideological implications of phenomenal, psychological, and surface research of empirical-analytical science; (5) its inability to appreciate the differences between a dialectical science and a functional, explanatory, and behavioral science, and their implications for the study of society as a whole; and (6) the differences in the logical rules of research procedure between the methods of critical social theory and the deductive, functional, and hypothetical categories and statements in critical rationalism. Like Thomas Kuhn, Habermas stresses that there is a real unresolved difference within critical rationalism between issues of ontology and truth and issues of utility and application.[89] If there is a correspondence between science and reality, it is only arbitrary and accidental, despite the epistemological claims of Popper. According to Habermas, "A factual agreement between the derived law-like hypotheses and empirical uniformities is, in principle, fortuitous and as such remains external to theory."[90] In analytical science, theory is reduced to a measuring unit, a testing summary, and an ordering model for statistical regularities. Since there is an epistemological indifference between the interests and goals of traditional objective theory and technical empirical research in the positivist tradition, the connection between the empirical method and theory is always problematic and eventually leads to "a distortion of the object."

Habermas discretely and succinctly summarizes the debate with a single sentence: "The structure of the object, which has been neglected in favor of a general methodology, condemns to irrelevance the theory which it cannot penetrate."[91] There is an unbridgeable divide within the neo-positivist tradition of empirical science between theory and method that makes it impossible to understand or create a critical social theory. Since theory is reduced to hypothetical experiments and functional categories capable of prognosis and causal predictions of objectified events in order to reproduce the logic of empirical science, it is incapable of developing a social theory that is not tied to technical and utilitarian purposes for administrative control. Objective theory is reduced to subjective and hypothetico-deductive social theory. Following Adorno, Habermas argues that this approach to science creates its own experimental experiences, controlled observations, technical method, and hypothetical laws of behavior, which in the end only reproduce the logic, method, and reified abstractions of exchange and utilitarian capitalism. Habermas summarizes these insights with his comment that "the whole . . . can never itself be reduced to particular experimental arrangements."[92] As a product of hypothetical and experimental laws, positivist social theory cannot by its very nature ever reproduce the underlying structure or system of society in its totality; it cannot know the object of its study other than through experimental observation of law-like hypotheses. It does not hermeneutically understand that object of study; it can only create it using its limited functional and deductive method of inquiry. Theory is simply the summary product, empirical regularities, or natural laws resulting from the comparison of the initial hypothesis to the observation and experience of the events predicted.

Habermas turns his attention to two logical problems associated with critical rationalism and analytical science. He recognizes that scientific statements can only be justified when compared to empirical observation and experience. "Logically correct hypotheses prove their empirical validity only when they are confronted with experience."[93] However, there is an inherent logical problem with this theory of knowledge based on the experiential confirmation of scientific theories. Habermas continues: "strictly speaking, however, theoretical statements cannot be directly tested by means of experience, however objectified it may be, but rather only by other statements."[94] Popper, too, is aware of this problem, because he rejects the possibility of the empirical verification of scientific statements and replaces this approach with the method of empirical falsification. A scientific statement cannot be proven true using experience or observation; it can only be provisionally accepted by means of observational statements that are accepted by a public consensus within the scientific community as true until they are later falsified by other experiments and observations. "This agreement rests, in the last instance, upon a decision; it can be neither enforced logically nor empirically."[95] Habermas refers to this dilemma within epistemology as "the hermeneutical circle."

This problem of knowledge verification calls into question the traditional views that science reflects or corresponds to empirical reality. Looking more closely at this issue, Habermas declares that in order to establish the validity of an accepted hypothesis or theory it is first necessary to define the object of research, the nature of observation, and the empirical facts, which will confirm or reject the initial hypothesis or theory. The problem arises with the recognition that both empirical facts and empirical confirmation are both defined and determined by the actual method of scientific inquiry. That is, the method defines the original problem, facts of observation, the procedure of confirmation and validation, and, finally, the nature of the hypothesis construction. "One cannot apply general rules if a prior decision has not been taken concerning the facts which can be subsumed under the rules."[96] The end of the process of scientific confirmation is already established at the very beginning of the inquiry by the manner in which scientific hypotheses and observation are defined by the historical and hermeneutical horizons.[97]

The hermeneutical circle presents a logical problem of confirmation, since the objects of inquiry are created by the method of science itself. The analytical method creates its own objects, logic, facts, and science. In the process, it confirms and verifies its own logic and objectivity of scientific discovery. In the very act of applying the method, the objectivity of experience and observation is also constructed. That is, there is no objectivity of experience and knowledge beyond the actual analytical method employed. The empirical reality is a construct of the empirical method, which is then used to justify and validate science itself. Science does not reflect reality, but the conceptual, ontological, and theoretical imperatives of its own method and interests. By the very definition of theory and hypotheses, the types of empirical facts that correspond to this form of analytical, causal, and deductive science are created along with its distinctive process of verification. Thus science creates its own empirical reality, method of inquiry, technical interests, and procedures of truth confirmation and validation.[98]

Social facts are social constructs. The method creates its own definition of what constitutes facts and observation at the same time that it justifies science by its formal procedures, technical success, and administrative applicability. The correspondence between science and method, consciousness and reality, and knowledge and truth, is a closed circle by which the method justifies itself. This vicious circle undermines a correspondence theory of truth because there is nothing external to the method applied.

Both method and objectivity participate in the construction of each component of science itself. Empirical objects and accumulated facts of scientific observation are not known through experience and reason as independent truths, but are pre-constituted by the scientific method. Experience is defined in terms of universal laws, causal hypotheses, and explanatory theories and not in terms of a hermeneutical understanding of human action and intentional meaning within the social totality. As a result of this forced limitation of facts and observation, "whole problem areas would have to be excluded from discussion and relinquished to irrational attitudes."[99] Facts do not exist independently of the method or theory of inquiry, which create the empirical world under investigation, according to the logical imperatives of control over nature similar to the logic of industrial capitalism and alienated labor. In the end, it is the technical and formal interest of science that justifies its logic and theory. Science creates its own objects and metaphysics according to whether it is studying nature or society (general concepts and universal causal laws) or history (spirit or cultural and mental life of individual actions and intentions).[100] The method creates the theory, hypotheses, and facts, and the facts, in turn, justify the theory, hypotheses, and method. The analytical method defines and creates its own social reality of facts and experience, which is then functionally applied by experimentation and prediction to justify positivist science. These facts are artificial and objectified, since they must conform to the method of technical experimentation and hypothetical calculation. If the facts cannot conform to this method, they are not considered privileged or legitimate. Facts legitimate the methods just as the method creates acceptable facts. This constructed reality is then used to confirm the validity of the hypothesis and theory. As a result "the source of knowledge—pure thoughts, established tradition, and sense experience—all lack authority. None of them can lay claims to immediate evidence and primary validity and consequently to the power of legitimation. The sources of knowledge are always contaminated."[101] This reflects the hermeneutical circle, since to comprehend the various component parts of the scientific method, one must first understand the scientific method as a functional and causally related whole, which influences our understanding of the parts because they are all intimately related to each other.

All understanding of something meaningful—like a historical event, piece of art, work of literature, or philosophical text—requires that we understand the context, traditions, and horizons from which it came. Parts make sense only in the context of the whole. According to Habermas, the same is true for the manner in which hypothetical experiments, functional experience, and causal laws are to be understood. Controlled observation only makes sense in the broader context of knowledge about the research project as a whole. "The meaning of the research process as a whole must be understood before I can know to what the empirical validity of basic statements is related."[102] Knowledge of observation is only possible after knowledge of the method clarifies the meaning and context of observable statements. What appears as an abstract foundation for hypothesis-testing and experimental observation is just another form of hermeneutic pre-understanding of the meaning of social norms of acceptable scientific behavior. Popper's understanding of the nature of scientific procedures and technical reason is based on the same hermeneutic pre-understanding of the technical rules of behavior of specialization and technical reason as found in the industrial labor process of factory work. The rationalization of production and the rationalization of reason and science follow the same unconscious path of technical and formal procedures, prediction, causal relationships, and enforced control and domination over nature, humanity, and the objective process of knowledge organization, even when "the illusion of pure theory can preserve itself"—that is, even when the illusion of formal objectivity and value freedom are consistently maintained.[103] The fabrication of facts and data through specialized labor, controlled observation, mechanical prediction, and functional causality mirrors the specialized and mechanical fabrication of commodities and property. Both processes create technical knowledge and saleable products for economic and administrative consumption and control over their immediate economic and methodological environments.

Habermas argues that the idea of "value freedom" in the research process is a theoretical and academic myth, constructed to hide the reality of the logic of natural science, which reflects not the objective physical or social reality, but the reality of the social labor process. It reflects the technical cognitive interests of the reality of industrial production by means of its formal, functional, causal, and predictive categories for technical cognitive interests. Science is not value-free, because it contains the valuation of capitalist work based on technical and mechanical labor and not common, shared, or democratic labor. Habermas is clearly aware of the historical and sociological connection between science and modern economics and mechanical production. "The historical situation in which during the seventeenth century empirical science in the strict sense emerges with the new physics, is by no means external to the structure of empirical science."[104] The cognitive interests of scientific research and knowledge are historically tied to a particular form of human labor and production for the technical domination of nature, which are part of "the new modes of manufacture." The underlying metaphysics of science, as discussed in chapter 2 of the book on the positivism debate, is a product of the underlying metaphysics, logic, and structure of the modern machine in the workplace, with its fragmentation and division of labor and its private control of production. Both science and bourgeois manufacturing emerged at the same historical moment and were intimately connected in their logic and method.[105] This connection between cognition and work, between knowledge and manufacturing, and between science and economics, further linked these two apparently distinct areas in the manner of concept formation and the capitalist organization of human labor. The concepts, method, and theses of science reflect the logic of capital in industrial production and market exchange. The reality or worldview of science reflects the objective reality of early mechanical production, as it reifies and neutralizes natural and social objectivity in the form of labor and reflection into serviceable and mechanical objects of scientific perception and exchange. Habermas calls this process the "illusion of autonomy." Science is manufactured to conceive of the world as a useful machine for mechanical production and knowledge. Social relations and scientific categories are reified ideal objects or scientific commodities of social production that are then taken for objective reality. By this means, science unconsciously "incorporates the natural and social world into the labor process and transforms them into productive forces."[106] The logic underlying both modern science and mechanical work is the same: both appear to be reified and abstract forms of value freedom, even as they are mechanically geared to the domination and mastery of nature and humanity. They are both abstractions from the system of production and from the cultural lifeworld. The world as an objective reality of use values, exchange values, surplus, profits, property and the world of mechanical physics are both artificially produced forms of objective realty which conceal their historical and sociological origins and connections. However, over time their connection is absolved into the unconscious memory as they are separated into distinct and indifferent entities which refuse to recognize any technical or historically related interests.

Habermas continues this line of argument in his second contribution, "A Positivistically Bisected Rationalism" (1964), in which he expands and deepens a few of his earlier arguments. In particular, he focuses on Kant's epistemology and theory of representations, and on a critique of traditional foundationalism in empiricism and rationalism, the difference between scientific verification and methodical validation, the differences between the methods of understanding and explanation, and the role of conjecture and criticism in Popper's analysis of analytical science. Habermas is aware that Popper refuses to recognize his own residual "positivist prejudice," even as "he assumes the epistemological independence of facts from the theories which should descriptively grasp these facts and the relations between them. Accordingly, tests examine theories against 'independent' facts."[107] Habermas rejects Popper's position as he maintains that the latter fails to recognize the logic of the hermeneutical circle as he continues to assert the existence of an independent reality and objectivity of observation and experience in the hypothesis confirmation process. Habermas distinguishes between the technical method of science and application and the hermeneutical self-reflective understanding of the meaning and application of technique and science within the total picture of the method itself. Implicit in this aspect of Popper's theory of knowledge is an acceptance of both realism and objectivism—that is, a correspondence theory of truth and the existence of an independent, external world of objective facts.[108]

This presents a profound internal logical inconsistency surrounding Popper's belief in the "mythical and objectivistic illusion" that scientific theories represent autonomous experimental facts. Habermas calls for a deeper analysis of the meaning of natural and social facts, which lie in a more complex hermeneutical understanding of factual statements and empirical validation. Each component of the scientific procedure, rules, and method leaves an imprint that helps define the other components of the total system. The major categories of initial theory, systematic observation, and empirical testing must be understood as part of the complex method that defines the nature of these very categories, which do not exist independently of the method itself; the parts make sense only in the context of the whole. There are no independent components within the scientific method because each element is defined and has meaning only in terms of its relationship to the other functional elements. As stated above, science creates its own objects and facts which do not exist independently of the scientific procedure and its co-related cognitive interests, for the technical control and productive force over nature and human labor. As a result, both the analytical theory and pre-formed facts are made to fit the methodical testing of the original hypothesis. According to Habermas, these three usually unarticulated and unconscious moments of the scientific process—neo-Kantian epistemology, the hermeneutical circle, and metaphysical and pragmatic interests— help to clarify the normative underpinnings of modern science, which are instrumental in understanding the meaning of its functional and technical terms.

Habermas turns to the Kantian critique of pure reason as evidence that sense experience cannot be the basis of scientific observation, experience, theory verification, and the final justification of scientific knowledge, since there is no perception of the world without a categorical framework of intuition and the understanding. There is no independent objective world without the mediation of the transcendental subjectivity of human consciousness, which changes what it experiences by its own mental categories. There is no knowledge of things in themselves (noumena), but only conceptually transformed objects of experience (phenomena). "The search for the primary experience of a manifest immediacy is in vain."[109] The transcendental categories of functionalism and pragmatism in method reflect the transcendental categories of intuition and the understanding of cognition. There are no privileged or controlled representations or primary experiences independent of the act of cognition. There is no objectivistic knowledge of empirical reality independent of the intervention and prejudice of the human mind. Empirical facts are not reflections of reality, but only the constructed appearances and interpretations of the scientific theories themselves, which in the end cannot be proven, but only provisionally validated by scientific tests, consensus, and technical practicality. Facts are not derived from immediate, unfiltered, and unprejudiced observation, but are formed through a complex system of institutional rules and scientific procedures (hermeneutical circle) based on open criticism, prognosis, testing, and utility.[110] It is only these types of questions that have claims to empirical validity. "The system of laws and the facts of the case are not given independently of one another. On the contrary, the facts of the case are even sought under the categories of the system of laws."[111] To understand the meaning of controlled observation and empirical facts, one must first understand the meaning of the uniform empirical theories and natural laws of regular human behavior and ideas, along with the procedures by which they are created.

The scientific method is a transcendental method within neo-Kantian epistemology, since method has replaced subjectivity in the creation of the world of experiences. Just as there are no independent appearances in Kantian epistemology, there are no autonomous empirical facts or statistical data in modern science. In both cases, the appearances and facts are mental constructs of the mind and method. Habermas finds that although Popper is aware of elements of Kant's theory of knowledge as he moves beyond empirical verification to a form of temporary validation through falsification, he is still caught in the positivist illusion of autonomous facts, hypotheses, and observation.[112] Popper is aware of the critique of objectivism and realism in epistemology, but, according to Habermas, fails to apply this same criticism to the scientific method itself, especially the application of hypothesis-testing. Popper is aware of the innovation of Kant's theory of appearances and reality, but does not apply it to his understanding of the scientific method. From Habermas's perspective, both the transcendental consciousness of knowledge and transcendental method of science are two ways of interpreting subjectivity, as a form of experiential and phenomenal consciousness or as a form of scientific and methodological consciousness. Popper recognizes the false objectivity of empiricist epistemology, but fails to see it as part of the scientific method. This is why it is necessary to develop a self-reflective understanding of the nature of scientific inquiry that goes beyond outlining the main elements of analytical science and its functional method. Science itself must be viewed within a more comprehensive and critical appreciation of how each component of the empirical method helps define the limits of our understanding of terms such as *experience, observation, testing,* and *validation.* And when these very limits define the expanse of science itself, it becomes a form of political ideology for the purposes of authoritarian control and administrative domination. Science and ideology are both productive forms and forces of alienated labor and consciousness in which the academic products of experience and facts and the corporate products of objects and profits are fabricated under highly organized and technical rules of experimental and industrial control. Habermas maintains that the logic and method of positivism reflect the logic and method of industrial production in modern society. Any approach that does not conform to the contours of the logic and method of analytic philosophy and science, or reach the heights of the explanatory and causal laws of science, cannot become a true science of objective social reality.

Beyond the cognitive interests of science, the limits that science sets upon itself impact the human imagination, the range of theoretical questions that may be raised, and the possibilities for social change. Social theory cannot be reduced to such a narrow and ideological range of legitimate questions and issues. The notion of objectivity of experience runs well beyond that of hypothetical functions, causality, and explanations. As already mentioned, social objectivity includes the analysis of structures (political economy); history; dialectics (immanent critique and economic and structural contradictions); consciousness (phenomenology and ethnography); culture (social norms, values, and ideals); traditions (classical humanism, classical social theory, and critical theory); critical hermeneutics (hermeneutics, psychoanalysis, and depth hermeneutics); and ethics and politics (social justice). These traditions involve the importance of critique, dialectics, understanding, and structural analysis as opposed to a sociology of explanation, functional causality, and utility.[113] The central theoretical question overriding all others in sociology is whether, using the method and logic of analytical science, one is able to raise these types of critical, historical, and holistic social questions. This is an especially interesting question, since these other approaches require entirely different methodological and theoretical orientations, whose subject matter is not open to the hypothetico-deductive approach to science. With this expansion of our understanding of the nature of science, there is also an expansion of new objects of study that take into consideration the totality and structures of society as a whole, including cultural ideals, social institutions, intellectual traditions, and economic forces and relations of production. These forms of knowledge do not conform to the analytical-positivist method of natural and social science, and as a result they are repressed into the academic unconscious and lost to intellectual history, producing a silence of reason and a stultifying moral nihilism and political conformism.

In the end, theory has little value in itself, since its real contribution is to validate and aid the positivist method of inquiry. Theory has become a mechanism for the justification of particular research methods and operational statistical tools, and those traditions that do not conform to its approach are lost in both the philosophical and sociological traditions. And with them a critical, self-reflective understanding of the total structure of society is silenced and repressed. Theory is useful only when it conforms to and services the purpose of a particular technical research method, the history of theory, content analysis, and literature review, all designed to help articulate the initial research problem and hypothesis. We live in a post-theoretical, voiceless world unable and unwilling to conceptualize or understand the grand traditions and their classical horizons from the ancients to the moderns. And without theory, there are no dreams; without dreams there can be no social justice; and without justice, there is no future—no ways to think about or act against injustice in the world or to reflect upon the possibilities of alternative forms of political economy and social systems.

The search for social justice has been replaced by the quest for statistical evidence; social philosophy by technical observation; theory by techne and hypothetical method; critical thought by utilitarian data; and social justice by authoritarian conformity and political ideology.[114] Without social theory we are left speechless in an alienated, rationalized, and disenchanted world; we are left without heart and spirit, without social ethics and communal democracy in the face of utilitarian capitalists and social technicians. No matter how many social problems, experimental hypotheses, functional tests, controlled observations, data collections, and theoretical conclusions one may draw from scientific research, the classical and contemporary theories of continental sociology and philosophy cannot be reproduced or expanded. The evolution of the metaphysics and method of the natural sciences has resulted in the death of nature and continued domination and exploitation of the physical environment, whereas the development of positivism in the social sciences has resulted in the death of substantive and critical reason—the death of social theory itself.

Science and the Domination of Reason and Humanity: Debate Within Critical Theory between Marcuse and Habermas

OVER THE COURSE OF THIS BOOK, the idea that science reflects an objective and external reality has been called into question. This dilemma of modern science and reason requires a rethinking of the nature of modern science at the philosophical and sociological level. As we saw in chapters 1 and 2, neo-Kantian philosophy and phenomenology have raised a number of key issues that have called into question the traditional theories of knowledge and their epistemological defenses of natural science in empiricism and rationalism. Husserl's phenomenological critique of objectivism and realism and his theory of transcendental subjectivity, combined with Scheler's sociology of knowledge and theory that science involves the domination of nature, has produced a new range of theoretical questions about the true nature of Western science. It has opened a whole new avenue of investigation that stresses the role of science as a theoretical and methodological form of machine production and technological rationality, whose ultimate purpose is to dominate the area of its technical application. We have already examined the ideas that the formative and historical purposes of science were to dominate nature, work organization, production technology, humanity, and even the social sciences themselves. This chapter will examine the debates within the Frankfurt School of critical theory—in the writings of Max Horkheimer, Herbert Marcuse, and Jürgen Habermas—over the nature of pure science and its role in the rationalization and repression of society by facilitating the efficiency and productivity of capitalist industries.

Starting from Kant's initial critique of pure reason and his theory of the a priori forms of knowledge, there were four major directions in the evolution of a critical theory of science. Each of these new theories added another dimension to Kant's original epistemology, which rejected the narrow views of traditional positive science and their immediate successors: (1) the critique of the limited view of positivist objectivism in phenomenology; (2) the construction of objective reality and natural science as social and not subjective phenomena or products of pure human consciousness; (3) the transcendence of structuralism and social theory in positivism's inability to develop a totalistic, macro, and integrative view of society, and (4) the loss of ethics, dialectics, and immanent critique in positivist science. The first form of critique began with epistemology and its emphasis on the nature of subjectivity and the latter's role in the construction of knowledge of the objective phenomenal world. This knowledge was not given either by innate ideas of rationalism or direct empirical correspondence of objective reality by the reflecting mind of empiricism. Rejecting the mathematical a priori and dogmatic objectivism, this critique emphasized the importance of subjectivity, consciousness, and values in the construction of knowledge, science, and objective reality. This was viewed as an advancement, but still a very inadequate understanding of subjectivity. The second form of a critique of positivism involved the need to broaden the understanding and range of subjectivity and its technical and social a priori forms of sensibility and the understanding to include sociology and the social construction of reality and science. This will help us better appreciate the technological rationality and the domination of nature that are essential elements in the formation of consciousness and science. The third critique of positivism in the social sciences involved a recognition of the sociological and theoretical loss or transcendence of a holistic and critical social theory capable of examining the structural and functional relationships of the complex institutions within society. Working under the metaphysics and metatheory of positivism, science was relegated to the mechanical, formal, and quantitative collection of empirical data through induction and the deductive formulation of hypotheses, testing, and empirical confirmation of experimental results. This third form unfolded with the recognition that knowledge and science were a priori and historical constructs of a social subjectivity—that is, constructs of the political economy and culture of modern capitalism itself. The fourth form of critical theory focused on ethics and social criticism by examining the implication of realism and nominalism and the loss of ethics and immanent critique, which made it logically impossible to imagine future possibilities based on an immanent critique of society's own social ideals. Thus the critique of positivism involved a critique of objectivism, sociology, technological rationality, and dialectical ethics.

The weakness of positivism, especially when applied to the social sciences, rested upon its narrow and psychological theory of objectivity (Husserl and Scheler); inability to move beyond philosophy into sociology and social theory; loss of transcendence and a structuralist social theory (Adorno, Habermas, and C. Wright Mills); and the loss of dialectical reasoning and immanent social critique (Horkheimer and Marcuse). That is, positivist sociology rested upon its inability to raise certain types of questions about the social construction of reality and objectivity beyond phenomenological subjectivity and individual human consciousness; its inability to develop a broad and comprehensive social theory based on alternative methods and theories of knowledge beyond positivism, one that challenged the underlying assumptions, values, and

institutions of social reality; and its inability to pursue an immanent and ethical critique of society which encourages us to look
beyond the present to future possibilities and new forms of work,
production, and politics. These different forms resulted in turning
positive social science into an ideology incapable of questioning
the underlying structures, norms, and ideals of modern capitalist society. This ideology of positivism distorted both philosophy
and sociology by creating disciplines that reflected a distortion
and eclipse of reason. This characterization of critique in terms of
objectivity, transcendence, and ethics moves beyond epistemology
and phenomenology, and beyond a philosophy and psychology of
knowledge, into a critical social theory. The goal of the latter is to
develop a detailed analysis of the relationship among knowledge,
science, and technology and the broader structures of work, management, and political economy. This approach forms the heart
of a critical theory of the domination of humanity and reason, as
formulated by members of the Frankfurt School.

Weber and Marcuse on the Rationalization of Science and Society

In *One-Dimensional Man* (1964), Marcuse moves beyond a positivist understanding of society in order to develop a more critical
perspective on the nature of modern science, technological rationality, and human emancipation. He begins with a summary of
Marx's theory of alienation and exploitation, based on Marx's
labor theory of value and the organic composition of capital.
However, quoting from the *Grundrisse*, Marcuse argues that
with the mechanization of work, surplus value and profits are no
longer derived directly from the exploitation of labor, but from the
increased intensity and productivity of industrial automation. This
requires a rethinking of the role of science, technology, and work
in the creation of value in production in an evolving social system.
With this insight, Marcuse begins to redirect his understanding of
alienation and exploitation by exploring his analysis of science and

technological rationality in modern industry, including machines, tools, techniques, knowledge, and social organization. Building on the traditions we have already examined in this book, he extends the analysis of positivism and critical theory of science beyond the domination of nature into a social theory of the domination of work and production.

Marcuse's theory of technological rationality moves from the domination of nature to the domination of humanity, work, and industry, in his analysis of the constructed objectivity of society through scientific management. Our perception and understanding of objective reality have shifted from the transcendental subject to the social subject as the object of investigation. Along with these changes, the a priori categories of intuition and the understanding which help consciousness construct the world of objects is now laden with political and ideological categories through which our perception of reality is filtered and measured. The Enlightenment categories of reality are transformed categories of capitalist relations of production, as pure reason is itself transformed into technological reason, which in turn changes our relationship to nature, the environment, and society. Marcuse is quite clear when he writes that "'the objective order of things' is itself the result of domination."[1] "The objective order of things" is measured by the mathematical and quantitative laws of economic behavior, which block out any consideration of worker alienation and wage exploitation in the sphere of production because of the defensive ideology of economic science and reason. The eclipse and repression of reason has penetrated deep into the science and laws of economics and has developed "a mode of thought and behavior which is immune against any other than the established rationality."[2] Because economics is a pure science of reason, it cannot by definition interject alternative sets of ethical and political values and ideals into an analysis of the economic system without undermining its own claims to rationality and science. Economics continues the nominalist quantification and mathematization of nature, but now into the very institutions and structures of society itself. Alternative considerations through immanent critique or alternative social values are made illegitimate, unscientific, and impossible. The critique of pure reason has turned into a critique of formal reason that organizes and justifies the organization and management of production and the division of labor, the market and commerce, and wealth distribution and class. A new objectivity is maintained by the subjective consciousness with its a priori forms and laws of perception. Access to a different ancient or medieval understanding of nature and the economy is made impossible by the objective reality of capitalism and the forms of consciousness that protect and enshrine that objectivity.

Quoting from a variety of contemporary philosophers of science, Marcuse begins to unpack a critical theory of objectivity. He raises the question as to the exact nature of objective reality: its inanimate objects, substances, movements, empirical reality, etc., and their relationship to the method of natural science (hypothetical observation, quantitative calculation, causal prediction, and mathematical relations and laws). Does science reflect reality or create reality? If the latter, by what means and method and for what purpose is objectivity constructed? Moving beyond transcendental subjectivity, Marcuse treats the method, categories, and theories of science as the a priori forms of pure reason that create empirical reality that we see and understand. Does the nature of pure science lie in the objectivity of the external reality or in the objectivity of the scientific method? In a brief section of *One-Dimensional Man*, Marcuse quotes Herbert Dingler, Willard Van Quine, H. Reichenbach, Max Born, Adolf Grünbaum, Werner Heisenberg, Philipp Frank, and Gaston Bachelard, as he surgically questions the meaning of external objects and physical reality in nature. His conclusion, drawing upon these scholars of idealism, is that the belief in a world of physical objects to be examined by science is an obsolete but convenient and necessary mythic construction and cultural posit that creates an Enlightenment metaphysics and mathematics of nature.[3] The mathematization of nature represents a moving away from physicalism and realism, since the physical objects are real only to the extent that they are observable and measurable by mathematical and logical calculation, and it is the latter that has become the basis for natural science. Nature is a construct of the quantitative and mathematical mind that defines objective reality in observable, measurable, and experimentally testable categories that are never truly justified other than through hypothetical and experimental testing.

The central philosophical point is that this form of knowledge and justification proves only that something is experimentally true and works but does not say anything about the reality of the objective world. It is capable of observation, calculation, manipulation, and observable control, but says nothing about its objective reality and absolute truth. Marcuse concludes that "it suspends judgment on what reality itself may be, or considers the very question meaningless and unanswerable."[4] Science appears to have given up the search for objective truth and reality as it settles upon a utilitarian foundation of the physical sciences. In contemporary science, truth, objectivity, and reality are replaced by utility and control.[5] Science is now no longer grounded in traditional metaphysics but in experimental validation and functional utility. This ultimately defines its view of nature, experience, and reality in terms of a priori functional and utilitarian categories for the control of both experiments and nature itself. This is a contemporary and radical variation of the transcendental subjectivity of Kant, which Marcuse pushes to its formal and idealist conclusions in mathematical equations and logical relationships. This is the position taken by the various authors quoted by Marcuse, as they move away from the traditional metaphysics of science in physical nature. Science is no longer interested in the search for absolute truth or access to being-in-itself, but to a form of knowledge whose goal lies in the ability to predict and control the workings and relationships within nature. However, Marcuse recognizes that the scientific creation of its own world of metaphysical entities based on mathematical time and space results in artificial and fictional products of human consciousness. He inquires into the formation of this reality of objects of scientific inquiry, which replaced Galilean and Cartesian dualism and, by implication, the ancient and medieval view of nature as an organic living whole of actuality, essence, form, and potentiality.

The traditional views of natural science and physical nature still held for the belief in the search for an objective and essential reality independent of subjective consciousness. However, Marcuse is aware that with the development of the more radical form of idealism this inquiry into truth and reality was relinquished and replaced by the search for utility and management of experiments and nature. Marcuse summarizes the contemporary forms of objectivism in his analysis of science as a metaphysical and political construct. The traditional epistemologies of pure science in the Enlightenment searched for an objective reality based on a physical landscape of metaphysics defined in terms of time, space, and motion. This has now turned into a new form of radical idealism that explains the external world in terms of ideational and mathematical relationships. But if this idealism is a construct of the transcendental, phenomenological, mathematical, or historical subject, this does not explain or justify how and why this particular view of the metaphysics and method of science and nature developed at a particular time in history and claimed it as reflecting an axiomatic and absolute truth.

Husserl and Scheler helped with the view that the modern form of objectivity was technically crucial for the development of the categories and knowledge necessary to dominate and control nature. They never reflected on the nature of phenomenal subjectivity, because their critical reflection was directed mainly at empiricist and rationalist forms of objectivity. Unanswered are the questions of why nature had to be controlled in a market economy and, perhaps more importantly, how nature is controlled in work and production. These questions bring our understanding of science, method, and nature to the historical and sociological foundations and justifications for this view of objective reality. Scientific truths and facts are reduced to measurement, calculation, and prediction in order to anticipate and control natural occurrences, events, and forces. For Marcuse, this position results in the idea that "matter itself would be objectively of the structure of mind," that is, that the natural world of matter and substance as appearances reflect the structure of mind.[6] But then the question must be raised: what exactly is the structure of the mind? This question requires a deconstruction of the nature of transcendental subjectivity that goes beyond the traditional philosophical categories of the mind and metaphysics of science. Where does this form of subjectivity come from and what are the underlying metaphysical issues grounding modern science? These profound insights of contemporary philosophy of science only recapitulate, with certain adjustments, the key insight of Descartes from the mid-seventeenth century that reality (*res extensa*) is mathematical and understandable by the human mind as *res cogitans* (thinking substance).

Whether the physical world is viewed as an extended and independent substance consisting of observable and quantitative objects and forces (as in the Galilean and Cartesian universe) or as mathematical and ideational relationships (as in the world of Heisenberg and Quine), Marcuse contends that it is the a priori categories of the mind—that is, categories that are prior to all technical application—that formulate a world of utilitarian advantage and control, which is the key to understanding modern science. It is crucial to appreciate that these approaches to science have surrendered the search for meaning and truth regarding physical nature in the quest for the domination of nature itself. After careful if brief consideration of these different ideational formulations and idealist theories of the foundation of knowledge in human consciousness, Marcuse moves his analysis into a deeper understanding of the objective reality and absolute truth of matter and substances. He redirects his attention away from the underlying idealist foundations of the metaphysics of science and its mathematical belief system to a materialist approach to science and questions about the domination of nature, technological rationality, and the historical dynamic of the rise of capitalism. He moves from the idea that nature is an objectivity of the mind to the idea that nature is an objectivity of society mediated through the mind; that is, the Kantian forms of intuition and knowledge are historical forms of consciousness and not ahistorical, universal forms of science. The world we perceive, understand, experience, and know is a world of technical reason and social and historical objectivity.

Although a product of human consciousness and the categories of Western thought, science is no longer a neutral or indifferent observer, but has invested its categories and method with a distinct a priori political content of control over nature. We have moved from epistemology, idealism, phenomenology, and contemporary and postmodern philosophy of science to a sociology of historical materialism and critical theory of the rise of capitalism. With the evolution of modern society and capitalism, positive reason has been modified to reflect the objective reality and technical reason of capital. Thus, a dialectic is created between subjectivity and objectivity, between consciousness and the economic system; they reinforce and validate one another at the same time that they conceptually invalidate and restrain any attempt to see or move beyond the present system to an alternative social and economic system.[7] This movement from epistemology to sociology also represents a change from the transcendental subject and a priori categories of intuition and the understanding to the a priori categories of political and economic liberalism. Following the path established by Husserl, Scheler, and Heidegger, Marcuse argues that "the science of nature develops under the *technological a priori* which projects nature as potential instrumentality, stuff of control and organization."[8] According to Marcuse, this technological a priori is the foundation stone for modern science. Technology is not simply the application of science to particular problems in modern industry and production. Marcuse's position is much more radical, in that the underlying and innate forms of pure reason are embedded in a political directive and ideology of control over nature.

In this manner Marcuse has started to integrate Marx's theory of work with Kant's a priori principles of the mind that create the objective world in experience. Marcuse summarizes his position: "the technological a priori is a political a priori in as much as the transformation of nature involves that of man."[9] The implications of this idea are revolutionary, as Marcuse raises the question about the concepts that define nature and asks if they are a priori technological and political. The application of science to increased industrial production and the organization of work is a technical feature of science that reduces external objectivity to quantification, management, and control. Marcuse also argues that the a priori concepts that create the physical and mathematical world—which science claims is objective reality—are an ideological, political, and social construct. The values of modern industrial society are part of the very categorical and theoretical structure of science itself. To clarify his point Marcuse asks if science is indifferent to the type of society that applies its theories and methods. That is, is science itself neutral to its technological application, or are the very categories and method of science political by nature? Is the world that science creates, the world that we perceive and understand and that surrounds us in our everyday life and in the scientific academy, indifferent to its application to nature? Or does this world reproduce the values and institutions of the political world that originally created it? If science is a priori political, does that not mean the science itself is a product of a certain type of society, thereby expressing, reinforcing, and implementing the values of that society? This is an extremely profound and complex issue that moves Marcuse beyond many others dealing with similar questions.

Here, with his explanation of the concept of "political a priori" when referring to the "science of nature," Marcuse relies upon Marx's theory of historical materialism. The concept and thought of science is inherently political not just because of its technological use, but also because of the values and principles embedded in the deepest regions of science itself that are grounded in "the historical mode of production" and the structured class organization of political economy. That is, science is political because its concepts and its formalistic method, as well as its application, are grounded in the abstraction and the fetishism of human labor of a particular form of industrial production and organization. The social mode or social relations of production are the key determining factor in the conceptualization of humanity's relationship to nature, observation of empirical reality, and science itself. Technological rationality or technical reason is a product of the "universal form of material production."[10] Science is political in the very depths of its underlying conceptual and theoretical foundations, not only because of its potential technological application, but also because it is a product of the inherent technical, instrumental, and operational formation of its very categories that create a technical and practical reason by means of which humans distinctively and historically observe, know, and dominate nature. Without the prior existence of material production and its social organization of production, science would not have developed, or not developed in the way it did. Its sociological foundations preceded its epistemological and methodological foundations. Science is both a priori technological and a priori political because it was formed within a historically specific material and social mode of production that reduced human life and labor to a quantifiable abstraction for the purposes of exploitation and manipulation.[11] Science became a more efficient and productive form of exploitative knowledge of commodity production. This position goes well beyond the issue of the politics of machine metaphysics examined in chapter 3.

Marcuse's statement about "the technological" and "the political a priori," quoted above, represents the heart of his theory of technological rationality and modern society and the underlying ambiguity of his intentions. The idea that science is both a technological and political a priori inherent in the deepest categories and structures of pure and practical science is central to his thesis about scientific rationality. However, because of his manner of presentation, the notion of "politics" could be interpreted in two different ways. First, it refers to "political" as the oppressive effects of technological science in the domination of nature and humanity. The hierarchical and class organization of production based on scientific rationality is political in its application and usage in modern industry. However, it could also refer to the structural origins of technological rationality and its organizational technique of domination in the historically based class politics and power of capitalism—in the nature of abstract labor, private property, and class politics. He has argued both positions throughout this essay, since positive science contains a priori categories of domination and is itself a construct and product of society. The following interpretation is that Marcuse is defending both definitions of science—its political origins in class warfare and the needs of industrial expansion, and in its technical application in environmental and social domination.[12]

Technological rationality is a broad and comprehensive term that refers to science and technology, the productive forces, social relations of production, scientific management, advertisement, forced consumption, and the domination of nature and humanity. Western science is capitalist and thus a particular historical and social form of knowledge; that is, science has an a priori political imperative that governs the creation and legitimation of the bureaucracy and direction of a capitalist economy. The politics of science are a central aspect of the categories and consciousness of knowledge, the description of the physical and natural objectivity of science, and its application to increased productivity and efficiency. Politics is a priori embedded in its very categories and forms of thought, as well as its application and justification. The politics of science is best expressed in the following manner: (1) the abstraction and quantification of science, human labor, and surplus extraction results in the confirmation of the rationality of the Enlightenment and capitalism and the domination of nature and humanity; (2) the a priori categories and forms of perception, experience, and science are abstract, formal, and technological, as they are oriented toward the domination and control over nature and production; (3) science provides the metaphysical foundations for a dead, mechanical, machine-like world defined in terms of time, space, forces, and mathematical calculations that can be exploited; (4) science is an important element in the technical machinery and nature of the productive forces for greater productivity and efficiency; (5) science provides the cultural legitimation, ideology, and metaphysical solace of universal truth and essential objectivity for the exploitative and oppressive class division of labor, the organization of production, and private appropriation of the means of production and capital; (6) science is a political ideology due to its abstract and formalistic epistemology and methodology of positivism, naturalism, nominalism, and disenchantment, and thus its inability to conceive of essence, form, potentiality, meaning, dialectics, or critical social theory; (7) science silences substantive reason by repressing and eliminating alternate and conflicting views of critical reason and normative thought as unscientific and illegitimate, thereby further justifying its form of reason and society, leading ultimately to "the abandonment of thought"; (8) science is not neutral and value-free in its concepts, method, or application, thereby expressing its underlying political orientation toward oppression; and (9) the theories of science and practical reason are understood as incorporating Weber's theory of formal scientific reason and the historical process of rationalization with Marx's theory of historical materialism and the social relations of production, which only furthers the belief that science is historically constructed and socially determined. The scientific mind does not reflect an objective reality, nor is it neutral in the manner and content of its application. Rather, science and technology impose their concepts, methods, and theories upon the external world with the intent of controlling its normative and productive structures to maintain and expand the privileged position of the wealthy over alienated workers.

Marcuse simplifies the question by asking if an electronic computer can be used in a capitalist and socialist society, implying that the technology is useful and neutral and can be employed in opposing social systems. The question is deceptively simple and enticing, but extremely complex to answer. The central issue involved is the nature of physical science and its relations to technical knowledge. That is, is there a dualism between pure and applied science, natural and technical science, and scientific inquiry and scientific application? Does science search for the truth about an independent, objective reality, but then apply its knowledge to the technical control of the external world? The traditional philosophical discussion about the nature of subjectivity and objectivity, human consciousness and nature, is now revived in the realm of social theory and the critique of reason. Marcuse argues that this traditional discussion about the subjectivity of a priori categories and the objectivity of physical matter, experimental relations, and mathematical laws is a myth of science, created to facilitate and obscure the technique of the domination of both nature and society.

The mathematization of nature and the instrumentalization of science are related to the historical rationalization of society. That is, technological rationality is inherent in the very categories and method of science itself. Science has become a technique of management and control over nature as it also dominates the workplace since its very a priori categories are themselves formal, technological, and functional. The subjective inner structure of the human mind and the epistemological search for objectivity (ontology and methodology, reality and truth), with their dialectical interplay between consciousness and reality, have been replaced by a social subjectivity with the normative imperatives of technological rationality. Observation, causation, and prediction have become mathematical relationships of the general laws of motion. The objectivity of nature in terms of the observation, measurement, and calculation of physical objects and the laws of motion has become a convenient myth to rationalize and justify the physical domination of nature and humanity, as nature is reduced to a technical reality and humanity to abstract labor and private property. Subjectivity acts as a conduit through which the social norms and values of modern capitalism are transmitted to our pure and practical knowledge of nature and society. Subjectivity, consciousness, experience, and science and the objective reality they create are all products of industrial production and the labor exploitation of humanity in the workplace. The everyday world we live in, perceive, and experience, know and understand, is a construct of an historical subject overwhelmed by social objectivity. Nature is a construct of alienated labor and consciousness. This is an updated variation of historical materialism, applied to human consciousness and natural science. Marcuse recognizes that this mathematical world of experiments and hypothetical testing creates a psychological and epistemological need for a concrete and functional world of extended substance, structured form, and bodily motion which, in turn, is used to justify this artificial construct of technical knowledge and control over nature. Marcuse is blunt and direct in referring to modern science and its world of objective physical objects as a rational form of repression which has the same reality as metaphysical and natural laws.

Marcuse broadens the discussion, introducing elements of Marx's theory of historical materialism into his argument by claiming that science is a product not of simple technological advancement, but of the total social mode of production and labor of capitalist society. If technology is not simply the application of science to human and natural problems, but rather reflects the underlying values and imperatives of the technology and machinery of industrial production, does that not mean that modern science is a reflection of the social system that produced it, whether capitalist or socialist? Narrowing his historical response, Marcuse maintains that the a priori categories of science reflect the political ideals and ideology of modern capitalism in its quest to dominate both nature and society. The a priori forms of intuitions and understanding by which we construct our relationship to the immediate physical environment, and by which we articulate and picture the world we observe and experience, are part of the process of industrial production. "The evolution of the scientific method merely 'reflects' the transformation of natural into technical reality in the process of industrial capitalism."[13] Marcuse further clarifies

his position when he states that it is not the theoretical categories or operational method of technical knowledge that dominates
our culture and organizes and defines our universe, but rather the
social modes of industrial production. "Technological rationality
is a system of domination which operates already in the concepts
and construction of techniques."[14] Science and technology are not
only applied in industry for greater efficiency, increased productivity, and the justification of organizational control; they are applied
because they contain the very concepts and logic necessary for
technical manipulation, management control, and ideological justification. If modern science and technology were neutral forms of
the productive forces, their forced application might be possible,
but not their transformation of consciousness. The two components of rationalization of science are necessary for the modern
form of advanced industry. Science legitimates and rationalizes
the quantification of nature, and in the process justifies the class
relations of capitalist production. It is the most rational form of
economic and social organization. In this manner, Marcuse rejects
Weber's thesis of the neutrality of scientific inquiry, which presents the latter as economically and politically independent of its
application in modern industry.

Western science is a cultural phenomenon reflecting the capitalist spirit, since its a priori categories and technical reason—by
which it constructs its view of nature and physical objectivity,
applies its method and theories, and technically manages and
controls its immediate natural environment for the "advancement" of humanity—reproduce the social relations of production
of modern society that have created science's very categories
and forms of thought. Marcuse hints at an emphasis on both the
technology and social organization of modern industry and production. His key points and their theoretical implications are not
clearly and definitively outlined. However, he does state that it is
the "social mode of production" which defines, delineates, and
constructs being and the objective reality of science. Science is
a socially determined form of technical knowledge. The human

mind and natural world are not reflections of the ego's search for innate ideas, empirical reality, or the a priori categories of pure reason, but rather the reflection of the economic totality of the production and class process. The human mind in all its endeavors is a product of its own society and distinctive mode of production. Marcuse has added another dimension to the issue of the mechanical manipulation and domination of nature, which is itself a reflection of the domination of humanity in its social relations of production and class structure. Thus, science is a priori political and technological, reflecting the priorities and needs of natural and social control within industrial production: science is a political ideology, no different from the ideologies reflected within the social sciences examined in the previous chapter. Kant's critique of pure and Enlightenment reason has been transformed into a critique of technical and political reason.

Although Marcuse does not commit fully to a theory of historical materialism, he stands at the edge of this insight. If knowledge is socially determined and defined, he needs to show how scientific concepts and theories reflect a particular political ideology, beyond merely restating the phenomenological insight that it also contains a priori concepts and methods for the domination of nature. Science is socially determined and thus political, not because it is simply focused on the domination of nature, but because the domination it performs manifests the priorities of a certain type of social discourse and institutional arrangement. Although he has connected Husserl and Scheler to a materialist foundation in his critical theory, Marcuse has not fully drawn the connecting historical links. Science reflects the logical and structural priorities of the economic system because it has reduced all knowledge and objectivity to a quantifiable and mathematical knowledge capable of the management and control of nature through modern industry. Science is a form of political knowledge because it has turned the labor of species beings—which was capable of expressing the essence of human creativity, political and aesthetic freedom, and communal responsibility—into an alien ideology that justifies a particular historical form of production and industry. The alienation of the senses, the quantification of labor time, the exploitation and commodification of abstract human labor in production and exchange, and the organization and management of human labor for profit and property accumulation have turned all human experience and nature into a measure of capitalist management and manipulation. These historical and social relationships have over time become embedded in the conceptual framework of modern science, which reflects the values and institutions of industrial and commercial capitalism. This is similar to the later process by which the social system becomes reflected in the concepts, theories, and methods of economics, political science, psychology, and sociology. The natural sciences are no different, as their forms of consciousness have become a social product and commodity unable to reflect upon or criticize the society out of which they came.

Science thus represents a new form of rationality and objectivity of instrumentality and operational control over physical matter. Science appears to be formal, mathematical, and neutral regarding the purpose of nature, as it calls for an objective neutrality of traditional goals or teleological ends. It has been released from any connection to Cartesian natural law. Freed from the traditional dependence on a teleology of final causes and specific ends, abstract mathematical science is now its own pure ideational ideal, which reduces everything to quantifiable figures and relationships—including "abstract labor power" which, like substances in nature, is reducible to quantifiable and measurable labor time in the production process, in order to ensure the maximum extraction of surplus value. Abstract labor is framed and measured by practical reason as this quantification of nature and work justifies both the domination of nature and humanity. Through this process labor is turned into an exploitable and monetary object or thing that does not express the ethical conditions for human creativity and freedom. Humans are quantitatively leveled and reduced to replaceable objects as their labor time, space, and energy are mathematically calculated to ensure economic profitability with lower costs, since workers have no other value that their productive capacity in a market economy defined by business success, profit accumulation, levels of consumption, and property ownership. The categories of science and the objects of production and consumption become marketable commodities and reflections of private property. The reduction of nature to the measurement and calculation of mathematical relations is made possible for the purposes of control over production by the reduction of human labor to commodities in the market. This is, in itself, made possible by the abstraction of labor from its particular social uses and common purposes as it is turned into pure forms of quantifiable and marketable commodities that are defined and calculated by the efficiency and productivity of work and by the profitability of market sales and consumption patterns. Neither labor nor nature has any purposes other than that promoted by the technical need for increased commodity production and property acquisition. Both nature and human labor are fetishized and mathematized by the same categories of domination and logic of capital accumulation; this is what Marcuse means by the rationalization and alienation of nature and society. A central implication of this position, outlining the historical and social bond between science and production, is that they are both historically and sociologically embedded in the same structures and values of modern capitalism. A desire to move toward a more democratic and free society would entail a radical change in the economy and culture of this type of society—a radical change in the nature of control over both the means of production and natural science itself.

Science and industrial technology are inherently connected, because they are grounded in the same a priori categories of scientific technology. The technological and political application of science for the purposes of economic exploitation and political domination within a capitalist economy is not something that is externally imposed upon science in opposition to its own search for objective truth and objective reality. These epistemological and

teleological goals of the ancient and medieval universe have long
been forgotten by science's own subjective and internal priorities,
built into its categories and logic of inquiry as a historically and
socially specific product of industrial capitalism. Science is a form
of knowledge constructed not by a transcendental subjectivity,
but by the a priori imperatives and goals of the industrial system.
Marcuse writes: "Specific purposes and interests of domination are
not foisted upon technology 'subsequently' and from the outside;
they enter the very construction of the technical apparatus. . . .
Such a 'purpose' of domination is 'substantive' and to this extent
belongs to the very form of technical reason."[15] The formal application of industrial and political technology is not something that is
arbitrarily or inadvertently applied in a given social system, undermining its original and truth-seeking telos. Science is not distorted
or transformed by the power and exploitation of an alien economy
and life culture. Science is instead an intimate and necessary part
of the institutional totality of this type of political economy, and
reflects its inherent value system and culture of domination.

Marcuse does not elaborate on this brief comment, but he seems
to be making a clear correlation between the formal quantification
and instrumental measurability of science and the quantification
and measurability of human labor: its necessary costs, exercise,
and profits in surplus labor. The mathematization of nature as
a hypothetical objectivity or "matter-in-function" is now correlated with the commodification and measurability (wages and
profits) of human labor and industrial production. He seems to
imply that, historically and sociologically, the logic of capital is
theoretically internalized in the very categories, concepts, laws,
and metaphysics of science. Unfortunately, Marcuse only hints at
this relationship between science and matter on the one hand and
machinery and labor on the other, which he names the "rationalization of the modes of labor," as he links "scientific and societal
quantification."[16]

A potential weakness in Marcuse's analysis is that he does not
state whether there is a parallel or causal link between science

and society, between the domination of nature and the domination of humanity, and between science and industrial capitalism. He recognizes there is a clear co-determination and historical interconnection between the culture and rationality of science and the structures of production and work. He recognizes the contextual relationship between the transformations of modern science and the institutions of society, but only hints at the historical relationships in this essay. The drive to dominate humanity in society precedes the domination of nature. The actual form that domination takes is framed by the capitalist system. This is a historically unclear idea, but it expresses more the relationship and debate between the phenomenology of Weber and Husserl and the historical materialism of Marx. It does not help the reader with the economic and sociological question of the historical origins of science. It expresses the physiological and psychological need for survival and the later social form that survival takes. Marcuse has a dialectical understanding of the relationships between the domination of nature (science) and the domination of humanity (capitalism), idealism and materialism, and consciousness and capitalism, as he moves back and forth between the forces of society. Marcuse is trying to avoid a deterministic view of the relationship between science and society as he emphasizes the biological drive for life and survival, but informed by the imperatives of the social system. For him, the relationship is interconnected and dialectical, even as he emphasizes the primacy of production over science.

The rationalization of the "modes of labor" precedes the "universe of science." The modes of labor in industrial production are formed using the technique and rationality of formal science in the technology, organization, management, accounting, and division of labor in the workplace. The justification of labor fragmentation and organization is based on the rationality of modern science and technology. However, this is the point where Marcuse fails to develop, even in outline, the nature of the social determination of this form of rationality. He uses terms like "concrete social practice," "modes of labor," "abstract labor power," and a "universe of discourse and action."[17] These terms only create confusion, because of their historical and social vagueness. He does say that "society freed men from the 'natural hierarchy' of personal dependence [in the feudal world] and related them to each other in accordance with quantifiable qualities—namely, as units of abstract labor power, calculable in units of time."[18] Marcuse quotes this important sentence from *Dialectic of Enlightenment* by Theodor Adorno and Max Horkheimer.

Marcuse does not examine the historical foundations of formalistic science, but focuses instead on the universal and abstract connection between capitalist labor as quantifiable and abstract and positive science as having the same social and metaphysical characteristics. It is this connection between science and society that frames Marcuse's theory of scientific and economic abstraction and his theory of the a priori political categories of science. It is these two aspects of science which bond science and society together and make them politically and socially inseparable, as well as making the neutrality and methodological and formal objectivity of science impossible. Western science is dialectical in that it is both a cause and effect of the commercial and industrial revolution and Enlightenment of Western society. Marcuse focuses on this theory of the abstraction of both science and labor because of its emphasis on the idea that both culture and political economy, both science and the reorganization and restructuring of modern work, are socially defined by quantification and calculability and socially determined by the implementing of science in industrial production. It is a historical form of society which both produces modern formal reason and technical science and applies them to the organization of human labor, since every aspect of society is rationalized by the standards of practical, formal reason in science and production. In this manner, science integrates social history and political economy for technological rationality and operational control. The politics of science thus lies in its metatheory, metaphysics, concepts, and technical application for the domination of nature and production.

According to Adorno and Marcuse, this structural process of abstraction in both science and labor is a form of political oppression, because it administers work and knowledge according to the logic of mechanical and formal laws and industrial machines, and because it no longer is capable of thought beyond quantifiable relations. Issues of hope, concept, essence, theory, ethics and the meaning and purpose of human life, are lost in a void of positivism and scientific hypotheses. There are no longer universals capable of deep reflection and analysis, just mathematical abstractions of the mind and body in all aspects of society. Human consciousness and thought are reduced to the control of mathematics, machines, and organizations. In the process, human labor loses its qualitative and ethical dimension as it becomes a universal and abstract object—a measurable quantity and a saleable commodity. For Horkheimer and Adorno, this transformation of science has important epistemological and sociological implications. Science does not reflect an objectivity of physical and social reality, but rather the domination of nature and humanity by class power over the means of production. In very strong terms, they argue that the Enlightenment represents the death of nature, human senses, and reason—"the abandonment of thought."[19] They write: "The universality of ideas as developed by discursive logic, domination in the conceptual sphere, is raised up on the basis of actual domination."[20] The foundations for the evolution of the Enlightenment, modern science, and the productive forces lie in the logic of capital and its class structure.

This theory of the social abstraction and quantification of labor (labor value, fetishism, and commodification) and science (empirical observation and hypothesis verification) also clarifies and adds another dimension to Marcuse's notion of the political a priori components of science itself. Together these two epistemological and sociological theories highlight the internal, a priori, and ideological connections and dependencies between science and capital. They emphasize the deep historical and sociological foundations of science in the logic and structures of capitalist organization and industry. The politics of science and labor are profoundly grounded in the same logic and formal categories of abstraction and the same a priori politics of oppression and domination of nature and humanity.

Although Marcuse focuses his attention on the traditional issues of subjectivity and the a priori categories of the mind, his own arguments drive him toward a materialist interpretation of the critique of reason. He states that he is not interested in exploring the historical connections between the rise of modern science and modern society in *One-Dimensional Man*, and thus not interested in developing a theory of historical materialism. But he does hint at their relationships when he argues that "the principles of modern science were a priori structured in such a way that they could serve as conceptual instruments of self-propelling, productive control . . . which led to the ever-more effective domination of nature . . . as well as the instrumentalities for the ever-more-effective domination of man by man *through* the domination of nature."[21] Mind does not reflect reality or even attempt any longer to achieve this goal, as it moves away from epistemology toward a critical sociology of knowledge. The categories and logic of industrial capitalism have infused and informed the categories of pure reason and technical science.

At first, with all these modern changes in subjectivity and objectivity, science appears to be instrumental and operational in its inherent conceptual design, just as it appears to be neutral in relation to any final goals, such as those which defined the ancient and medieval worlds and their views of the ends and purpose of humanity and nature. But even this is deceptive. Science is not neutral, since it is connected to the deep structures of rationalization (Weber) and the contemporary modes of labor (Marx). Science is intimately connected to the quantification and commodification of human labor within a capitalist society that attempts to exploit the surplus labor and profits that it can extract from its specific form of social organization. It is at this point in his analysis that Marcuse raises the question that connects epistemology and sociology, pure and technical reason. He finally asks the historically specific question of the connection between the historical rise of Western science and industrial capitalism; he asks if the relationship between scientific and technical quantification and the domination of nature and humanity is one of "parallelism or causation."[22]

But just as quickly as the question arises, Marcuse states that this is not the purpose of his work since his goal is to focus on issues of subjectivity (a priori categories of technical reason) and objectivity (mathematical quantification and control over nature). But even with this strong reservation, there is a dialectical opening since science is formed within a broader social setting in which the control over nature and humanity requires a control over the process of production. Control over nature through the quantification of both nature and production through labor, efficiency, capital accounting, and production involves the domination of humanity itself. Science does not develop in a historical or economic vacuum, but pure science and theory become integrated into the concrete, real world with the operational and instrumental logic of technical reason and the organization of production. The relationship between science and society is dialectical and interactive. Marcuse completes the Kantian critique of pure reason as it traces the transformation from pure to operational and technical reason, but continues to hold onto the idea of a dualism between pure and technical reason. The first is a theoretical abstraction, independent of traditional views of nature and teleology, and the second is a practical application in modern society.

By maintaining the divide between these two forms of reason, Marcuse inhibits investigation into the analysis of the rationalization of society with a detailed examination of the organization, structure, and management of technical reason in the workplace.[23] However, keeping separate pure and practical reason helps to continue the traditional myths of science. The illusion of pure science helps maintain the myth and ideology of scientific methodological objectivity, neutrality, and truth, while the practical application of technical reason justifies the efficiency and productive rationality of the historical social organization of production. Marcuse sees the two interpretations of science as intimately interconnected, since all forms of science occur within "a given universe of dis-course and action"—a different universe of a priori categories of technology that frame both empirical observation and scientific understanding.[24] It is society which determines the exact nature and content of the mathematical abstractions and the particular form of domination that science will assume in an ever expanding and aggressive market and industrial economy. Marcuse is clear that the economy implements the historically specific manner of domination, but is also clear that the characteristics of abstract and pure science are not a defense of a normative and political neutral-ity of science. The technology and politics of capitalist production is a priori inherent in the very categories and forms of thought of pure science. However, there is an interesting fine line between pure and practical science that could potentially lead to theoretical complications and confusions. This is not Marcuse's intention. He is, in fact, attempting to show the dialectical framework of theoret-ical and practical reason, abstract science and instrumentality, and science and society which now permeates all spheres of society, from its structures of political economy to its normative culture. He is clear that the logic and technique and the domination of nature are part of the a priori categorical structure of science, prior to any technical application in the real world. Marcuse's constant refer-ence to a priori technology and a priori politics is a reconfirmation of the initial Kantian insights that the categories of intuition and understanding are part of human consciousness prior to the act of perception and experience. The mathematization of nature created the illusion and prejudices of objective truth and a world of physi-cal objectivity having "certain basic concrete forms, shapes, and relations"—the abstract and ideational reality of mathematics—based on the prior determination of its instrumental and political categories and structure to observe, calculate, predict, and control nature. In this manner, science creates its own practical reality of the *Lebenswelt* or everyday life in perception, experience, and knowledge. Science as "technics becomes the universal form of material production, it circumscribes an entire culture; it projects a historical totality—a world."[25] Marcuse, following Husserl, calls this the "instrumental horizon" of pure (abstract mathematics) and practical (technical and instrumental) reason.[26]

Because of the conceptual and economic imperative toward the technological and political rationality of work organization, efficiency, productivity, and aggressive and unceasing industrial and market expansion, science is able to justify its historical form and place in the domination and control over production and the state. This a priori industrial imperative only reinforces and reconfirms the rationality of the political domination of humanity through the class exploitation of production and work, as it also confirms the irrationality of any alternative form of economic and political activity, i.e. socialism and democracy. Science provides the theoretical, logical, and rational justification of industrial capitalism, since it is the only rational form of the organization and logic of production and consumption. If an important goal of society is industrial development, expansion, efficiency, increased consumerism, happiness, and a better quality of life, science and technology are central to this American dream. But this form of material and economic rationality leads only to irrationality because the internal logic and instrumentalization of science—the categories, theories, and method it applies—are a reflection of the logic and operation of the machine and capital. The mathematization of science and the quantification of nature "would be the horizon of a concrete societal practice."[27]

This technical and political view of science also provides the conceptual foundation for the justification of law, liberties, rights, and personal freedom. Freedom, rights, and liberties, in turn, can only be defined and justified in terms of the capitalist system. To free humanity from the burdens of material life and the need for increased production only reinforces oppression through scientific rationality. Marcuse has developed his theory of technical science upon the writings of Galileo and Husserl, who have argued that theoretical or pure science is built upon the physical objectivity created by prior perception and experience of the general lifeworld (*Lebenswelt*). Marcuse moves beyond their approaches to the recognition that perception and experience are themselves products of a historical and social reality that pervades its a priori conceptual structure. This is all hidden by the false objectivity and technological ideation of mathematics. The world we experience and the world configured by mathematical equations and relationships are technically the same, just with different appearances. The commodification and abstraction of quantitative labor has permeated the abstract quantification and mathematization of nature. The world of perceptual sight and theoretical experiments, the world of practical and pure reason, is a conceptually pre-structured universe based on the technical nature and organization of society for domination over the process of production and nature. In *One-Dimensional Man*, Marcuse expands his understanding of technical rationality beyond science and production to include the totality of society in consumption, culture, the academy, and the inner psychological needs of the individual. He also recognizes the ideological and repressive power of natural science as the rational foundation of modern society, since all other forms of freedom outside of a capitalist economy are viewed as illegitimate, oppressive, and totalitarian.[28]

At the end of the book, Marcuse opens a new avenue of discussion by observing that mathematical science does not challenge the underlying epistemological or existential assumptions of the physical world we inhabit. Though the worlds of sight and mathematics are different, they share a common conceptual foundation in the formal a priori categories of technical domination, and thus do not threaten each other or call for "qualitatively new ways of seeing" or new ways of organizing one's existential and social life. It is at this point that Marcuse calls for a consideration of a new type of science, with new categorical forms underlying subjectivity and objectivity.[29] Here, he raises a new question: With a new "discourse and action," a new social universe with different economic and political priorities based on social justice and communitarian values, would the very nature of science fundamentally change? Would there be a new social form of political economy and a new form of science, no longer attached to the domination of nature but to another set of ethical and political priorities? This would and must occur since science is a priori technological and political. It is not a neutral form of knowledge reflecting objective reality and truth, but a socially constructed form reflecting the objectivity of historically defined social relations of production.

The categories and method of modern science are historical and cultural phenomena based on the prior structures and values of modern political economy. Culture and knowledge are social and thus predetermined and pre-formed in human consciousness by institutional and normative priorities of society, thereby creating the world of both everyday experience and positive science. This is the instrumental and mathematical world of practical and theoretical reason. Marcuse summarizes his work on the innate political implications of science and technology in the following manner: "The point which I am trying to make is that science, *by virtue of its own method* and concepts, has projected and promoted a universe in which the domination of nature has remained linked to the domination of man—a link which tends to be fatal to this universe as a whole."[30] According to Marcuse, this form of the social relations of production or economic hierarchy may increase the material wellbeing of some individuals in a limited fashion, but it also intensifies the class system of economic oppression. It is at this point that he raises a different type of question: Would a radical transformation of this distorted rationality and work organization also affect the relationship between humanity and nature?

Science is informed and encumbered by its political and technical categories for greater control over nature that give the appearance of epistemological objectivity and methodological

neutrality based on the prior technological and political imperatives of the social system. Would a social transformation toward
democratic socialism force a reconsideration of the very nature
of science itself? Because of the a priori and internal intimacy
between concepts and reality and between politics and science,
would a change in the nature of society force a reconsideration
and change in science and, thus, our relationship to our immediate physical environment? If the categories of Western science
are so intimately and internally connected to technological
advancement, instrumentality, and the political structure and
organization of work, would a new science have to be constructed
that expressed a more emancipated society and a more organic,
symbiotic, and liberated relationship to nature?[31] This new science
would represent a change from the domination of humanity and
nature to a modern form of stewardship, teleology, and respect
for all forms of planetary life. Marcuse is raising a central question of whether science, although a technical and instrumental
factor in nature and production, is neutral and, thus, capable of
being utilized in an alternative and classless social system. This
question implies that science is both naturalistic and realistic as
it reflects an objective reality that can be utilized effectively and
fairly in any type of social system, whether capitalist or socialist. If
science is neutral in its method of observation, hypothesis formation, empirical testing, and causal conclusions, and if, because of
this neutrality, science has been instrumentalized for the domination of nature and humanity in a capitalist system, it still has the
potential to be applied in a non-oppressive and liberating manner
in a new type of social organization. Science has no inherent or
a priori biases or political imperatives toward one type of social
system over another. However, in his concluding remarks at the
end of *One-Dimensional Man*, Marcuse reaffirms that the domination of nature entails the domination of man. The concepts and
method of science are inseparable from industrial and commercial
capitalism because their ideas and method of the appropriation of
natural goods and abstract labor reflect a common foundation of

capitalist production and class structure. Rational questions about nature would continue to be raised by scientific hypotheses and experiments, but science would have different concepts, facts, and an entirely different view of objective reality and truth. The end result would be a radical change in the nature of science and its relationship to both nature and society. In this way "the rational society subverts the idea of Reason."[32]

Because a social revolution would transform both the technically rational and bureaucratic organization of production and other social institutions, Marcuse does recognize that this would necessarily entail a revolutionary restructuring of science, technology, and the workplace. Recognizing the breadth of such a radical transformation of the public and private spheres of rationalization, he states that such a revolution "would involve a change in the *technological structure itself* in all spheres of private and public life" and in both consciousness and the external social reality.[33] In his essay "Industrialization and Capitalism in the Work of Max Weber" (1964) Marcuse details his expanded understanding of science and technical rationality with his examination of Weber's theory of rationalization and disenchantment.[34] The irrational structural and logical foundations of modern society are best expressed for Marcuse as the contradictions between the private ownership of the means of production (private property) and the social productivity of communal wealth. Overcoming the contradictions between the technical and operational means of production and the social or class relations of production was viewed as the central idea in Marx's later economic writings.[35] Marcuse maintains that Soviet communism held that with the socialization of the productive forces it would no longer be subservient to the logic and rationale of capitalist production at the same time that private property would be communally redistributed under a communist system, but Marcuse is quite clear here: "Neither nationalization nor socialization alter *by themselves* this physical embodiment of technological rationality."[36] Revolutionizing the class system and social property will radically transform and liberate humanity, but

it will not change the inner structure and categories of technological rationality. The latter is a form of both pure and practical
reason, but also contains the inner logic and mechanical workings
of scientific management and the wage slavery and automation of
the social relations of production. Even the public nationalization
of property and production or the social redistribution of productive wealth will not change the character and structure of technical
rationality and scientific management. The productive and technical forces are intimately, socially, and historically interconnected
with technological rationality. That is why such rationality is political by nature: it reflects the social relations of production in its
particular form of reason. Reason is never truly pure and abstract
from physical or social reality. The values of capitalism are embedded in technical reason and thus to radically transform only the
social relations of production is unfortunately to miss the Trojan
horse and ideology hidden in science and technology themselves.

Marcuse begins *One-Dimensional Man* with an analysis of
advanced industrial society and bureaucratic rationalization that
call for a rethinking of Marx's labor theory of value, the organic
composition of capital, the role of surplus value in production,
and the nature of alienation and exploitation in the workplace.
For his insight, he draws upon Weber's theory of rationalization and Marx's later analysis of production in the *Grundrisse*
(1857–1858).[37] The rationalization of science and production
have produced a new advanced economy of scientific management and Taylorism, expanded production and efficiency, capital
accounting, automation and technical progress, machine productivity replacing human labor, blue collar workers, increased
advertising-induced consumption, a deepening of psychological
and existential problems, and so on. The workplace has become
modernized and automated, changing the nature of labor exploitation and worker consciousness as well as changing the very nature
of the social pathology of capitalism. What is stressed in the workplace are not the structural contradictions of work, but the need
for worker integration and participation, as alienation is socially

and psychologically sublimated into a domination of administration and bureaucratic organization and is no longer viewed as the extraction of surplus labor and value. Technological rationality has been altered by the rationalization and bureaucratization of the workplace. Technological and scientific rationality replace and sublimate the traditional forms of labor exploitation, resulting in a soft alienation that becomes more and more difficult to recognize and critique.

Where Marcuse develops a critical theory of science and technology based on historical phenomenology, neo-Kantian and anti-foundational philosophy of science, classical social theory, and historical materialism, Habermas continues this line of thinking by building upon the classical social theory of Marx and Weber and the system theory of Talcott Parsons, with its total system of structures of political economy and the modern cultural lifeworld. As we have already seen, Marcuse emphasized the transcendental subjectivity and consciousness of the objective physical and social world by combining Weber's theory of the rationalization of science and the technological heart of formal and abstract rationality with the phenomenological theory of the domination of nature. He then combined these insights with Marx's ideas of economic exploitation, political oppression, and the domination of humanity. Habermas expands upon Marcuse's theory of scientific oppression and the domination of humanity by adding a broader and more comprehensive structural theory of society that he borrows from Parsons' theory of the structures, functions, and historical interconnectedness among systems of political economy and social institutions and the cultural foundations of the everyday world of experience and normative cultural values. That is, Habermas combines technical-purpose reason and communicative interaction. Marcuse's critical social theory expanded the phenomenological critique of science and domination by combining it with classical social theory in order to focus on the technical and political nature of the categories and theories of natural science, while Habermas continues to expand Marcuse's theory by combining it with Parsons' holistic social theory of the structures and functions, system and lifeworld of modern society. Marcuse focuses on the political nature of science and the expanded application of science in modern technology, factory and corporate organization, political bureaucracy, and the culture industry. Habermas, too, is interested in the expansion of Enlightenment rationality beyond work and industry into new social spheres that are articulated in Parsons' expanded systems theory.

In *Economy and Society* (1921), Weber developed a theory of rationalization which examined the quantification and methodical and mathematical calculation of technical science and rational accounting as it was incorporated into everyday experience, bureaucracy, law, and hierarchical and corporate organizations. His goal was to understand the nature of modern technology in the corporate economy and bureaucratic state, in order to show the form of rationality and domination in corporate capitalism. This form of technical reason and specialized knowledge requires the existence of free labor, a market economy, and private ownership of the means of production.[38] These elements of a modern corporate economy are essential for economic control, calculation of general costs of labor and technology, and greater efficiency and control over production. The system of formal reason becomes more rational, disciplined, and technically productive, giving this new system of bureaucratic control and domination the illusion of rationality, realism, and neutrality. Through this means the labor process becomes more organized and specialized from the top down, reinforcing and confirming the corporate power structure, worker discipline and domination, social leveling and passive compliance, and the advances of industrial capital.

The technical rationality of science is used to implement the formal rationality and order of the organization of production through free labor in a free market, as well as the formation of an autocratic mass democracy. It is interesting that Weber contends that socialism would simply be an alternative social system built upon the same logic and principles as advanced capitalism, since formal science is value-free and neutral in its technical application. Marcuse supports Weber's analysis of the rationalization of society as the key to understanding the corporate and bureaucratic structure of modern capitalism, but rejects Weber's view that technical science is value-free and neutral. Marcuse reinforces this position at the end of his essay on Weber: "Specific purposes and interests of domination are not fostered upon technology 'subsequently' and from the outside; they enter the very construction of the technical apparatus. Technology is always a historical-social project: in it is projected what a society and its ruling interests intend to do with men and things."[39] The domination of humanity in the workplace has always been an essential and a priori element in the formation of Western science, which is a form of "capitalist reason." The technological domination of nature and humanity is not external to science but lies in the depth of the concepts and method of science itself. Science is the intellectual and theoretical form of domination and not simply its practical form. Weber abstracted from the material foundations of science and thus failed to see its a priori political dimension. An important implication of this critical position is that a reorganization of society based on a humanistic ethic of communal responsibility, individual freedom, and personal dignity would also require a rethinking of the very history, structure, and logic of modern science and its relationship to issues of the environment and social justice.

HABERMAS AND THE RATIONALIZATION OF SCIENCE AND IDEAL COMMUNICATION

Habermas builds upon Weber's theory of rationalization by joining it with Parsons' holistic system theory of the structures and life-world of modern society as the basis for understanding personal and social action. One reason Habermas switches to Parsons and his holistic theory of social systems of action is that Habermas was critical of Marx's theory of labor and its apparent methodological positivism as articulated by the analytical Marxists. Parsons was also viewed in the United States as a classical social theorist who dominated the academic scene. Habermas also incorporated the ideas of U.S. pragmatism from the writings of John Dewey and George Herbert Mead with those of Scheler, Husserl, and Alfred Schutz, in order to expand and join together his understanding of the rationality of the system and lifeworld in Parsons' own theory. The phenomenologists emphasized the transcendental and a priori forms of consciousness and their relation to physical and social objectivity. This positioning of their historical analysis of the evolution of consciousness was too individualistic and too mechanical and instrumental when applied to science and technology. Parsons provided a way of broadening the theoretical framework away from an emphasis on the inner structure of consciousness and toward explaining the relationship between technical reason and the totality of society. His emphasis was on the relationship between individual actions and motivations and their integration into the structures of the social system. The social system is viewed as a living organism affecting the motivation and action of individual agents. With phenomenology and pragmatism, Habermas attempts to complete the project with their analysis of consciousness, subjectivity, language, and symbolic interaction. He is able to expand his critical theory of communicative action to include both systems theory and symbolic action theory. By this means he is able to connect the logic and interaction of the system or structures of political economy and domination on the one hand and the language, culture, and institutions of the social lifeworld on the other. Habermas approached the study of society by examining the relationship of personal motives, intentions, and cultural values to specific actions within society. In his study of personal action within the social system, he integrates culture, society, and the personality—the cultural values and institutions, political and economic structures of society, and personal and biological motivations based on physical and cultural needs—as the basis for determining the nature of individual action within the social system. Unlike Parsons, who used his macro-sociology to examine the nature of behavioral and social integration, Habermas instead focuses on intentionality, conflict, change.[40] His sociological goal is to emancipate human reason, the Enlightenment, and social and communicative action from the pessimism and positivism of traditional science and capitalism.

Habermas also relies upon the writings of Weber and Marcuse, but is at the same time critical of the weaknesses he perceives in their works. In particular, he rejects Marcuse's connection between a priori technological rationality and the politics embedded in the scientific categories and method of inquiry. Instead, Habermas argues that the rationality of science became part of the rationality of the lifeworld in its culture, values, institutions, and consumption as the rationality of the system dominated the lifeworld. However, there is no necessary inner logical connection between the two, only a historical connection of capitalist domination. By this means he can sustain the belief, as with Weber, that science is neutral and objective and not touched by a priori connections to the logic of the political and economic system of capitalism. Science is not just pure instrumentalism. Although a member of the Frankfurt School, Habermas rejects the intellectual pessimism of the first generation of critical theorists in the writings of Adorno, Horkheimer, and Marcuse, who held that the Enlightenment resulted in totalitarian domination, the loss of critical reflection, and the death of reason and philosophy.[41] Finally, borrowing from structuralism and functionalism of systems theory permits Habermas to detail more finely a broader picture of social domination and oppression in the tradition of classical social theory at the same time that he develops his own emancipatory theory of communicative action and discursive rationality. Using this structural and functional approach to the study of society permits Habermas to move beyond the dialectic of enlightenment and a one-dimensional view of society to uncover the emancipatory potential of human liberation of practical (ethics and praxis) action based on cultural values and intersubjective discourse. It is a way of moving beyond the traditional notions of reason and understanding as transcendental, objectivistic, technical, and practical rationality in the tradition of Bacon, Kant, Hegel, and Marcuse to the liberation of reason in intersubjective discourse, cultural hermeneutics, and political language. Knowledge is not of a physical thing or social object, but of shared values, norms, and ideals communicated in public language.[42] In this manner, Habermas is able to rediscover the lost essence, form, and reason of the public and private life-world that has been repressed in the rationality of the modern social system.[43]

By blending Marx's critique of political economy; Weber's theory of economic and administrative rationalization and bureaucracy, technological rationality, and domination; and Parsons' structuralism and functionalism, Habermas thinks he is better able to explain the historical transition of liberal capitalism and the market economy to advanced capitalism and the administrative welfare state. The result is a new critical theory of scientific and technological application and development, placed within the macro-structures of Habermas's theory of social action, which includes the social system and cultural lifeworld. To accomplish this task, he grounds his theory of how social systems function and maintain stability on two fundamental and different forms of social action—the instrumental, efficient, and technical action of work, and the intersubjective cultural and normative action of intersubjective communication (social interaction). This structural approach separates technical from practical or instrumental from ethical and normative action based on the key distinctions between system and lifeworld. Habermas develops his own critical social theory by readjusting classical and Parsonian sociology in the following ways. He argues that in advanced capitalist society there have been changes in the relationships between the basic subsystems and structures and their functions, including: (1) the base and superstructure, (2) productive forces and social relations of production, (3) state and the economy in areas of social welfare and economic stabilization and order, (4) changes in the nature of political ideology and social displacement and justification, (5) separation of science from culture and science from politics, and (6) the explanation of science and technology by juxtaposing and connecting the system and lifeworld.

Borrowing from Parsons' system theory, Habermas argues that these changes occur within his broader and more comprehensive understanding of the structures and subsystems of the social system as a network of social interaction among individual actors. There are four key structural prerequisites and integrative functions which are essential to the continued stability and maintenance of society, represented by the acronym AGIL: adaptation (A), adjustment, and control over the physical environment and the provision of resources and goods for the economy and market through production and distribution; the setting of political priorities, objectives, and collective goal (G) attainment, as well as the necessary resource allocation to achieve them; the societal community, social institutions, and subsystems of the law, family, education, and religion necessary for social solidarity, coordination, integration (I), and socialization for "latent pattern maintenance and tension maintenance" by transmitting and integrating the cultural patterns or underlying cultural values and moral commitments that define social action; and latency (L), or the hidden cultural patterns of moral values, social norms, language, role expectations, and empirical knowledge for pattern maintenance and social integration, conformity, and harmony.[44] This AGIL scheme represents the economy, state, social institutions, and culture, which are the necessary structural and functional foundations of all societies. Parsons develops these ideas in the early 1950s, in *The Structure of Social Action*. Habermas would use this broad view of the interactions among the total social subsystems throughout his later writings to help develop the social foundations for his own theory of communicative action, discursive rationality, and the legitimation crisis, as well as to aid in the formation of a new and emancipatory theory of democracy. This approach allows Habermas critical insights into the class domination of the structures of modern political economy and their continued stability, maintenance, and justification by the cultural phenomena of the lifeworld. But these very distinct institutions and forms of social action also allow for the possibility of a critical reflection on the immanent potentialities of a renewed public sphere and democratic communication in the lifeworld.

Habermas begins to pull this material together in his theory of the rationality of science and technology by undertaking a general critique of the macro social theory of Weber, Marcuse, and Marx in *Toward a Rational Society* (1967). Habermas's focus is initially on Weber's theory of rationalization in science and technology, economic production, human labor, bourgeois law, and the state bureaucracy, and the corresponding forms of purposive-rational and technical-instrumental action appropriate to maintain these central elements in society. The same type of formal rationality of modern science permeates and justifies the various systems of collective action within society. This is the beginning point for Marcuse's critical analysis of Weber's theory of scientific and societal rationalization. Habermas builds his social theory on this integration of the broad conceptual frameworks of classical social theory, grounded in the ideas of Weber's theory of rationalization and disenchantment and Freud's theory of the unconscious and repression. He also contends that Marx's economic theory contains a serious theoretical problem that revolves around the relationship between two of Marx's key concepts: the productive forces and the social relations of production. Habermas argues that this problem is especially acute when considering the revolutionary changes in the nature of capitalist production in an advanced industrial society.

Marx argued that with the increasing development and expansion of scientific, technological, and industrial developments within capitalism, the productive forces and growing material wealth of society would lead to a serious reconsideration of the ethical and technical need for the continuation of the exploitative class structure within the industrial workplace. That is, the increasing rationalization of production and the immense expansion of social wealth would produce a call for emancipation from the oppressive and hierarchical social relations of production and exploitation of surplus labor value and economic profits. Starting from this issue, Habermas begins his critique of Marcuse by outlining an alternative view of economic expansion in which the productive forces continue to expand the material base of society, but also undermine any emancipatory potential by rationalizing and repressing any thought of alternative ethical and political ways of economic and social organization of the material production and distribution of social wealth. The productive forces of technological rationality in contemporary society now have an a priori political dimension to justify technical reason and repress any awareness of social oppression. All aspects of modern industry, whether at the level of technical production or bureaucratic and class organization, become immunized from social critique. Where Marx saw an emancipatory potential in science and technology, Weber and Marcuse see the opposite—further exploitation of human resources, labor, and energy, leading to the increased dehumanization and degradation of humanity and nature. This integration of the forces and relations of production results in the loss of emancipatory potential, along with a loss of traditional, reflective, and dialectical reason and critical social theory. The result in advanced capitalism is continued economic growth and capital accumulation, accompanied by the repression of social ethics, ideals, and hopes for an alternative form of political and economic system— that is, a loss of social justice which is only magnified by the split in the U.S. academy between natural science, social science, and the humanities. It is this which leads to a one-dimensional society without hope and without a vision for the future.

According to Habermas, by fusing the productive forces and social relations of production in his theory of the political and technological foundations of modern science into his grand theory, Marcuse has politicized science and technology, since scientific knowledge is no longer viewed as an objective and neutral form of knowledge seeking objective truth and reality. At the same time, it undermines the ability to reason and act toward the creation of a more open and free society based on scientific and technological rationality. The latter has restructured both nature and society, leading to the rationalization of the economy and the domination of society. Against this position, Habermas maintains that in order to understand the nature of the modern science and its relationship to the social system, it is necessary to separate the productive forces and social relations of production. In this way, he is able to depoliticize science and technology and separate its potential inquiry and use from the capitalist organization of production, while connecting it instead to the cultural and phenomenal superstructure. Habermas historically and socially disconnects the productive forces and the social relations of production in order to disconnect emancipation from domination, social production from capitalist production, and communicative action from instrumental, purposive-rational action. In a capitalist society, the social system, social relations, and superstructure lose their independence, because they are organized around the immanent political imperatives of technological rationality. The domination of nature through an ideological and politically laden science also requires the domination of humanity according to the same logical principles and categories of scientific and technological rationality that required the metaphysics of science and the domination of nature. However, according to Habermas, Western science is not itself one-dimensional or narrowly and historically specific. It does not reflect the logic of capitalism, although he recognizes that it has been used in a technologically specific manner within that type of social system. It is conceptually and methodologically capable of being the basis for economic growth beyond capitalism in a truly free and democratic society; there is no a priori political imperative within science, only a historically and socially defined manner of expression and application of technical reason. Habermas recognizes the instrumental and technological a priori of modern science, but rejects the theory of a political a priori developed by Marcuse. The technical imperative built into science itself does not reflect the domination of a particular social system, but is a universal characteristic of modern science. By taking this position, Habermas has separated the productive forces from the relations of production, thereby keeping the former as a potentially progressive instrument for human liberation. This is an essential reason for his later separation of the system and life-world, political economy and cultural values, norms, knowledge, and ideals of a society. The lifeworld is the key to the social integration and rationalization of the social life, as it is composed of the culture, personality, and social institutions. The social system of capitalist political economy does not necessarily share the same form of rationality as the cultural lifeworld. The domination of humanity infects the relations of the social organization of production and the cultural superstructure.

Habermas recognizes the central importance of Weber's theory of rationalization but refuses to push it to the extremes that Marcuse holds. Although science is embedded in a universal and instrumental rationality for the domination of nature, this does not mean that it is politically and economically determined for the domination of humanity. The rationalization of science has been abused within the capitalist system for the purpose of industrial expansion, cultural justification, and political ideology—colonization and distorted communication of the lifeworld—but the inner logic of capital does not penetrate into the deepest recesses of human consciousness and categories of scientific reason and actions. Science, as it is utilized in advanced industrial society, plays a dual role as instrumental rationalization and political justification of the domination of humanity in the class hierarchy of the workplace. But unlike Marcuse in his search for a "new science," Habermas contends that science is conceptually, theoretically, and methodologically independent of capitalist domination; it has only been appropriated for a historical moment by class power. Much of Habermas's writing is an attempt to expand his understanding of the theory of rationalization and the relationship between instrumental or purposive-rational action and the disenchantment of cultural traditions (Weber) and the relationships between scientific rationality and political domination (Marcuse), between the productive forces of science and industrial production and the social relations and class organization of production (Marx), and between social domination and the unconscious repression of distorted reason and thought (Freud). Disenchantment becomes disassociated and displaced symbols and ideology, which subsume any possible differences and conflicts between the base and superstructure and hide the above-mentioned dualisms within the mode of production.

Habermas thinks modern science has a crucial role in expanding production, oppressing workers, and hiding the economic and political domination from critical reflection and refutation. The expanded rationality of science and increased productivity and efficiency of the modern productive forces occur at a cost of meaningful and productive personal and community lives and social democracy, since they do not call into question the apparent and assumed rationality of both the theory and application of science itself. Thus capitalism is seen as a rational form of social organization because it is grounded in the legitimacy of scientific rationality as both a technical and productive force, as well as a theoretical and conceptual reflection of objective reality. This legitimates the need to dominate both nature and society because "the existing relations of production present themselves as the technically necessary organizational form of a rationalized society."[45] Marx had believed that, with the expansion of material wealth and growing products of industrial society, there would be a call to change the class structure with its social relations of domination. Habermas argues the opposite: that with industrial expansion, modern science only further supports and justifies the continued oppression of the social relations of capitalist work. Science rationalizes, in the Weberian and Freudian meaning of the term, the continued social organization of production rather than revealing its oppressive structure. In this way, "rationality is weakened as a critical standard" for the evaluation of the history and structures of political economy by its unconscious and distorted political fusion of the productive and scientific/technological forces and the social relations and organization of production. The dialectical and critical interplay between the technical and social forms of production are ideologically repressed and unconsciously forgotten, resulting in the continuation of an oppressive social system that has expanded the rationalization of society to include both political economy and cultural legitimation in a class system destructive of both democracy and the natural environment.

According to Habermas, technical science and industrial work are historically conjoined to the point that the former is no longer capable of offering critical insights into the nature of domination or alternative social forms of work organization. The class nature of science and work are viewed as both logical and legitimate expressions of human reason and also progressively necessary for continued economic expansion and enjoyment of the good material life. The critical and dialectical reason that recognizes the inner structural contradictions of modern society—between science and work, the productive forces and social relations of production, and instrumental rationality and communicative reason—is repressed and disappears into a social unconsciousness incapable of developing a memory of true reflections and insights. Rationalization has resulted in the loss of reason and social critique, as it has been turned into a form of technical rationality which expands the productive and technological forces of production. In the process it unconsciously legitimates their continued application toward further "objectively obsolete domination" within a class society by the outdated and oppressive social relations of production.[46] The oppressive nature of the rationality of science and work is divorced from any reflective ability to make ethical and political judgments about them. The forces of scientific and technological production have rationalized the productive and social organization of the economy to such an extent that they can no longer be the basis of critique, but only the basis for ideological legitimation.[47]

It is at this point that Habermas critically turns against Marcuse's view of the political values at the heart of modern science and its legitimation of capitalist industry, work hierarchy, and purposive-rational action. The former views the fusion of the productive forces and technological science as a distinct historical and socio-logical moment in time that results in their failure to recognize their own material, social, and emancipatory potentiality and the need to move beyond the capitalist organization of production. This is the failure of the productive forces and their inability to form a critical social theory of advanced industrial society. The productive forces have enormously expanded the industrial reach of modern industry even as they have lost their critical, dialec-tical, and emancipatory function in society. Marcuse views their relationship quite differently: for him, the dialectic is not between ethics and work or justice and production, but between the pro-ductive forces and logic of capital. He joins together science and politics, technology and domination, which only furthers the loss of essence, concept, theory, and critique.[48] It is the political content of modern science and technology that is the focus of Marcuse's theoretical attention. Since science is internally constructed along distinct political categories and method that reflect the underlying structures and logic of advanced political economy, the produc-tive forces could never be the basis for critical enlightenment. That demands a rethinking of the very nature of science itself.

Habermas contends, following Marx, that the problem lies in the loss of the dialectic between the productive forces and social relations of production, and in the transition of the role of science from emancipation and critique to legitimation and ideology. This distinction and debate with Marcuse frames much of the development of Habermas's later critical theory of communica-tive action. By taking classical social theory and integrating it with aspects of the macro sociological approach of Parsons, and by expanding the structures and subsystems of society and their internal functions and stabilizing effects, Habermas believes he is able to broaden his theory of rationalization beyond Weber and

Marcuse. By doing so he sees the connections, but also the critical separations and distinctive subsystems and functions within society, between the productive forces and relations of production, between science and work, between purposive-rational action and communicative action, and between science and ideology. By separating science and the political a priori of the domination of humanity and by studying society in which political economy is only one component of a broader social system, Habermas opens up new fields of inquiry.

Science is no longer tied to the logic of capital; it is no longer socially determined by "class interests and historical situation," and thus may become part of a truly revolutionary transformation of society without itself becoming a "new science."[49] Science has been used by the class system as an instrument of domination and control, but Habermas rejects the idea that science is inherently political and determined by the logic of capital. If this remains true, then the dogmatic and ideological symbols of domination come not from science and technology, but from another part of the social system. This, too, expands Habermas's theory of rationalization and critique of domination, just as it opens up two other distinct social possibilities. First, if it is not science and technology which act as the basis for political domination, then there is no need for a "new science" and, second, the opportunity for social critique and a critical social theory outside the logic of capital is reenergized. For Habermas, science does have an a priori imperative for technical reason and instrumental control that has been used for class oppression under capitalism. However, its underlying concepts and method are not corrupted and abused by an inner political content defined and determined by capitalist production. Technical reason has not been reduced to politics and domination. Thus, Habermas is not interested in developing a new science, a new view of nature, or a new form of application. Science does have an instrumental core that is based on technical rationality, the nature of work, human nature, and the need for self-preservation. Science is instrumental and is used for control over nature, but does not determine the specific historical and social organization and power relations in society. He replaces the political domination of science with the universal instrumental control of purposive-rational action over physical nature by the human species. Technology has been used throughout human history for the mastery over nature as necessary for the continuation of human existence.

Science's conceptual imperative is technical utility and control, not political domination, and thus science does not rationalize the social relations of production. Habermas switches from a focus on science and technology as domination to science and technology as forms of purposive-rational action; the latter is an important element in the very survival of the human organism. It is less a political and sociological issue and more a biological issue of the continuance of the species itself. In this sense, science is politically neutral with regard to the manner and purposes for which it is applied. Habermas recognizes that it has been used for capitalist domination, but also holds that it can be the basis for social liberation. This represents a return to Marx's position regarding the power of critique and change of the productive forces. In the end, the manner of its applications is defined by society itself. From this perspective, science and technology have no predetermined goals set by capitalism, and, therefore, may be the basis for changing the class system. The real problem lies in the social relations of production and the method of ideological justification of domination. Habermas ends his critique of Weber's and Marcuse's theory of rationalization with the recognition that the productive forces are no longer viewed as inherently and mechanically political, but tied to the instrumental action of the human species. The legitimation and ideology of advanced capitalism do not lie in productive capacity and rationality of science and technology, but in the distortion and corruption of science's cultural values. The productive forces will be the basis for social critique and change, as well as economic expansion and the potential material wellbeing of society.

The central insight of this perspective for Habermas is that although there must be a social revolution to escape the oppressiveness of a class society, there does not have to be a revolution in reason and science. Also, he argues, previous theorists never fully appreciated the internal dynamics, tensions, and conflicts within and between the subsystems of advanced society, nor did they appreciate the role each subsystem played in maintaining the economic development, political direction and stability, cultural integration, value-orientations and pattern maintenance of cultural values, and ideological justification, and the emancipatory potential of critical theory that lies within these complex structural and functional relationships. By broadening social theory in this manner, Habermas contends that he is able to overcome the weaknesses of traditional social thought. He concludes his critique of Marcuse by maintaining that the answer to the dilemma of whether the productive forces of science and technology represent the continued oppression of human labor or the potential to create the material conditions for a more democratic society—a choice between ideology and emancipation, oppression and reason—lies in his theory of social action.

Habermas's rejection of elements of the traditional theories of rationalization in classical and critical theory helps to articulate and explain the direction that his later theoretical research will take. In his early writings he broadens his theory of rationalization by navigating and reintegrating the components of the social system by distinguishing between two forms of social action—purposive-rational action or work and symbolic or communicative action. He begins with a general critique of traditional social theory by distinguishing between these two forms of action based on different parts or subsystems of the capitalist system. Later, Habermas moves beyond these forms of rationality and action to a structural and functional analysis of the legitimation crisis, consisting of the pathologies and dysfunctions within the total social system. These transformations arise from his incorporation of Parsons' system theory into a more critical analysis of advanced capitalism.[50] Responding to critics who have argued that

Habermas, too, is guilty of idealism and abstractionism from the concrete historical reality in his theory of communicative action and the ideal speech situation, Thomas McCarthy presents an alternative interpretation. He emphasizes Habermas's attempt to move beyond the idealism of Hegel, the reductionism and economic determinism (mechanical integration of productive forces and social relations of production) of Marx, the culture critique of critical theory, and the social abstractions and individualism of Parsons. Habermas, McCarthy argues, does so through a creative synthesis of historical materialism with both structural and systems theory and the progressive rationalization of communication, discursive or consensual rationality, discourse ethics, practical or moral reason, and culture.[51] That is, Habermas's goal is to integrate a critical examination of the subsystems and structures of society, which are part of a contemporary legitimation crisis, with the pragmatic structure of communication free from domination and ideological distortion. In this way he joins together both a critique of political economy and culture—the productive forces with the "force of a better argument" in open and free dialogue of the ideal speech situation freed of social and psychological pathologies and crises of distorted economic growth, communication, and personality development. Following Habermas, McCarthy irretrievably links truth and discursive consensus, practical reason and ideal discourse, with the structures, institutions, and values of social justice. "'Truth,' therefore, cannot be analyzed independently of 'freedom' and 'justice.'"[52]

This creative joining together of moral and political discourse with the social institutions of a just society can also lead to a more progressive relationship between science and technology and the physical environment. It also represents the return of the use of "essence," "ideas," and "critique" in social ethics, which Marcuse contended had been lost with the rise of scientific rationalization and the technological and political justification of capitalism. Habermas's perspective is also a critical response to the rise of postmodernism, discussed in the first chapter of this book. It is a way of creating the social conditions for an open and free dialogue about political and moral issues that moves beyond the substantive criticisms of postmodern theorists, who hold that there is no rational way of establishing the justification for morals, ethics, and politics. Traditional idealism and practical reason are now incorporated into the language of communication and public discourse.[53] Habermas moves beyond the discussion of particular theories of morality and politics grounded in traditional philosophy and metaphysics to argue for the ideal conditions of social discourse within which these issues could be discussed, beyond the structures of domination in the system and lifeworld. These are the structures of social justice, as well as the basis for the justification of particular social action and public consensus. Habermas focuses upon the central importance of knowledge and truth as the foundation of communicative action and social justice as the structural and material preconditions of that search. Although he does not discuss Marx's own theory of social justice, the latter could potentially act as both an important critique of all forms of domination of nature and humanity, as it provides the ideal structural boundaries in the economic, political, ethical, and cultural systems for such a public discussion.[54]

In *Knowledge and Human Interests* (1968), Habermas outlines the historical and philosophical evolution of the epistemological understanding of objectivity and subjectivity in German idealism and materialism. He traces the philosophical evolution of the forms of human consciousness from the categories of the understanding to the formal categories of instrumental action. Hegel begins the *Phenomenology of Spirit* with a critique of Kantian epistemology and theory of pure reason, tracing the historical evolution of phenomenology and consciousness throughout Western thought from the subjective and objective spirit to the absolute spirit. The categories of consciousness are historical and social in nature. Hegel undertakes this critical analysis by tracing the evolution of the mind from the natural Consciousness of the physical world in sense certainty, perception, and the understanding; the

Self-Consciousness of the position and power over others in ancient slavery; and the modern Reason of utilitarian liberalism, individualism, and Kantian moral philosophy. He then turns to the development of the Objective Spirit in the ideals of the ancient ethical community and natural law to the modern Enlightenment, utilitarianism, culture of alienation, and French Revolution and Terror ending in the Absolute Spirit of religion, art, and science.[55] Hegel has moved from the phenomenological experience of everyday life (in terms of our perception and understanding of the objective world) to the social world of categorical morality and communal ethics of the Enlightenment to the breakdown of community during the French Revolution and the unhappy retreat to the theoretical abstractions of different modes of knowledge in metaphysics, aesthetics, and science. Marx's theory of social justice, our understanding of which has been evolving over the past few decades, may be viewed as a positive attempt within the self-formative process of the ethical spirit to replace the failure of the Enlightenment and French Revolution by an alternative reconstruction of Western consciousness, from the ancient Greeks to German idealism, French socialism, and British political economy.

However, despite Hegel's phenomenological advances and critique of Kantian epistemology, Habermas asserts in a return to Kant that "there can be no concept of knowledge that can be explicated independently of the subjective conditions of the objectivity of possible knowledge."[56] Kant's theory of the synthetic unity of apperception in the creative imagination of the human mind is his major contribution to a theory of knowledge and the understanding of objective reality. Habermas continues to develop his argument by slowly dismantling the abstract foundations and categories of pure reason as the mechanism for supplying the actual synthetic unity of our knowledge of the physical world that surrounds us. The synthetic unity of consciousness in German thought—which creates the conditions for perception and understanding, experience and knowledge—begins with the transcendental consciousness of Kant, the phenomenological and historical mind of

Hegel, the social labor of Marx, and, finally, the social consciousness of knowledge and the technical and communicative interests
of Habermas. This transition within the self-reflection of philosophy follows Habermas's claim that "a radical critique of knowledge
is possible only as social theory."[57] These stages of self-reflection on
the transcendental, phenomenological, and social subject (labor
and cognitive interests) are part of the "universal history of mankind" and the self-formative process by which the human species
understands itself and the potentiality of material production and
social freedom. But with his concept of the mode of production,
Marx blends the productive and technical forces of production
with the class structure and social organization of production.
Habermas argues that "Marx reduces the process of reflection
to the level of instrumental action," and by doing so "eliminates
reflection as such as a motive force of history."[58]

Reflection on the self-constitution of the spirit and moral community is replaced by the constitution of society and the power of
social labor, with a loss of reflective thought of cultural and rational self-conscious reflection as found in Hegel's phenomenology.
"That is why labor, or work, is not only a fundamental category of
human existence but also an epistemological category," Habermas
writes.[59] Objectivity, or the objective world of experience, is now
understood as part of the process of self-understanding and human
liberation in the creation of the objective world in both consciousness and work. And the categories of the transcendental subject
become the categories of social labor and the instrumental activity
of the productive forces of science, technology, and human labor,
which "determine" the social organization of production and the
social reality of the lifeworld—that is, the categories of the material and cultural lifeworld by which we perceive and understand
social reality. Habermas is aware of the advancement in transcendental philosophy but is critical of Marx for reducing social labor
to the productive and technological forces of modern industry.
Habermas stresses the point that objectivity as experience and
knowledge is a production of the development and evolution of

the human mind. For Marx, however, the epistemological question of logic and thought turns into an issue of instrumental reason and the technical forces of production that provide the transcendental conditions for knowledge and consciousness. In transforming Hegel's theory of the phenomenological evolution of human consciousness in history, Marx, according to Habermas, has reduced human reason to technical reason, thereby losing the possibilities inherent in human interaction and reflection. "The unity of the objectivity of possible objects of experience is formed not in transcendental consciousness but in the behavioral system of instrumental action."[60] The objective world of experience and knowledge is formed by human labor and not the transcendental or phenomenological categories of experience. The categories of the intuition and understanding are replaced by the displaced unconscious, ideology, and fetishism of the productive forces and categories of technical control. Knowledge is reduced to the technical control over nature and labor for the purposes of the domination over nature and political economy. "Consciousness is formed in each case in dependence on the historical stage of the development of the forces of production," thereby making self-consciousness in history impossible.[61] Since epistemology and knowledge are not oriented toward the technical control over nature and work, there is a corresponding loss of self-reflection of history and knowledge—social sciences and philosophy—resulting in a "dialectic of understanding" and a world that is ideologically incomprehensible to human understanding and, thus, to human change. Transcendental subjectivity is replaced by the domination of nature and humanity.

Habermas contends that, because of this form of a theory of knowledge based on the workings of political economy, Marx has lost critical thought and social reflection. The world as objectivity of the natural and social world of experience is a construct of subjectivity or human consciousness; the difference between idealism and materialism is that the former results from the evolution of the human mind, whereas the latter is a production of human activity in work. Unfortunately, in the end, Habermas falsely and uncritically claims that Marx is a mechanical materialist, economic determinist, and a positivist who has lost the German tradition of tracing the self-development of the consciousness and knowledge. "Marx reduces the process of reflection to the level of instrumental action" and by implication "eliminates reflection as such as a motive force of history."[62] There is no longer a need to trace the unfolding of the history of knowledge in culture and self-consciousness (phenomenology) and nature and science (epistemology). And by no longer knowing how Western consciousness evolved over time, the human species is no longer capable of serious reflection on the nature of the social oppression of humanity, through the loss of self-consciousness of ethics and politics and the domination of nature through scientific and instrumental rationality. To emphasize his point, Habermas finishes his analysis of Marx by claiming that the latter's theory of social labor is just another form of natural science and positivism. The main characteristic of positivism in the natural and social sciences is a loss of self-reflection and of the possibility of challenging and overcoming the domination of nature and society. Both areas of traditional self-reflection in phenomenology and epistemology are lost, thereby reducing the human mind to technical reason and the forces of production. Self-reflection on the social and cultural evolution and the self-constitution of the human species ends with the coming of positivism and capitalism, because humanity is no longer capable of asking: What is the good life and what is the meaning of life? These questions are lost because the answer is already contained in the logic of science and industry—greater expansion of material goods and consumer happiness, even if the latter is displaced, sublimated, and repressed happiness.

The main result, according to Habermas, is that Marx had lost the central importance of cultural values and ideals necessary for social critique, as well as the ability to see through the false consciousness, distorted language, and political ideology of a free labor market-based commodity exchange, free labor, surplus value, and just exchange value. This results in the philosophical and socio-logical self-liquidation of the possibility of theory, reason, and critique.[63] This represents an important development in German thought and an important change in the nature of transcendental activity—the creation of objectivity by subjectivity. However, the real problem is the reduction of human labor to its technical pro-ductive forces and instrumental activity. In addition, the oppressive conditions of the social organization of production are excluded, along with the cultural and political superstructure, as merely reflexive and not reflective activities, with no independent role in human evolution and, thus no role in the self-conscious recogni-tion and activity for human emancipation. The social relations of production and superstructure, the class system of work, and the cultural system of ideological symbols and language are unable to provide the foundation for self-enlightenment and social change. Because of the power of scientific rationality and instrumental activity, humanity has lost the heart of traditional epistemology— the self-formation process of consciousness. The latter is reduced to the technical conditions of political economy, as the self-reflec-tive process is lost as an epiphenomenon of history and has been integrated into a culture of ideology and suppression of inde-pendent reflective thought. The material conditions of industrial production (*Produktionswissen*) have repressed the ability of the human mind to reflect on its own social conditions, because the categories of "critique and self-reflection" (*Reflexionswissen*) are no longer relevant or even possible in a society consumed by the distractions of the culture industry. In the end, *Reflexionswissen* disappears and is replaced by the political imperatives for control over production, nature, and society. Technical knowledge and natural science make this possible.

Habermas believes that Marcuse makes a serious mistake when he follows Marx down this dark path, and by doing so loses the progressive and emancipatory potential of the productive forces of modern science and technology. Habermas also holds that Marx and Marcuse accept the theory that the productive forces are too closely tied to the oppressive class structure of work, which had become the synthetic unity by which experience and knowledge of the world had been filtered. By reducing the cultural lifeworld to the economic mode of production, interaction to labor, Marx loses to social repression the emancipatory potential of culture, in the form of social ideals, self-reflective epistemology, dialectical reasoning, social action, and history. Marx's major mistake, according to Habermas, is the reduction of the synthetic categories of consciousness to technical social labor, which eliminates the "structure of synthetic intuition and the role of cultural tradition" from the critique of knowledge and the transcendental formation of subjectivity. This reduction represents a critique of the failure of epistemology and consciousness to understand the nature of ideology and distorted consciousness and the corresponding idealized need for symbolic interactionism and political and cultural consensus. In the cases of both Marx and Marcuse, the ability to develop a broad overview of the history of Western consciousness and the potentiality for species liberation are displaced and forgotten by the politicization of technological rationality and the disappearance of cultural reflection and critique. This forces Marcuse to view the world as one-dimensional, since it has lost the dialectical and critical theory. The fusion of the productive forces with the social relations of production and the fusion of the economic system with the cultural system both undermined the development of self-consciousness and self-understanding of the economic and cultural potential of the human race. The Hegelian dream of the study of the transcendental and phenomenal evolution of human consciousness and freedom disappeared. Both fusions produced a reified consciousness, unable to imagine creatively and critically a new society based on the ethical principles of classical and modern humanism of mutual love, friendship, human dignity, freedom, moral community, and the democratic polity.

Habermas rejects what he views as economic determinism and reductivism, by which the productive forces are innovatively

retranslated and represented as the integrative and synthetic categories of human experience, knowledge, and potentiality. This is
the transcendental consciousness as redefined by modern positivist epistemology and scientific methodology. In an unusual and
unexpected turn, Habermas argues that epistemological positivism parallels the productive forces in advanced capitalist society
since it also unfortunately halts the self-reflective and self-formative evolution of human consciousness and human freedom
as it developed from Kant to Marx. Positivism only confirms this
economic reductivism and nominalistic exclusionism, by which
the cultural superstructure is explained only as a product and
reflection of the historical mode of production.[64] The irony of
intellectual history for Habermas is that it is positivism, not only
historical materialism, which reduces self-consciousness, reason,
and culture to a deterministic and mechanical self-understanding of the evolution of the human species; it is positivism which
stops this self-reflective learning process of history from critically
examining the evolution of self-consciousness within the capitalist social system, by directly and indirectly reducing natural and
social knowledge to the technical sciences and productive forces
of capital. Theorists in the analytic and positivist tradition have
argued that Marx was an economic determinist who reduced the
cultural superstructure to the economic mode of production; but
a closer look reveals that it is modern positivism—in its various
contemporary forms of empiricism and logical rationalism, scientism and nominalism—which eliminates dialectical and critical
thought in the name of pure reason, false objectivity, and technical
science. This reduction of all knowledge to technical and instrumental rationality parallels the misplaced critique of historical
materialism and its reduction of culture and the superstructure
to the instrumental productive forces and social relations of production. Habermas is also critical of the reduction of science to
technological and political rationality, which results in the loss of
an objective, neutral natural science and instrumental rationality.
In the process science and positivism lose concepts, reason, ethics,

and the ability of reflective critique—social justice—as it creates a world of rigid objectivity, distorted ideology, and a non-reflective and mechanical form of positive knowledge in both the natural and the social sciences. Positivism ends the self-reflective process of transcendental and phenomenal consciousness, and with it the whole of epistemology is replaced by a formalistic philosophy of science.[65]

Habermas focuses on Marx's expansion of transcendental and phenomenological thought into historical materialism. The latter transforms transcendental subjectivity into the history of social labor. Labor becomes the "species-subject" that creates phenomenal objectivity and human consciousness, not logic or thought; the synthetic categories of human experience become the product of human labor and not the transcendental subject or spirit. The self-constitution of the human species occurs not because of the history of the critique of the forms of knowledge, individual reflection, and consciousness of Kant, or through social labor and the historical form of production. Habermas writes: "Marx reduces the process of reflection to the level of instrumental action. By reducing the self-positing of the absolute ego to the more tangible productive action of the species, he eliminates reflection as such as a motive force in history, even though, he retains the framework of the philosophy of reflection."[66] By reducing Kant's transcendental subject and Hegel's Absolute Spirit with the "mode of production," Habermas has conjoined his criticisms of both Marx and Marcuse. For him, both have retained the framework of transcendental logic and subjectivity, just as both have lost the ability to see history as the evolution of self-reflection and critical ideals which would become the basis for the critique of advanced capitalism.[67]

Habermas's theoretical goal is twofold: retranslate and expand Marx's critique of political economy into the cultural lifeworld, and develop the self-reflection of the evolution of human consciousness into the realm of language and symbols, concepts and consensus, in order to revive the lost epistemological foundations of public dialogue and debate. In this manner, Habermas believes

that he is able to continue this line of reasoning by expanding subjective consciousness into both work and language, social labor
and discursive rationality. By doing so, he places Marx's materialist
theory of the mode of production within the theory of knowledge
and formation of consciousness of German idealism. Habermas
wishes to expand German idealism into both work and democracy,
in order to fully understand the historical evolution of the human
species and its constructive creation of the physical, spiritual,
scientific/technological, and industrial world. It is an interesting
phenomenon that where Marx turned to the classical horizons of
ancient Greece to support his initial and early rejection of capitalism, it appears, however unconsciously, that Habermas turns to
American pragmatism and classical Greek philosophy as the basis
for his rejection of modern capitalism. His view of democracy and
freedom is grounded not in the technological rationality of science
and the logic of capital, but in the logic of discursive reason and
political communication and consensus. By integrating the social
and political thought of Parsons, Dewey, and Aristotle, Habermas
believes he has found the key missing elements in the Frankfurt
School's critique of capitalism—culture and democracy, Parsons
and Aristotle.[68]

Habermas has made a major philosophical advance in his
critique of positivism and integration of the various schools of
thought within German Idealism to reaffirm the notion of the
self-constitution of the human species in reason, production, and
interaction. He continued in the German tradition of expansion
and integration of different traditions to develop a more comprehensive and critical social theory. However, in spite of this,
Habermas makes a crucial error in his investigation of Marx. He
maintains that Marx reduces morality, knowledge, culture, and
critical consciousness to the framework of production, with its
class consciousness and struggle, thereby reducing the cultural
system to the values and interests of social labor. What is right or
wrong is defined by the class struggle over the control of the means
of production and by expansion of the capacity of the productive

forces, which only lessens the class struggle and represses human needs. It is here that Habermas misses a crucial opportunity to expand his understanding of knowledge and critique in Marx's theory of social justice.

Habermas is mistaken in his attempt to reduce Marx's theory of morality to production and his theory of knowledge to positivism. Marx has an extensively developed theory of social justice that Habermas does not take into consideration, and which could have required Habermas to seriously readjust his whole theory of communicative action. In a complex and comprehensive manner, Marx in his theory of social justice does integrate work with interaction, production with ethics and politics, communication with public discourse and democracy, and modernity with classical humanism. Although never explicitly formulated as a comprehensive theory, this theory does run throughout all Marx's writings and pulls together in a comprehensive totality the history of Western consciousness. The very things Habermas criticizes him for not doing, Marx in fact impressively accomplishes. All the crucial elements in social theory and a history of Western consciousness that Habermas argues are missing in Marx are there, including social critique, theory, reason, communicative rationality, and democracy. These traditions and their distinctive social methods, presumed missing by Habermas, include (1) the cultural values of ethics and politics from classical humanism; (2) moral economy and democracy, from Athenian democracy and the Paris Commune of 1871; (3) individual and political rights, liberties, and freedom, from the French Revolution; (4) the labor theory of value, and industrial surplus value and profits, from British classical economics; (5) transcendental consciousness of social labor, from the German idealism of Kant, Schelling, and Hegel, and the dialectical critique of the structural and logical contradictions of industrial production and a class society, derived from Hegel's logic; and (6) ecological crisis of industrial production and scientific rationality, from historical and empirical social science analysis. These traditions and their distinctive methods constitute

the heart of Marx's theory of social justice and the self-constitution of the species. Social justice is the means by which they are
integrated into a broader theory of society, incorporating work
and interaction, production and justice, from the ancients to the
moderns.[69]

Throughout his work, Marx relies on a complex variety of
non-positivist philosophical and methodological traditions necessary to undertake his historical and social research in political
economy and historical materialism. He does not reduce reflection, consciousness, and communicative interaction to industry
or the productive forces. Perhaps these various forms of research
went mainly unnoticed in the history of modern thought because
there was an implicit understanding that there was a major difference between his early philosophical and later economic writings,
which appeared to represent a linear evolution of his thought
and not an integrated understanding of the relationship between
ethics and virtue at one end and moral economy and democratic
polity at the other. By using the methods of immanent and dialectical critique, hermeneutics and history, political economy,
and the critique of classical economics and ideology, Marx has
moved beyond the productive forces in his understanding of
history, epistemology, consciousness, and the self-constitution
of the species. The latter takes shape in political, economic, and
cultural institutions, as Marx uses the ethical and political ideals
of Ancient Greece; modern human and civil rights and liberties
in Prussia, France, and England; political rights and democracy
of the French Revolution; and economic rights, democracy, and
federalism of the Paris Commune. Of central importance here is
that Marx did not rely on an ethical or political critique of capitalism from an external, abstract, or utopian rejection of capitalism.
Unlike the Frankfurt School and other Marxist traditions, Marx's
ethics and critique are grounded in a phenomenological history
of the consciousness, structures, and institutions of social reality,
as he incorporates the actual ethical and political ideals of evolving societies, from classical humanism to democratic socialism,

into his analysis and rejection of industrial capitalism. He uses the dialectic and immanent critique to unmask the illusions and ideologies of liberalism and bourgeois rights to self and property, the class oppression and control over work, the degradation of human labor, the contradictions between the potentialities of productive forces and the reality of labor alienation in the social organization of production, and the conflicts between the social ideals and human needs of production against the logical and historical contradictions of a capitalist economy. The actual historical evolution of social ideals and institutions are the basis for ethics and critique. True consensus, discursive rationality, and democratic institutions arise not out of the abstract categories of the lifeworld and social subsystems, but out of the concrete historical praxis and struggle for human rights, liberties, and freedom in the real world.

In his analysis of Marx and Marcuse, Habermas believes that their interpretations of the logic of science as expressing the inner logic of capitalist production and class oppression provided little opportunity to imagine and dream of alternative social systems. In this way, positive science became part of the productive forces and, thus, a form of ideology and false consciousness supporting the existing social system. This is a main reason why Habermas turns to Parsons' theory of the structures and functions to broaden his understanding of the complex relationships within the social system and avoid Marcuse's integration of scientific rationality, technological imperatives, and political domination. Habermas's goals are fourfold in his attempt to create a social theory around social systems, critique, culture, and ideology: (1) to study the complex transformation of positivism in different schools of thought that continue the repression of critical social theory; (2) to reengage the powers of social observation—based on the ideas of essence, dialectics, and social critique—that revolve around the ideal speech situation, discursive/democratic rationality, and communicative interaction; (3) to investigate the role of culture among the other subsystems of society in both maintaining social integration and systems stability, but also its role in distorting consciousness, maintaining ideology, and repressing social critique, thereby creating the conditions for serious economic and political legitimation crises; and (4) to rediscover the centrally important role of norms, values, and cultural ideals in the study of communicative action and the ideal speech situation, which had been excluded by Marx's theory of the mode of production and positivist social science. These theoretical needs lead Habermas to pursue a broader social theory based on Parsons' theory of the social system and the complex inner workings of the subsystems of society within traditions informed by both Marxism and critical theory. These new areas of social research on positivism, economic and cultural crises, and social critique based on the discursive reason and the ideal speech situation, ultimately found their way into the his major writings on these subjects: *Knowledge and Human Interests* (1969), *Legitimation Crisis* (1973), and *The Theory of Communicative Action* (1981).[70] These writings expand upon ideas that Habermas developed in his earlier writings and critiques of the epistemological, methodological, and metatheoretical analyses of German idealism and materialism, and British and American positivism. If science is a pure, objective, and neutral abstraction, then the solution to its abuse within capitalism is not to transform science and technology themselves, but to change our understanding of the social and political manner in which science is utilized in the social relations and organization of production (A: economy); restructuring the economic and political process to allow for a more democratic and socialist society (G: state); and transforming the social and cultural variables and values in our self-consciousness about its role in maintaining the human species, as well as changing our positivistic understanding of science itself (IL: culture and social institutions). By emancipating the economic, political, and cultural subsystems from legitimation crises, repressed cultural symbols, cultural ideologies, distorted communication, and lack of political consensus, Habermas believes that scientific rationality could become the technical basis for an emancipated and free society. These various sub-areas reflect the direction of his later sociological writings in critical theory.

Habermas continues the German Idealist themes of the self-formative process of consciousness and society. The human species has a real interest in maintaining its cultural values and moral and technical knowledge, and in internalizing these values to assure social stability, communication, and sharing of public ideals and virtues, and political consensus. Habermas calls this the "interest structure of a species." The practical and cognitive social interests are internalized in consciousness and acted upon in social institutions, as they provide the knowledge necessary for human survival, reflective consciousness, and individual freedom. These interests—formed in work, language, and power—are institutionalized in the economy, culture, and state, and expressed in different forms of knowledge as instrumental scientific knowledge (*techne*) and cultural understanding and shared meaning, and in social communication and political legitimation (*phronesis*). In this way the self-constitution of humanity in history and society is maintained, as well as the self-understanding and awareness of its various forms of reflection, knowledge, and reason which only aid in the articulation and realization of its practical values and ideals. Note that these forms of knowledge and institutions— which constitute the basis for human emancipation, freedom, and democratic communication—represent Habermas's expansion of Parsons' AGIL schema. Whatever the limitations of Habermas's critique of Marx and his failure to see Marx's theory of social justice, Habermas's critique of positivism and ideology, and his theory of moral virtue and democratic politics, do not undermine the theoretical important contributions in his theory of communication, ideal speech situation, and discursive democracy. These are an important expansion of critical theory and neo-Marxist thought. But a more developed understanding of Marx would have greatly helped Habermas's own understanding of culture, values, and consensual politics.

Although Habermas maintains a comprehensive structural view

of society and the relationship between political and economic systems and the cultural patterns, personality, and socialization of the lifeworld, he alters Parsons' AGIL to emphasize the social interests for species survival or the "interest structure of the species" through work (A), power (G), and language (IL) or technology and industrial economy, political direction and the state, and culture, communication, and consensus.[71] In this way Habermas is able to introduce to both critical theory and systems theory his two main theoretical concerns: First, he is able to give a broad theoretical framework for the examination of the various social systems that constitute modern society; he is also able to give a critical theory of the practical interests of the different forms of knowledge as they are related to the different structures of society, including technical knowledge and scientific information in the economy, interpretive knowledge of cultural meaning and language in the social lifeworld, and discursive knowledge and power to persuade within a free and open dialogue and political consensus. By this means Habermas is able to create a social theory grounded in political economy and social structures; cultural values, language and knowledge grounded in social and cognitive interests; and political discourse and democracy. Also, by distinguishing in his adaptation of systems theory between the system and lifeworld and between system integration and social integration, Habermas is able to divide Weber's theory of rationalization into two different forms of rationalization and social crises based on industrial production and social interaction. By so doing, he is able to divide society into two distinct and separate dimensions, one of which would provide the basis for the revival of the lost critique in the dialectic of enlightenment.[72] By knowing the range of knowledge and science, the technical and communicative interests behind science and culture, and the social institutions which would best respond to an open and free society, Habermas has framed his social theory by blending many different intellectual, philosophical, and theoretical traditions geared to understanding the complexities and cognitive interests of all kinds of knowledge, institutions, and political orientations.[73] These new questions about the nature of the social system expand the forms of knowledge within the social sciences to include phenomenology and hermeneutics of subjectively intended meaning (Weber and Schutz); the objective meaning of social institutions of politics, religion, and social ethics; the depth hermeneutics of Freud; public meaning and symbols of political communication and discourse; structuralism and history; and the political economy of advanced capitalism, capital accumulation, and the state welfare system and cultural legitimation. In the end, Habermas's goal is to move beyond the traditional means of grounding knowledge and reflection in the essence of pure reason and transcendental and phenomenological subjectivity, toward a more postmodern view of a linguistically based idea of intersubjectivity and consensus.[74]

PART IV

Beyond the Dialectic of Enlightenment by Integrating Science and Social Justice

Conclusion: Rediscovering Reason, Science, and Social Justice

CRITICAL THEORY OFFERS AN EXTENSIVE and comprehensive overview of modern society by combining so many different traditions and expanding our understanding of the complexity of the modern social system. It pushes us to the edge where a host of new questions arise, carrying us to another level of critical analysis. Jürgen Habermas's work is embedded in a complex web of philosophical issues which are central to his major themes. He is critical of what he sees as Marx's mechanical and deterministic economic theory—he views Marx's theory as a form of positivism in which the productive forces determine the following components of society: social organization and class hierarchy of production, the expansion of the material conditions of society, the revolutionary consciousness for social change, and the form and content of the social and cultural superstructure. These positions of positivism and economic determinism only reinforce the major problem of critical theory: that the philosophical space necessary to develop an ethical and political critique of capitalism no longer exists. It reinforces the major themes of the dialectic of enlightenment, the contempt for reason and social theory, and the loss of any critical understanding of advanced capitalist society.

The critical theorists believed that it was very difficult to maintain an enlightened position in a society where reason had been repressed and lost. The rise of postmodernism, with its undermining of traditional epistemology and social ethics, also added to this problem of justifying the ethics and values necessary to emancipate humanity from the oppressive conditions of modern society. The traditional areas of transcendental and phenomenological subjectivity and historical materialism were no longer viewed as adequate responses to the social pathologies and crises of modernity. As we have seen in previous chapters, Horkheimer and Adorno recognized the problem but were theoretically frozen in their response. Marcuse moved away from theoretical reflection and critique to art as the imaginative and aesthetical basis for social criticism. And Habermas attempted to justify his rejection of modern capitalism by moving beyond the traditional methods of reflection in German idealism and materialism, turning instead to language, communication, and consensus as the main form of critique, built into the very logic of human consciousness and species development. The problem boils down to the structure of "critique."

Habermas believed he had uncovered a new epistemological and sociological approach to the critique of capital in the structure and logic of the lifeworld itself. The social norms and values inherent in culture, socialization, and personality development assumed that there was a common consensus and agreement to their value and validity that was undermined by the distortion, repression, and ideological corruption necessary to justify the oppressive nature of the class mode of production. By separating the system and lifeworld, Habermas believed that he was able to distinguish between the instrumental rationality of action found in modern science and the communication and consensus within the cultural lifeworld. Truth of verbal or written statements is a product not of observation or experience, but of rational consensus within discursive and communicative interaction.[1] By keeping communicative action and scientific and technical reason separate in two different social subsystems, Habermas is able to overcome the dialectic of enlightenment to some degree. There is always a place within the cultural system for dialogic consensus and cultural values that are independent of the formal imperatives of technological rationality and domination. The values, norms, and ideals found in this aspect of society contained the basis for social reflection and critique of economic oppression, political ideology, and cultural distortions. This fact is not based on the substantive content of the culture, but on the implicit logical notion that the norms and values are the potential product of a universal social consensus.[2] Habermas's approach was able to overcome the social pathologies and legitimation crises that were characteristic of modern society, as well as the epistemological criticism of postmodern epistemology and philosophy of science. He recognizes the epistemological and methodological difficulties in the social sciences faced by the critical theorists, these advances were important for the continued evolution of Marxist thought.

The raising of these questions was key to the evolution of critical thought, which nevertheless remained too philosophical, abstract, and speculative to appreciate the real historical and social complexities of the world of the social system. Habermas believed that Marx had erred by integrating the system and lifeworld, making social critique impossible. His arguments at such a high level of philosophy and metatheory made the understanding of political economy and the social system difficult. Habermas's distinction between the economic base and cultural superstructure, system and lifeworld, purposive-rational action and communication, work and interaction, social labor and language, and system integration and social integration, expanded the basis for the search for a critical social theory. Included in these dialectics are his examinations of the various sociological methods and traditions necessary to gain access to these social structures and subsystems. Although representing an expansion of social theory, Habermas's work did move away from the more practical, historical, and political economic issues necessary to establish the basis for social critique and social change. To do so, social theory must provide an analysis of the real concrete institutions and structures that would make enlightenment, emancipation, and social change possible.

To develop a comprehensive and holistic social theory would require that our understanding of the complexity of the social system be revised from its internal logic, language, and symbolic interaction to its real objective structures. The latter affect our social and natural environment, including the nature of work; the organization of production; the class system; the relationship to nature and the environment; scientific consciousness and technology; and the cultural values of ideology, consumption, and repressed ideals. Objectivity of the world takes place through language, cultural institutions, and work, and it is upon these foundations that consciousness of the natural and moral world arises. This knowledge requires a more radical rethinking of the substance and relationship among science, political economy, the ecological crisis, and cultural ideals. Both Marx and Habermas construct their social theories around the constitution of objectivity as a material, moral, and social form, but Habermas retreats into a more speculative social form of idealism.

Habermas remains more in the field of German idealism and transcendental subjectivity—philosophical metatheory of the foundations of human experience and knowledge through observation, meaning, and consensus—while Marx forms his social theory of objectivity in terms of labor, morals, and culture within the history of Western consciousness and the actual structures of political economy, judged by the ideals of social justice. This position argues that the basis of language, reflection, and critique lies in the history of Western consciousness and social institutions, which have been the locus of human struggle for emancipation throughout history. The injustices of capitalist production are exposed throughout Marx's writings, on topics including human labor, the Industrial Revolution, the capitalist mode of production, the history of capitalist formation, and political revolutions

in France. Marx also addresses the internal structural contradictions within capitalism, between the economic rights of man
and the political rights of the citizen, the poverty of reason and
human dignity in work, productive forces and social relations of
production, accumulation of material wealth and overproduction,
surplus value and exchange value, economic growth and crises.
From the nature of work, production, and capital accumulation,
the call for social emancipation and justice is present throughout
his writings. Unfortunately, Marx never wrote a systematic treatise
on the topic, which has led to enormous confusion and misunderstanding of his writings, and has moved many scholars to see him
as a positivist and economic scientist. It is this aspect of Marx's
social theory—that is, his theory of social justice—that Habermas
is unaware of.

For Habermas, social theory is grounded in language, consensus, and interests (technical and practical, instrumental and
communicative). Thomas McCarthy has succinctly summarized
the epistemological problem of the method of grounding social
critique within a complex grouping of social systems. Habermas
rejects Parsons' approach to systems theory, which involved questions surrounding the maintenance of systems stability and social/
cultural integration and legitimation. Instead, he views the social
system as an opportunity to investigate the nature of language and
consensus within the cultural tradition as a way of creating the
basis for the formal and logical analysis of social critique, independent of particular historical examples. McCarthy writes:

> The question is: To what standard does this materialist phenom-
> enology appeal in unmasking ideological vices and forms of life?
> To what perceptions or theory of reality does it appeal in char-
> acterizing other perceptions and theories as distorted? To what
> theory of history does it appeal in distinguishing progressive
> from regressive modes of thought and practice?[3]

For both Habermas and McCarthy, the answer lies in language

and a consensus theory of truth, based on the logical prerequisites for agreement and truth claims. Theory is grounded in language and the phenomenology of self-reflection. Perhaps a better way in which to ground ethics and social critique is not in a metatheory of language and discourse, but in the actual values and virtues of ethics and the institutions of human rights and liberty, moral economy, social equality, and communal democracy. Although Habermas expands our understanding of the integral complexities of the social system and lifeworld, he remains caught in the abstractions and speculations of German idealism. Even his consideration of the nature of political economy is always tied closely to the structures of language and discourse, social integration and systems integration.

The goal of this book is to supplement the ideas of work and interaction, system and lifeworld, with a more historical, empirical, and structural analysis of ethics and politics, virtue and democracy, moral values and political economy. This makes social theory and critique more relevant and practical, by detailing the actual structures and institutions necessary for human emancipation, individual freedom, and true democratic communication and consensus. The end result is a social theory based on an empirical and historical analysis of the interaction and interdependence of science and technology, nature and the environment, and political economy and culture (virtue, morals, and social ideals). This view of social theory, already established by Marx, replaces work and interaction with work and social justice, in an implicit phenomenological theory of the self-development of the human species within Western culture, from the ancients to the moderns. In this way, self-reflection and reason are embedded in the actual history, values, and institutions of modern society in its various attempts at reaching out for human liberation and freedom at various times. Marx, in a creative impulse, pulls together these key ethical and political traditions into a comprehensive theory of society. The ethics and values Habermas seeks in language and discourse are already present in the historical ideals of different societies and demands for social change that Marx integrates into his view of social justice and communal democracy.[4] Although these views are integrated into his writings, they are never fully explicated or developed into a comprehensive theory of social justice. However, the ethical and political theory does exist just below the hermeneutical surface of his writings.

To place Marx within the parameters established by Habermas's systems theory, we can say the following. Without the cultural ideals and social institutions of social justice, (1) there is no concrete foundation for the possibility of communal social consensus, classless discursive democracy, and a moral economy; (2) nor can there be the basis for a restructuring of the social relations and organization of industry and production that emphasizes human dignity, beauty, creativity, and communal responsibility; (3) nor can there be a symbiotic and organic interaction and stewardship of science and technology with nature and the physical environment; and, finally, (4) nor can there be an economic system that is not built on historical and logical contradictions and continuous economic and legitimation crises and breakdowns. Even with his enormous accomplishments, Habermas overlooks the pervasive influence of social justice in Marx's writings on politics, economics, classical and modern humanism, work, and more. This is because Habermas focuses more on a mechanical and deterministic view of Marx, the split between the mode of production and the superstructure, and Parsons' distinction between system and lifeworld. Also, in advanced capitalism, the ideological justification of the social system lies within the rationalization of society in the form of scientific and technological reason. Traditional cultural ideals and values become unnecessary in a one-dimensional society, having gone through a dialectic and transformation of enlightenment justified by the rational expansion of the productive forces. This loss of reason and critique makes it difficult for critical theory to justify the rejection and transformation of the present society into an emancipated social system. It was just this problem recognized by members of the Frankfurt School that became the basis for creating a theory of communicative and symbolic interaction implicit within the very logic and phenomenon of language and the need for social integration. However, this approach is just an extension of transcendental and phenomenological self-reflection—a continuation of the abstract and philosophical formation of the human species in the mind, spirit, or language. The result is that Marx's theory of social justice was not noticed and appeared not to play a role in his overall critique of political economy. This was part of the thesis which emphasized the difference between his early philosophical writings and his later economic and scientific works. But with the integration of his earlier humanistic works and his later political economy, the theory is quite visible if one looks beyond the traditional economically focused views of Marx.

After careful consideration of the issues discussed in this book, it seems clearer that a partial solution to the problem of knowledge and language is to recognize that the issues of economic and cultural crisis in a rationalized world of science and technology call for a more historical and empirically based social critique, and not simply the continuation of a transcendental self-reflection, whether in the form of phenomenology, pragmatism, symbolic interactionism, or critical theory within idealism or materialism. The ethical foundation for social critique lies in the emancipatory potential for communication and consensus or discursive and dialogical rationality, but only within real social institutions that can be the basis for social critique and social change. Such change can only be accomplished by the integration of the various structures and subsystems within society, through an expanded form of Marx's theory of social justice that includes issues of science and technology, nature, the environment, cultural and ethical traditions from the ancients to the moderns, and the various political and economic forms of justice in industry and the polity. This is the concrete form that language, discussion, and consensus must take; otherwise we have just returned to another form of idealism and metaphysics. This approach provides a better mechanism for both social critique and social praxis, as it again separates poiesis from phronesis, techne, and praxis. It also separates the productive forces from the social relations of production, as well as the system of political economy from the cultural lifeworld. These are the key elements in Habermas's own critical theory. But Marx's approach attempts the reconnection of ethics and political economy, emancipation and social reality, in ways that provide a more vivid and sociological critique of modern society and permit a true reflection of the real possibilities of social change and the concrete realization of social justice in history.

By comparing the issues of social labor in his early writings and social justice of his total writings, we see that Marx develops a materialist continuation of phenomenology, not in the form of an explicit thesis tracing the historical evolution of human consciousness throughout history; but rather through the integration of that history into his initial critique of the philosophy of social labor, and later into his critique of the structures of political economy and capitalism. In his early philosophical and political writings Marx borrows the overall framework of Aristotle's arguments by beginning with issues of ethics and traditions. In this way he integrates the phenomenology of Hegel with the ethics of Aristotle. That is, he creatively combines the self-constitution of humanity in Western consciousness with the spirit of the classical humanism of the Athenian polity. This is the very thing Hegel lost in his transition from modern reason and social ethics to the Absolute Spirit in his work *Phenomenology of the Spirit*. In his earliest works, Marx outlines his theory of labor and its value to production by juxtaposing the structures of alienation and dehumanization from the product, process, community, and the individual self to the social and historical ideals and ethics of (1) the inherent divinity of humanity and critique of idolatry (Isaiah and the Ancient Hebrews); (2) the economic goal of the satisfaction of fundamental material and spiritual human needs of love and friendship (the Old and New Testaments and Aristotle); (3) the goal of human life of the political animal (species being) defined in terms of virtue, happiness, love, friendship, and community in the ethics and politics of Aristotle; (4) the primacy of human activity and praxis, dignity, creativity, and self-development (Aristotle and the German Idealism of Kant and Hegel); (5) work as an aesthetic form of creative art and beauty (Friedrich Schiller and German and French Romanticism); (6) political democracy and moral economy in the writings of Aristotle, Benedict Spinoza, and Jean-Jacques Rousseau, and the German and French socialists and communists Wilhelm Weitling, Moses Hess, Charles Fourier, and Pierre-Joseph Proudhon; (7) belief in the central importance of political emancipation, individual liberties, personal dignity, and human rights for the protection of free thought, speech, assembly, and the press, in the tradition of John Locke, Thomas Jefferson, Abraham Lincoln, the Marquis de Lafayette, and Ferdinand Lassalle; and (8) the centrality and importance of human labor (British political economy) in creating the material conditions for the formation of society and the good life and happiness. Social labor became the basis for the formation of human consciousness, species development, and the integration of the phenomenological history of Western thought. Labor is the melding force in society by which humans create and constitute their economic, political, spiritual, and cultural lives with dignity and purpose to form a moral community and democratic polity. And social labor is a category that is a summary of the major ideals of Western society, articulated through its major cultural representations.

Marx continues to apply this same approach in his later writings where he focuses more on the structures and institutions of political economy and industrial production. Here again, he centers his attention not on a mechanical or technical science of economics, but on another integrative force that pulls together these same earlier traditions that now become the basis for his comprehensive theory of social justice, thereby integrating language and work, social integration and systems integration, ethics and politics, and classical humanism and factory labor. By linking the ethics and structures of social labor and social justice, Marx connects philosophy and sociology in a more relevant and concrete way. The totality of his writings becomes analytically and socially clearer, because now we see the connections and contradictions between the classical Greek and German traditions on one hand and the structures of alienation and political economy on the other. These contradictions between ethics and politics, and between ethics and political economy, continue throughout Marx's writings, as he sees the contradictions and possibilities between the ethical ideas of human work, creativity, and free self-determination and the alienation of private property, the fragmented and specialized division of labor, and the loss of the wellbeing of the community in the workplace.

This dialectical approach continues during Marx's middle period with the contradictions between the emancipatory potential of the productive forces of science, technology, and industry and the continued and expanded oppression of the class system and social relations of production, between the capitalist mode of production and the institutional and cultural superstructure, and, finally, between the logic of capitalist expansion and its historical contradictions in the form of overproduction, unemployment, human suffering, and economic crises. Throughout his scholarly life, Marx sought to reveal the inner logical contradictions and dialectic between social ideals, virtues, and ethics of the ancients and moderns with the historical reality of capitalism, the contradictions within the mode of production itself, and, finally, the contradictions between capitalist production and its self-realization of wealth and private property in commerce and profit accumulation. These are the contradictions between ethics and the social institutions of labor, production, and capital. The capitalist system—as seen from classical ethics and scientific and technological possibilities—and the structure of capitalist production itself reveal that this particular social system contradicts the values and ideals, the theoretical and material potentialities, of modern science and technical reason, and the very structures of industrial production itself. By this means Marx extends the reach of the connections between labor and social interaction within a dialectical framework of its own alienation and contradictions.

In his later writings, Marx recapitulates the central importance of politics, moral economy, and social institutions. In this way he completes Aristotle's plan of integrating ethics and politics, virtue and political economy, and philosophy and sociology. Marx undertakes a similar theoretical approach as he integrates the various philosophical and historical forms of justice into a comprehensive and holistic theory of justice that includes praxis, work, and industrial production. These ideas are not a late afterthought or theoretical final summary, but run throughout his writings, as he closely follows both the form and substance of the ethics (values and ideals) and politics (institutions and structures) of Aristotle, retranslated and updated for modern industrial society. The historical and social structures of justice range from (1) the protection of political rights and civil liberties of public assembly and free speech, derived from the constitutions of the French Revolutions of 1789 (declaration of natural rights), 1791, 1793, and 1795; (2) the dignity and self-determination of material labor, from German moral philosophy and aesthetic Romanticism; (3) ecological justice, from German theories of knowledge of the relationship between humanity and nature and British newspaper reporting on industrial pollution; (4) distributive and communal justice, from Aristotle and French socialism; (5) communal and political democracy, from the Athenian constitution of the fourth century BC (for an analysis of fairness and just price in the market), as well as the inner workings of the structural components and political institutions of the Athenian democratic polity in the council (*Boule*), assembly (*Ekklesia*), and the jury courts (*Dikasteria*), the Iroquois Confederacy of Nations and the Iroquois constitution (*Great Law of Peace*) of 1451, Abraham Lincoln's Emancipation Proclamation of 1862 and Gettysburg Address of 1863, and the *Declaration to the French People* of the Paris Commune of 1871 by Charles Delescluze, Jules Valles, and Pierre Denis; and (6) the underlying logical and structural contradictions and economic

crises of capitalism, from an immanent critique of British economic theory and German idealism. Marx fuses the ideals of
individual and social life with the ethics and politics of social justice, into a critique of political economy. This approach contains
both a reflective history of human consciousness, from the ancient
Hebrews and Greeks to the modern Europeans, and a theory of the
structures of political economy, in both an immanent critique and
an institutional analysis of the historical potential for an emancipated society, built on the ideals that run through the history of
Western consciousness. By this means, the issues of social labor
and social justice are integrated into a critical theory of advanced
capitalism that itself must be connected and updated to more contemporary issues of political economy; intolerance and abuse of
racial, sexual, and cultural minorities; and the crisis of nature and
the ecology. After careful consideration of these issues, it becomes
clear that Marx is not reducible to economism or scientism, or to
having a deterministic and mechanical view of political economy.[5]

It should be noted that Marx does not outline or delineate the
different sociological and philosophical methods of inquiry in his
writings, nor did he write about the epistemology and metatheory
that were necessary for the development of his own social theory.
He does incorporate a rather diverse approach to the methods of
the social sciences which rests on an analysis of history, hermeneutics and interpretive sociology, phenomenology, ethnography,
dialectics, immanent critique, structuralism, functionalism, and
classical economic theory.[6] Capitalism is an economic and political system guided by its own cultural ideals, which are irrational
and immoral at their core. The productive forces are arranged to
produce enormous amounts of social wealth for the purposes of
maintaining a class system; the hierarchical and class organization of production only reaffirms and justifies the alienation and
exploitation of workers within the system; politics is ultimately
controlled by the powerful, as it is ideologically justified by the
appearance of public participation and elections; and science and
technology justify further economic expansion that maintains

class difference and ecological crises. On the ethical side of the equation, economic expansion does not lead to material wellbeing for the majority of citizens; it does not lead to communal solidarity, common will, or a participatory democracy; nor does it lead to greater worker emancipation and control over their own organizations, skills, and the political conditions of work. Economic expansion does not lead to greater economic stability and integration that solve the system's structural problems and crises. Finally, increased scientific rationality and applied technology do not lead to a more virtuous, creative, and happy life, a life of practical reason and discursive rationality, and a life of a moral and democratic community. Alienation has a twofold meaning: the worker is alienated from the social ideals of the community and from the economic and political benefits of industrial production. This makes the issues and ideals of a moral economy and democratic society impossible, either structurally or logically, to realize under the present conditions of the social system. Political participation, democracy, and social consensus can only be brought about by the transformation of language and interaction, by collective consciousness and cultural reflection. But this is only the beginning. The social system is contradictory at its core of ethics and structures, moral values and political economy. These must change for a truly open and free democracy and the potential for practical reason and discursive rationality to begin to take place.

Throughout his early and later writings, Marx's theories of ethics and social justice are grounded in the various forms of contradictions between the social ideals of Western culture and the structural reality of capitalism. These contradictions within and between ethics and structures are manifested in a variety of different historical and social ways: (1) the contradiction between civil rights and human rights, the rights of man and the rights of the citizen, and liberalism and democracy in the French Revolution, in *On the Jewish Question* (1843); (2) the social ethics of human creativity, beauty, self-determination, nobility, dignity, individual freedom, and the community and brotherhood of man grounded in classical and contemporary humanism and the alienation, exploitation, and dehumanization of human labor, through the industrial product as private property and the process and organization of work, in the *Economic and Philosophical Manuscripts* (1844); (3) the potential emancipation and material wellbeing resulting from productive forces of science, technology, and industry, and the oppressive social relations and class organization of production, in *The Communist Manifesto* (1848) and *A Contribution to the Critique of Political Economy* (1859); (4) the economic and material productive forces for the potential betterment of humanity and communal prosperity matched against the unequal class distribution, barbarism, and human suffering, again in *The Communist Manifesto*; (5) democracy compared to capitalism and civil society; the newly formed French government of the Third Republic to the progressive democratic ideals in *The Paris Commune* (1871) and the critique of the party platform of the proposed Social Democratic Party in Germany compared to Marx's own view of socialism, in *Critique of the Gotha Program* (1875); and (6) the expansive production and the technological and industrial overproduction and material waste, followed by continued structural crises and economic breakdown, in the *Grundrisse* (1857–58) and *Capital*, vol. 1 (1867). Capitalism is ethically, logically, and structurally incompatible and contradictory to the social ideals, premises, and potentialities of a true and open democracy and the social ideals of Western society. This is the common theme in Marx's work and forms the basis for his ethical and political rejection of both political liberalism and economic capitalism. Marx is either detailing the internal inconsistencies of the theories, ideas, and ideals of liberalism, or revealing the inner contradictions and structural fault lines about to burst asunder in the production process itself. From this perspective in his core writings, capitalism is a social system that is both immoral and irrational in its very structural and moral foundations. It wastes scientific and technological potentialities and creates environmental disasters as it undermines any sense of the ethical and social

ideals of a moral economy and social democracy. It is this continued juxtaposition of the social structures of industrial work and
social ideals of cultural interaction throughout that frames Marx's
theory of social justice.

Habermas argues that Marx's understanding and articulation of
the historical and theoretical relationship between the productive
forces and social relations of production is extremely problematic.
It is a relationship that Marx never truly clarified, and which had
serious implications for the full development of his social theory.
Marx had hoped that the expansion of the productive forces would
lead to class consciousness and radical social change, but he never
truly developed a theory that explained their historical and social
relationship or potential for an emancipatory consciousness. Marx
recognizes that the two parts of the capitalist mode of production
were intimately related and interdependent, but, Habermas writes,
"the two developments do not converge.... Marx tried in vain to
capture this [interdependence] in the dialectic of forces of production and the relations of production." However, he never developed
these ideas and was later "misinterpreted in a mechanical manner."[7]
Nevertheless, as stated above, this connection between the emancipatory potential of the productive forces of science, technology,
and industry and the oppression of the class system and organization of human labor is expanded within Marx's broader
themes of the relationship between human labor and social justice. Ethics and social justice are more comprehensive categories
than symbolic language and social interaction, and better reflect
the ideals of the self-formative process (*Bildungsprozess*) of the
species being and human spirit. Unfortunately, Marx does not
develop these earlier technical terms in his later clarification of
his theory of the cultural and social ideals and real possibilities of
social change in the manner anticipated. Instead, he focuses his
attention in his later writings on the productive forces and their
relationship to the structural and economic crises within the class
system of capitalism. His purpose seems to be to stress the oppression and irrationality of capitalism to his readers, rather than their

emancipatory potential.[8] He seems more interested in writing for the moment of praxis, raising class consciousness, and providing the foundations for the possibilities of real social change.

Horkheimer and Adorno wrote in their *Dialectic of Enlightenment* during the Second World War that the rise of scientific and technological rationality during the Enlightenment in the eighteenth century also eventually gave rise to the fascism in the twentieth century. This was due to the actual internal workings and dialectic of enlightenment, where Western reason and critical reflection were lost in the rise of positivist rationality. They attempted for many years to search for a legitimate foundation for the reason lost in the Enlightenment. A possible solution to the epistemological dilemma created by modern science and its positive method lies in the total reconstruction of Western thought as the basis for social reflection, concepts, and critique. Marx presents the opportunity to rediscover the answer to the dialectic of enlightenment with his theory of the history of the ethics and structures in his social theory. He concluded his famous work *Capital* not with an analysis of the historical and economic inevitability of the breakdown of capitalism, as is generally believed, but with a recognition of the structural, logical, and ethical contradictions (*Widersprüche*) of the capitalist system that cannot be negated or overcome. His writings end where they began in the mid-1840s, with an emphasis on Aristotle and Hegel and an ethical critique of the moral and political failures of modern society with an economic system that is alienating and exploitative, irrational and immoral. The analytical Marxists of the 1970s mistook Marx's rejection of isolated and ahistorical moral philosophy and its separation of ethics and politics for a rejection of any attempt at constructing a critical theory of social justice. The analytical Marxists eliminate any theory of justice in Marx by misreading and misinterpreting his critique of ideology and moralism, and his theories of science, dialectics of ideals and economic structures, the logic of history, historical materialism, and political economy. Finally, in perhaps their most serious error, the analytical Marxists forget the ancient and modern traditions upon which Marx developed his theory of modern industrial society. By doing so, they lose the soul (ancient Hebrews and early Christians), the heart (ancient Greeks), and the spirit (modern French and Germans) of his social theory, ideals, and vision; they, in turn, lose the ability to see, imagine, and to dream.

Marx's theory of social justice is not limited to civil law or issues of workers' wages, fairness, or economic redistribution. It is much broader, more comprehensive, and more profound than that. It delves into the question of the emancipation and self-realization of the historical essence of humanity in ethics, culture, law, politics, production, work, and its species being as a "political and productive animal." Marx's theory focuses on issues of happiness; moral and intellectual virtue; friendship; moral economy; political and economic democracy; human and natural rights; self-realization and self-determination of species being in political economy; individual freedom, dignity, beauty, and human creativity in material, cultural, spiritual, and political work; and economic distribution based on reciprocity and the satisfaction of fundamental human needs. Marx's true goal is the realization of the ethical values and political ideals of classical humanism in modern society in order to create a moral economy and self-government "of the people, by the people," for the common good. At one point in his addresses on the Paris Commune, Marx attempts to integrate the classical ideals of Aristotle and Lincoln. The goal of justice is to affirm the existential meaning, purpose, beauty, and dignity of human life in its various social forms; it is to elevate humanity to a higher level of existence and value than as a commodity of production, exchange, and consumption. Following closely the development in Aristotle's thought between the *Nicomachean Ethics* and the *Politics*, Marx, too, emphasizes in his theory of justice the distinctions among morality, ethics, and virtue; social institutions and social structures and social ethics. He incorporates Aristotle's ethics and politics into his general social theory by expanding the nature of virtue, goodness, and happiness into a critical theory of political economy and the nature of a moral economy, physical, intellectual and moral labor, and economic democracy.

Ethics is an area of study that reflects the highest moral values, principles, and ideals of the good and virtuous life, while *politics* examines the social institutions of the state and political economy that nurture, protect, and ensure the existence of that moral life of humanity; these very institutions make virtue, happiness, and communal existence possible. The overall structure, logic, and substance of Marx's theory of justice mirrors very closely that of Aristotle's theory. The latter begins with the classical humanism of ethics, moral virtue, happiness, and friendship in the *Ethics*, and then evolves into a concrete historical and institutional examination of the Athenian polity and assembly, household and moral economy, and critique of unnatural wealth acquisition in a commercial market economy (*chrematistike*) in the *Politics*. Marx, in turn, begins in his early philosophical writings with an examination of the political rights of the citizen and ethical humanism of species being and aesthetic human labor, and then advances into a study of political and economic democracy, moral economy, and a critique of the irrationality and immorality of unnatural capitalist production, consumption, and market exchange in his later writings on capital. Although for all practical purposes Marx does not have or use the terms *justice* or *social justice* in his writings, the overall formal, logical, and substantive structure of both authors' works and the evolution of their theories parallel each other closely. The totality of Marx's writings are thus part of a comprehensive theory of social justice, reflecting Aristotle's influence, that may be divided into the following general areas.

The traditional view of Marx's writings in the secondary literature is that he evolved over time from his philosophical and humanistic writings to his more dialectical, economic, and scientific works. Others have argued that if Marx did have a theory of justice, it focused on the economy and the proper and fair distribution of property and social wealth for the benefit of all members of society. The latter position, however, is only one aspect of Marx's

broader and more comprehensive theory of social justice. His ultimate goal is to restructure the political economy in such a fashion
as to realize the secular and historical natural law or distinctive
essence and historical potentiality of humanity as a free, creative,
and social being—to make ethics and social philosophy applicable, practical, and real. Marx reveals how the essence of humanity
was distorted and undermined in an alien and exploitative political economy; this provides the basis for his ethical humanism by
allowing him to show the distinction between the real and the
ideal (ethics). The above interpretation is intended to show that,
rather than a one-dimensional linear evolution of his works from
his early to his later period, Marx develops his own social theory
based on the ideals of classical antiquity. Between Aristotle's ethics
and politics, and between Aristotle's theory of moral philosophy,
virtue, and happiness and his theory of moral economy and democratic polity, Marx inserts his understanding of work and the value
of human labor, modern industrial society, alienated labor, factory
organization, the labor theory of value, and political economy.

In rethinking the importance of Aristotle for modern society,
Marx blends elements of ethics, phronesis, and praxis into his
theory of work, since *work* now refers to technical and mechanical skills, artistic sensibilities and impressions, ethical aspects of
self-realization and human freedom, and an essential and creative imperative toward wisdom, politics, and democracy. Work
integrates ethics and politics, virtue and communal responsibility, technical knowledge and aesthetics, economics and politics,
production and kindness, through the creativity of the subject in
history; work is primarily an ethical and aesthetic activity because
it provides for the material common good of the polity and is a
way of constructing the institutions which manifest the essence
and beauty of humanity as creators of its own world. This is the
essence of work and humanity for Marx. For Aristotle, there are
elements of both technical knowledge and art in his concept of
techne, which Marx then incorporates into his theory of praxis
as physical, moral, and political labor. According to Marx, labor

is a form of a moral, aesthetic, and technical work—an art form and a human virtue. For both Aristotle and Marx, virtue is moral excellence, but each uses different characteristics to describe the ethics and virtue of their distinctive historical times and philosophical horizons. Aristotle describes the virtuous life in terms of practical reason, political wisdom, and the democratic polity, whereas Marx refers to it more in terms of human labor, social creativity, equality, freedom, and democratic socialism. Thus, Marx is explicating and expanding upon the various themes and components in Aristotle's theory of social justice and applying them to the modern industrial world, thereby fusing the ancients and the moderns into a comprehensive critical theory of liberalism and capitalism. Praxis also plays an important role in framing Marx's critique and transcendence of Hegel and the creation of his theory of historical materialism—an integration of idealism and materialism, consciousness and nature, consciousness and society, and science and modern industry. Marx, like Aristotle, moves from his early ethics and humanistic writings on social ideals, happiness, self-determination, and creativity to his later writings on economics and political economy—that is, from his abstract humanistic philosophy to a concrete institutional sociology.

However, between Aristotle's *Ethics* and *Politics*, Marx, as mentioned above, adds the primacy of work which includes issues of aesthetics, art, beauty, creativity, and both poiesis (making and using technical/artistic knowledge or techne) and praxis (doing). According to Aristotle, praxis is an ethical form of moral activity and intellectual virtue. This concept lies at the center of Marx's theory of work of the aesthetic artisan, creative worker, and moral and deliberative citizen within a democratic polity and moral community. Marx understood that the Aristotelian concept of praxis included both practical/political knowledge (prudence and political wisdom of phronesis) and creative, economic and artistic making (poiesis); he expanded the concept into the ethical dimension of human labor in economics, politics, and culture, thereby making the concept relevant to modern industrial society. Work is practical in that it refers to both "technical" and "moral" labor; it also connotes a "technical" and "artistic" dimension that exists in Aristotle's notion of "making" (poiesis). In his early writings, it is clear that Marx emphasizes the moral and aesthetic aspects of human labor in the workplace as the foundations of his ethical humanism and critique of capitalism. Marx also incorporates poiesis into the concepts of subjectivity and objectivity, from the German Idealism of Kant and Hegel, since human consciousness and reason create not only a realm of ideas of perception, consciousness, and self-consciousness (*Phenomenology of Spirit*), but empirical, scientific, moral, and historical reality (materialism). Aristotle connected ethics and politics by joining together his analysis of the good life of moral virtue (courage, moderation, nobility, honor, love, compassion, goodness, friendship, and justice) and intellectual virtue (*episteme, phronesis,* and *techne*) in the *Nicomachean Ethics*, with the best political constitution of the democratic polity in the *Politics*. In this way, the virtuous life of happiness would be made concrete and real within the economic and democratic polity.[9]

Marx takes this analysis and adds his understanding of the creative and constitutive potential of human labor, which constructs the social, cultural, economic, and political institutions that make the integration of ethics and politics possible. It is physical, spiritual, and political work that creates the good life and makes the dreams of Aristotle relevant and possible for the modern age. This creative fusion of the ancients and the moderns through "work" helps create a new critical and dialectical theory of society and political economy. That is, to Aristotle's ethics, Marx adds German moral, epistemological, historical, and phenomenological constructivism; the French, German, and British philosophy of art, creativity, harmony, and beauty; and the British theory of labor and value. To Aristotle's politics, Marx adds French and German political theory and the ideals and institutions of the French Revolution, the Paris Commune of 1871, and the Gotha Program. It is communal work which creates the existential meaning and social purpose in life, and provides the foundation for natural law, secular and classical humanism, and the social critique of political economy. Marx expands the classical views of a democratic polity to include the economic democracy of workers' associations and workers' control over the process and means of production. He also expands Aristotle's ideals of moral and intellectual virtue, the good and happy life of political deliberation and citizenship, practical wisdom, and moral economy, to incorporate the social values of species-being, human creativity, beauty, harmony, friendship, and self-determination in work, communal democracy, and socialism.

Distortion of these ideals leads to *chrematistike* (the unnatural wealth acquisition of a trading or commercial market that destroys the moral economy and democratic polity) and *Entfremdung* (workers' alienation and loss of control over production, politics, and the possibilities of humanity's future). Both Marx and Aristotle ground their views of ethics and democracy in the highest moral ideals of virtue and happiness. In opposition to liberalism, Marx defines freedom not in limited economic and materialistic terms of free market choices, wealth acquisition, and individual liberty (Locke). Rather, Marx holds that freedom is an expression of each individual's humanity as a moral and species-being—as a universal creator of the social community. In this way, he blends Aristotle with German and French idealism, romanticism, and political and economic socialism, along with left-Hegelian materialism and British economic theory of labor and structural crises, thereby dialectically and synthetically reconfiguring and reconceptualizing the various elements of the classical traditions into a modern theory of justice. In the end, Marx recognizes the inner structural and cultural dialectic of capitalism: the possibilities of species-being and democratic socialism are incompatible and irreconcilable with the class irrationalities and oppression of material production; a virtuous life incompatible with incoherent commercialism and unrestrained consumerism; social ethics and collective morality incompatible with crude materialism and indifferent market self-interest; species-being incompatible with possessive individualism and economic competition; communal democracy incompatible with class, inequality, poverty, and human misery; and industrial and market rationality incompatible with the social irrationality, structural contradictions (*Widersprüche*) of capital, and the constant material waste and economic and ecological crises of industrial society.

Finally, capitalism is incompatible with the whole of Western ethical, political, and classical ideals and values. This is the unfortunate irony of intellectual and social history, since modern liberalism and capitalism are not pro-life, or pro–ethical community, or pro–moral economy, or pro-democracy; instead, they are pro–private property, militarism, economic and racial colonialism, and destructive class power. Marx's early writings use the dialectic in the form of immanent, humanistic, and political critiques of capitalism, whereas his later writings rely on a dialectical critique of the structures and contradictions of political economy. By pulling together these different traditions into a coherent theory of justice, Marx concludes that the essence of humanity lies in its ability to aesthetically and ethically create through praxis—work and communal democracy—the material and political worlds according to the laws of beauty and human dignity. The moral imperative and drive of the artistic imagination toward beauty inspires social justice, just as justice moves us to a world without contradictions and conflicts, nurturing balance, harmony, and elegance of the mind and the body, of the senses and reason, along with the integration of the real and the ideal, and the communal integrity and ethical wholeness of the individual and the collective spirit. Modern political and ethical issues of freedom, liberty, equality, and natural rights are now interpreted through the prism of romantic and classical dreams. Marx sees these political and ethical categories in terms of praxis as poetry and art; they are retranslated in terms of human creativity, self-determination, compassion, love, friendship, and beauty in the workplace, moral economy, and communal democracy.

Humanity is now viewed through the primacy of the ethical and political community in which humans define and create their own worlds for the purpose of individual meaning and wisdom, self-fulfillment of human potentiality, and the expansion of the ethical community of familial love and communal identity for public wisdom and democracy. Marx's theory of aesthetic or poetic labor becomes the key to his understanding of social justice, communal democracy, individual freedom and fulfillment, and his critique of alienation, exploitation, and the structural contradictions of class labor and surplus value. The early *Philosophical Manuscripts* remain the heart of his later critique of political economy. This integration of labor and the law of beauty—harmony, symmetry, moderation, balance, and humane—is only part of Marx's theory of beauty, self-determination, and human creativity, which is to be reflected in sensual perception, modern poetry, industrial production, democratic politics, and environmental concerns. The products of human creativity and beauty in the economy and polity are to be socially distributed according to the ancient Greek and Hebrew ethical principles of social justice and human needs (Luke and Aristotle). And these issues of aesthetics, beauty, human need, and the environment are to be considered a modern and expanded part of Aristotle's ethics and politics— that is, moral economy and political democracy.

Praxis is thus a form of ethics (phronesis) and art (poiesis), critical poetry, and imaginative dreams, through which the world is formed. Poetry can be an expression of the rhythm and intuition of the heart or a critical social theory of the mind, as both use a new vocabulary to reach beyond the immediate to the truth of human existence and its potentialities. Labor is a form of artisanship—that is, it is a form of art and poetry, not a form of alienation, humiliation, and dehumanization. Labor is a poetic experience and vision because it builds the social, economic, and political world around us through imagination, freedom, self-determination, and human creativity, not through capital, property, profits, exploitation, and class. Poetry expresses elegance, integration, grace, beauty, motion, and harmony in art, nature, work, and politics, not the antagonism, conflict, isolation, loneliness, poverty, and human misery in liberalism and capitalism. The beauty and harmony of nature are also reflected in the moral economy and democracy—in the beauty of society. For Marx, labor represents the fulfillment and integration of reason and society—of Kant's pure and practical reason (knowledge and morality) and Hegel's theory of phenomenology of spirit and the self-conscious constitution of humanity and reason in the economy and state—an integration of consciousness, self-consciousness, and the philosophy of right. At its highest form, modern art and poetry form the basis for Marx's theory of social justice as it is made real in the workplace and politics, history and society, consciousness and social institutions; it is the heart and sinews of political economy and human existence. At its height, poetry is art, labor, nature, democratic socialism, and social justice. Some Romantic poets wanted to return to the hopes and ideals of classical Greece, while Marx wanted to use those ideals to create a new type of moral society. By integrating Aristotle, Kant, Hegel, and Schiller, the foundations are set for a new vision of humanity, as Marx looks upon the darkness and despair of the capitalist factories in Manchester, Leeds, and London from the heights of the classical beauty and spiritual vision of the Acropolis.

What is distinctively and disruptively ironic in all this analysis is that Marx's theory of social justice is inherently and organically part of the history of Western thought, whereas the values and institutions of liberalism and capitalism are antithetical to these ancient and medieval traditions. Perhaps even more surprisingly, Marx's theory of social justice is broader and more comprehensive than that of the ancient Greeks, with its emphasis on political, ethical, and communal themes; and more Christian and moral than modern Christianity, with its emphasis on collective beneficence, social responsibility, and civic virtue. These ancient and medieval traditions eventually lost their social and religious ideals—moral community and social sin—as they were incorporated into the prevailing social systems of their times. By using a variety of methods—including philosophical anthropology, hermeneutics, historical analysis, Hegelian phenomenology, British economic theory, historical materialism, immanent critique of political and ethical ideals, and dialectics of economic structures—Marx was able to show that modern industrial society was inherently contradictory to the modern and ancient ideals of species-being, human potentiality, and human excellence. For each dimension of social justice, there is a specific social and historical method of scientific inquiry, which runs counter to the epistemology and methodology of the natural sciences.

Marx expanded his theory of social justice in his later writings to include racial justice. While acting as the European foreign correspondent in exile for Horace Greeley's *New York Daily Tribune* between 1852 and 1862, he broadened his understanding of justice by writing news dispatches on issues of racial justice, with expanding positions on race, ethnicity, colonialism, imperialism, labor exploitation, inequality, and slavery in India, Indonesia, China, Algeria, the Middle East, Poland, and Ireland, and in America during the Civil War. Marx continued to write about these subjects in his even lesser known *Ethnological Notebooks* from 1879–82.[10] A new and expanded work on the theme of social justice would involve moving beyond Marx's nineteenth-century theory to incorporate the fundamental structural, institutional, and cultural changes in contemporary society, closely examining the nature of twenty-first century American monopoly capitalism, neoliberalism, class inequality, poverty, fiscal policy, taxation, militarism, racism, sexism, and prejudice against gender differences—all in light of Marx's ethical and political theory of virtue, human dignity, freedom, moral economy, and democratic socialism. Today these issues of class, inequality, and oppressive wealth and power distribution are difficult to examine directly and publicly because they are hidden behind the phenomena of ideology and distorted language of "cultural issues" and the public policies of abortion restrictions and birth control; pro-life politics, gun rights, and critique of "welfare queens" and the welfare system; and race, Southern strategy, gerrymandering, and voter suppression. Also issues of global warming, climate change, and the ecological crisis are not being directly confronted and examined as products of capitalist production. The underlying structural and institutional foundations of Western capitalism—and thus the basis for any critical theory of social justice—continue to be ignored and unexplored. Finally, it should be noted that Marx's ideas and writings did not evolve in the same manner as those of many modern scholars: he never developed a systematic or comprehensive theory of social class, the modern liberal state, historical materialism, social praxis, human need, or social justice. Nevertheless, these ideas are integrated into the overall heart of Marx's writings and form the very foundation of the soul of his social theory and critique of modern political economy.

In the end, both Marx and Aristotle reach similar conclusions in their works: ancient and modern democracies are to be aligned with corresponding moral economies. Both recognize the normative and structural incompatibility between the uplifting ideals and reality of a democratic society and a capitalist economy characterized by profits, property, poverty, inequality, class divisions, distorted power relations, and exploitation. All these aspects of capitalism are logically and ethically contradictory to the compassion, friendship, freedom, political and economic equality, collective self-determination, and political wisdom necessary for a true democracy and human happiness. In an interesting and counterintuitive manner, Locke indirectly and unintentionally confirms this thesis in the second half of chapter V of his *Second Treatise of Government* (para. 50). Here Locke moves from a moral economy in the original state of nature based on natural reason, natural law, and property limits—founded upon the law and ethical principles of spoilage, labor, and sufficiency (paras. 31–34)—to a market economy consisting of a social contract, natural rights, and the modern state or Leviathan (paras. 28, 37, 46–48, 50, 85) grounded in money accumulation, private property, inequality, class, and possessive individualism.[11] Marx's penetrating and dialectical critique of liberalism and capitalism may now be understood as part of a broader and more comprehensive rejection of these Enlightenment political and economic values and market institutions found throughout the history of the classical traditions of Western thought, from the ancient Hebrews, Hellenes, and Hellenists to the modern French, German, and British artists, poets, philosophers, and economic theorists. This is similar to Habermas's attempt to justify and ground his theory of intersubjectivity, the lifeworld, and communicative action on the basis of a neo-Hegelian self-formative and creative process in history and the democratic community. Through his dialectical reasoning, romantic poetic imagery, philosophical imagination, and critique of modern political economy, Marx became the modern Aristötle with an umlaut. Seen through this lens, liberalism and capitalism are clearly incompatible with the whole of the Western traditions based on the belief and necessity of a moral economy, ethical community, and democratic socialism.

To further develop the full implications of a contemporary theory of social justice that integrates the phenomenological history of Western self-consciousness, reason, and the communal spirit would require a critical rethinking and creation of a new metaphysics of science, one that integrates the ancient Hebrew and medieval Christian traditions of stewardship and nature, along with the classical Greek tradition of metaphysics and a symbiotic and moral balance between humanity and nature.[12] This in turn would be connected to a rethinking of the role of modern science, technology, and industry and their relationship to the social relations within a moral and democratic political economy. Finally, a third element would involve a more comprehensive understanding and empirical-historical analysis of advanced capitalist society, with its multinational corporations, neocolonialism, neoliberalism, welfare state, post-Keynesian economics, and decline of liberal democracy. This contemporary integration of nature and socialist ecology, a renewed and living metaphysics of science and technology, and a comprehensive theory of the contemporary structures of political economy would expand in important ways a critical theory of social justice. The notion of the "domination of nature" is the underlying social imperative of modern natural science running throughout the work of Nietzsche, Weber, Scheler, Husserl, and critical theory. The joining of the various structural components and subsystems within the system and lifeworld in the manner of Habermas—economy, politics, social institutions, and culture—helps us better understand the complex interdependence and integration of society. Knowing these relationships forces us to consider both the increasing necessity to change the organization and power relations of work toward the creation of a moral community and democracy; and to change the manner and application of the natural and social sciences, to ensure stewardship and emancipation and not the technical domination and rational control over the environment and society. The shadows of the Enlightenment slowly disappear as reason and the classical horizons return to permit the imagination needed for a new creative and dynamic world that respects the potentialities of both humanity and nature. For all their major advances within critical social theory, most members of the Frankfurt School failed to develop the radical implications for epistemology and a theory of science posed by Marx's theory of historical materialism and his structural analysis of a theory of social justice. Only by blending historical materialism, postmodern philosophy of science, and ecological theory will we begin to forge a more comprehensive and holistic theory of social justice that truly emancipates all life from the domination of nature, humanity, and society.[13]

SUMMARY OF THE STRUCTURAL FOUNDATIONS OF THE ANCIENT AND MODERN THEORIES OF SOCIAL JUSTICE[14]

Marx's theory of social justice lies deeply buried and hidden within the structure of his writings. The reason it has taken so long to uncover these insights is that Marx never develops a systematic and methodical approach to the issue itself. Rather, he creates a structure running through his early and later works that mirrors

Aristotle's approach to social justice, supplemented by Hegel's phenomenological reconstruction of classical, medieval, and modern ethical and political traditions, and by Marx's own analysis of classical political economy and modern capitalist society. A brief overview follows as we trace the substantive, structural, and formal correspondence between Aristotle's ethics and politics and Marx's early philosophical and humanistic writings and his later economic and political works on the nature of democracy.

Part 1: Aristotle's humanistic ethics, moral excellence, and moral/intellectual virtues. Classical virtues of happiness, love, compassion, friendship, citizenship, praxis, good moral life (moral/political activity), and household or family economy (*oikonomia*), intellectual virtues of philosophical wisdom *(episteme)*, artistic or technical knowledge *(techne)*, and ethical and political wisdom *(phronesis)* and the moral virtues of courage, moderation, and justice. Marx continues this approach with his analysis of the modern virtues of creativity, beauty, human dignity, praxis (ethical and aesthetic work), human emancipation, economic and political democracy, brotherhood of man, friendship, citizenship, equality, freedom, cooperative sharing based on human need, self-determination of non-alienated human nature or species being (*Gattungswesen*), social justice, and ethical humanism. For both Aristotle and Marx, these humanistic and ethical values express the highest forms of human need, moral virtue, and human excellence, as well as the highest forms of individual freedom, human rights, and self-realization of human potentiality.

Part 2: Expanding the relationship between ancient and modern ethics and politics. Marx builds upon Aristotle's *Ethics* and *Politics* by adding another key dimension pertaining to human labor in an industrial society, whereby ethics-politics becomes ethics-work-politics. In the process Marx integrates ancient ethics, virtue, political wisdom, and the democratic polity with the modern emphasis on human labor, production, art, creativity, human dignity, and communal sharing and cooperation. Many of the characteristics of ancient ethics and politics thereby become fused with and expressions of human labor, especially the technical, moral, aesthetic, and political dimensions of labor. With Marx, human labor becomes a central economic (artisanship and production), political (democracy), aesthetic (art and beauty), and moral (dignity, creativity, and self-determination) category.

Part 3: Political and economic theory of the best constitutions. Aristotle turns to the democratic polity of Athens based on direct democracy (*demokratia*), political equality (*isonomia*), public accountability (*eisangelia*), and political wisdom (*phronesis*). Marx looks to the democratic commune of Paris based on class equality, public participation, worker self-determination, and the collective ownership of the means of production and the political rights of the citizen found in the French Revolution and French Constitutions from 1789–95 and the Communards of Paris in 1871. Both forms of ancient and modern democracy were built on a moral economy.

Part 4: Prerequisites for a moral economy. According to Aristotle, household or family economy (*oikonomia*) and distribution based on reciprocity, love, friendship, need, and grace provide the economic foundation for democratic politics. Marx follows with his analysis of the socialist or workers/cooperative economy based on fairness, need, and the democratic and collective ownership of production as the foundations of democracy.

Part 5: Critique of unnatural wealth acquisition. Compare Aristotle's rejection of ancient commercial trade (*kapelike*) to Marx's critique of modern capitalist production. Compare the structural contradictions (*Widersprüche*) and loss of virtue and reason found in the ancient exchange market and money/profit/ property accumulation of *chrematistike*, using the Socratic method and immanent critique of dialogue and dialectics to the logical and structural contradictions of capital, using Hegelian logic and the dialectic of capital, which destroys the moral economy, democratic polity, and the future possibilities of humanity as a community of virtuous and rational human beings. For both Aristotle and Marx, unnatural wealth acquisition and property accumulation of commercial trade and capitalism undermine the moral foundations of society and the possibility of human virtue, equality, freedom, and happiness—that is, a just society.

Part 6: Forms of social justice. Ancient universal or political justice (moral excellence, virtue, and happiness through politics) and particular justice (rectificatory, reciprocal, and distributive justice). Marx's theory of political justice runs throughout his writings, from his analysis of human emancipation and the "political rights of the citizen" to distributive/economic and political/communal justice in the Paris Commune and *Critique of the Gotha Program*. These various forms of ancient and modern justice are the structural and social means of insuring, nurturing and protecting the underlying ethical values and virtues of modern humanism and communalism, through emphasis on proportionate equality, freedom, dignity, and reciprocal fairness in a moral economy, concern for the common good and human needs in economic distribution, and the implementing of these economic and political ideals in democratic socialism: reciprocal exchange, need distribution, worker ownership and control, and political and economic democracy.

Part 7: Rejection of the values and ideals of the ancient and modern forms of capitalism. Both Aristotle and Marx accept the ideal of a moral economy that rejects the values of utilitarianism and possessive individualism, commercial trade, profit and capital accumulation, and the belief in the ideals of equality, freedom, happiness, and justice built upon a commercial, market, and class economy. These ideals are antithetical to the ethics and politics of both classical and modern democracy.

Part 8: Transition from ethics to politics; the critical research of applied philosophy and ethical sociology. Transition from classical ethics and virtue to the social institutions of political economy—household economy, polity, and Athenian democracy; and the transition from the ethics of Marx's early moral and humanistic writings to the institutions of political economy and democratic socialism in his later works on capital and the Paris Commune.

Both Aristotle and Marx create a new and integrated discipline of applied philosophy, critical sociology, and historical political economy. By turning to Aristotle's critical social theory, Marx rejects the idea of a mechanical, deterministic, and positivistic dialectical materialism. Both theorists are interested in grounding their ideals of a moral economy and virtuous life in the actual institutions of ancient Athens and modern industrial and cooperative society. Social justice is ultimately about the ethical ideals and moral values that make us human and the political and economic institutions which give them concrete life, purpose, and social meaning.

Part 9: The organic environment and the ecological crisis in agriculture and industry: Aristotle attempts to integrate his theory of ethics and nature into an environmental theory based on the moral responsibility of humanity to protect all living beings and to preserve the environment for the happiness and good life of future generations. This is a holistic and symbiotic view of the interconnectedness of all life and living entities. Nature is a living organism with a specific purpose and teleology and humans have a responsibility to care for it. In 1840 Marx translated Aristotle's work *De Anima* which examined the Greek view of biology and nature, and which he would later integrate into a broader theory of the alienation of humanity and nature. Since work and the environment are so intimately connected in the process of production, Marx is quite aware of the physical and ethical damage done to both. He is sensitive to this organic view of nature, as he integrated the Greek philosophy of Aristotle, Epicurus, and Lucretius; the German idealism of Kant, Hegel, and Schelling (*Naturphilosophie*); and the scientific writings on natural science, climate change, and agricultural and industrial pollution of Theodor Schwann, Julius Robert Mayer, John Tyndall, and Charles Darwin. In this manner, he was able to have a comprehensive appreciation of environmental issues and social justice.

Part 10: Summary: Classical ethics and politics of Aristotle expanded by Marx's critique of political economy. Just as Marx expands Aristotle's understanding of "ethics" (virtue, love, friendship, political wisdom, and justice) to include the beauty, dignity, and creativity of art and human labor (German idealism and British and German romanticism), he also expands Aristotle's notion of "politics" on the Pnyx (Athenian democracy and household economy) to include communal democracy, value of human labor, workers' control, producer associations, dismantling of the class system, economic and moral contradictions and crises of capitalist production, and distributive justice based on grace, reciprocity, and human need (British political economy, German idealism, and French socialism).

Marx uses the three key elements of Aristotle's general framework in his theory of ethics and politics—moral virtues, moral economy, and democratic polity—and integrates them into his understanding of modern society based on a number of ethical and political ideals, including: (1) the political institutions of Athenian democracy and its constitution in the council (*boule*), assembly (*ekklesia*), and the popular jury courts (*dikasteria*) of Athenian democracy in the fourth century BC, based on a moral economic and virtuous life of political wisdom, love, and communal responsibility; (2) the constitution and Great Law of Peace of the Iroquois Confederacy of Nations in 1451; (3) individual liberties, political emancipation, and the natural rights of the citizen for public assembly, free speech, and freedom of thought from the French constitutions of 1789 (declaration of natural rights), 1791, 1793, and 1795, in *On the Jewish Question*; (4) Abraham Lincoln's *Emancipation Proclamation* of 1862 and the Gettysburg Address of 1863 in the *Critique of the Gotha Program*; (5) the ideals of fairness, just price, reciprocity, human needs, and distributive justice, also in the *Critique of the Gotha Program*; (6) the expansion of the concept of democracy to include the ideals of worker associations, workers' control, and democratic socialism, in the *Declaration to the French People* of the Paris Commune of 1871 by Charles Delescluze, Jules Valles, and Pierre Denis, in the *Civil War in France*; (7) the ideals of species being, human dignity, aesthetic work, artisan creativity, human freedom, and self-determination in French socialism, German idealism, and British/German poetry in the early *Economic and Philosophical Manuscripts of 1844*; and (8) these ideals keep the same form in Marx's later writings and critique of political economy, which reveal the inner social irrationality of capitalism; its continuous and unavoidable structural contradictions and economic crises; and the immorality of a society based on unlimited material production, growth, and private accumulation, while maintaining continued class power, inequality, poverty, and human misery, dehumanization, and exploitation. The ethical and political ideals listed above are logically and socially incompatible with the institutions and structures of modern political economy within the capitalist system.

The result is that both Aristotle and Marx integrate their ethics and politics, philosophy and sociology, virtue and political economy, into their comprehensive and critical theories of civil/legal, economic, and political justice. Marx introduces and broadens our understanding of the Athenian moral economy and democratic polity and assembly for the modern age. Commercial trade (*kapelike*), industrial capitalism, and class structure are all viewed as incompatible with the ideals of ancient and modern democracy, equality, and freedom. By joining ethics and politics, both Aristotle and Marx agree that the life of true moral excellence and the happiness of a good life could only be achieved within a community characterized by a moral economy grounded in human need and a democratic polity and based on freedom and equality. For Aristotle, the foundation of ethics and politics lies in the love, respect, and compassion within the family, extended to the polity and fellow citizens of Athens; for Marx, by contrast, the foundation lies in the respect and dignity of cooperative workers and fellow citizens. Marx even uses terms such as *chreia* (need) and *praxis* (activity and work) to show that distributive justice and human labor are essential issues of rational and moral virtue of free individuals. He views labor, creativity, and beauty as fundamentally ethical actions which defined humanity as moral and rational beings. Ethics, work, praxis, and politics are all intimately interconnected for Marx, as they provide the basis for the meaning and purpose of his life's work and underlying critique of capitalist society. Thus, both Aristotle and Marx connect ethics, politics, and economics with the concept of praxis, since all are various forms of moral activity for the good of humanity.

Marx's theory of social justice is not limited to civil law or issues of workers' wages, fairness, or economic redistribution. It is much broader, more comprehensive, and more profound than that. His theory delves into the question of the emancipation and self-realization of the historical essence of humanity in ethics, culture, law, politics, production, work, and its species being as a "political and productive animal." It focuses on issues of happiness, moral and intellectual virtue, friendship, moral economy, political and economic democracy, human and natural rights, self-realization and self-determination of species being in political economy, individual freedom, dignity, beauty, and human creativity in material, cultural, spiritual, and political work, and economic distribution based on reciprocity and the satisfaction of fundamental human needs. Marx's true goal is the realization of the ethical values and political ideals of classical humanism in modern society, in order to create a moral economy and self-government "of the people, by the people" for the common good. The goal of justice is to affirm the existential meaning, purpose, beauty, and dignity of human life in its various social forms; it is to elevate humanity to a higher level of existence and value than a commodity of production, exchange, and consumption. Following the development in Aristotle's thought between the *Ethics* and the *Politics*, Marx, too, emphasizes in his theory of justice the distinctions among morality, ethics, and virtue, social institutions and social structures, and social ethics. He incorporates Aristotle's ethics and politics into his general social theory by expanding the nature of virtue, goodness, and happiness into a critical theory of political economy and the nature of a moral economy, physical, intellectual and moral labor, and economic democracy.

Ethics is an area of study that reflects the highest moral values, principles, and ideals of the good and virtuous life, while politics examines the social institutions of political economy which nurture, protect, and ensure the existence of that moral life of humanity; these very institutions make virtue, happiness, and communal existence possible. The overall structure, logic, and substance of Marx's theory of justice mirrors very closely that of Aristotle's theory: the latter begins with the classical humanism of ethics, moral virtue, happiness, and friendship in his *Ethics*, and then evolves into a concrete historical and institutional examination of the Athenian polity and assembly, household and moral economy, and critique of unnatural wealth acquisition in a commercial market economy in his *Politics*. Marx, in turn, begins in his early philosophical writings with his examination of the political rights of the citizen and ethical humanism of species being and aesthetic human labor, and then develops his social theory into a study of political and economic democracy, moral economy, and a critique of the irrationality and immorality of unnatural capitalist production, consumption, and market exchange in his later writings in *Capital*. Marx's theory of social justice lies buried in the overall formal, logical, and substantive structure of his writings and reflects his deep respect and admiration for classical Greek humanism and Aristotelian ethics. The content and evolution of their theories are very similar and parallel each other closely.

Here we realize that Marx's theory of social justice is only the beginning, since it must be expanded to include an examination of the history and structures of advanced capitalist society, including monopoly capitalism, the welfare state and neoliberalism, the taxation system, authoritarian democracy and voter suppression, the military-industrial system and neocolonialism, structural racism and sexism, the domination of nature and ecological crisis, the forms of capitalist science and technological rationality in the workplace and academy, and the evolution of an emancipated science of nature and society. It is at this point that the foundation is established for a society of communicative action, public discourse, and democratic socialism. Marx's theory of the different forms of social justice, resulting from an integration of ancient and modern ethics and politics, offers a framework for a comprehensive and critical theory of the potential for future forms of emancipation and democracy.

Notes

Introduction: Epistemology, the Crisis of Science, and the Twilight of Reason

1. Fritjof Capra, *The Turning Point: Science, Society and the Rising Culture* (New York: Simon and Schuster, 1982), 99–262.

2. Karl Popper outlines the principles and logic of scientific inquiry in his work *The Logic of Scientific Discovery* (New York: Harper & Row, 1968), 39–62, and in "The Logic of the Social Sciences," in *The Positivist Dispute in German Sociology*, ed. Theodor Adorno, trans. Glyn Adey and David Frisby (New York: Harper & Row, 1976), 89–90.

3. "Politics" in this context refers to any type of value or value system that frames or influences human consciousness, individual behavior, or our relationship to nature and society, including (1) metaphysics and theology (God, being, and the physical reality); (2) economics (utility, productivity, efficiency, and consumerism); (3) morality, ethics, politics (liberalism and individualism); and (4) aesthetics, social relationships, and the full range of the cultural values of the Enlightenment. Its more precise meaning, however, refers to the values produced by the rise of the Western economy, global commerce, and industrial capitalism. The hidden political values in natural science are expressed in its metaphysics, imperative to dominate nature, and its technical application in capital production and expansion; the hidden values in social science are expressed in its underlying disenchantment in its epistemology and methodology of empiricism and nominalism, the imperative to dominate humanity, the fragmentation of disciplines that does not permit deep structural analysis of political economy, and

in the nominalist ideology of science that separates ethics and science and undermines any form of critical and historical social theory.

4.   The innate, natural rights of life, liberty, health, and property of John Locke in the seventeenth century were reflections of a market economy and the primacy of private property. In a similar fashion, the concepts of the Enlightenment and modern science articulated by Francis Bacon and René Descartes were also reflections of the underlying social system.

5.   Friedrich Nietzsche, *The Gay Science: With a Prelude in Rhymes and an Appendix of Songs*, trans. Walter Kaufmann (New York: Vintage Books, 1974), book 3, sec. 108, 167. The "shadows of God" originally referred to Nietzsche's description of the history, logic, and phenomena of Western reason—the history of the decadence and decline of the Apollonian forms of human reason—from the Platonic idealism of Socrates and Plato, Christian theology of Augustine and Aquinas, scientific rationalism of Galileo and Descartes, political liberalism of Hobbes and Locke, and modern morality and practical reason of Kant, in his work "Twilight of the Idols" in *The Portable Nietzsche*, trans. and intro. Walter Kaufmann (New York: Viking Press, 1969). See also the reference to the "madman" who sought God in the marketplace in *The Gay Science*, book 3, sec. 125, 181. Dante in *The Inferno* also speaks of the "shadows"—the cowardly souls of the damned—who are the lost souls on the outermost region of Hell along the shores of the Acheron River that circles Hell. These souls cannot enter because of their silence and frozen impotence in the face of evil. Above them is the sign "Abandon all hope, you who enter here." Finally, silence also refers to the dark side of unarticulated political and ideological values hidden in the depths of modern science that remain unarticulated and silent but whose values cause real harm when not understood. A similar contempt for those who cannot morally decide or commit to action is found in the New Testament in the statement by God to the Laodiceans in Anatolia: "I know your deeds, that you are neither cold nor hot. I wish you were either one or the other! So, because you are lukewarm— neither hot nor cold—I am about to spit you out of my mouth." These people are "wretched, pitiful, poor, blind, and naked" (*Revelation* 3:15– 16). The references above to Nietzsche, Dante, and the New Testament are very applicable here since, with the rise of Enlightenment science and positivism in the social sciences, a key result has been the death of reason accompanied by nominalist indifference, objectivist arrogance, and the silence of moral convictions and critical theory in the academy. In summary, "shadows" refer to the moral indifference in the Bible; the shades or "ombra" of anxiety and incoherence along the Acheron

at the entrance to Hell in Dante; the existential despair and silence of the wasteland, iron cage, and last man in Nietzsche and Weber; the loneliness, isolation, and illness of radical individualism and liberalism in Fromm, Arendt, and Lasch; the terror of the exile and liquidation of reason of the Enlightenment in Horkheimer and Camus; the silence of the shadows of science in the face of rising fascism in the Frankfurt School; and, finally, the contemporary shadows of the Enlightenment and the repression and loss of social ethics, ecological balance, sociological theory, and political economy. In the context of contemporary capitalist society, the shadows of science and the Enlightenment include issues of the metaphysics, utility, politics, and domination of nature and the workplace.

6.   Nietzsche, *The Gay Science*; Max Weber, "Science as a Vocation," in *From Max Weber: Essays in Sociology* (New York: Oxford University Press, 1958); Max Horkheimer, *Eclipse of Reason* (New York: Continuum, 1947); Theodor Adorno and Max Horkheimer, *Dialectic of Enlightenment: Philosophical Fragments*, ed. Gunzelin Schmid Noerr, trans. Edmund Jephcott (Stanford, CA: Stanford University Press, 2002); Herbert Marcuse, *One-Dimensional Man: Studies in the Ideology of Advanced Industrial Society* (Boston: Beacon Press, 1964); Karl Marx, "Alienated Labour" and "Private Property and Communism," in *Karl Marx: Early Writings*, trans. and ed. T. B. Bottomore (New York: McGraw-Hill, 1964); and Leszek Kolakowski, *The Alienation of Reason: A History of Positivist Thought*, trans. Norbert Guterman (Garden City, NY: Doubleday, 1968).

7.   Jürgen Habermas, *Knowledge and Human Interests* (Boston: Beacon Press, 1971), 67–90.

8.   Richard Rorty, in *Philosophy and the Mirror of Nature* (Princeton: Princeton University Press, 1980), 308–11, derives his theory of representations and relativism from Donald Davidson in the latter's essay "On the Very Idea of a Conceptual Scheme" and his critique of the correspondence theory of truth in his "The Structure and Content of Truth."

9.   Max Scheler, *Die Wissensformen und die Gesellschaft* (Leipzig: Der Neue-Geist Verlag, 1926), 250.

10.   The term "mirror of production" used here represents a critique of the relationship between science and capitalist production, as well as a critique of rationalism and empiricism and its underlying epistemology of the "mirror of nature." It is not used as a critique of Marx's inability to rise beyond the capitalist theory of the mode of production and theory of value as outlined by Jean Baudrillard in *The Mirror of Production* (St. Louis, MO: Telos Press, 1975).

11. Marcuse, *One-Dimensional Man*, 154.

12. Alfred Sohn-Rethel, *Intellectual and Manual Labor: A Critique of Epistemology*, trans. Martin Sohn-Rethel (Atlantic Highlands, NJ: Humanities Press, 1978).

13. René Descartes, "Discourse on Method," in *Discourse on Method and Meditations*, trans. Laurence Lafleur (Indianapolis: Bobbs-Merrill, 1960), 45.

14. Carolyn Merchant, *The Death of Nature: Women, Ecology, and the Scientific Revolution* (New York: Harper & Row, 1983), 226-235.

15. E. A. Burtt, *The Metaphysical Foundations of Modern Physical Science* (Garden City, NY: Doubleday Anchor Books, 1954), 96.

16. Marcuse, *One-Dimensional Man*, 157-58.

Chapter 1: Social Epistemology and Radical Pragmatism of Postmodernism:

1. For an overview of early American pragmatism see C. Wright Mills, *Sociology and Pragmatism* (New York: Oxford University Press, 1966); Hans Joas, *G. H. Mead: A Contemporary Re-examination of His Thought*, trans. Raymond Meyer (Cambridge, MA: MIT Press, 1985); Hans Joas, *Pragmatism and Social Theory* (Chicago: University of Chicago Press, 1993); Cornel West, *The American Evasion of Philosophy: A Genealogy of Pragmatism* (Madison: University of Wisconsin Press, 1989); and Mitchell Aboulafia, ed., *Philosophy, Social Theory and the Thought of George Herbert Mead* (Albany: State University of New York Press, 1991).

2. David Hume, *An Inquiry Concerning Human Understanding*. Positivism is a complex web of different schools of thought ranging from Hume's empiricism to modern analytic philosophy which argued that there is a knowable objective reality and that science is capable of knowing, experiencing, and mathematically predicting that reality from empricism (Locke and Hume) and rationalism (Descartes) to logical positivism (Ayer, Wittgenstein, and Popper). There is an objective real world (objectivism) capable of being known by some form of scientific inquiry (scientism and naturalism).

3. David Hume, "An Enquiry Concerning Human Understanding," in *The Empiricists: John Locke, George Berkeley, and David Hume* (Garden City, NY: Doubleday, 1961).

4. Karl Popper, *Conjectures and Refutations: The Growth of Scientific Knowledge* (London: Routledge & Kegan Paul, 1991), 42.

5. Quote from H. Reichenbach's *Erkenntnis* in Karl Popper, *The Logic of Scientific Discovery* (New York: Harper & Row, 1968), 28.

6. Popper, *The Logic of Scientific Discovery*, 40.

7.   Karl Popper, "The Logic of the Social Sciences," in *The Positivist Dispute in German Sociology*, ed. Theodor Adorno et al., trans. Glyn Adey and David Frisby (New York: Harper & Row, 1976), 90.

8.   Roger Gibson, *Enlightened Empiricism: An Examination of W. V. Quine's Theory of Knowledge* (Tampa: University of South Florida Press, 1988), offers an expanded overview and summary of Quine's doctrines from all his writings, beginning with those already mentioned and including the following: indeterminacy of translation, inscrutability of reference, ontological relativity, holism (Duhem–Quine thesis), rejection of intentional objections, rejection of synonymy, rejection of quantified modal logic, acceptance of a holistic account of logic and mathematics, acceptance of a naturalist account of morality, and a pragmatic philosophy of science (9).

      See Paul Roth, *Meaning and Method in the Social Sciences: A Case for Methodological Pluralism* (Ithaca, NY: Cornell University Press, 1987), for a discussion about Quine and the apparent difficulty of integrating his negative theory of holism, truth, and the underdetermination of scientific theory with his positive defense of natural science, a new empiricism, evidentiary justification, and a naturalized epistemology (7 and 17). Roth examines Richard Rorty's argument that holism and naturalism, holism and empiricism (Quine's theory–independent reality as a first philosophy, natural science as truth, and empirical, objective evidence) are incompatible (44 and 56–58) and Donald Davidson's rejection of the dichotomy between holism and observation sentences (53). Rorty also disputes Quine's naturalism and psychophysiology in favor of his theory of intersubjectively validated empirical evidence within a community of scientists. Rorty rejects what he sees as a tension between the psychological and sociological elements in Quine's naturalized epistemology (55). It is Quine's critique of traditional epistemology and positivism which has been picked up by the postanalytic tradition. There is also a discussion about the discrepancies between his theory of truth and meaning, the underdetermination thesis and the indeterminacy of translation and meaning thesis, as well as the epistemological divergence between truth and meaning statements (11, 13, and 44). Roth's goal is to move beyond these discrepancies in order to integrate holism and empiricism.

9.   There is a debate over whether Quine is a Kantian. Gibson in *Enlightened Empiricism* argues against this thesis (49), while those who argue for the connection include Manley Thompson, "Quine and the Inscrutability of Reference," *Revue Internationale de Philosophie*, vol. 26 (1972); Kenton Machina, "Kant, Quine, and Human Experience," *Philosophical Review*, vol. 81 (October 1972); Rudiger Bübner, "Kant, Transcendental

Argument and the Problem of Deduction," *Review of Metaphysics*, vol. 28 (March 1975); Henry Veatch, "Is Quine a Metaphysician?" *Review of Metaphysics*, vol. 31 (March 1978); and Paul Roth, "Reconstructing Quine: The Troubles with a Tradition," *Metaphilosophy*, vol. 14 (July/October 1983), "Semantics without Foundations," *The Philosophy of W. V. Quine*, ed. L. Hahn (La Salle, IL: Open Court, 1987, and *Meaning and Method in the Social Sciences: A Case for Methodological Pluralism* (Ithaca, NY: Cornell University Press, 1987), 11.

10.   Willard Van Orman Quine, "Two Dogmas of Empiricism," in *From a Logical Point of View* (New York: Harper & Row, 1963), 43.

11.   Ibid., 42; and "Epistemology Naturalized," 82.

12.   Willard Van Orman Quine, "The Nature of Natural Knowledge," in *Mind and Language*, ed. S. Guttenplan (Oxford: Clarendon Press, 1975), 74.

13.   Roth, *Meaning and Method in the Social Sciences*, writes: "The positivists were right in believing that the evidence is sensory and not otherwise. They erred, rather, in thinking that there existed techniques that would allow them to make explicit the sensory content of individual scientific statements" (46).

14.   Gibson, *Enlightened Empiricism*, 46.

15.   Roth, *Meaning and Method in the Social Sciences*, 23; Pierre Duhem, *The Aim and Structure of Physical Theory*, trans. Philip Wiener (New York: Atheneum, 1981). For an analysis of the Duhem-Quine thesis, see Gibson, *The Philosophy of W. V. Quine: An Expository Essay*, 79–83.

16.   This is a position held by Weber because of his theory of value and concept formation. See Guy Oakes, *Weber and Rickert: Concept Formation in the Cultural Sciences* (Cambridge, MA: MIT Press, 1988), 32–40 and 94.

17.   Willard Van Orman Quine, "Epistemology Naturalized," in *Ontological Relativity and Other Essays* (New York: Columbia University Press, 1969), 75 and 83. For a further analysis, see Roth's examination of naturalized epistemology, theory of language, and empirical psychology in *Meaning and Method in the Social Sciences*, 46–55 and 59–65.

18.   West, *The American Evasion of Philosophy*, 185.

19.   Willard Van Orman Quine, *Word and Object* (Cambridge, MA: MIT Press, 1967), 21–25. See also Roger Gibson, *The Philosophy of W. V. Quine: An Expository Essay*, foreword by W. V. Quine (Tampa: University Presses of Florida, 1982), 168; and *Enlightened Empiricism*, 16–19 and 50–51; and J. Smart, "Quine's Philosophy of Science," in *Words and Objections: Essays on the Work of W. V. Quine*, ed. D. Davidson and J. Hintikka (Dordrecht, NL: Reidel Publishing Company, 1969), 3–13. Roth in *Meaning and Method in the Social Sciences* raises the issue of

the compatibility between Quine's empiricism (theory-independent world) and his Duhemian holism (theory-dependent scientific facts). He writes: "Quine qua empiricist adheres to the belief that all evidence is sensory evidence, yet his advocacy of holism suggests that there is no way to discriminate, as empiricists traditionally have, between the sensory contribution to knowledge and other sources such as cultural conditioning" (22). He argues that they are not incompatible because of Quine's transformation of empiricism from a theory of truth to a theory of evidence (53–55).

20. Cornel West, *The American Evasion of Philosophy*, 186.

21. Gibson, *Enlightened Empiricism*, 28–29.

22. Imre Lakatos in his essay "Falsification and the Methodology of Scientific Research Programmes," in *Criticism and the Growth of Knowledge*, ed. Imre Lakatos and Alan Musgrave (Cambridge: Cambridge University Press, 1979), 92, stresses the importance of Alexandre Koyré, *From the Closed World to the Infinite Universe* (Baltimore: Johns Hopkins Press, 1968); and *Metaphysics and Measurement: Essays in the Scientific Revolution* (Cambridge, MA: Harvard University Press, 1968); Edwin Arthur Burtt, *The Metaphysical Foundations of Modern Science* (Garden City, NY: Doubleday, 1954); Pierre Duhem, *The Aim and Structure of Physical Theory*; Karl Popper, *The Logic of Scientific Discovery*; Polanyi, *Personal Knowledge: Towards a Post-Critical Philosophy* (1958); and William Whewell, *History of the Inductive Sciences: From the Earliest to the Present Time* (London: 1847) to Kuhn's work.

23. Richard Bernstein in *Beyond Objectivism and Relativism: Science, Hermeneutics, and Praxis* (Philadelphia: University of Pennsylvania Press, 1983) argues that Kuhn's view of rationality and paradigm is closer to Aristotle's notion of *phronesis* (practical knowledge) and Hegel's notion of *Aufhebung* (negation and transcendence) (54 and 84, respectively).

24. Margaret Masterman writes in "The Nature of a Paradigm," in *Criticism and the Growth of Knowledge*, ed. Imre Lakatos and Alan Musgrave (Cambridge: Cambridge University Press, 1979) that she counted no less than twenty-one different uses of the term paradigm (61–65).

25. Thomas Kuhn, *The Structure of Scientific Revolutions* (Chicago: University of Chicago Press, 1971), 113.

26. Ibid., 24.

27. Ibid., 15 and 16–17.

28. Thomas Kuhn, *The Copernican Revolution: Planetary Astronomy in the Development of Western Thought* (Cambridge, MA: Harvard University Press, 1981), 165. See also *The Structure of Scientific Revolutions*, 154–56.

29. Kuhn, *The Structure of Scientific Revolutions*, 68 and 119.

30. Kuhn, *The Copernican Revolution*, 181.

31. Morris Berman, *The Reenchantment of the World* (Ithaca, NY: Cornell University Press, 1981), 40.

32. Kuhn, *The Structure of Scientific Revolutions*, 147.

33. For an analysis of two of Popper's students, Paul Feyerabend and Imre Lakatos, see Bernstein, *Beyond Objectivism and Relativism*, 64–71.

34. Kuhn, *The Structure of Scientific Revolutions*, 78.

35. Ibid., 26.

36. Ibid., 34.

37. Ibid., 97.

38. Ibid., 94.

39. Berman, *The Reenchantment of the World*, 50.

40. Kuhn, *The Structure of Scientific Revolutions*, 156.

41. Ibid., 206.

42. This argument will be examined in more detail in the next chapters on critical theory and Jürgen Habermas. In the United States, Roth, too, moves in the direction of replacing epistemology with a sociology of knowledge. Taking his cue from the Duhem-Quine thesis of underdetermination and holism and Kuhn's theory of paradigms, social practice, and revolutions, Roth begins to formulate a theory of the social construction of science. *In Meaning and Method in the Social Sciences* (152–82), he outlines the basic features of the "strong programme in the sociology of knowledge" by Barry Barnes, *Interests and the Growth of Knowledge* (London: Routledge & Kegan Paul, 1977); *T. S. Kuhn and Social Science* (New York: Columbia University Press, 1982); David Bloor, *Knowledge and Social Imagery* (London: Routledge & Kegan Paul, 1976); and *Wittgenstein: A Social Theory of Knowledge* (New York: Columbia University Press, 1983); and Barry Barnes and David Bloor, "Relativism, Rationalism and the Sociology of Knowledge," in *Rationality and Relativism*, ed. Martin Hollis and Steven Lukes (Cambridge, MA: MIT Press, 1982); and Steven Shapin, "The History of Science and Its Sociological Reconstruction," *History of Science*, vol. 20 (1982). See also Mary Hesse, "The Strong Thesis of Sociology of Knowledge," in *Revolutions and Reconstruction in the Philosophy of Science* (Brighton, EN: Harvester Press, 1980); and Michael Mulkay, *Science and the Sociology of Knowledge* (London: George Allen and Unwin, 1983).

43. Gibson, in *Enlightened Empiricism*, outlines Rorty's borrowings from Quine. However, he rejects Quine's inability to follow through on the logic of his own thought as he retreats back into a correspondence theory of truth, an integration of explanation and justification, and an empirical psychology as a replacement for traditional epistemology

(69–84). Quine falls back into a psychological grounding of knowledge after his critique of epistemology. But this is only another form of justification. The Quinean form of justification lies in science itself—in observation and predictions—and not in any form of knowledge prior to it. That is, there is no first philosophy (naturalism). Rorty radicalizes the argument further by claiming that what Quine sees as the empirical and psychological, objective and rational foundations of science, are really the general social practices and agreements within the psychological community. It was Hegel's historicism and dialectic and Nietzsche's nihilism and perspectivism that began the critique of foundationalism in the nineteenth century.

44. West, *The American Evasion of Philosophy*, 200–202.

45. In an interesting essay titled "Mirrors and Veils, Thoughts and Things: The Epistemological Problematic," in *Reading Rorty: Critical Responses to "Philosophy and the Mirror of Nature" (and Beyond)*, ed. Alan Malachowski (Cambridge, MA: Basil Blackwell, 1990), John Yolton challenges Rorty's view of seventeenth-century epistemology and his theory of the ocular metaphor of impressions as accurate or privileged representation of objective reality. Returning to Locke, Descartes, and medieval scholasticism, Yolton distinguishes between cognitive and physical reality. There is a real difference between sensations and physical objects, cognition and physiology; cognition is always an interpretation of that objective reality through ideas, never a direct reflection of it. Yolton argues that ideas are not proxy objects and metaphors and thus should not be mistaken for facts (62 and 69).

46. For an analysis of similar positions held by Rorty—critique of metaphysical realism, essential rationality, objectivity, and Cartesian method—see the work of Paul Feyerabend, *Against Nature: Outline of an Anarchistic Theory of Knowledge* (London: Verso, 1993); and *Science in a Free Society* (London: NLB, 1978).

47. Richard Rorty, *Philosophy and the Mirror of Nature* (Princeton: Princeton University Press, 1979), 11.

48. Ibid., 174 and 367.

49. In response to Rorty, Thomas McCarthy, "Reason in a Postmetaphysical Age," in *Critical Theory*, Thomas McCarthy and David Hoy (Oxford: Basil Blackwell, 1994), writes: "This sort of radical historicism lands him [Rorty] in familiar self-referential contradictions. If he is proposing notions of reason and truth relative-to-a-framework, then he cannot claim for himself any framework-neutral metaperspective from which to depict—in absolute terms, as it were—such framework-relative truths. The God's eye view implicitly claimed by this type of cultural relativism cannot exist, by its own account." (32).

50. Rorty, *Philosophy and the Mirror of Nature*, 157.

51. Ibid., 160.

52. Ibid., 139.

53. Ibid., 154.

54. Wilfrid Sellars, "Empiricism and the Philosophy of Mind," in *Science, Perception and Reality* (London: Routledge & Kegan Paul, 1963).

55. Willard Van Quine, "Things and Their Place in Theories," in *Theories and Things* (Cambridge, MA: Harvard University Press, 1981), 23.

56. Willard Van Quine, "Ontological Relativity," in *Ontological Relativity and Other Essays*, 50–51, quoted in Rorty, *Philosophy and the Mirror of Nature*, 196.

57. Rorty, *Philosophy and the Mirror of Nature*, 202.

58. Thomas Upton, "Rorty's Epistemological Nihilism," *Personalist Forum*, vol. 3 (Fall 1987), concludes from Rorty's idea that truth is justified by conversation and social practices and that dialogue produces only contingent truths. Since there are no absolute standards or ultimate principles "nothing really is or can be known" (142). In his own interesting twist to the myriad of Rorty interpretations, Upton contends that Rorty makes a "subjective turn" back to the Cartesian-Kantian view of knowledge as a product of the power, creativity, and freedom of the human mind (146–50). Since meaning and truth can only be found in the subjective for Descartes and Kant and in the intersubjective social practices for Rorty, he reproduces the traditional paradigm in the social context. For a discussion of the importance of conversation to Rorty see Kenneth Gallagher, "Rorty on Objectivity, Truth, and Social Consensus," *International Philosophical Quarterly*, vol. 24 (1984), 111–24.

59. Rorty, *Philosophy and the Mirror of Nature*, 170.

60. Ibid., 174 and 178.

61. Ibid., 178.

62. Ibid., 330.

63. For a further analysis of Gadamer see George McCarthy, *Romancing Antiquity: German Critique of the Enlightenment from Weber to Habermas* (Lanham, MD: Rowman & Littlefield, 1997), chap. 6, 209–40.

64. Book review of *Philosophy and the Mirror of Nature* in *Review of Metaphysics*, vol. 33 (1980): 800. S. R. writes, "If there is no overarching structure of rationality, then it seems to me to be impossible to follow any conversation, let alone to think of interesting ways to continue it" (801).

65. Many interpreters of Rorty have stressed this connection between postmodernism and liberalism, including Peter Dews, *Habermas: Autonomy and Solidarity* (London: Verso Books, 1986), 6–7; Richard

Bernstein, "One Step Forward, Two Steps Backward: Richard Rorty on Liberal Democracy and Philosophy," *Political Theory*, vol. 15, no. 4 (November 1987): 555; and *The New Constellation: The Ethical-Political Horizons of Modernity/Postmodernity* (Cambridge, MA: MIT Press, 1992), 248; Eric Weislogel, "The Irony of Richard Rorty and the Question of Political Judgment," *Philosophy Today* (Winter 1990): 308–10; William Connolly, "Identity and Difference in Liberalism," in *Liberalism and the Good*, ed. R. Douglass, G. Mara, and H. Richardson (New York: Routledge, 1990), 59–85; Ronald Beiner, "Richard Rorty's Liberalism," *Critical Review*, vol. 7, no. 1 (Winter 1993): 16, 19, and 26; Honi Haber, "Richard Rorty's Failed Politics," *Social Epistemology*, vol. 7, no. 1 (1993): 61–62; J. M. Fritzman, "Thinking with Fraser about Rorty, Feminism, and Pragmatism," *Praxis International*, vol. 13, no. 2 (July 1993): 114–15; Richard Shusterman, "Pragmatism and Liberalism: Between Dewey and Rorty," *Political Theory* (August 1994): 396–98; and Michele Marsonet, "Richard Rorty's Ironic Liberalism: A Critical Analysis," *Journal of Philosophical Research*, vol. 21 (January 1996): 394. The central focus of these authors is either on the idea that the liberal ironist is incapable of committing to liberal institutions or that the ironist is co-opted by these institutions. That is, the split between public and private, politics and culture, the social bond and private self-description is too wide in the former case or that the public is ultimately absorbed into the private in the latter one. It is Weislogel who contends that, in the end, the individual is integrated into an apathetic, cynical, and depoliticized liberalism (210). According to Beiner, the split between the public and private leads to the incoherence of liberalism (24).

66. Richard Rorty, "Postmodern Bourgeois Liberalism," *Journal of Philosophy*, vol. 80, no. 10 (October 1983): 583–89; and in *Objectivity, Relativism and Truth* (Cambridge: Cambridge University Press, 1979). Roy Bhaskar in his essay "Rorty, Realism and the Idea of Freedom" in *Reading Rorty*, places Rorty's defense of freedom in the philosophical context of the Kantian distinction between pure and practical reason, explanation and understanding, nature and history, scientific determinism and individual freedom (217).

67. Charles Guignon and David Hiley, "Biting the Bullet: Rorty on Private and Public Morality," in *Reading Rorty*, 346.

68. Rorty, *Contingency, Irony, and Solidarity*, 52. For an examination of the implications of Rorty's theory of a "conversation of mankind" without the Enlightenment metaphysics of a search for truth and foundations, see Steven Hendley, "Putting Ourselves Up for Question: A Postmodern Critique of Richard Rorty's Postmodern Bourgeois

Liberalism," *Journal of Value Enquiry*, vol. 39, issue 2 (1995), 243–53. Hendley fears that without a common ethical language or universal narrative, the basis for our conversation and our definition of the community could never be reached; we could never know who the "we" is, since everything is open to redescription by the ethnocentric and historicist ironists. Rorty wants speech without rational content; dialogue without reasons. "A democratic community is perpetually launched onto an unstable search in which the issue of justifying our political institutions and practices is permanently raised but also permanently deferred as every justification, every resolution and consensus, must be upset as it is once again put up for question in this debate without end" (248). Hendley is also concerned that Rorty's view of the liberal community is too narrow and insular, resulting in a suspicion of ideas and truth claims that appear to come from outside the community of believers and that radically question the liberal social system (249). See also Guignon and Hiley, "Biting the Bullet," 341. Guignon and Hiley outline the fundamental criticisms of liberalism by communitarian philosophers: liberalism undermines community values and institutions, as well as the possibilities for self-fulfillment (Christopher Lasch, Daniel Yankelovich, and Robert Bellah); it creates socially undesirable individuals (Alasdair MacIntyre and Charles Taylor); and, finally, it leads to the philosophical incoherence of relativism and a problematic anthropology (Michael Sandel). Guignon and Hiley also contend that Rorty radicalizes Heidegger's thought by accepting his antifoundationalism and being in the world, but refuses to define the individual's goal as authentic self-focusing. The result is a decentered individual in continuous search for self-fulfillment and self-interpretation seeking new narrative vocabularies and expressions without any inner center or unity in reason, being, or existential purpose (346–50).

69. Marsonet, "Richard Rorty's Ironic Liberalism," 395–96. Marsonet is suspicious that liberalism could rest on the private dreams and hopes of the individual without some philosophical grounding. But Rorty introduces ideas of solidarity and tradition which are supposed to provide what philosophy can't. However, many secondary interpreters of Rorty have voiced concern that a poetic ironist, because there is no inner rational core of reasons to his or her political choice, will not have the strength of commitment or dedication to liberalism that a traditional metaphysician would have who believed in human nature, natural rights, personal utility, or rational choice (400–401). Marsonet is concerned that there would be no rational reason to resist totalitarianism. To choose liberalism over fascism has the same

rational basis as choosing basketball over football. Everything is simply a linguistic game without any objective moral or political principles that lie behind the actions of the will. See Richard Bernstein, "Rorty's Liberal Utopia," in *The New Constellation: The Ethical Political Horizons of Modernity/Postmodernity* (Cambridge, MA: MIT Press, 1993), who writes that the public and private spheres are futilely joined into an irreconcilable apartheid. Solidarity of the public sphere has no grounding (264), as Bernstein maintains that liberalism goes the way of the Enlightenment; if there is no grounding for the latter, there is no justification for the former.

On this issue see also Robert Foelber, "Can an Historicist Sustain a Diehard Commitment to Liberal Democracy? The Case of Rorty's Liberal Ironist," *Southern Journal of Philosophy*, vol. 32 (1994). He asks how nominalist and arbitrary fictions, relative and contingent values, can sustain democratic institutions over time; he calls this the "relativist predicament" (23). There is no need for justification, for the system works at protecting self-overcoming in the search for meaning, happiness, and purpose (24). Foelber concludes that in the end "ironism will inevitably subvert liberalism (or liberalism will subvert ironism)" (32). He does not develop this line of reasoning. But, if he is correct, the political result will be nothing like a just society. Foelber is more concerned with offering an alternative political view to Rorty's, one that emphasizes his liberal and leftist orientations in a critique of poverty, inequality, discrimination in America (33–34). "Rorty's utopian society, in other words, is a society that celebrates and encourages cultural diversity, freedom of expression, multiplicity of views, and material equality to enable everyone to realize their own personal fantasies. It is more diverse, socialistic, cosmopolitan, consensual, and tolerant of all points of view than the traditional liberal society envisioned by (say) the founders of the American republic" (37). Liberalism is better than any other form of society not because it protects rights and liberties, but because it "works better" —it is utilitarian and thus better at ensuring the search for aesthetic freedom and moral autonomy. In the final analysis, all this discussion about historicism, relativism, and ironism is just another form of Western metaphysics. Michele Moody-Adams, "Theory, Practice, and the Contingency of Rorty's Irony," *Journal of Social Philosophy* (1994), writes that the connection between irony and contingency, private and public, is tenuous at the least (212–13).

Nancy Fraser, in "Solidarity and Singularity: Richard Rorty between Romanticism and Technocracy," in *Reading Rorty*, ed. Alan Malachowski (Oxford: Basil Blackwell, 1990), 303–21, worries about the damage done to social solidarity by the romantic poet's contempt for the familiar. There is a tension between pragmatism and romanticism, democracy and self–expression, between the social need for community, commitment, and kindness and the individual's search for narcissistic difference and elitist distancing (262). She concludes that both culture and theory become depoliticized. And because modern society is characterized by the end of ideology, its replacement by technical reason and piecemeal engineering (*poiesis* and *techne*), and the reduction of politics to ironic poetry, the postmodern human is both apolitical (existential individualism) and atheoretical (anti-foundationalism). "Moreover with no deep rifts or pervasive axes of domination, practice can float entirely free of theory" (266). Keith Topper also stresses the conflict between liberalism and ironism in his essay, "Richard Rorty, Liberalism and the Politics of Redescription," *American Political Science Review*, vol. 89, no. 4 (December 1995): 956–57; whereas J. M. Bernstein, "De-Devinization and the Vindication of Everyday Life: Reply to Rorty," *Tijdschrift Voor Filosofie*, vol. 54, no. 4 (1992), sees it in much less threatening language. In fact, he contends that Rorty's distinctions between the public minimizing of cruelty, private self-description, and technical science is similar to Habermas's distinction between the three validity spheres of moral rightness, aesthetic authenticity, and truth (673–74).

70. Richard Rorty, *Contingency, Irony, and Solidarity* (Cambridge: Cambridge University Press, 1996), xv. Rorty borrows this definition of liberalism from Judith Shklar, *Ordinary Vices* (Cambridge, MA: Harvard University Press, 1984), 8. See also Bernstein, "Rorty's Liberal Utopia," 278.

71. Moody-Adams, "Theory, Practice, and the Contingency of Rorty's Irony," 215. Moody-Adams makes the argument that because of his beliefs, Rorty would not be sympathetic to the idea, which is at the heart of critical theory, of false consciousness or the unconscious.

72. Rorty, *Contingency, Irony, and Solidarity*, 84–85.

73. Beiner, "Richard Rorty's Liberalism," 23.

74. Richard Rorty, *Consequences of Pragmatism* (Minneapolis: University of Minnesota Press, 1983), 166. In his recent work, *Achieving Our Century: Leftist Thought in Twentieth–Century America* (Cambridge, MA: Harvard University Press, 1998), Rorty defends the pragmatic, experimental, and reformist left-leaning politics of Dewey and Whitman and those who "struggled within the framework of constitutional democracy to protect the weak from the strong" (43)—from Debs, Du Bois, Wilson, Brandeis, Lewis, and Reuther to Schlesinger, Hook, Harrington, and Galbraith. He rejected the radical and revolutionary

left of the New Left of the 1960s and the later postmodernists. Rorty
concludes his work with the words: "As long as we have a functioning
political Left, we still have a chance to achieve our country, to make it
the country of Whitman's and Dewey's dreams" (107).

75. Richard Rorty, *Objectivity, Relativism and Truth* (New York: Cambridge
University Press, 1991), 192.

76. Shusterman, "Pragmatism and Liberalism," 399. Habermas has
rejected Rorty's view of a decentered and privatized notion of the self
as dangerous to the development of a free society. For an analysis of his
view of distorted personality development, depoliticization, culture
of narcissism, the McDonaldization of society, and the colonization
of the lifeworld, see Jürgen Habermas, *The Theory of Communicative
Action,* vol. 2: *Lifeworld and System: A Critique of Functionalist Reason,*
trans. Thomas McCarthy (Boston: Beacon Press, 1989), 332–373. Also
compare their views on Freud. See also Haber, "Rorty's Failed Politics,"
63. Shusterman argues that Rorty borrowed heavily from Davidson's
reading of Freud: Donald Davidson, "Paradoxes of Irrationality,"
Philosophical Essays on Freud, ed. R. Wollheim and J. Hopkins
(Cambridge: Cambridge University Press, 1982); Rorty, "Freud and
Moral Reflection," *Philosophical Papers, Essays on Heidegger and Others*
(Cambridge: Cambridge University Press, 1991); Jürgen Habermas,
Knowledge and Human Interests, trans. Jeremy Shapiro (Frankfurt/
Main: Suhrkamp Verlag, 1971), 214–300. See also Bernstein, "Rorty's
Liberal Utopia," 269; and Guignon and Hiley, "Biting the Bullet," 351–
55.

For an analysis of the influence of Nietzsche on Rorty, especially
the former's rejection of epistemology and objective reality, as well
as Rorty's view of the relationship between Nietzsche's perspectivism
(anti-foundationalism and nihilism) and residual metaphysics
(Heidegger's interpretation of metaphysics as the philosophy of the
Übermensch, eternal return, and will to power) see Daniel Conway,
"Disembodied Perspectives: Nietzsche contra Rorty," *International
Studies in Philosophy,* vol. 21 (1989): 281–89; and "Thus Spoke Rorty:
The Perils of Narrative Self-Creation," *Philosophy and Literature* (1991):
103–10; Daniel Shaw, "Rorty and Nietzsche: Some Elective Affinities,"
International Studies in Philosophy, vol. 21 (1989): 3–14; and Gary
Madison, "Coping with Nietzsche's Legacy," *Philosophy Today* (Spring
1992): 3–7.

77. Fritzman, "Thinking with Fraser about Rorty, Feminism, and
Pragmatism," 121; and Beiner, "Richard Rorty's Liberalism," 21. Beiner
contends that other than examining issues of civil rights and the welfare
state, Rorty's truncated concepts of liberalism prove unable to get

beyond issues of economic distribution. The broader questions about the meaning of human life and the structures of class and power in liberal society are suppressed by the "inadequacy of liberal theorizing." Rorty has produced a liberal society with very shallow moral standards (26).

78. McCarthy, "Private Irony and Public Decency," 366-67.

79. Haber, "Rorty's Failed Politics," 66-67. Haber contends that there are fundamental contradictions at the basis of Rorty's politics that exist between the public and private, pluralism and solidarity, liberalism and aestheticism, liberal and ironist, critique of metaphysics and belief in common human essence, and the voicing of marginal groups with the speech of elite intellectuals.

80. Shusterman, "Pragmatism and Liberalism," 398. Quoted section from Rorty comes from *Objectivity, Relativism, and Truth* (Cambridge: Cambridge University Press, 1991), 211. For an analysis of pragmatism and Dewey see Richard Bernstein, "Philosophy in the Conversation of Mankind," *Review of Metaphysics,* vol. 23, no. 4 (1980); Isaac Levi, "Escape from Boredom: Edification According to Rorty," *Canadian Journal of Philosophy,* vol. 11, no. 4 (1981): 589-602; Kai Nielsen, *After the Demise of the Tradition: Rorty Critical Theory, and the Fate of Philosophy* (Boulder, CO: Westview Press, 1991), 127-48 and 169-81; Larry Hickman, "Pragmatism, Technology, and Scientism" in *Pragmatism: From Progressivism to Postmodernism,* ed. Robert Hollinger and David Depew (Westport, CT: Praeger, 1995), 72-87; and for an overview of the convergences and divergences between Dewey and Rorty see James Campbell, "Rorty's Use of Dewey," *Southern Journal of Philosophy,* vol. 22 (Summer 1984): 175-87; and Konstantin Kolenda, *Rorty's Humanistic Pragmatism: Philosophy Democratized* (Tampa: University of South Florida Press, 1990), 88-95.

81. Rorty, *Contingency, Irony, and Solidarity,* 84. But Rorty is also aware of the differences between the two, since Habermas has a sophisticated critique of ideology. Topper, "Richard Rorty, Liberalism, and the Politics of Redescription" points to the problem in Rorty that though he accepts the importance of free and open communication as the basis for the pragmatist view of rationality and truth, he cannot describe empirically or transcendentally what this might mean: "Yet he also fails to examine those social practices and institutions that inhibit the development of a more free, open, inclusive, and democratic public discourse. Instead, he offers vague suggestions that circumvent entirely the difficult practical issues" (963). Rorty's postmodern liberalism with its insistence on educational quality and opportunities, freedom of the press, political freedom, etc. never does get at the underlying structural issues in

American society that affect participatory discourse, rationality, and social justice. As Topper correctly recognizes, Rorty's search for the "we" ignores structural issues of racism, class, and inequality. Mary Hesse puts it nicely in an article on Habermas titled "Habermas's Consensus Theory of Truth": "The attainment of truth is not independent of conditions of freedom and justice" (380–81). Bernstein in his essay, "Rorty on Liberal Democracy and Philosophy," writes: "[Rorty] never faces the hard issue of clarifying what *historical* standards and criteria ought to be employed in evaluating the experimental discipline of politics" (241–42). Thomas McCarthy in *Ideals and Illusions: On Reconstruction and Deconstruction in Contemporary Critical Theory* (Cambridge, MA: MIT Press, 1991), is also critical of Rorty's unwillingness to articulate a sense of the political beyond a very privatized and aestheticized view (26). See also Tony Couture, "Review: Bernstein, McCarthy and the Evolution of Critical Theory," *Philosophy and Social Criticism*, vol. 19, no. 1 (1993): 59–75. Jo Burrows, in "Conversational Politics" in *Reading Rorty: Critical Responses to Philosophy and the Mirror of Nature and Beyond*, ed. Alan Malachowski (Hoboken, NJ: Wiley-Blackwell, 1991), 327, argues that Rorty's view of ironic liberalism with its values of openness and pluralism has no room for social critique by the marginal. His view of the end of ideology, reduction of social and political problems to technical solutions, his critique of socialist and Marxist theory, and his pragmatism tend only to support the status quo. Burrows writes: "We have ended up with the rather bland conclusion that despite his protests, to the contrary, Rorty is peddling liberal ideology" (331). Burrows makes the interesting observation that Rorty's political ideology is supported and enhanced by his critique of epistemology and foundationalism. By accepting liberalism as an empirically given phenomenon, there can be no political language or perspective from which to challenge this view (329). She concludes that the interesting aspect of Rorty's liberalism is that it does not allow for diversity and pluralism but results in a "swallowing up [of] political differences and spitting our apologies" (333–34).

82. Mario Moussa, "Misunderstanding the Democratic 'We'": Richard Rorty's Liberalism and the Radical Urge for a Philosophical Foundation," *Philosophy and Social Criticism*, vol. 17, no. 4 (1991); and Jo Burrows, "Conversational Politics: Rorty's Pragmatist Apology for Liberalism," in *Reading Rorty*, 327.

83. Bernstein, "One Step Forward, Two Steps Backward," 539–43; and *The New Constellation*, 231–36. See also Brian Hendley, "The Conversation Continues: Rorty and Dewey," *Process Studies*, vol. 20, no. 2 (Summer 1991), who writes that "in the end, his [Rorty's] sense of irony wins

out over his liberal sentiments" (108); and Topper, "Richard Rorty, Liberalism and the Politics of Redescription," 954 and 964. Both Bernstein in "One Step Forward, Two Steps Backward" and Moussa in his "Misunderstanding the Democratic 'We'" (300) state that Rorty abandons theory altogether. J. M. Bernstein, "De-Devinization and the Vindication of Everyday Life," is critical of Rorty's view of liberalism since it does not account for issues of "technology, bureaucracy, the invisible hand of the market, societal rationalization, the system's theoretic colonization of the lifeworld, and the like." He continues that "each are societal universals that subsume and dominate persons" (679). Bernstein argues that Rorty's analysis needs to be examined in light of the work of Heidegger on technology, Habermas on colonization, Weber on rationalization and bureaucracy, and Smith and Marx on the invisible hand of the market. Bernstein points out that with the loss of the public sphere and the privatization of social values of religion, ethics and politics, values "look futile, meaningless, or worse" (678). The problem with Rorty's position is that autonomy is reduced to the anxiety and existential fear of a few authors and cruelty to inadequate vocabulary or narrative. Both lose an appreciation for the nature of politics and the implications of the separation of the public and private spheres. Most important, we repress the recognition of the institutions of power and domination, as well as the institutions necessary for our political ideals and the real possibilities for social change.

84. Shusterman, "Pragmatism and Liberalism," 391–92.

85. Bernstein, "One Step Forward, Two Steps Backward," 541. See also William Connolly, "Mirror of America," *Raritan* (Summer 1983): 134–35; and West, *The American Evasion of Philosophy*, 206.

86. Beiner in "Richard Rorty's Liberalism" asks how a story becomes false and untrue for Rorty (17).

87. Rorty, *Contingency, Irony, and Solidarity,* 52.

88. For the response of critical theorists to Rorty see Thomas McCarthy, "Private Irony and Public Decency: Richard Rorty's New Pragmatism," *Critical Inquiry*, vol. 16 (Winter 1990): 355–70; Rorty's response in the essay "Truth and Freedom: A Response to Thomas McCarthy," *Critical Inquiry*, vol. 16 (Winter 1990): 633–43; and McCarthy's critique once again in "Ironist Theory as a Vocation: A Response to Rorty's Reply," *Critical Theory*, vol. 16 (Spring 1990): 633–55; "An Exchange on Truth, Freedom, and Politics," *Critical Inquiry*, vol. 16 (Spring 1990); and "Philosophy and Social Practice: Richard Rorty's 'New Pragmatism'" and "Postscript: Ironist Theory as a Vocation," in *Ideals and Illusions: On Reconstruction and Deconstruction in Contemporary Critical Theory* (Cambridge, MA: MIT Press, 1991), 11–42, and "On the Idea

of a Critical Theory and Its Relation to Philosophy" and "Reason in a Postmetaphysical Age," in *Philosophy and Critical Theory: A Reprise*, ed. Thomas McCarthy and David Hoy (Oxford: Wiley-Blackwell, 1994). See also the essays from the *Symposium on Critical Theory* by Thomas McCarthy and David Hoy, especially Richard Rorty, "The Ambiguity of Reason" and Thomas McCarthy, "Philosophy and Critical Theory: A Reply to Richard Rorty and Seyla Benhabib," *Constellations*, vol. 3, no. 1 (1996): 95–103; and Bernstein, "One-Step Forward, Two Steps Back" (1987); Rorty's reply in "Thugs and Theorists," *Political Theory*, vol. 15 (November 1987); and Bernstein's rejoinder, "Rorty's Liberal Utopia" (1990). Also see Richard Rorty, "Habermas and Lyotard on Postmodernism"; and Jürgen Habermas, "Questions and Counter Questions," in *Habermas and Modernity*, ed. Richard Bernstein (Cambridge, MA: MIT Press, 1985), 161–75.

For other commentaries on this issue see Dieter Misgeld, "Modernity and Social Science: Habermas and Rorty," *Philosophy and Social Criticism*, vol. 11, no. 4 (Fall 1986): 355–72; Tony Couture, "Habermas, Rorty and the Purpose of Philosophy," *Eidos*, vol. 6 (June 1987): 53–69; Kai Nielsen, "Skeptical Remarks on the Scope of Philosophy," *Social Theory and Practice*, vol. 19, no. 2 (Summer 1993): 117–60; and *After the Demise of the Tradition*, 195–216; David Hall, *Richard Rorty: Prophet and Poet of the New Pragmatism* (Albany: State University of New York Press, 1994), 146–54; Hauke Brunkhorst, "Rorty, Putnam and the Frankfurt School," *Philosophy and Social Criticism*, vol. 22, no. 5 (1996), 1–16; and Józef Niżnik and John Sanders, eds., *Debating the State of Philosophy: Habermas, Rorty, and Kolakowski* (Westport, CT: Praeger, 1996), 1–29 and 97–103.

For a feminist critique of Rorty see Seyla Benhabib and Drucilla Cornell, eds., *Feminism as Critique: On the Politics of Gender* (Minneapolis: University of Minnesota Press, 1987); Dorothy Leland, "Rorty on the Moral Concern of Philosophy: A Critique from a Feminist Point of View," *Praxis International*, vol. 8 (October 1988): 273–83; Fraser, "Solidarity or Singularity," 303–21; and "From Irony to Prophecy to Politics: A Response to Richard Rorty," *Michigan Quarterly Review*, vol. 30, no. 2 (Spring 1991); and Fritzman, "Thinking with Fraser about Rorty, Feminism, and Pragmatism," 113–25.

89. Isaiah Berlin, *Four Essays on Liberty* (Oxford: Oxford University Press, 1969); and Karl Popper, *The Open Society and Its Enemies*, vols. 1 and 2 (Princeton: Princeton University Press, 1971).

90. Rorty, *Contingency, Irony, and Solidarity*, 178.

91. Bernstein, "Rorty's Liberal Utopia," 264.

92. Bernstein in "Rorty's Liberal Utopia" argues that, in fact, there are

hidden universals or reasons in Rorty's theory of utopian liberalism—defense of liberalism, argumentation, beliefs worth dying for, rejection of cruelty, negative liberty, and a public/private split.

Chapter 2: Phenomenology of Scientific Consciousness and the Domination of Nature

1. Susan Gottlöber, "The Problem of Reality: Scheler's Critique of Husserl in *Idealismus–Realismus*," in Rodney B. Parker, ed., *The Idealism-Realism Debate Among Edmund Husserl's Early Followers and Critics* (New York: Springer, 2021), 119–33. Gottlöber argues that Scheler's idealism and anti-realism are best represented by the phrase *esse est percipi*, or "existence is perception." It refers to the idea that there is no existence independent of consciousness. Scheler contends that this idea comes from the writings of Heinrich Rickert, Wilhelm Schuppe, and Hans Cornelius, and represents a rejection of critical realism and its notion that knowledge is a correspondence of ideas to objective reality and that objects exist independent of consciousness and knowledge. This is part of the idealism-realism debate that was revived in the 1930s.

2. Dietmar Heidemann, "Kant and the Forms of Realism," *Synthese* 198 (December 2021): 3231–52.

3. Edmund Husserl, *The Crisis of European Sciences and Transcendental Phenomenology*, trans. David Carr (Evanston, IL: Northwestern University Press, 1970), 88–89.

4. Ibid., 91.

5. Ibid., 87.

6. Ibid., 88–91.

7. Ibid., 52. This work on the crisis of European sciences and transcendental phenomenology was published in 1936 and based on two earlier writings: a letter read at the International Congress of Philosophy at Prague entitled "The Mission of Philosophy in Our Time" (September 1934), and a lecture delivered in Vienna entitled "Philosophy in the Crisis of European Mankind" (May 1935). The work is divided into three main parts: Part I examines the meaning and crisis of European science and humanity; Part II outlines the method and objectivity of science in Galileo and Descartes, leading to the conflict between objectivism and subjectivism, realism and idealism, in the search for meaning in natural science, philosophy, and the various forms of European consciousness; and Part III deals with the central importance of Kant's transcendental philosophy and subjectivism as the foundation of Husserl's theory of critical phenomenology, as well as the distinction between the lifeworld of sense experience and mathematical science. For the purposes of this chapter, it is Part II which represents the key section because of its analysis

of scientific methodology and the distinction between rationalism and empiricism (objectivism) and the central importance of Kantian epistemology (subjectivism) for the foundation of Husserl's historical phenomenology of consciousness and experience in the ontic and sense experience lifeworld and pure science. The book may be further divided into an analysis of the crisis of Western science and reason, the evolution of the methodology of modern science from Descartes to Kant, and the theory or meaning of science itself regarding issues of objectivity and subjectivity, realism and idealism, and the central role of consciousness and reason. From crisis, methods, and theory of science, Husserl tries to uncover the evolution of our understanding of the crisis of reason in Western society.

8.   Ibid., 5.
9.   Ibid., 64.
10. Ibid., 6.
11. Ibid., 7, 68–69, and 299.
12. Ibid., 12.
13. William Leiss points out that Husserl mentions the issue of the technological domination of nature only two or three times *in The Crisis of European Sciences* (Evanston, IL: Northwestern University Press, 1970) on pages 22, 66, and 271. Leiss, *The Domination of Nature* (Boston: Beacon, 1974), 126–27.
14. Husserl, *The Crisis of European Sciences*, 23.
15. Ibid., 51–54. The goal of phenomenology is to return to the meaning, motivation, and origins of modern science in the idealities of subjectivity. This is where Scheler would play a central role in starting the conversation about science and the technical domination of nature.
16. Ibid., 51.
17. Ibid., 52.
18. Ibid., 57. Husserl contends that any previous attempt to undertake a phenomenological history of the origins and meaning of scientific consciousness has been dismissed by scientists themselves as "metaphysical." For this reason Husserl wishes to return to the origins of the modern view of science and nature in the writings of Descartes. Those who resisted this approach held to a self-enclosed world of bodies embedded in mathematical and mechanical laws of causality, splitting reality into the experience of nature and spirit. This resulted in the mathematization of nature and natural science which became the model for the study of everyday consciousness and the spirit of the lifeworld itself. Philosophy itself must be built on this modern view of science, which evolves well into the analytic philosophy of logical positivism, especially in the British and American tradition.

The result is the loss of spirit in ethics, politics, science, and classical humanism.

19. Ibid.
20. Ibid., 113.
21. The real problem here is that Husserl does not stop his analysis to consider the real meaning of science beyond his own critical phenomenology and move into other areas of investigation, such as political economy and historical materialism and structuralism.
22. Husserl, *The Crisis of European Sciences*, 66.
23. Ibid., 244–65.
24. Ibid., 91 and 265.
25. Ibid., 94–95. Rationalism and empiricism did not consider the nature of subjectivity in their theories of knowledge, and thus did not understand the nature and origin of science and reason, 74, 94, 97, and 100. Kant rejected both psychologism and objectivism as he undertook a critical analysis of pure reason based on the question of the universal and necessary preconditions for perception, experience, and knowledge in the forms of human sensibility and understanding. Husserl, summarizing the whole of Part II, states that the goal of phenomenology is to uncover "the true ontic meaning of the objective world—precisely as a transcendental subjective meaning" (*The Crisis of European Sciences*, 100). In this way, "the most important and most profound concept of all—objectivism," would take on a new meaning and relevance. With an analysis of the notion of critical subjectivity, the true and relevant meaning of objectivity—objective truth and objective reality—will be revealed. These are the very things that are taken for granted and, because of the work of Kant, would finally be examined. Husserl refers to this as the "meaning-construct [*Sinngebilde*] . . . of functioning subjectivity" (ibid., 113).
26. Ibid., 262–63.
27. Ibid., 88.
28. Theodor Adorno, *Against Epistemology: A Metacritique. Studies in Husserl and the Phenomenological Antinomies*, trans. Willis Domingo (Cambridge, MA: MIT Press, 1983).
29. Max Scheler, *Problems of a Sociology of Knowledge*, trans. Manfred Frings (London: Routledge and Kegan Paul, 1980), 101. For a helpful overview of Scheler's theory of *Herrschaftswissen*, see William Leiss, *The Domination of Nature* (Boston: Beacon, 1974), chapter 5, 101–23; for a critical overview of Scheler's thesis of the domination of nature, see pages 114–19. It should be noted that the concept of *Herrschaftswissen* took a number of different forms in Scheler's work, including *Herrschaftswille* (will to dominate), *Herrschaftswissenschaft* (science of

domination), *Herrschaftstrieb* (drive to power), *Herrschaftsgeist* (spirit of domination), *Macht* (power), *Machtbetrieb* (operation of power), and *Machtwille* (will for power). A number of these categories were found in the second essay, "Cognition and Work," in *Problems of a Sociology of Knowledge*, 1–8, 15–22, 67–74, and 78–83.

30. Ibid., 80.

31. Ibid., 100.

32. Ibid., 101.

33. Ibid., 133.

34. Ibid., 134.

35. Robert Wolff, "A Reconstruction of the Argument of the Subjective Deduction," in *Kant: A Collection of Critical Essays*, ed. by Robert Wolff (Garden City, NY: Doubleday, 1967), 94–108.

36. Arthur Schopenhauer, *The World as Will and Representation*, trans. E. F. J. Payne (New York: Dover, 1969), 3.

37. Ibid., 15.

38. Ibid. 12.

39. Ibid., 205. For a further analysis of the nothingness of our world of will and representations, see 364–66 and 411–12.

40. Ibid., 275.

41. Ibid., 364.

42. For a more detailed understanding of the relationship between Kant and Nietzsche, idealism and existentialism, see George McCarthy, *Dialectics and Decadence: Echoes of Antiquity in Marx and Nietzsche* (Lanham, MD: Rowman & Littlefield, 1994), note 17, 357.

43. Schopenhauer, *The World as Will and Representation*, 412.

44. Ibid., 364.

45. Ibid., 378–391. See also McCarthy, *Dialectics and Decadence*, 192–200.

46. Ibid., 357. It is obvious that Kant is not an existentialist. However, his critique of reason and traditional epistemology led to those with even more radical tendencies, such as Schopenhauer and Nietzsche. For the connection between Kant and Nietzsche, see George McCarthy, *Romancing Antiquity: German Critique of the Enlightenment from Weber to Habermas* (Lanham, MD: Rowman & Littlefield, 1997), note 60, 294, note 67, 285, and note 72, 296.

47. Friedrich Nietzsche, *Philosophy in the Tragic Age of the Greeks*, trans. Marianne Cowan (Chicago: Henry Regnery, 1962), 41.

48. Friedrich Nietzsche, "On Truth and Lies in a Nonmoral Sense," in *Philosophy and Truth: Selections from Nietzsche's Notebooks of the Early 1870s*, trans. and ed. Daniel Breazeale (Atlantic Highlands, NJ: Humanities Press, 1979), 86.

49. Schopenhauer, *The World as Will and Representation*, 12.

50. Ibid., 196.

51. Ibid., 364.

52. Martha Nussbaum, "The Transfigurations of Intoxication: Nietzsche, Schopenhauer, and Dionysus," *Arion: Journal of Humanities and Classics* 1, no. 2 (Spring 1991): 105.

53. Friedrich Nietzsche, *The Birth of Tragedy*, in *The Birth of Tragedy and The Genealogy of Morals*, trans. Francis Golffing (Garden City, NY: Anchor, 1956), 29–30.

54. Ibid., 30.

55. Friedrich Nietzsche, *The Genealogy of Morals*, in *The Birth of Tragedy and The Genealogy of Morals*, 251.

56. Nietzsche, *The Birth of Tragedy*, 34.

57. Ibid., 102.

58. Karl-Otto Apel, "The Common Presuppositions of Hermeneutics and Ethics: Types of Rationality beyond Science and Technology," *Research in Phenomenology* 9 (1979): 42.

59. Nietzsche, *The Genealogy of Morals*, 299.

60. Friedrich Nietzsche, *The Will to Power*, trans. Walter Kaufman and R. J. Hollingdale (New York: Vintage, 1968), section 397, 214. For a brief analysis of Nietzsche's concept of the *Wille zur Macht* and its influence on Scheler's concept of *Herrschaftswissen*, see Leiss, *The Domination of Nature*, 106–07.

61. Friedrich Nietzsche, *The Antichrist*, in *The Portable Nietzsche*, trans. Walter Kaufmann (New York: Viking, 1969), 577.

62. Ralph Schroeder, "Nietzsche and Weber: Two 'Prophets' of the Modern World," in *Max Weber, Rationality and Modernity*, ed. Scott Lash and Sam Whimster (London: Allen & Unwin, 1987), 219. For a more extensive bibliography on Nietzsche and Weber, see McCarthy, *Dialectics and Decadence*, 348–49, and *Romancing Antiquity*, notes 52–53, 304–306.

63. Wilhelm Hennis, "The Traces of Nietzsche in the Work of Max Weber," in *Max Weber: Essays in Reconstruction*, trans. Keith Tribe (London: Allen & Unwin, 1988), 158. Hennis argues that the key principles of Weber's *Wissenschaftslehre* (theory of science), including his concepts of objectivity and value relations, must be viewed in the context of Nietzsche's philosophy.

64. Max Weber, "Science as a Vocation," in *From Max Weber: Essays in Sociology*, trans. and ed. Hans Gerth and C. Wright Mills (New York: Oxford University Press, 1968), 141.

65. Ibid., 143.

66. Friedrich Nietzsche, *Thus Spoke Zarathustra*, in *The Portable Nietzsche*, 130.

67. Max Weber, *The Protestant Ethic and the Spirit of Capitalism*, trans. Talcott Parsons (New York: Charles Scribner's Sons, 1958), 181.
68. Weber, "Science as a Vocation," 150.
69. Rogers Brubaker, *The Limits of Rationality: An Essay on the Social and Moral Thought of Max Weber* (London: Allen & Unwin, 1984), 2.
70. Weber, "Science as a Vocation," 155.

Chapter 3: The Metaphysics and Method of Natural Science

1. E. A. Burtt, *The Metaphysical Foundations of Modern Science* (Garden City, NY: Doubleday, 1954), 34.
2. S. V. Keeling, *Descartes* (Westport, CT: Greenwood Press, 1970), 75–76.
3. René Descartes, *Meditations Concerning First Philosophy*, in *Discourse on Method and Meditation*, trans. Laurence Lafleur (Indianapolis: Liberal Arts, 1960), 82.
4. Descartes, *Discourse on the Method of Rightly Conducting the Reason and Seeking Truth in the Field of Science*, in *Discourse on Method and Meditation*, trans. Laurence Lafleur (Indianapolis: Liberal Arts, 1960), 24.
5. Ibid., 125. Frederick Copleston, in his *History of Philosophy*, vol. 4: *Modern Philosophy: Descartes to Leibniz* (Garden City, NJ: Doubleday, 1960), 114–15, argues that the logical justification of the self (*cogito*), reason, and God ultimately rests on a fallacious and circular argument since it presupposes the validity of clear and distinct ideas. The problem is that clear and distinct ideas had not been justified until after the existence of the non-deceptive God was proven based on the assumed validity of clear and distinct ideas. Since God is not a deceiver, the intuitive ideas of consciousness must also be true. But the very existence of God rested on these earlier unproven innate ideas. The very thing that Descartes is attempting to prove—the criterion of truth based on clarity and distinctiveness—is assumed to be true to prove the existence of the perfection and divinity of God. The conclusion is based on presuppositions that had yet to be justified.
6. Descartes, *Meditations Concerning First Philosophy*, 24.
7. Copleston, *History of Philosophy*, vol. 4, 90.
8. Ibid., 91. Copleston in an insightful comment contends that these innate or a priori forms of thought of Descartes anticipate Kant's theory of pure reason (94). But Copleston is also clear that Descartes' method is a logic of discovery of innate ideas existing internally within human consciousness and not a logic of construction of reality from the a priori structure of the mind.
9. Descartes, *Meditations Concerning First Philosophy*, 119.
10. Ibid., 120.

11. Ibid., 125.

12. Gerald Galgan, *The Logic of Modernity* (New York: New York University Press, 1982), 60-61.

13. Descartes, *Meditations Concerning First Philosophy*, 125.

14. Galgan, *The Logic of Modernity*, 73.

15. Copleston, *History of Philosophy*, vol. 4, 90, 93. "For Descartes innate ideas are *a priori* forms of thought which are not really distinct from the faculty of thinking" and thus the principles and laws of natural science are part of the "innate constitution of the mind" (94).

16. Galgan, *The Logic of Modernity*, 60, 72.

17. Keeling, *Descartes*, 58-59.

18. There is a distinction in this chapter between the metaphysics of divine cosmology from the *Meditations on First Philosophy* and the metaphysics of science from the *Discourse on Method*. Descartes himself makes the distinction between metaphysics and theology. In metaphysics, God's existence is based on philosophical and rational grounding of first principles and pure reason. In theology, his existence is grounded in belief and faith. Descartes applies the term using the first meaning. This chapter is using metaphysics differently from that found in Descartes' writings in that there are two forms of metaphysics—the metaphysics of God's perfect being and infinite existence or medieval cosmology and the metaphysics of nature or the structural and logical presuppositions of physics. For more on Descartes' usage of these terms and distinctions among metaphysics and theology and physics and reason, see Keeling, *Descartes*, 58-60. "Without it [knowledge of God's nature and existence] there can be no knowledge of any body of science, nor even of single, isolated propositions belonging to science or metaphysics" (110). Clear and distinct ideas related to physics and nature refer to three-dimensional space in mathematics as "the ultimate constitution of material bodies" in geometry and kinematics (115) and "to metaphysics falls the responsibility of conferring validity . . . on Method" (78).

19. Carolyn Merchant, in *The Death of Nature: Women, Ecology and the Scientific Revolution* (New York: Harper & Row, 1983), writes that "Descartes' method depended on the manipulation of information according to a set of rules" which was "the key to power over nature" (231).

20. Descartes, *Meditations*, 87. For a more detailed discussion on the primary and secondary characteristics of wax and their relationship to the Cartesian theory of matter, see Daniel Garber, *Descartes' Metaphysical Physics* (Chicago: University of Chicago Press, 1992), 63-93.

21. Descartes, *Meditations*, 118–19. These quantitative, mathematical, and innate ideas of Descartes closely parallel the irreducible, immutable, and inalienable rights of man in Locke. Both nature and politics are grounded in a metaphysics of God that ensures their existence, validity, and durability.

22. Ibid., 125–26.

23. Ibid., 120, 134.

24. For an analysis of Descartes' critique of Aristotle and return to the ancient atomism of Democritus, Epicurus, and Lucretius, see Garber, *Descartes' Metaphysical Physics*, 117–20. Descartes uses atomism as a central element in his distinctive methodological or mathematical atomism of reducing problems to the smallest component parts. Descartes argues that all extended bodies and their primary characteristics, such as physical and geometric extension, are divisible into an infinite number of parts. The atomists, on the other hand, believed that bodies were made of non-infinitely divisible parts or atoms "or as Descartes often prefers to put it, indefinite divisibility of geometrical extension to the infinite or indefinite divisibility of extended substance." He concludes: "And so bodies cannot be made up of indivisible parts, as the atomists claim they are" (123).

25. Copleston, *A History of Philosophy*, vol. 4, 90, 93, 94–95. The universal laws of physics or natural philosophy are deduced from the simple nature and first principles of physics of extension and motion, that is, metaphysics.

26. Descartes, *Discourse on Method*, 15. The method of science consists of radical doubt, intuition of pure ideas, clear and distinct ideas, analysis, synthesis, and general scientific theory.

27. Garber, *Descartes' Metaphysical Physics*, 64, 66.

28. Descartes, *Discourse on Method*, 31.

29. Ibid., 45.

30. Ibid., 45–46.

31. Ibid., 41. For Descartes' analysis of the rules of mechanics and its connection to modern machinery, see 34–41.

32. Fritjof Capra, *The Turning Point: Science, Society and the Rising Culture* (New York: Simon and Schuster, 1982), 60.

33. Ibid., 43.

34. Merchant, *The Death of Nature*, 234.

35. Morris Berman, *The Reenchantment of the World* (Ithaca, NY: Cornell University Press, 1981), 34.

36. Edwin Arthur Burtt, *The Metaphysical Foundations of Modern Science* (Garden City, NY: Doubleday, 1954), 17.

37. F. S. C. Northrop, "Introduction" to Werner Heisenberg, *Physics and*

Philosophy: The Revolution in Modern Science (New York: Harper & Row, 1958), 25.

38. Ibid., 9.
39. Floyd Matson, *The Broken Image: Man, Science, and Society* (Garden City, NY: Doubleday, 1964), 14.
40. Alexandre Koyré, *From the Closed World to the Infinite Universe* (Baltimore: Johns Hopkins University Press, 1957), vii.
41. Matson, *The Broken Image*, 13.
42. Northrop, "Introduction" to *Physics and Philosophy*, 4.
43. Ibid., 13.
44. Heisenberg, *Physics and Philosophy*, 81. Heisenberg's focus is on the growth of science after Descartes and the seventeenth century.
45. David Hume, *An Enquiry Concerning Human Understanding*, in *The Empiricists* (Garden City, NY: Doubleday, 1961), section 4, 322–33, and section 12, 417–22.
46. Merchant, *The Death of Nature*, 179.
47. Ibid., 193. Berman in *The Reenchantment of the World* takes an interesting approach, arguing that "the scientific paradigm has become as difficult to maintain in the late twentieth century as was the religious paradigm in the seventeenth" (23). The colonization of the lifeworld and science have resulted in "an inherent instability that severely limited its [modern epoch and science] ability to sustain itself for more than a few centuries" (ibid.).
48. Ibid., 50.
49. Ibid., 49.
50. Ibid., 143–52.
51. Jürgen Habermas, *The Theory of Communicative Action*, vol. 2: *Lifeworld and System: A Critique of Functionalist Reason*, trans. Thomas McCarthy (Boston: Beacon, 1989), 199–373. There were some minor changes in the constitution of the lifeworld to better fit the ideas of classical social theory.
52. Matson, *The Broken Image*, 62. Matson, referring to B. F. Skinner, writes in *The Broken Image* that the "central tradition of Western thought, which has cherished the essential dignity and liberty of the individual is, quite simply, no longer tenable in the face of modern scientific knowledge of the nature of man." In a mechanical and deterministic universe, human beings are "hapless creatures," 14. The social sciences are based on the premises of behavioral engineering and technological rationality. Politics, too, as the science of behavior, has been replaced by polling, the manipulation of symbols and propaganda to change attitudes, neutrality, bureaucratic administration, and the replacement of democracy by scientific choices; economics becomes an expression

of self-interest, competition, social Darwinism, and the consumer laws of supply and demand; and psychology is simply the study of the imbalances of the biological organism adjusted through medication. Matson writes that "by the thirties a school of thought closely parallel to psychological behaviorism had become established in sociology." (67).

53. Errol Harris, *The Foundations of Metaphysics in Science* (London: Allen and Unwin, 1965), 18–33; Mary Hesse, *Revolutions and Reconstructions in the Philosophy of Science* (Indianapolis: Indiana University Press, 1980), vii ff.

54. Larry Laudan, *Progress and Problems: Towards a Theory of Scientific Growth* (Berkeley: University of California Press, 1978).

55. Richard Rorty, *Philosophy and the Mirror of Nature* (Princeton, NJ: Princeton University Press, 1980).

56. Hesse, *Revolutions and Reconstructions in the Philosophy of Science*, xi; Laudan, *Progress and Problems*, 13–14; Jürgen Habermas, *Knowledge and Human Interests* (Boston: Beacon, 1971), 121; and Willard Van Orman Quine, "Two Dogmas of Empiricism," in *From a Logical Point of View* (New York: Harper and Row, 1963), 44.

57. Henry Veatch, "Is Quine a Metaphysician?" *Review of Metaphysics* 31, no. 3 (March 1978): 414.

58. Paul Feyerabend, *Science in a Free Society* (London: New Left, 1978).

59. Pierre Duhem, *The Aim and Structure of Physical Theory*, trans. Philip Wiener (New York: Atheneum, 1981), 7.

60. Ibid., 20–21.

61. Ernst Cassirer, *The Problem of Knowledge: Philosophy, Science, and History since Hegel* (New Haven, CT: Yale University Press, 1978), 111.

62. Cassirer, 113.

63. Quine, "Two Dogmas of Empiricism," in *From a Logical Point of View*, 78.

64. Ibid., 44. "As an empiricist I continue to think of the conceptual scheme of science as a tool, ultimately, for predicting future experience in the light of past experience. Physical objects are conceptually imported into the situation as convenient intermediaries—not by definition in terms of experience, but simply as irreducible posits comparable, epistemologically, to the gods of Homer.... But in point of epistemological footing the physical objects and the gods differ only in degree and not in kind. Both sorts of entities enter our conception only as cultural posits. The myth of physical objects is epistemologically superior to most in that it has proved more efficacious than other myths as a device for working a manageable structure into the flux of experience."

65. Ibid., 43.
66. Rorty, *Philosophy and the Mirror of Nature*, 170.
67. Duhem, *The Aim and Structure of Physical Theory*, 14–15.
68. E. A. Burtt, *The Metaphysical Foundations of Modern Science* (New York: Doubleday, 1954), 90.
69. Alexander Koyré, *Metaphysics and Measurement* (Cambridge, MA: Harvard University Press, 1968), 19–20. See also his *From the Closed World to the Infinite Universe*.
70. Hans Jonas, *Philosophical Essays* (New York: Prentice Hall, 1974), 10.
71. Quine, "Two Dogmas of Empiricism," in *From a Logical Point of View*, 78.
72. Joel Whitebook, "The Problem of Nature in Habermas," *Telos* 40 (1979): 41–69.
73. Maurice Merleau-Ponty, *Themes from the Lectures at the Collège de France 1952–1960*, trans. John O'Neill (Evanston, IL: Northwestern University Press, 1970), 71–72.
74. Georg Lukacs, *History and Class Consciousness*, trans. Rodney Livingstone (Cambridge, MA: MIT Press, 1968), 14.
75. Merleau-Ponty, *Themes from the Lectures at the College de France 1952–1960*, 73.
76. Alfred Schmidt, *The Concept of Nature in Marx*, trans. Ben Fowkes (London: New Left, 1971), 120.
77. Ibid., 119.
78. Rorty, *Philosophy and the Mirror of Nature*, 359ff.
79. Jürgen Habermas, *Theory and Practice*, trans. John Viertel (Boston: Beacon, 1973), 142ff.

Chapter 4: From Epistemology to Historical Materialism

1. Arthur Schopenhauer, *The World as Will and Representation*, trans. E. F. J. Payne (New York: Dover, 1969), 3–18. See Schopenhauer's interpretation of Kant's *Critique of Pure Reason* at the beginning of his work, where he introduces the epistemology of German idealism and subjectivity as the basis for his existentialism and theory that all knowledge is a result of representations, dreams, and illusions.
2. Immanuel Kant, *The Critique of Pure Reason*, trans. Norman Kemp Smith (New York: St. Martin's), 93.
3. This interpretation of Hegel moves beyond the traditional view of him as an abstract idealist. It might be more useful to view Hegel as a cultural idealist who incorporates into his theory and method a strong materialist element.
4. George McCarthy, *Marx and Social Justice: Ethics and Natural Law in the Critique of Political Economy* (Chicago: Haymarket, 2018), 163–65.

5.	A. Kiarina Kordela, "Materialist Epistemology: Sohn-Rethel with Marx and Spinoza," *History of the Human Sciences* 29, no. 2 (2016): 114.

6.	Peter Bulthaup, *Zur gesellschaftlichen Funktion der Naturwissenschaften* (Frankfurt am Main: Suhrkamp, 1973), 84–114.

7.	Karl Marx, *A Contribution to the Critique of Political Economy*, introduction by Maurice Dobb (New York: International Publishers, 1970), 20–21. Note that the term "intellectual production" is used twice in the third volume of *Capital: A Critique of Political Economy*, vol. 3: *The Process of Capitalist Production as a Whole*, ed. Friedrich Engels (New York: International Publishers, 1975), 81–82, to refer to the natural sciences and thus places the natural science in both the productive forces of production and the cultural and ideological superstructure.

8.	Ibid., 21.

9.	Karl Marx and Friedrich Engels, *The German Ideology* (New York: International Publishers, 1965), 14.

10.	Ibid., 21.

11.	Friedrich Engels, *Dialectics of Nature* in *Marx Engels Collected Works* (*MECW*) (New York: International Publishers, 1975), vol. 25, 465. Engels wrote three books on natural science: *Anti-Dühring: Herr Eugen Dühring's Revolution in Science* (1885), *Ludwig Feuerbach and the End of Classical German Philosophy* (1888), and *Dialectics of Nature: Engels's Explanation about Dialectical Materialism* (1925).

12.	Marx, *Capital*, vol. 3, 167–70, 209, and 385. Marx is not trying to predict prices, profits, or economic crises in his theory. This is why he details the nature of exploitation, dehumanization, and alienation in the workplace at the micro level in his early writings and at the macro or structural level in his later writings. This is why his methodology stresses the internal logic of capital rather that an empirical description of economic crises. There is a coherent theme throughout his writings, since his main focus is on outlining a comprehensive and critical theory of social justice.

13.	It is important to note here that at the very end of the twentieth century, the natural science notebooks of Marx and Engels were published in the 31st volume of the *Marx-Engels Gesammtausgabe*. This publication contained the hitherto unpublished notes of Marx on inorganic and organic chemistry and electricity, as well as Engels's notes on physics and ecology.

14.	Isaac Balbus in his work *Marxism and Domination: A Neo-Hegelian, Feminist, Psychoanalytic Theory of Sexual, Political, and Technological Liberation* (Princeton: Princeton University Press, 1982) argues that there are two different approaches in both Marx's own writings and later Marxist literature tracing the relationship between the productive forces of science and technology and the class and power structure of the social relations of production. These two different approaches are inconsistent and contradictory. Balbus traces in exegetical detail the changes and inconsistencies in Marx's position throughout his writings from his early *Paris Manuscripts* and *The German Ideology* to the *Grundrisse* and *Capital*. What is most interesting is that both approaches may be found in the same works.

Later Marxist social theorists may be divided on this issue into two distinct groups: The "instrumental or optimist view" (129-141) maintains that science and technology are neutral, objective, and independent forms of knowledge and instrumental applicability that can be applied in both a capitalist and socialist economy for oppressive or for emancipatory purposes. The second and more critical approach contends that Enlightenment science and modern technology are products of a capitalist system whose purpose is the domination of nature and humanity and, thus, cannot be used for human liberation in a free society. Balbus writes: "The 'pessimistic theory' (141–163 and 234–265) upholds the primacy of capitalist social relations over the forces of production and thus points to the conclusion that the construction of socialism cannot rely on, but rather demands a qualitative break with, the logic of technological progress under capitalism . . . the possibility of socialism cannot be grounded in the development of technology under capitalism since this technology is an intrinsically capitalist technology. . . ." (141). From this perspective the Enlightenment and Industrial Revolution are a product of the logic and institutions of repressive capitalism and primitive accumulation, since "the imperatives of machine technology of production are present within the very structure of machine technology itself" (144). Western science and technology are a priori political and repressive. The Enlightenment is a capitalist revolution at the level of concepts, ideas, and science. According to the alternative theory, the organization of production and class system—the totality of capitalist social relations—are historically, economically, and logically built into the cultural fabric and conceptual and methodological framework of science and technology. Science is a form of alienated consciousness which would exploit human labor in both a capitalist and socialist society. Finally, Balbus writes that the factory and modern machinery are utilized in factory production not because they are the most rational, productive, and efficient forms of economic production, but because they are the most effective ways to exploit labor power and profit maximization (144). A parallel historical argument emphasizes that the capitalist revolution was not preceded by the scientific and technological revolution of the productive forces, but by the transformation of the class structure and property ownership from feudal to capitalist relations and control over production. The logic and values of capitalism are inherent in the very logic and metaphysics of science, technology, and machine production. The application of science and technology in production is more effective at the extraction of surplus value than alternative approaches. They are more effective at the control, manipulation, exploitation, and alienation of human labor for the purpose of profit maximization and class oppression. See Marx, *Capital*, vol. 1, 338, 360-61, 367, 371, 422, 436-437, 714, and 737.

Representatives of the Structural or Pessimistic theory of science argue that natural science and technology are manifestations of capitalist production and social order, thereby making them impossible to be used in a socialist society:

Shlomo Avineri, *The Social and Political Thought of Karl Marx* (Cambridge: Cambridge University Press, 1968).

Harry Braverman, *Labor and Monopoly Capital* (New York: Monthly Review Press, 1976).

André Gorz, "Technical Intelligence and the Capitalist Division of Labor," *Telos*, no. 12 (Spring 1972) and "On the Class Character of Science and Scientists," in *The Political Economy of Science: Ideology of/ in the Natural Sciences* (London: Macmillan, 1976).

Herbert Marcuse, *One-Dimensional Man* (Boston: Beacon, 1964).

Stephen Marglin, "What Do Bosses Do? The Origins and Functions of Hierarchy in Capitalist Production," *The Division of Labour: The Labour Process and Class-Struggle in Modern Capitalism*, ed. A Gorz (Hassocks, UK: Harvester, 1976).

Ramesh Mishra, "Technology and Social Structure in Marx's Theory: An Exploratory Analysis," *Science & Society* 43 (Summer 1979): 132–57.

Bertell Ollman, *Alienation: Marx's Concept of Man in Capitalist Society* (Cambridge: Cambridge University Press, 1975).

Karl Polanyi, *The Great Transformation* (Boston: Beacon, 1957).

Representatives of the Instrumental or Optimistic theory of science argue that science is objective and neutral, and can be used in either a capitalist society to create surplus value or in a socialist society to create the material social wealth and economic democracy necessary for a moral community:

Ben Cohen, *Marx's Theory of History: A Defense* (Princeton: Princeton University Press, 2000).

Jürgen Habermas, *Knowledge and Human Interests* (Boston: Beacon, 1971).

Alfred Schmidt, *The Concept of Nature in Marx* (London: New Left Publisher, 1971).

15. Wal Suchting, "'Productive Forces' and 'Relations of Production' in Marx," *Analyse & Kritik* 4 (1982): 164. Suchting contends that the productive forces do not mechanically determine the formation of the social relations of production, but that there is a dialectical interplay between these two components of production. He quotes from *Capital*, vol. 2, 461 (*MECW*, vol. 24, 384) that "the production of absolute and relative surplus-value determines . . . the whole social and technical shaping of the capitalist process of production" (163). Suchting also writes that "the relations of production have a very considerable degree of autonomy with regard to the level of development of the productive forces" (164). See also *Capital*, vol 3, 798; *MEW* 25, 826ff.

16. Balbus, *Marxism and the Domination*, 153. Balbus summarizes the Marxist structural theory of science and technology by quoting directly from Marx's *The German Ideology* (149): ". . . the natural sciences interiorize the logic of capitalist relations of production and must therefore be understood as specifically capitalist sciences" (151). Balbus then adds that capitalism is the historical and economic cause for the rise of industrial revolution (144). To apply modern science and technology to the workplace is to reinforce and ideologically legitimate the class system of economic oppression. However, in another section of chapter 4 of his work entitled "Marxist Theories of Repressive Technology," Balbus articulates the instrumental theory of science and technology found in *The German Ideology*, *Grundrisse*, and *Capital*, vols. 1 and 3 (129-141). He summarizes these two Marxist schools of thought by claiming that Marx did not have a consistent position throughout his writings and that his treatment of these issues was quite ambivalent and confusing. Balbus concludes that neither position within Marx's writings helps to create a theory of "liberatory technology." (153).

17. Marx and Engels, *The German Ideology*, parts I and III, 13-14.

18. Ibid., 19.

19. Alfred Sohn-Rethel, *Intellectual and Manual Labor: A Critique of Epistemology*, trans. Martin Sohn-Rethel (Atlantic Highlands, NJ: Humanities, 1978), 15.

20. Marx, *A Contribution to the Critique of Political Economy*, 205f. Toward the end of this work, Marx undertakes a methodological analysis of how the traditional empirical science of political economy outlines its study of a country by beginning with certain types of categories, which appear to be concrete and particular, but are in reality abstractions from more foundational concepts. To understand the nature of population

and its economic importance, one must first examine those elements of society which underlie it. Therefore, Marx argues that political economy usually begins "with the division of the population into classes, town and country, the sea, the different branches of production, export and import, annual production and consumption, prices, etc." (205). According to Marx, this represents an abstraction of science from "the real and concrete elements, [from] the actual pre-conditions." These economic categories which act as the foundation of economic science are only abstractions from the more important issues of classes, wage labor, capital which, in turn, presuppose an understanding of exchange, division of labor, prices, value, money, price, etc.

21.   Hilary Rose and Steven Rose, "The Incorporation of Science," in *The Political Economy of Science: Ideology of/in the Natural Sciences*, ed. Hilary Rose and Steven Rose (London: Macmillan, 1976), 14–15.

22.   Richard Clarke's summary of a paper delivered by Boris Hessen at the International Congress of the History of Science in London (1931) entitled "The Socio-Economic Roots of Newton's *Mathematical Principles of Natural Philosophy (Principia)*" in "What Can a Marxist Approach Tell Us About Science?" *Culture Matters*, November 27, 2017, http://culturematters.org.uk.

23.   Marx and Engels, *The German Ideology*, 36.

24.   Karl Marx, letter to Engels, June 18, 1862, in *Marx Engels Collected Works*, vol. 41, 380.

25.   Marx and Engels, *The German Ideology*, 35.

26.   Ibid., 29.

27.   Ibid., 19.

28.   Friedrich Tomberg, *Bürgerliche Wissenschaft* (Frankfurt am Main: Fischer Taschenbuch, 1973). The nature of modern science and technology has evolved over time from the craft knowledge, guild system, and trade economy of the feudal period and the scientific revolution and machine technology of the Industrial Revolution to the scientific management, Taylorism, and human relations technology of the contemporary economy. Harry Braverman in *Labor and Monopoly Capital: The Degradation of Work in the Twentieth Century* (New York: Monthly Review Press, 1974) maintains that at the heart of the modern scientific revolution in the workplace is the Babbage principle whose ultimate goal is to further management control over the labor process and profit maximization in order "to cheapen the worker by decreasing his training and enlarging his output" (118). The goal of the scientific studies by Frederick Taylor at the Midvale Steel Company in 1880 was for management to maintain control over production and the factory by the monopolization of technical and scientific knowledge

(85-121). In this way, management was able to undertake the following reorganization of production based on three fundamental scientific principles: (1) divorce the labor process and knowledge from workers' skills, craft, and tradition. Control over knowledge and production shifted from the skilled workers to the owners and managers of capital; (2) the intellectual organization and conceptualization of industry plans were to be concentrated in the hands of management, thereby "divorcing conception from execution" and reducing labor to "its animal form"; and (3) the application and control of scientific knowledge and the planning of labor, that is, the labor process itself is to be in the hands of management (112-121). Thus, the knowledge, planning, and control over production is to rest with management as this class system is rationalized and justified by the application of scientific knowledge and theoretical experiments. Later scientific studies would expand management's self-understanding and control over the workplace by using less overtly authoritarian methods of control. This was to be accomplished by introducing more psychologically friendly and less intrusive forms of worker manipulation which would reduce alienation by the use of behavioral science as in the Elton Mayo experiments at the telephone equipment plant of the Western Electric Company in 1927. These experiments only deepen our understanding and appreciation of the primacy of the social relations and class system of production over the technical and scientific forces of production. It is the former that has historical, structural, and logical priority over the latter since science is used to maintain the class system of production and not expand production for the benefit of workers. For more information on these topics, see Robert Blauner, *Alienation and Freedom: The Factory Worker and His Industry* (Chicago: University of Chicago Press, 1964); Braverman, *Labor and Monopoly Capital*, 138-139; David Jenkins, *Job Power: Blue and White Color Democracy* (New York: Penguin Books, 1974), 18-61 and 155-175; Paul Blumberg, *Industrial Democracy: The Sociology of Participation* (New York: Schocken Books, 1976), 14-46; and Richard Edwards, *Contested Terrain: The Transformation of the Workplace in the Twentieth Century* (New York: Basic Books, 1979), 67-89 and 90-110.

29. Ollman, *Alienation*, 17, 259, note 23, and Balbus, *Marxism and Domination*, 22.

30. Marx and Engels, *The German Ideology*, 36; see also 18 and 26.

31. Marx, *A Contribution to the Critique of Political Economy*, 30-31.

32. Karl Marx, *Capital: A Critique of Political Economy*, vol. 3, 216-19, 223-25, 240, and 247. For an analysis of the decline in the rate of surplus value extraction, see pages 25, 26, and 30.

33. Karl Marx, *Grundrisse: Foundations of the Critique of Political Economy*, trans. Martin Nicolaus (New York: Random House, 1973), 402.

34. Ibid., 415.

35. Ibid.

36. Ibid., 421.

37. Ibid., 432 and 434.

38. Ibid., 770.

39. Ibid., 432. On the decreasing value in each commodity due to the decrease of living labor in each raw material, Marx writes that the determination of value has nothing to do with the market mechanism of supply and demand (433).

40. Ibid., 412.

41. Ibid., 404.

42. Ibid., 410.

43. Ibid., 705.

44. Ibid., 748. This tendential fall in the rate of profit is developed further in chapter 13 of *Capital*, vol. 3, 211–31. The concept has a long history within classical economics in the writings of Adam Smith, John Stuart Mill, David Ricardo, and Stanley Jevons.

45. Marx, *Capital*, vol. 3, 212. The scientific and technological rationality as the overproduction of constant capital and disproportionality between production and consumption (257) is what produces the economic crisis, because it leads to a relative decline in the rate of profit (240), overpopulation of labor (216), growing unemployment, overproduction of commodities, economic stagnation, crisis, and the rise of concentrated capital (monopolies).

46. Paul Mattick, *Marx and Keynes: The Limits of the Mixed Economy* (Boston: Porter Sargent, 1969), 60.

47. Ibid., 63.

48. Karl Marx, *Capital*, vol. 3, 255. For a comprehensive overview of the various forms of crisis theory in *Capital*, vol. 3, see McCarthy, *Marx and Social Justice*, 358–59.

49. Marx, *Capital*, vol. 3, 257.

50. McCarthy, *Marx and Social Justice*, 27–71.

51. Ibid., 21.

52. Sohn-Rethel, *Intellectual and Manual Labor*, 6.

53. Alfred Sohn-Rethel, "Historical Materialist Theory of Knowledge," *Marxism Today* (April 1965): 119.

54. Sohn-Rethel, *Intellectual and Manual Labor*, 36.

55. Ibid., 28.

56. Ibid., 65.

57. Ibid., 128. Sohn-Rethel writes: "Our explanation of the principle of

inertial motion is that it derives from the pattern of motion contained in the real abstraction of commodity production. This motion has the reality in time and space of the commodity movements in the market and thus of the circulation of money and of capital" (128 and 72). More explicitly, Sohn-Rethel maintains that Galileo's theory of inertia and natural movement is derived from exchange abstraction or "the commodity movements in the market" (128).

58. Ibid., 115.

59. Bulthaup, *Zur gesellschaftlichen Funktion der Naturwissenschaften*, 110–11.

60. Kordela writes in "Materialist Epistemology," 113–29: "The exclusivity of exchange as the source of abstraction (partly) explains Sohn-Rethel's concentration on (coined) money . . . and his thesis that 'the critique of epistemology must be undertaken independently from that of political economy.'" Kordela also writes that "what eludes Sohn-Rethel is that Marx argues that labor is abstracted already within production only under the precondition that the labor in question is waged labor, commodified labor." Commodity exchange already presupposes the existence of abstract labor and commodity production and "the two processes occur at the same time and presuppose each other."

61. Franz Borkenau, *Der Übergang vom feudalen zum bürgerlichen Weltbild. Studien zur Geschichte der Philosophie der Manufakturperiode* (Darmstadt: Wissenschaftliche Buchgesellschaft, 1971), 9.

62. Ibid., 14.

63. Sohn-Rethel, *Intellectual and Manual Labour*, 8. Sohn-Rethel maintains that the "constituent elements of the exchange abstract unmistakably resemble the conceptual elements of the cognitive faculty emerging with the growth of commodity production" (6). Sohn-Rethel goes even further in his analysis of intellectual and manual labor with his comment that "true identity exists between the formal elements of the social synthesis and the formal constituents of cognition" and that "the conceptual basis of cognition is logically and historically conditioned by the basic formation of the social synthesis of its epoch" (7). Kant's critical epistemology outlines the a priori conditions of cognition. Sohn-Rethel argues that these a priori categories of the mind are social categories of the form of production. The concept of the "*Mathematisierung der Natur*" (315) was developed by Borkenau to emphasize that nature is a social production of the human mind (*Denkform*) that appears as an alien object that "is the result of the 'self-alienation' of humanity in capitalism" (317). Science and nature are a product of capitalism and the structures of alienation. Epistemology is thus grounded in the history and materialism of capitalist society. The

reduction of empirical nature to the deduction of pure mathematical laws is an attempt to escape this recognition of this connection between thought and economics (353). But it is an essential connection since to change our relationship to nature requires a transformation of society and its method of production and exchange, along with its method of distribution and consumption. Metaphysics must be replaced by a historical materialism and critical social theory.

64. Borkenau, *Der Übergang vom feudalen zum bürgerlichen Weltbild*, 15.

65. Sohn-Rethel, "Historical Materialist Theory of Knowledge," 116.

66. Marx and Engels, *The German Ideology*, 36. In a dramatic flourish, Marx says that if Ludwig Feuerbach's experience of the world were interrupted for a period of just one year, upon returning, the natural and human world he remembered would have disappeared. Our experience and knowledge of the world—our categories of intuition and the understanding—are tied to the dramatic changes of industry and trade, and the world we experience is a reflection of that underlying economy.

67. Balbus, *Marxism and Domination*, 144. Balbus is here quoting from Marx's *Capital*, vol. 1, 371. The purpose of modern science and technology is to shorten the working day for necessary labor, cheapen the costs of market commodities, and lengthen the time spent on the exploitative production of surplus value and profits. Also see Mishra, "Technology and Social Structure in Marx's Theory," 147–48.

68. For an attempt to develop that missing theory of social justice in Marx's writings, see McCarthy, *Marx and Social Justice*.

Chapter 5: The Rise of Positivism and the Decline of Critical Reason in the Social Sciences

1. Jeffrey Dixon, Royce Singleton, Jr., and Bruce Straits, *The Process of Social Research* (New York: Oxford University Press, 2016), 74–102.

2. Leszek Kołakowski, *The Alienation of Reason: A History of Positivist Thought*, trans. Norbert Guterman (Garden City, NY: Doubleday, 1968), 31. Kołakowski calls Hume the "father of positivist philosophy."

3. David Hume, *An Enquiry Concerning Human Understanding*, in *The Empiricists* (Garden City, NY: Dolphin, 1961), chapter 2, 316–17. A helpful summary of Hume's argument may be found in Frederick Copleston, S. J., *A History of Philosophy*, vol. 5, *Modern Philosophy: The British Philosophers, Part II: Berkeley to Hume* (Garden City, NY: Image, 1964), 68–101.

4. Hume, *An Enquiry Concerning Human Understanding*, 320.

5. Ibid., 324.

6. Ibid., 325.

7.   Ibid.
8.   Ibid., 326
9.   Ibid., 332.
10. Kołakowski, *The Alienation of Reason*, 1–10; Jürgen Habermas, *Knowledge and Human Interests*, trans. Jeremy Shapiro (Boston: Beacon, 1971), 67–90.
11. Hume, *An Enquiry Concerning Human Understanding*, 333.
12. Copleston, *A History of Philosophy*, vol. 5, 74. Copleston writes that this rejection of the notion of substance or objects could be a product of the impressions based on the senses. However, there is no sensation of an object or substance, only the products of the senses and feelings. We see only perceptions, not objects. He then states that this is "the general line of Berkeley's criticism of Locke's notion of material substance."
13. Ibid., 98–99.
14. Hume, *An Enquiry Concerning Human Understanding*, 419.
15. Ibid., 420. At this point in his argument Hume rejects Descartes' attempt to justify the existence of an external world beyond perception by appealing to the existence and nature of a kind, non-deceptive supreme Being in the *Meditations*.
16. Ibid., 330–31.
17. This critique of empiricism continues in the writings of Max Horkheimer, C. Wright Mills, Karl Popper, Thomas Kuhn, and Richard Rorty.
18. C. Wright Mills, *The Sociological Imagination* (New York: Oxford University Press, 1976), 50–99. Mills is aware that the method of the social sciences can only reflect conscious opinions, thoughts, and action, and is unable to access repressed thoughts, feelings, and ideologies, class consciousness, or changes in the nature of democracy toward totalitarian democracy. The method within the social sciences has "an inadequate view of the national structure of class, status, and power" (54). Mills is critical of the application of the method of the natural sciences to the study of society, politics, and class because these issues are beyond the understanding and explication of the method employed by abstract empiricism. It makes the epistemology and methodology of the social sciences arbitrary, technical, and thin. "The kinds of problems that will be taken up and the way in which they are formulated are quite severely limited by The Scientific Method." Methodology, in short, seems to determine the problems. (57).
19. The term "metaphysics of science" used by Mills has a strong negative connotation, similar to its usage in E. A. Burtt, *The Metaphysical Foundations of Modern Science* (Garden City, NY: Doubleday, 1954). Burtt defines metaphysics as an historical, speculative, and

philosophical theory about the physical characteristics of nature, which permits the creation of a particular universal worldview. Metaphysics reflects less an accurate description of nature and is more a reflection of the essential assumptions and values of the prevailing historical moment. Burtt's main argument is to distinguish between the metaphysics of medieval and modern thought (17). These assumptions and worldviews operationalize their different views of science and knowledge. Medieval physics emphasizes a view of nature through the scholastic categories of substances, essence, ideas, matter, form, quality, and quantity, tied to a theological and teleological belief in God and the spirituality and purpose of human beings, while modern physics in the seventeenth century transitioned to a new focus on a mechanical, technical, and causal view of the simplest parts of nature, described in terms of time, space, mass, energy, atoms, and motion, and embedded in a thoroughly meaningless and empty world of disenchantment (18 and 24). Both Burtt and Mills describe these presuppositions and ultimate postulates in the metaphysics of science in terms that resonate more with philosophical and theological speculation. They reflect unexamined and unarticulated religious and cultural belief systems projected onto nature and society. Gerald Galgan, in *The Logic of Modernity* (New York: New York University Press, 1982), quotes from the writing of S. V. Keeling, *Descartes* (London: Oxford University Press, 1968), 81: "Science . . . cannot establish for itself the legitimacy of its own procedure; methodology cannot of itself demonstrate that the character, connection, and order of our thoughts exactly represent, correspond point for point, with the character, connection, and order of independent fact" (58). This is very similar to what we have already seen in Hume's skeptical reading of our scientific knowledge about the world. There is no direct knowledge of the external natural world independent of our imaginative reconstruction of it, and there is no way to compare our perceptions of objects to the objects themselves. Galgan responds to Keeling's idea: "Scientific method requires a support outside itself in the certitudes of a metaphysic; this metaphysics can appeal to no prior proposition taken on faith or even taken as self-evident" (ibid.). A few pages later, he writes about Descartes' epistemological position: "What I really know in knowing this object (wax object) or any other thing in the world is the nature of my mind—the nature of myself as a 'res cogitans'" (60).

It is interesting that Descartes juxtaposed the metaphysics of the self (Meditations 2), God (Meditations 3–4), and nature (Meditations 5) and the method of logic, ideas, and science as he, too, sought to establish the foundations of knowledge, science, and truth beyond illusions and skepticism in his work, *The Meditations Concerning First Philosophy* (1637) in *Discourse on Method and Meditations*, trans. Laurence Lafleur (Indianapolis: Library of Liberal Arts, 1960). Descartes saw that the metaphysics of consciousness, God, and nature provided the ultimate foundations for belief in the existence and justification of objectivity—an independent and knowable physical reality. Metaphysics justified his analytic/synthetic method, his clear and distinct ideas, and ultimately geometry and science. Without the metaphysical foundations in the belief in a non-deceiving God, our knowledge of method, science, and nature could not be known or justified. Metaphysics justifies the objectivity of nature (existence) and science (truth). Galgan summarizes the Cartesian position: "Modern science is fated to deal, not with nature as given or pregiven, but with nature as assimilable to the thinking of the finite human subject" (72). In knowing the world, we are really only knowing ourselves, and within the history of Western philosophy we know the world only by knowing the cogito (Descartes), the imagination (Hume), the transcendental subjectivity (Kant), the Spirit (Hegel), and human labor and the materialist economy (Marx).

20. Mills, *The Sociological Imagination*, 68. Mills develops his methodological theory of psychologism on pages 61, 66–71, and 86. Sociology turns into a form of psychologism or data collection of social opinions and the likes and dislikes of political consumerism. Mills will juxtapose the method and logic of empiricism and positivism based on psychologism to the structuralism and history of political economy, which require other sociological methods and theories of knowledge than the method and logic of positivism and natural science. It is interesting how this distinction between psychologism and structuralism also reflects the consumerism of values and opinions found in mass media and television news entertainment. What is accepted as daily news is only a discussion of various competing social surveys and public opinions offered as insightful scientific and objective political discussions and statistical analyses. There is no discussion about the structures of society and how they impact people's lives, the consumption of political commodities, or the power and class structure in society.

21. Ibid.

22. Ibid., 54–55.

23. Ibid., 67. The methodological emphasis on pluralism is discussed on pages 66, 68, 73, 85–87.

24. Ibid., 55.

25. Ibid., 63. Also see pages 57, 64, 66.

26. Ibid., 73.
27. Mills, *The Sociological Imagination*, 80–82, 92. For an overview of these
     different theoretical traditions within sociology, see Irving Zeitlin,
     Rethinking Sociology: A Critique of Contemporary Theory (Englewood
     Cliffs, NJ: Prentice Hal, 1973).
28. Ibid., 80. Mills views sociology as an ideology of liberal reform and
     piecemeal analysis and pluralistic fact-gathering which represses any
     consideration of structural and social issues that would call the validity
     of social institutions and political values into question (80–96).
29. Ibid., 90. Mills calls this the "metaphysics of liberal practicality" (86).
30. Max Horkheimer, *The Eclipse of Reason* (New York: Continuum, 1974),
     3–9; Max Weber, "Science as a Vocation," in *From Max Weber: Essays
     in Sociology*, trans. H. H. Gerth and C. Wright Mills (New York: Oxford
     University Press, 1968), 138–40.
31. Max Weber, *General Economic History* (New Brunswick, CT:
     Transaction, 1981), 275–351; David Westby, *The Growth of Sociological
     Theory: Human Nature, Knowledge, and Social Change* (Englewood
     Cliffs, NJ: Prentice Hall, 1991), 379–94.
32. Weber, *General Economic History*, 352–69; Anthony Giddens,
     *Capitalism and Modern Social Theory: An Analysis of the Writings of
     Marx, Weber, and Durkheim* (London: Cambridge University Press,
     1971), 178–84; and Irving Zeitlin, *Ideology and the Development of
     Sociology Theory* (Englewood Cliffs, NJ: Prentice Hall, 1968), 124, 155–
     56.
33. Weber, "Science as a Vocation," 140–43. Detailing the social evolution
     of human consciousness throughout history by Weber and Horkheimer
     parallels closely the phenomenological method of Hegel in his
     Phenomenology of Spirit (1807) which, in turn, expanded the categories
     of intuition (perception) and the understanding (experience) of
     Kant's *Critique of Pure Reason* (1781) to include the sociological and
     historical foundations of the moral life and self-consciousness of the
     Objective Spirit. Hegel's method presented the social evolution of
     human reason within an ethical and political community (*Sittlichkeit*)
     of self-conscious and free human beings floundering on the modern
     Enlightenment rationality of liberalism, utilitarianism, hedonism,
     individualism, and the law of the heart and romanticism and Kantian
     morality and the modern Objective Spirit of the ethical order; the loss
     of community and its ethical ideals (*Sittlichkeit*); the Aristotelian polity,
     and the alienation of culture in the bourgeois zoo and civil society
     (state); and the French Revolution and Terror. He temporarily salvaged
     the situation by retreating into the realm of the Absolute Spirit (art,
     religion, and philosophy), but returned years later to the ethical and

political community with his *Philosophy of Right* (1820). Nietzsche, on the other hand, saw the last man of the iron cage as a product of the decadence, idolatry, and shadows of God in Enlightenment science (Descartes and Galileo), liberalism (Hobbes and Locke), and individual morality (Kant). There seems to be a consensus among the great minds that something was amiss with the rise of modern reason and the decline of traditional values and the community spirit and polity. For a detailed overview of Weber's theory of rationalization and the crisis of reason, see Rogers Brubaker, *The Limits of Rationality: An Essay on the Social and Moral Thought of Max Weber* (London: Allen and Unwin, 1984), 21, 27, 37–38, and 86–87.

34. Weber, "Science as a Vocation," 144.

35. Ibid.

36. Ibid., 143.

37. Friedrich Nietzsche, "Prologue" to *Thus Spoke Zarathustra*, in *The Portable Nietzsche* (New York: Viking, 1969), 129.

38. Max Weber, *The Protestant Ethic and the Spirit of Capitalism*, trans. Talcott Parsons (New York: Charles Scribner's Sons, 1968), 182. Specialists without spirit are without the communitarian and political guidance of Aristotle and Hegel; sensualists without heart are without the virtue and ethics of Aristotle and the moral philosophy of Kant. This work ends with the recognition that the Protestant Reformation, with its principles of asceticism and specialized labor, was fundamentally necessary for the rise of rationalization, capitalism, and the spirit of the iron cage. However, returning to the origins of this new consciousness of religion and human reality, we also see a new metaphysics of nature upon which science, technology, and formal rationality will be based. This new religious worldview will help pave the way for the rise of the spirit of capitalism, but also the metaphysics and rationalization of science itself (105, 109, 115–26). That is, this new view of nature is itself also grounded in the implications of the Calvinist principles of predestination, asceticism, calling, hard work, specialized labor, and most importantly, the theological principles of *Deus Absconditus* and Pauline Indifference. God has abandoned and absconded from the world, has transcended and hidden from it, and is indifferent and apathetic to it because it is a world of meaninglessness, sin, insufferable torment, evil, fear of the loss of grace and damnation, and anxieties over friendships and community. The world is a place of decadence and terror, as it establishes a form of individuality characterized by inner loneliness, emptiness, fear, insecurity, pain, and isolation (103–05, 111– 12, and 119–21). This world represents the spirit and consciousness of the commercial market and modern capitalism, since it is inhabited by

the psychology of the last man in the iron cage, who provides the very foundations of liberalism, natural rights, and individual freedoms and liberties within a capitalist society. But this last man also provides the later legitimacy for the rationalization and domination of nature and humanity. From this perspective, capitalism and the Enlightenment were founded upon seriously impaired social, political, and economic principles of a distorted and sickened individual without reason and virtue.

39. Weber, "Science as a Vocation," 145–46.

40. Ibid., 149–50.

41. By drawing the distinction between subjective and objective reason, Horkheimer seems to be placing his critical theory within the framework of Hegel's phenomenology and the distinction between objective (social ethics, moral philosophy, and social institutions) and subjective spirit (consciousness, science, and knowledge of the external world). Objective reason is substantive and reflective, but also includes the social institutions and history within which the values, ideals, and concepts are concretely and objectively embedded, thereby joining together both philosophy and sociology, Hegel and Marx, in his concept of critical reason and theory. The subjective spirit and reason represent the consciousness of human perceptions, experience, and knowledge, whereas the objective spirit and reason reflect virtue and ethics, moral community and polity, and traditional concepts and social justice.

42. Horkheimer, *Eclipse of Reason*, 5.

43. Ibid., 14, 15.

44. Ibid., 20.

45. Ibid. "The factory is the prototype of human existence and which models all branches of culture after production" (50). Horkheimer appears to give primacy to political economy and the logic of industrial production upon which all aspects of culture, including science and knowledge, are produced. Natural science "is above all an auxiliary means of production" (59).

46. Ibid., 18.

47. Richard Rubenstein, in *The Cunning of History: The Holocaust and the American Future* (New York: Harper Torchbooks, 1987), also sees the connection between the process of rationalization and bureaucracy and the death camps of the Nazis (4, 21, 29–31).

48. Horkheimer, *Eclipse of Reason*, 23.

49. Ibid., 40.

50. Ibid., 75. Horkheimer emphasizes his point about the circularity of neo-positivist reasoning by mentioning the circular reasoning recognized by Hume that observation cannot be the justification for

observation. In the same way, positivism cannot serve as the ultimate justification of positivism; method cannot justify epistemology, theory, and subjective reason. He emphasizes his main point by contending that the "irrational dogmatism" within the Catholic church is more rational that positivism's attempt to justify itself based on its own use of the scientific method. This is not only circular reasoning but also authoritarian reasoning. The philosophy of positivism "has meaninglessness as its meaning" (79). In the end, the scientific procedure based on facts and methodology, which reduces the world to objects and things, is "a product of social alienation" (82). Without the social ideals and intellectual reflection of substantive reason, which are repressed and forgotten, individuals become the ultimate arbiter of their own values and ideals in a narcissistic and liberal society of self-interested mediocrity in a consumer-oriented market economy. This only leads to further adaptation and conformism to the existing social system (97). When discussing neo-positivism, Horkheimer specifically refers to the writings of Sidney Hook, John Dewey, and Ernest Nagel.

51.   Nietzsche, *Thus Spoke Zarathustra*, 129–30.

52.   Horkheimer, *Eclipse of Reason*, 82. Positivism lacks self-reflection because it lacks its own epistemological and methodological foundations; the implications of its claims to universalism and nominalism; and its inability to develop a holistic and critical social theory. Its only concern is with immediate phenomena that can be technically organized and socially measured, but not critically evaluated because ethics, politics, and theory are simply forms of metaphysics. Truth, ideals, and ethics are sacrificed on the altar of utility and facts created by the positivist method, which becomes another form of mythology (86).

53.   Ibid., 73.

54.   Karl Popper, *The Logic of Scientific Discovery* (New York: Harper, 1968), 29. What is very interesting is that Popper begins his work by equating hypotheses with "systems of theories." This would become very important in the later debates with members of the Frankfurt School, who argue that Popper's position leads to the disappearance of social theory as the latter becomes integrated into the deductive method of natural science. Under positivism, traditional classical and contemporary critical social theory becomes impossible, and with it serious totalistic understanding of the structures and systems of political economy.

55.   Ibid., 59–62.

56.   Ibid., 61. Although Popper is highly critical of empiricist natural science and positivism, especially with its failure to get beyond the narrow issues of empiricism and method, it is Popper who also reduces

500 NOTES TO PAGES 314–316

theory in the social sciences to a particular method of inquiry and in the process loses the ability to reflect on historical and philosophical issues of substantive reason.

57. The logic of scientific discovery and the method it employs will become very problematic when Popper later applies it to the social sciences, because it is not capable of explaining the origins of theory other than by a historical accumulation of the data from the logic of scientific discovery itself. This will leave unexplained and unexamined the history of social theory in the social sciences and sociology in particular. As we have already seen, the methods employed by classical and contemporary European social theory do not conform to this view of science or its method and logic of discovery. In the natural sciences, the method of hypothesis observation and testing informs the object of investigation, whereas, in traditional sociology, it was social theory and the historical, hermeneutical, and structural questions of political economy which defined the actual areas of interest and methods of study. In the social sciences theory defines and delineates the appropriate method employed, whereas in the natural sciences, already informed by a speculative and abstract metaphysics of a mechanical and deterministic nature and science, it is method which produces theory. The distinction between the two approaches may be succinctly summarized in the following manner: In the positivist tradition, method creates theory, while in European sociology, theory creates method. This will be a major stumbling block in the later discussions about positivism and the scientific methodology of the social sciences during the 1960s, because positivism does not respect the actual distinctive and complex forms of knowledge and logic of inquiry within nineteenth- and twentieth-century sociology. In this way both epistemology and theory are reduced to the method of scientific discovery.

58. Popper, *The Logic of Scientific Discovery*, 39.

59. Ibid., 40.

60. Ibid., 41.

61. Ibid., 31.

62. Ibid., 94. Popper has systematically rejected empiricism throughout his work as logically not justifiable. He follows the logic of Hume's earlier critique of basing universal statements on inductive reasoning since the opposite occurrence and conclusion is always possible. In this part of his reemerging critique of empiricism, he takes up Hume's other critique of empiricism—the fact that an object (substance) and causality cannot be known through sense experience. Popper offers the example that I can see a glass of water. As with Hume, Popper's

response is that one cannot see a "glass of water" through experience. The universal concept of glass and water cannot be verified through any observational experience. "The reason is that the *universals* which appear in it [the statement] cannot be correlated with any sense-experience" (95). Both Hume and Popper recognize that the logical problem with empiricism as a theory of knowledge is that it cannot explain or justify the use of universals in statements. Experience does not give us access to this form of knowledge. Kant would argue in his *Critique of Pure Reason* (1781 and 1787) that universals of intuition and understanding are products of pure reason and not immediate perception.

63. Ibid., 79.

64. Popper maintains that Otto Neurath and Rudolf Carnap, who were members of the Vienna Circle, and Robert Reininger, a guest of the group, held views similar to the school of empirical psychologism. The group, chaired by its founder, Moritz Schlick, held an epistemological theory known as logical positivism, and met regularly to discuss issues of analytic philosophy of science at the University of Vienna from 1924 to 1936. This school of epistemology held that the logical foundation of scientific knowledge did not lie in the correspondence between statements and experience, but between statements and other statements.

65. Popper, *On the Logic of Scientific Discovery*, 96.

66. Ibid., 108–9. Popper does agree with the conventionalists that the initial statement of the scientific problem is defined by logic and conventional agreement. These statements are singular statements of facts and problems confirmed by scientists, not unlike the process that occurs in the confirmation of a legal judgment and verdict by a jury following legal procedures and rules of logic whose goal is the "discovery of objective truth" (110). These statements are not the universal law. Later in his analysis Popper argues that scientific theories are always interpretations of the facts (423) and thus are "testable, but non-verifiable hypotheses transcending experience" (424).

67. Herbert Keuth, "The Positivist Dispute in German Sociology: A Scientific or Political Controversy," *Journal of Classical Sociology* 15, no. 2 (May 2015): 154–69.

68. Karl Popper, "The Logic of the Social Sciences," in *The Positivist Dispute in German Sociology*, trans. Glyn Adey and David Frisby (New York: Harper, 1976), 88.

69. Ibid., 89.

70. Ibid., 90.

71. The method and logic of scientific discovery articulated by Popper

beginning with theory (content analysis and literature review) and a social problem may be found in Dixon, Singleton, and Straits, *The Process of Social Research*, 75–78 and 84–101.

72.   Popper, "The Logic of the Social Sciences," 99.

73.   Ibid., 100. Also see Popper, *The Logic of Scientific Discovery*, 59–60.

74.   Theodor Adorno, "On the Logic of the Social Sciences," in *The Positivist Dispute in German Sociology*, 106.

75.   Adorno derives this notion of social contradiction in the workplace from Georg Friedrich Hegel, *Philosophy of Right*, trans. T. M. Knox (London: Oxford University Press, 1967), section 243, 149–150.

76.   Adorno, "On the Logic of the Social Sciences," 69, 112.

77.   Ibid., 109.

78.   Ibid.

79.   Ibid.

80.   Theodor Adorno, "Sociology and Empirical Research," in *The Positivist Dispute in German Sociology*, 71.

81.   Adorno, "On the Logic of the Social Sciences," 112.

82.   Adorno, "Sociology and Empirical Research," 81.

83.   Adorno, "On the Logic of the Social Sciences," 118.

84.   Adorno, "Sociology and Empirical Research," 69.

85.   Ibid., 71. In the empirical sciences, theory has been reduced to summary and classification of empirical data, content analysis, literature review, and the history of ideas as it is separated from its intellectual origins in philosophy, epistemology, and social history.

86.   Popper, "The Logic of the Social Sciences," 99.

87.   Adorno, "Sociology and Empirical Research," 73.

88.   Ibid., 84.

89.   Ibid., 133, 137, 141, 145, and 148. See also Thomas Kuhn, *The Structure of Scientific Revolutions* (Chicago: University of Chicago Press, 1971), 106, 206.

90.   Jürgen Habermas, "The Analytical Theory of Science and Dialectics," in *The Positivist Dispute in German Sociology*, 133.

91.   Ibid., 134. On the theme that empirical science cannot reproduce empirical reality, see pages 78, 100, 207, 216–20.

92.   Ibid., 136. These criticisms also apply to the application of the analytical-empirical method to the social sciences, historical sciences, and the cultural sciences (134–40).

93.   Ibid., 149.

94.   Ibid.

95.   Ibid., 151.

96.   Ibid., 152.

97.   Hans-Georg Gadamer, *Truth and Method* (New York: Seabury, 1975),

269-74. For an analysis of the connection between the hermeneutical circle, the fusion of horizons, and Aristotelian politics, see 259-67, 274-89, and 350-51.

98. For a deeper and more profound analysis of the concept of technical interests directing scientific inquiry, see Habermas, *Knowledge and Human Interests*, 67-139.

99. Jürgen Habermas, "A Positivistically Bisected Rationalism," in *The Positivist Dispute in German Sociology*, 199.

100. None of the traditional classical and contemporary schools of continental sociological theory in Germany or France, with their distinctive epistemologies and methodologies, could be created using positivism, whether in the form of empiricism (Locke and Hume), rationalism (Descartes), logical positivism (Carnap and Neurath), or critical rationalism (Popper and Albert). See also F. S. C. Northrop, "Introduction" to Werner Heisenberg's *Physics and Philosophy: The Revolution in Modern Science* (New York: Harper & Row, 1958), 13 and 25. Northrop emphasizes that a scientist does not empirically confirm a scientific investigation because although the latter is a product of empirical inquiry, it is also framed by a distinctive scientific method and natural theory. Metaphysics, theory, and method precede, predefine, and prestructure what is empirical and what is objective reality; scientific inquiry confirms these foundational components of science. On this point see *Physics and Philosophy*, 79-85, where Heisenberg refers to this as "metaphysical realism," which he differentiates from "practical" and "dogmatic realism," 81.

101. Habermas, "A Positivistically Bisected Rationalism," 202.

102. Habermas, "Analytical Theory of Science and Dialectics," in *The Positivist Dispute in German Sociology*, 152-53.

103. Ibid., 155.

104. Ibid., 156.

105. Habermas is drawing his comparison between the method of work and science from Franz Borkenau, *Der Übergang vom feudalen zum bürgerlichen Weltbild. Studien zur Geschichte der Philosophie der Manufakturperiode* (Darmstadt: Wissenschaftliche Buchgesellschaft, 1973), 1-15.

106. Habermas, "Analytical Theory of Science and Dialectics," 157.

107. Ibid., 203.

108. Popper seems to confirm Habermas's criticism in his essay "The Logic of the Social Sciences," where he clearly states that "we term a proposition 'true' if it corresponds to the facts, or if things are described by the proposition. This is called the absolute or objective concept of truth" (99). The hermeneutical circle calls this an epistemological

claim to absolute truth, even with the admission that observation cannot absolutely verify claims to truth, but only temporarily support those claims and observations (the falsification principle of science). Habermas maintains that Popper has a residual positivism in his writings. In the end, justification rests on scientific consensus and the technical success and applicability of the theory itself since realism is ultimately replaced by utility.

109. Habermas, "Analytical Theory of Science and Dialectics," 201. This epistemological position undermines the traditional view in empiricism and rationalism that there is an objective and knowable reality independent of the knower. These two traditions differ on the nature of knowledge in experience or reason and the methods of inquiry through inductive or deductive logic. The Copernican revolution of Kant was to integrate both traditions with his recognition that both perception and reason were essential for human knowledge of the external world.

110. Habermas likens the process of the interpretation of facts to the structuring of facts within the context or horizons of the process of discovery within hermeneutics and the law. This is true for science, textual analysis and exegesis of literature, and a trial jury decision in a legal proceeding. "The facts of the case are even sought under categories of the system of laws" (ibid., 205). Basic interpretations, statements, and decisions are only made clear when viewed from within the broader interpretive whole—legal code and procedures, horizons and context of the text, and the functional and analytical method and theory of science. Without this broader context, there are no legal decisions, no scientific facts, and no literary interpretations. Habermas writes, "I think that the area of the empirical is established in advance by means of theoretical assumptions concerning certain structures" (205). These a priori structures of interpretation ground the hermeneutical circle which is based on the Kantian notion that objectivity is created by subjectivity in the form of legal codes, textual analysis, and functional hypotheses, all of which are constructed before the objectivity and facts of law, literature, and science can be asserted. Hypotheses are empirical qualities, behavioral regularities, and statistical projections. In the final analysis, scientific facts are the product of experimental hypotheses, theoretical assumptions about the nature of knowledge and structure of research, and technical and functional utility. Facts are not reflected in experience, but created through the formal procedures of investigation and argumentation. Thus experience cannot justify the experiment and theory, since it was the experiment and theory which created the facts from the beginning. Experimental and privileged facts are constructs

of the experiment itself, and the latter cannot verify its own creation of facts beyond their predictive capacity, operational utility as productive forces, and the public consensus resulting from the application of the appropriate scientific method of criticism, discussion, consensus, and refutation or validation. Those facts that do not conform to these procedures and predictions are not considered falsifiable or justifiable.

111. Ibid., 203.

112. Habermas argues that Popper, despite his insightful criticism of empiricism and positivism, falls into an acceptance of some of their main presuppositions, especially those surrounding residual positivism, independence of facts, and the testing of theories against independent facts in themselves (203). Habermas concludes that Popper is inconsistent in maintaining a correspondence theory of truth and the existence of "facts in themselves." Because of the hermeneutical circle, facts can exist only as logical statements within the scientific method and have no autonomous existence outside of theory itself. The nature of the method of hypothesis construction and empirical testing assumes a certain type of facts that are compatible with the method employed. The real danger of this approach is that "whole problem areas would have to be excluded from discussion and relinquished to irrational attitudes" (199). As in the case of human labor and the production of commodities, hypothetical facts are produced by the technical methods of scientific production. Experience cannot be reduced to experimental observation. Facts and their traditions created by different hermeneutical, dialectical, historical, structural, and symbolic methods would be excluded as non-scientific and not part of social theory. As critical of analytical science as Habermas is, he does not reject their particular empirical-analytical studies, which he admits can be valuable for explaining "empirical regularities of social behavior." His main objection is to the metatheory—epistemology, methodology, ontology, and politics—that underlies the inquiry as well as its scientistic claims to universalism and its reduction of knowledge to "technically utilizable knowledge" (221).

113. Habermas is aware that even those traditions in qualitative sociology that do not conform to any variation of neo-positivism and reject naturalism, scientism, and realism still retain positivist elements in their theories of knowledge based on realism, objectivism, and nominalism.

114. In his novel *The Fall*, Albert Camus outlined the middle-class hell of Jean-Baptiste Clemence, created by humanity that was a traitor to its own values and ideals but fell silent in the face of the mass extermination in the Nazi concentration camps. Camus' novel represents an extension

of Horkheimer's thesis of the eclipse of reason twelve years later. The silence in the face of unspeakable political and ethical crimes, the disenchantment of reason and moral nihilism, and the liquidation of theory and humanity expresses the unspeakable modern void of moral, spiritual, and theoretical emptiness, creating an unimaginable intellectual wasteland with no focus or future, no horizons or hope. And without social theory, there is no understanding why and how this happened and no possibility of avoiding it in the future. This is the eclipse and liquidation of reason in the iron cage. Sociology was once considered applied philosophy, by which abstract thoughts, ethics, and ideals could be made concrete and real in history. Now it has become an applied tool for social control. In the end this silence of theory is an ethical and political betrayal of the inherent dignity and purpose of humanity—of its dreams and future.

Chapter 6: Science and the Domination of Reason and Humanity

1. Herbert Marcuse, *One-Dimensional Man* (Boston: Beacon Press, 1964), 144.
2. Ibid., 145.
3. Ibid., 148–53. Kant's critique of pure reason and theory of the a priori categories of sensibility and understanding are transformed by Marcuse into an examination of scientific a priori forms and metaphysics of science.
4. Ibid., 151.
5. The epistemological and methodological claims of physical science to explain objective reality and natural truth have been called into question in the previous chapters of this book. Positive science has clearly surrendered any claims to be the model for scientific engagement in the social sciences, since the latter inquire into historical and social reality as the foundation for claims to social justice. The traditional foundation of modern science in realism, naturalism, and nominalism has been called into question as truth and reality have been reduced to experimental observation and technical utility. Here Marcuse combines the work of Quine and Scheler, as he writes that the myth of physical objects is a construct created to produce utility and not truth, created to dominate nature. Marcuse provides a more detailed summary of the contemporary history of philosophy and analysis of the nature of objectivism and the a priori categories of subjectivism. See Willard Van Orman Quine, "Two Dogmas of Empiricism," in *From a Logical Point of View* (New York: Harper, 1963), 44. Marcuse quotes from the writings of Martin Heidegger and C. F. Von Weizsaecker to articulate and justify his understanding of the technical nature of modern science.

6. Marcuse, *One-Dimensional Man*, 150.

7. This issue of the dialectic between subjectivity and objectivity, consciousness and the economy, reflects an earlier dialectical relationship between religion and economics, the Protestant ethic and the spirit of capitalism. The debate between Max Weber and R. H. Tawney was over the issue of which component of reality had historical priority—religious consciousness or the capitalist economy. That is, did capitalism in Europe arise from the transformation of medieval Catholicism into modern Protestantism, or was religion the product and justification of the new economic system? Was it a dialectical and interactive relationship between religion and the economy, or did one element have historical priority and influence over the other? The debate ultimately rested on whether one took the side of Marx's historical materialism or Weber's cultural idealism. See Max Weber, *The Protestant Ethic and the Spirit of Capitalism* (New York: Charles Scribner's Sons, 1958) and R. H. Tawney, *Religion and the Rise of Capitalism: A Historical Study* (Gloucester, MA: Peter Smith, 1962). Now the discussion focuses on the relationship between consciousness and the economy, science and capitalism. It should be noted that Weber at the end of his academic career gave a series of lectures on economic history at the University of Vienna and Munich that were then collected in his 1923 work, *General Economic History* (New Brunswick, NJ: Transaction, 1981) in which religion played a relatively minor role in his analysis of the structural origins of Western capitalism in the bureaucratic state, feudalism, medieval city, and modern capitalism (private property, market freedom, formally free labor, rational technology, and the commercialization of economic life). By this time Weber appears to have moved to a more materialist interpretation of history. See David Westby, *The Growth of Sociological Theory: Human Nature, Knowledge, and Social Change* (Englewood Cliffs, NJ: Prentice Hall, 1991), 379–94.

8. Marcuse, *One-Dimensional Man*, 153.

9. Ibid., 154.

10. Ibid. Science is both technological and political because of the ways in which it experiences and uses nature, which is a cognitive and technical expression of the underlying structures of industrial production and capital accumulation. Science is the cognitive, theoretical, and cultural manifestation of the values and institutions of political economy, and thus could never be methodologically objective or politically neutral.

11. Max Horkheimer and Theodor Adorno, *Dialectic of Enlightenment*, trans. John Cumming (New York: Herder and Herder, 1947), 39, 41. Horkheimer and Adorno maintain that the Enlightenment created

mathematical and scientific abstractions resulting in "the leveling domination of abstractions" that "liquidated" the objective natural world and in the "suspension of the concept" that mirrored what historically occurs in modern industry and its abstraction, fetishism, and liquidation of human labor (40–41). Nature and labor are turned into forms of abstraction or manipulable objects of domination (13, 39, 41). "Not only are qualities dissolved in thought, but men are brought to actual conformity" (12). In this manner abstract labor is the basis and foundation for abstract science. Later they write that with positivism and nominalism there is a dialectic of enlightenment that results in "the abandonment of thought, which in its reified form of mathematics, machine, and organization avenges itself on men who have forgotten it, enlightenment has relinquished its own realization" (41).

12. Ibid., xvi.
13. Ibid., 154.
14. Ibid., xvi.
15. Herbert Marcuse, "Industrialization and Capitalism in the Work of Max Weber," in *Negations: Essays in Critical Theory*, trans. Jeremy Shapiro (Boston: Beacon, 1968), 224.
16. Marcuse, *One-Dimensional Man*, 157, 23.
17. Ibid.
18. Ibid. Technical science is tied "prior to all application and utilization to a particular societal project" (159). This only reconfirms in an abbreviated fashion the social foundation for scientific enquiry. Marcuse emphasizes the link between the domination of nature and the domination of humanity (166–67).
19. Marcuse borrows his analysis of labor abstraction and abstract labor power from Horkheimer and Adorno, *Dialectic of Enlightenment*, 12–14, 21–22, 26–27, 30.
20. Ibid., 14.
21. Marcuse, *One-Dimensional Man*, 158.
22. Ibid., 157.
23. The further analysis of the quantification and mathematization of production would involve a detailed historical and sociological analysis of the contemporary forms of the organization of production, division of labor, scientific management, power structure of modern corporations, etc.
24. Marcuse, *One-Dimensional Man*, 157.
25. Ibid.
26. Ibid., 152, 154, 159–160, 162–164.
27. Ibid., 160.

28. Milton Friedman, *Capitalism and Freedom* (Chicago: University of Chicago Press, 1962), 15–18, 24, and 110–12.

29. Andrew Feenberg, "Marcuse or Habermas: Two Critiques of Technology," *Inquiry*, 39, no. 1 (March 1996): 47–48.

30. Marcuse, *One-Dimensional Man*, 166. Marcuse emphasizes the nature of class oppression and hierarchy in the organization and structure of modern industry, undermining any possibility of democracy and worker self-determination, creativity, and dignity. It should be added that in the twenty-first century the logic of capital expansion may undermine its own environmental foundations by the overexploitation of both labor and nature, resulting in greater class inequality and an ecological crisis.

31. For more on this question of the nature of science and technology and possibilities of a new science in Marcuse and Habermas, see Andrew Feenberg, *Critical Theory of Technology* (New York: Oxford University Press, 1991), 176–79 and 168–71; and *Lukacs, Marx and the Sources of Critical Theory* (New York: Oxford University Press, 1986), 249–55. Feenberg argues that Marcuse held two contradictory views of science. Marcuse held that science is not neutral or objective but reflected the political interests of the ruling class for domination and control over nature and workers, but at the same time also argued that science could be the basis for human liberation in a socialist society. In *Critical Theory of Technology*, Feenberg writes: "Despite his sharp criticism of 'technological rationality,' [Marcuse] still maintains the old Marxist faith in the liberating potential of the technological inheritance" (75) and "ends up asserting the neutrality, validity, and instrumental effectiveness of science and technology despite their 'ideological' character" (76). To confirm his position that Marcuse held ambiguous and contradictory views about the politics of science and call for a new science, he quotes from a few of Marcuse's writings: See Marcuse, *One-Dimensional Man*, 154, 168, 231–32, 251. For Feenberg, these apparent contradictory statements about the nature of science "reveal the limitations of Marcuse's approach" (76). Opposed to the ahistorical theory of science of both Marcuse and Habermas, Feenberg calls for a more historical, sociological, and cultural understanding of the nature of science and reason over time and how it has adjusted and changed according to the social conditions (177–78). He criticizes Habermas's approach to the critique of science and technology as a too abstract and philosophical approach to system and lifeworld. He also rejects an external ethical critique of the social system.

32. Marcuse, *One-Dimensional Man*, 167. Marcuse's call for a "new science" only reconfirms the idea that the notions of "a priori technological"

and "a priori political" were meant to encompass both issues of application and origins. Science in a capitalist system of production and consumption has been used for the domination and exploitation of both nature and society in its application in industrial production. However, by questioning science's inherent neutrality, logic, and theory of objectivity, Marcuse is also recognizing that science is a product and ideology of a particular type of social system that also must be radically altered in the future. It cannot be adjusted to fit the needs of a new social system with an adjusted new metaphysics of abstract mathematics and practical science and a new technology and organization of liberation. But just as quickly as Marcuse develops his thesis about the politics of metaphysics and science, he dialectically adjusts his argument by first criticizing John Dewey's juxtaposition of ancient and modern reason, and then seemingly arguing that *politics* refers to the use of technology in a particular type of exploitative society, thereby apparently undermining his own theory of political technology (166–67). He seems to imply that the ends of technological rationality are supplied by "pure objectivity" or the social system itself. At this point Marcuse appears to return to Husserl by stressing the idea that objectivity is a construct of subjectivity: "pure objectivity reveals itself as an object for a subjectivity which provides the Telos, the end" (168). It is the inner structure of political rationality contained in the pure subject or consciousness itself. Here he does not mention the broader foundations of consciousness and objectivity (Husserl) and its relation to the objective reality of the politics of control and organization within capitalism. Here he seems to be stressing a Weberian view of scientific rationality as part of the total organization of reason in modern bureaucracy. Marcuse seems to downplay his Marxist heritage, replacing elements of it with Weber's theory of science and reason. Marcuse will return to a more historical and materialist interpretation of subjectivity and objectivity, science and political economy, in his essay on Weber's theory of science, industrialization, and capitalism. The notion of objectivity contains the connotation of both subjective or human consciousness and objective social relations of production and bureaucracy. It does not appear that the conclusion represents a change of position, just a change in emphasis from political economy to bureaucracy—that is, a reemphasis on Husserl's theory of transcendental subjectivity and Weber's theory of technological rationality and bureaucracy. This is only an expansion of Marcuse's broader thesis, not a replacement of it.

33. Ibid., 23.
34. Marcuse, "Industrialization and Capitalism in the Work of Max Weber," 201–26.

35. Marx held that modern industrial society was ethically and logically contradictory. In his early writings he wrote that his version of modern ethics, art, and classical humanism was contradicted by the crude materialism, dehumanization, and individualism of modern society; the notion of contradiction was used differently in his later writings, to emphasize that there were structural and logical contradictions between modern production, economic growth, technical rationality, and property accumulation contrasted against rising unemployment, overproduction, economic waste, pollution, repression, and economic crises. See George McCarthy, *Marx and Social Justice: Ethics and Natural Law in the Critique of Political Economy* (Chicago: Haymarket, 2018), 309–60. Marcuse argues that social and dialectical critique is no longer possible, because the structural antagonisms in advanced capitalism are absorbed by the ideology of scientific rationality resulting in a one-dimensional society. With the rationalization of science and the economic system, there is no longer a contradiction between the culture and economy, ethics and politics, social ideals and industrial production. Thus, traditional cultural and political values cannot be the basis for an analysis of the structural and logical contradictions of capitalism or for the foundations of a critical social science.

36. Marcuse, *One-Dimensional Man*, 22.

37. Ibid., 24–29, 35–36.

38. Marcuse, "Industrialization and Capitalism in Max Weber," 204, 222.

39. Ibid., 224. Marcuse maintains that Weber did not see the material and social foundations of modern science and technology and abstracted them from their political origins in capitalist domination (222–25). "Technical reason thus reveals itself as political reason" (225). The main issues that predominate in Habermas's analysis of Weber and Marcuse are: (1) What is the process of rationalization and how far does it extend into structures and consciousness of society? (2) What does the rationalization of science and technology mean and is it a socially determined reflection of the logic and institutions of advanced capitalism? (3) What is the relationship between the productive forces and the social relations of production—is it simply a case of economic reductionism and positivist determinism of historical materialism, as the logic of the former overwhelms the social and cultural institutions, making it impossible for culture to provide a critical and progressive impulse—the loss of ethical reason? (4) Does culture simply reflect the logic of capital? (5) From where does social critique and practical reason come or has reason been totally repressed in a one-dimensional society? (6) Did the Frankfurt School in its search for practical reason lose political economy? And (7) did Habermas in his search for an

objective standard of consensual reason and social ethics also lose
political economy?

40. John Holmwood, "From 1968 to 1951: How Habermas Transformed
     Marx into Parsons," in *1968 in Retrospect* (London: Palgrave Mac-
     millan), 59.

41. Nasrullah Mambrol, "Key Theories of Jürgen Habermas," Literary
     Theory and Criticism blog, March 5, 2018, http://literariness.org.
     Against the pessimism of positivism with its accompanying loss of
     reason and reflection, Habermas wishes to complete the ideals and
     emancipatory potential of the Enlightenment.

42. Thomas McCarthy, "Translator's Introduction," in *The Theory of
     Communicative Action*, vol. 1: *Reason and the Rationalization of Society*
     (Boston: Beacon, 1981), vi. McCarthy stresses that the three major
     areas of theoretical innovation by Habermas are the incorporation
     into his social theory of: (1) a new theory of linguistic reason and
     symbolic interaction; (2) a separation of the heterogeneity of the social
     subsystems of political economy and the cultural and social lifeworld;
     and (3) a critical movement beyond the dialectic of enlightenment
     toward a new form of emancipation and social ideals. See also Thomas
     McCarthy, *The Critical Theory of Jürgen Habermas* (Cambridge, MA:
     MIT Press, 1978), 34–36. Habermas's early incorporation of the various
     elements of a theory of rationalization from classical social theory,
     psychoanalysis, and critical theory leads to his later incorporation of
     the structural-functionalism of the system theory of Parsons and Niklas
     Luhmann, which only further expands macro-sociology and aids in
     his expanded analysis of communicative action and the legitimation
     crisis of modern society. See John Murphy, "Talcott Parsons and Niklas
     Luhmann: Two Versions of the Social 'System,'" *International Review
     of Modern Sociology* 12, no. 2 (Autumn 1982): 291–301.

43. Horkheimer and Adorno, *Dialectic of Enlightenment*, 4–5, 12–16,
     21–23, 36, 41. Horkheimer and Adorno reject the fetishism of
     reason, the dialectic of enlightenment, and the impoverishment and
     abandonment of thought with the loss of reason beyond technical
     rationality. Habermas's theories of communicative action and ideal
     speech situation were an attempt to move beyond the limits of pure and
     practical reason and beyond the limits of scientism and objectivism
     of modern positivism, which resulted in the loss of reason, critique,
     and social theory capable of making political and ethical judgments
     about the nature of society. Positivism had created a view of science—
     scientism and nominalism—that corrupted reason by limiting its
     scope of application to technical rationality as it repressed the need
     for social critique. See also Jürgen Habermas, *Toward a Rational*

Society, trans. Jeremy Shapiro (Boston: Beacon, 1971), 67–69, 71, 74–80. Habermas's theory of discourse consensus, communication, and ideal speech is a response to the rejection of ethical foundationalism in scientific positivism. He examines the nature of cultural consensus within perception, assertions, needs, ethics, religion, politics, and law. An initial and similar position resembling his consensus theory of truth and discursive rationality as a response to anti-foundationalism may be found in John Stuart Mill, *On Liberty* (Indianapolis: Bobbs-Merrill, 1956), 21–28. Truth is determined not by correspondence to objective reality or sense certainty, but to discursive justification based on the "ideal speech situation." McCarthy, in *The Critical Theory of Jürgen Habermas*, writes: "This notion of an 'ideal speech situation' presupposed in discourse is central to Habermas's efforts to provide moral-practical foundations to critical theory. . . . Truth claims can ultimately be decided only through critical discussions and not through a direct appeal to sense certainty" (307). Truth is not a matter of correspondence or reflection of objective reality, but as "communicative ethics" it involves a rational consensus regarding the truth (325–26).

44. Habermas, *The Theory of Communicative Action*, vol. 1, 4–5, *The Theory of Communicative Action*, vol. 2: *Lifeworld and Systems: A Critique of Functional Reason*, trans. Thomas McCarthy (Boston: MA: Beacon, 1989), 239–50, and the *Legitimation Crisis*, trans. Thomas McCarthy (Boston: Beacon, 1975), 4–6. For a summary overview of the AGIL schema, see Jacek Tittenbrun, "Talcott Parsons' Economic Sociology," in *International Letters of Social and Humanistic Sciences* 13 (2014): 21. The earliest version of the AGIL appears in Parsons' collaborative work with Robert Bales and Edward Shils, *Working Papers in the Theory of Action* (New York: Free Press, 1953), 180–208.

45. Jürgen Habermas, *Toward a Rational Society: Student Protest, Science, and Politics* (Boston: Beacon, 1970), 83.

46. Ibid.

47. Ibid., 84.

48. Horkheimer and Adorno, *Dialectic of Enlightenment*, note 40, 40–41.

49. Habermas, *Toward a Rational Society*, 85–90. Habermas summarizes the tradition that has called for a new science due to the intimate political relationship between capitalism and the Enlightenment. Among the authors calling for a rethinking of the nature of modern science are Friedrich Schelling, Franz von Baader, Marx, Ernst Bloch, Adorno, Horkheimer, Walter Benjamin, and Marcuse.

50. Habermas is critical of the list of pattern variables and value choices in Parsons' social theory. He views them as one-dimensional and

abstracted from the historical and social context. He also argues that it is too oriented toward individual action within the social system. Habermas himself has been criticized for falling into this theoretical dilemma, since he, too, is guilty of social abstraction. By contrasting the technical values of work to the cultural and political orientations of communicative action of culture (pattern maintenance) and social institutions (pattern integration), he believes he has redirected Parsons' theory into the structures of advanced capitalist society. But the level of abstraction in his analysis separates the structures, action, ideals, and culture from empirical and historical political economy. Habermas seems to connect his theory of social action to an abstract human nature corrupted by the ideology of the culture industry, rather than taking key elements of Parsons' theory as the basis for an expanded historical and empirical study of advanced capitalism. For an alternative reading of Habermas, see Thomas McCarthy, "Translator's Introduction," in Habermas, *Legitimation Crisis*, xxii–xxiii.

51. Ibid., xix. McCarthy quotes from the Preface to *A Contribution to the Critique of Political Economy*, arguing that Marx reduced consciousness and culture to deterministic interpretation of economic production as the productive forces and material production—the economic base—determines the social relations of production and the cultural superstructure. McCarthy immediately pulls back from this formal and mechanical interpretation, as he recognizes that Marx's analysis of the economic foundations of society also involves issues of language and culture. Habermas views the potential danger of the Frankfurt School as lying in the attempt to restore practical reason and ethics but with the loss of political economy of Marx. Habermas calls for a dialectical reintegration of the study of political economy as *system* and the social-cultural superstructure as *lifeworld*. However, the integration remains only at the level of abstract idealism.

52. Ibid., xvii.

53. Unusually, this represents a modern return in a quite different fashion to the classical horizons and humanism of Aristotle, in that the institutions of political discourse and democracy become the foundations for ethics, virtue, and the good life. Habermas adjusts these relationships to fit the criticism of postmodern thinking, but there is still a clear and recognizable integration of practical and moral reason with a democratic polity.

54. McCarthy, *Marx and Social Justice*, 129–360.

55. Robert Solomon, *In the Spirit of Hegel: A Study of G. W. F. Hegel's Phenomenology of Spirit* (New York: Oxford University Press, 1983), 212–13, 480–90. The French Revolution and Terror ended Hegel's

attempt to create a moral community and social ethics within modern society in chapters 4–6 of the *Phenomenology*. Due to the unraveling of civil society during the French Revolution and Terror, he replaced the search for the ideals of classical humanism and *Sittlichkeit* with another form of unhappy consciousness and German idealism in the Absolute Spirit. However, he later revives his original insights and goals of the *Phenomenology of Spirit* (1807) in his more social and political writings of *Natural Law* (1803), *System der Sittlichkeit*, (1802–03), and *Philosophy of Right* (1821) that can be viewed as replacing the French Revolution and the Absolute Spirit by reestablishing the primacy of the ethical community and natural law that was broken by the French Revolution and Enlightenment moral individualism. Science is the history of self-reflection and the self-constitution of the human species in transcendental consciousness of the mind, cultural self-consciousness of the Spirit, social justice, and language and communicative action. This process has been disrupted by the rise of positive science, distorted consciousness, colonization of the lifeworld, and the loss of meaning and practical reason.

56.   Habermas, *Knowledge and Human Interests*, 11.

57.   Ibid., vii.

58.   Ibid., 44.

59.   Ibid., 28.

60.   Ibid., 34.

61.   Ibid., 39.

62.   Ibid., 44. Habermas contends that Marx reduces social critique to the logic and method of natural science (45–47) and that it is the natural sciences and the productive forces that determine the system of social labor (54). Habermas believes that Marx was aware of the problem related to the historical development of consciousness, reflection, and social critique within a capitalist society propelled by the logic of the productive forces. However, Marx fails in his attempt to develop a materialist theory of production and solve the problem of the priority and social imperatives of the productive forces and social labor by creating a dialectic between the productive forces and the social relations of production (55). This results in the loss of reflection and the self-consciousness of the human species in understanding the relationship among the various components of society that allowed for a self-consciousness about its history, institutions, and the possibilities of social change in the "organization of society linked to decision-making processes on the basis of discussion free from domination" (55). The result is that reflection becomes impossible, since there is no public space available within the logic of production for social self-reflection

and discourse. The self-constitution of the human species would have to wait until Habermas adapted Parsons to expand his social theory and critique of knowledge into the realm of communicative freedom and democratic discourse.

63. Ibid., 61. According to Habermas, Marx failed to expand his theory of the self-constitution of the human species beyond material production and social labor to include a critique of ideology and theory of communication, that is, he failed to integrate work and interaction, social theory and epistemology (materialist critique of knowledge and science). The result is that Marx failed to expand his theory of historical materialism, production, and work to include social interaction, theory of knowledge, and democratic consensus for social change.

64. Thomas McCarthy in his introduction to the *Legitimation Crisis* argues that the apparent economic determinism and reductivism found in the relationship between the economic mode of production and the forces of symbolic interaction and the superstructure are even more dialectically complex in Marx's writings (xix). Writing about Marx's apparent reductivism of culture and symbolic interaction to the economic mode of production, McCarthy moderates his initial statement by saying: "His [Marx's] empirical analyses incorporate in an essential way the institutional framework, the structure of symbolic interaction and the role of cultural traditions."

65. Understanding Habermas's reading of Marcuse and his criticisms of positivism, the correspondence theory of truth, and foundationalism, the former still accepts the post-modernist theory of knowledge and the loss of reason and social critique in Marcuse's one-dimensional society and in positivist epistemology. Marcuse's critical theory (society's loss of social ideals) and positivist theory of knowledge (nominalism and the loss of values), for entirely different reasons, rejected the foundationalism of social critique, i.e. reason, essence, concept, and ethics. In both cases, the dialectical and immanent critique of traditional ethics and politics became impossible. The rejection of ethical foundationalism due to philosophical nihilism, cultural relativism, sociological disenchantment, and scientific positivism created a "dialectic of enlightenment," the loss of the self-formative process of species thought, and the repression of reflective rationality. This forced Habermas to turn to a theory of communication and the ideal speech situation within a Parsonian framework of interactive social subsystems of the system and lifeworld. By moving in this direction Habermas overlooked the real power of Marx's critique of capitalism in his reliance on the ethics and politics of classical humanism and his holistic theory of social justice which could have

provided the real historical and social foundations upon which to build discursive rationality and democratic communicative action.

66. Habermas, *Knowledge and Human Interests*, 44.

67. Ibid. This criticism that Marx reduces the history of self-reflection and the history of rising self-consciousness to instrumental action and social labor is an interesting insight. However, Habermas misses the fact that Marx's incorporation of classical humanism in his early writings with the dialectical rationality and critique of the structural foundations and contradictions of capitalism in his later writings is the basis for his ethical theory of political economy. Nevertheless, Habermas appears to be correct in his argument that German thought had lost the dimension of symbolic interaction and the cultural system in these analyses which, in the end, would provide not just a "critique" in the form of alienation and contradiction, but a critical framework for outlining a political and social critique grounded in the self-constitution of human reason and public discourse (general will and common good).

68. This expanded notion of society, which includes the process of social integration and cultural values (Parsons) and democratic dialogue and consensus (Aristotle) along with political economy (Marx), provides the foundation for a reemergence of self-reflection within history—the integration of reflection on knowledge, history, and the structures of society. For an analysis of the influence of pragmatism on Habermas and his theory of democracy by George Herbert Mead and John Dewey, see Jürgen Habermas, *Theory and Practice*, trans. John Viertel (Boston: Beacon, 1973), 41–42, 47–49, and 272, and *Theory of Communicative Action*, vol. 2, 5–15, 21–22, and 92–105. See also, *Habermas and Pragmatism*, eds. Mitchell Aboulafia, Myra Bookman, and Cathy Kemp (New York: Routledge, 2002).

69. McCarthy, *Marx and Social Justice* integrates natural law and natural rights in Marx's theory of social justice, articulated in its various forms and structures of civil and legal justice, workplace justice, ecological justice, distributive justice, political justice, and economic justice. These areas cover the full range of issues in political economy, political and social theory, cultural values and norms, and political and economic democracy, well beyond a reliance on a system and logic of social labor and industrial production. Marx is also able to retranslate and incorporate Aristotelian social philosophy, with its integration of ethics and politics, into his own theory of social justice, by using a variety of different social methods, including history, hermeneutics, dialectics, immanent critique, ethics, and empirical research. Thomas McCarthy, in his introduction to Habermas, *Legitimation Crisis*, writes that the

early Frankfurt School replaced political economy with a Marxist *Kulturkritik* which incorporated psychological, social, and cultural issues. Habermas, on the other hand, makes the interaction between work and social interaction the key to his understanding of modern industrial society. His goal is to distinguish between the negative rationalization and domination of political economy and the positivist rationalization of communicative action and practical (ethical) reason, xxi–xxii. But Habermas's reception and incorporation of political economy is tied to Parsons' systems theory, the distinction between system and lifeworld, and the need for both systemic and social integration and legitimation. Economic crises and legitimation or cultural crises lead to serious problems in an advanced capitalist society. Thus, the critique of political economy is tied to Habermas's systems theory and communicative, linguistic, and symbolic interaction. It is the open and free communication disrupted by economic, social, and cultural problems of legitimation which supply him with his critique of political economy and the need for emancipatory change.

70. These are important advances in the development of a critical social theory because they respond to the weaknesses of previous theories in a dialectical manner of internal analysis, immanent critique, and theoretical inclusion and expansion. Habermas focused on a meta- and epistemological critique of science and positivism, and the need to introduce a new theory of political and emancipatory ideals unattached to the system of distorted logic, symbols, and communication. However, there still remains the need within social theory to reaffirm the central importance of the critique of history and political economy, and the need to respond to the ideology of contemporary economics and political science with detailed historical and empirical analyses of the internal dynamic and structural contradictions of advanced industrial society.

71. Habermas, *Knowledge and Human Interests*, 313. The brilliance of Habermas's social theory lies in its wide reach across the whole of classical and modern social theory. To resolve the pressing problems articulated by Adorno, Horkheimer, and Marcuse in critical theory, he broadens the range of social theory by introducing the systems theory of Parsons. By so doing he is able to better respond to the social problems and pathologies articulated by the classical tradition— alienation, rationalization, disenchantment, anomie, nihilism, loss of reason, and ideological repression. By using Parsons' AGIL schema Habermas is able to sketch the interconnections between the full range of social structures and actions including politics, economics, culture, socialization, communication, personality development,

and social integration. Even more interesting is how he explains these factors in terms of the major intellectuals of the time and their theories explaining social institutions and human behavior. As stated in this chapter, Habermas's main concerns deal with the rise of science and technological rationality, the displacement of reason through the social pathologies by the ideology of science and technology, the dialectic of Enlightenment, loss of substantive reason and social critique, and the repression of ethics and politics. In this way, Habermas is able to integrate systems theory with classical social theory, especially Weber's theory of rationalization, Marx's theory of alienation, Durkheim's theory of anomie, and Freud's theory of unconscious repression, into his own theory of external and internal colonization, social reification, and cultural impoverishment of the lifeworld in *The Theory of Communicative Action*, vol. 2, 283–373. By expanding our understanding of the internal dynamics and workings of the social system as a whole with its structures and subsystems within the system and lifeworld, Habermas is able to approach the major concerns of classical social theory and his general concerns about the revival of reason and the dialectic in social critique. Other concerns include the following: (1) critique of ideology; (2) placement of the analysis of science and technology within a broader cultural framework of social integration and the lifeworld; (3) examination of culture through language, cultural symbols, values, communication, and consensus; (4) revival of the lost traditions of reflection, reason, and critique; (5) relinking of system integration with social integration, science and technology with culture, in the AGIL schema; (6) revival of the dialectic of enlightenment and the means of overcoming it; (7) movement beyond Marx's apparent historical determinism and economic reductionism, mechanistic view of the world, methodological positivism, and technological determinism of the productive forces; and (8) insight into the causes of social pathologies lying in alienation, rationalization, and anomie.

Habermas's theory of communicative action provides an interesting account of the epistemological and methodological weakness of transcendental and phenomenological subjectivity and the history of consciousness, as well as the postmodern critique of realism and foundationalism. However, his theory never gets to the heart of the real question, about the nature of a just and free society where communication and symbolic interaction would take place and that would provide the concrete and historical basis for a critique of capitalist and class production and the emancipatory possibilities of democratic socialism. Beyond these areas of interest, there is one that remains untouched by Habermas: he never recovers the lost traditions of political economy or social justice ignored by the critical theory tradition of the Frankfurt School. His examination of science and society would have been positively expanded if he engaged with the contemporary theories of political economy of Harry Braverman, Herbert Gintis, Samuel Bowles, David M. Gordon, Bennett Harrison, and Barry Bluestone. These theorists would have been able to supply Habermas with alternative historical examples of worker associations and control, economic democracy, and the social relations of production, based on entirely different forms of the social organization of production and industry. These new structures would reflect the ability to form free and open consensus and communication within the workplace of a democratic and socialist system. Finally, it would also expand the nature of reason and the cultural values of the lifeworld.

72.   Habermas's revival of reason and critique is viewed by Thomas McCarthy, in *The Critical Theory of Jürgen Habermas*, as the means of moving beyond Marx's integration of the mode of production of productive forces and social relations of production with the social institutions and cultural values of the superstructure. By so doing, Marx only exacerbates the problem of enlightenment in an oppressive and deterministic class system. Marcuse takes a similar approach in his analysis of a one-dimensional society that has lost the emancipatory potential of the productive forces, a consumer society of distorted cultural symbols and displaced language in the process of socialization and integration, making critical reflection impossible. What would have been the basis for critical reflection instead became the foundation for distorted consciousness and ideology (17–18, 21–22, and 34–36).

73.   Thomas McCarthy, introduction to Jürgen Habermas, *The Theory of Communicative Action*, vol. 1, xx–xxiii, and Habermas, *The Theory of Communicative Action*, vol. 2, 95, 140, 399. Habermas borrows extensively from a wide variety of philosophical and sociological traditions, including classical social theory, symbolic interactionism, hermeneutics, critical theory, phenomenology, Freudian psycho-analysis, psychology, systems theory, language philosophy, analytic philosophy, etc. In fact, Habermas's theory of communicative action and critique of modern capitalism is based on the suppression of discursive rationality and open communication in the lifeworld. He supports his own theory of language, communication, and the modern history of cultural phenomena by beginning with a reconstruction of Hegel's phenomenology and the self-constitution of human consciousness and self-consciousness. Methods provide us with access to the study of culture and language which can then be used to broaden

our understanding of language and culture. Each of these traditions provides substantive meaning and clarification to the various structural components of the system and the lifeworld, further expanding the social theories of both Marx and Parsons. For more on this issue, see Jürgen Habermas, *On the Logic of the Social Sciences*, trans. Shierry Weber Nicholsen and Jerry Stark (Cambridge, MA: MIT Press, 1988). From another perspective, Marx had incorporated into his theory of social justice the self-constitution of humanity from the ancient Greeks to the modern German, French, and British philosophers and economic theorists. But even the anti-foundationalist argument rests on some form of epistemological foundation in the logic and idealism of pragmatic linguistics and symbolic interaction, which provides a weaker argument of consensus, rational speech, and the ideal speech situation than Marx's theory of social justice embedded in the history of Western consciousness, which itself is open to intersubjective reflection. For Habermas, essence and reflection turn into communication and interaction. The latter, although it aligns well with postmodernism, is left conspicuously formalistic and critically empty. While Marx's theory of social justice must be adjusted to incorporate contemporary social issues of racism, sexism, antisemitism, etc., he provides the very integration of ethics and politics with a historical and empirical understanding of the social structures and pathologies of modern capitalism.

74. For a discussion about the nature of foundationalism versus consensus theory, see Hudson Meadwell, "The Foundation of Habermas's Universal Pragmatics," *Theory and Society* 23, no. 5 (October 1994): 711–15; and Eva Knodt, "Toward a Non-Foundationalist Epistemology: The Habermas/Luhmann Controversy Revisited," *New German Critique* 61 (Winter 1994): 77–80; McCarthy, *The Critical Theory of Jürgen Habermas*, 325; Marcin Kilanowski, *The Rorty-Habermas Debate: Toward Freedom as Responsibility* (Albany: State University of New York Press, 2021).

Chapter 7: Conclusion: Rediscovering Reason, Science, and Social Justice

1. Thomas McCarthy, *The Critical Theory of Jürgen Habermas* (Cambridge, MA: MIT Press, 1981), 299–310.

2. Jürgen Habermas, *The Theory of Communicative Action*, vol. 1: *Reason and the Rationalization of Society*, trans. Thomas McCarthy (Boston: Beacon, 1984), and vol. 2, *Lifeworld and System: A Critique of Functionalist Reason*, trans. Thomas McCarthy (Boston: Beacon, 1987), and *Moral Consciousness and Communicative Action*, trans. Christian Lenhardt and Shierry Nicholsen (Cambridge, MA: MIT Press, 1990).

In the first volume of *The Theory of Communicative Action*, Habermas investigates the historical evolution of the philosophies and theories of communicative action, while the second volume examines the structural constraints on democracy and public communication. By accepting Talcott Parsons' theory of society, divided between the system and instrumental reason on one side and the cultural lifeworld and public consensus on the other, Habermas creates the conditions for his theory of the ideal speech situation, communicative competence, and universal pragmatics separate from the imperatives of the domination and control of technological rationality and science. See C. Fred Alford, *Science and the Revenge of Nature: Marcuse and Habermas* (Gainesville: University Presses of Florida, 1985), 51, 100. Alford writes: "For Habermas the purpose of social theory is to enunciate the conditions under which the good life may be decided upon rationally . . . [and] by demonstrating what constitutes a genuinely and comprehensively rational decision-making process" (175). However, Alford concludes this idea with a critique of Habermas: "The substance of the good life remains a consideration beyond the boundaries of Habermas's system." This insightful criticism could be overcome by connecting Aristotle's ethics and politics and Marx's social theory—creating the "substance" of the social system and institutional structures of social justice for the material foundations of discursive reason and public discourse and consensus. In this way, the analysis of democracy would be grounded in historical and social structures that make democracy real and relevant, and not simply the speculative and idealist theories of cognitive development and public discourse. The language of the structures of classical ethical humanism and modern political economy have to be recalled, remembered, and re-enchanted in order to revive the loss of substance reason and the critical traditions.

Hegel took years to integrate his early writings on the ethics and phenomenology of the communal spirit in *The Phenomenology of Spirit* (1807) with his later work on the politics of the modern state in *Philosophy of Right* (1820). From a Marxian perspective, the ethical critique of capitalism lies in the systematic and phenomenological reconstruction of the self-constitution of the human species in the Hebrew, Hellenic, Hellenistic, and the modern humanistic and romantic traditions of Western consciousness, integrated into the political and institutional critique of political economy in Marx's theory of social justice.

3.   McCarthy, *The Critical Theory of Jürgen Habermas*, 108.

4.   In his early work *Marx and the Ancients: Classical Ethics, Social Justice, and Nineteenth-Century Political Economy* (Savage, MD: Rowman &

Littlefield, 1990), 272–96, George McCarthy attempts to detail how Marx, borrowing from the political theories of Aristotle and Rousseau while emphasizing the importance of *praxis* (free, aesthetic, and self-creative activity) and *phronesis* (practical wisdom), offers a more critical and materialist interpretation of a consensus theory of democracy and socialism than that offered by Habermas in his more ahistorical and idealist communication theory of knowledge and action. In a later book, *Marx and Social Justice: Ethics and Natural Law in the Critique of Political Economy* (Chicago: Haymarket, 2018), McCarthy continues this approach by showing how Marx's theory of social justice provides the actual historical institutions and structural foundations—from the Athenian polity to the constitutions of the French Revolution and Paris Commune in the eighteenth and nineteenth centuries—for rational communication, public discourse, true democracy, and a moral economy, that are missing in Habermas's critical social theory.

5. Although the analytical Marxists are very different in their intellectual approaches and the philosophical traditions they have relied upon, there is still an interesting overlap in their common understanding and interpretation of Marx's theory of historical materialism. See Joseph Heath, "Habermas and Analytical Marxism," *Philosophy and Social Criticism* 35, no. 8 (2009): 891–919; and Kai Nielsen, "Analytical Marxism: A Form of Critical Theory," *Erkenntnis* 39, no. 1 (July 1993): 1–21. With some exceptions, analytical Marxists rejected the idea that Marx had developed an ethical, political, and economic theory of justice, as he remained focused on economic theory and the deterministic connections within the mode of production and its relation to the social institutions, cultural values, and social norms of the reflexive superstructure.

6. For an analysis of the full range of sociological methods—including history, normative-analytic and empirical-analytic method, functionalism, phenomenology, linguistics, and hermeneutics—see Jürgen Habermas, *On the Logic of the Social Sciences*, trans. Shierry Weber Nicholsen and Jerry Stark (Cambridge, MA: MIT Press, 1988). To this list, other outstanding methods of classical and contemporary social theory might be added, with ties to Hegel, Kant, Marx, the Frankfurt School, etc.

7. Jürgen Habermas, "Labor and Interaction: Remarks on Hegel's Jena Philosophy of Mind," in *Theory and Practice*, trans. John Viertel (Boston: Beacon, 1973). See also Thomas McCarthy's analysis of this essay in *The Critical Theory of Jürgen Habermas*, 34.

8. In his essay on "Labor and Interaction," Habermas outlines his analysis of Hegel's Jena lectures 1803–05 and 1805–06 by adjusting Hegel's

dialectical formation of human spirit, reason, and self-consciousness (mutual recognition) in the form of language, tools, and family, which Habermas borrows for his theory of symbolic representation, labor, and interaction in the formation of the spirit. Interaction takes place in moral action, reciprocity, the community, and the family (158–61). According to Habermas, it was Karl Löwith, in *From Hegel to Nietzsche: The Revolution in Nineteenth-Century Thought*, trans. David Green (Garden City, NY: Anchor, 1967), who recognized that Marx had relied on these same Hegelian lectures for his understanding of the dialectical relationship between the productive forces and the social relations of production. However, in *The German Ideology* things changed, as "Marx does not actually explicate the interrelationship of interaction and labor, but instead, under the unspecific title of social *praxis* reduces the one to the other, namely communicative action to instrumental action. . . . Everything is resolved into the self-movement of production" (168–69). For Löwith, Marx joined the two together in a mechanical and deterministic economics, whereas for Habermas, the relationship was never truly clarified and "could very quickly be misinterpreted in a mechanistic manner" (169). It is possible here that Habermas may be confusing the social relations of production with the political and cultural superstructure. The former could be integrated into labor and industry, while the latter remains critical and potentially emancipatory. However, the argument made in Habermas's book is that although Marx never clarifies the dialectical relationship between the technical forces and social relations of production, he, too, is following in the same Hegelian tradition, with his theory of the historical creation of the communal and democratic spirit in the form of human labor and the social interaction and cultural ideals of social justice.

Habermas ends this essay with the statement that "the self-formative process of the spirit as well as of our species essentially depends on the relation between labor and interaction." Given his extensive writings on this subject, he has made an incomparable contribution to critical social theory. However, to replace "interaction" with "social justice" may expand the history, sociology, and potentiality of the history of the human species, since it also includes not just language and interaction, but the history of Western culture and beyond, humanity's relationship to nature, and workers' self-consciousness and self-determination in the social relations within economic democracy and the moral community. It is this approach which maintains the essential distance between practical reason and technical reason, ethics and instrumental rationality. Habermas, under his concept of social interaction, combined both social institutions and cultural values based on communication, mutual recognition, and general consensus. Marx, on the other hand, had accomplished much of the same with his combination of the social relations of production and critique of political economy in his notions of social structures and social ethics within his theory of social justice. Finally, it is interesting and ironic that on the very page of his analysis of Habermas's critique of Marx, Thomas McCarthy argues that Habermas, like Hegel, rejected Kantian liberalism and individualism, as both returned to the integration of ethics and politics (35). An argument can easily be made that this is similar to a position held by Marx throughout his life by his integration of ethics and politics, moral virtues and social structures, and classical ethics and political/economic democracy in his integration of Aristotle into his own writings. Finally, fearing the mechanical integration of the productive forces and social relations, Habermas integrated the social institutions with the cultural subsystem. In the process, he seems to lose an important spirit of his social theory—the structures of political economy in an advanced capitalist society. *Legitimation Crisis* attempts to keep political economy prominent in the form of the system, systems integration, and economic legitimation crises, but that may require a more in-depth empirical and historical study and analysis of the institutions of political economy. From this perspective, Habermas's notion of the historical constitution of the human species through work and interaction was actually expanded earlier by Marx through his integration of Aristotle into his writings, which concluded with the self-constitution of the human species through ethics, work, and politics or cultural morals and virtues, aesthetic and productive labor, and political economy of democratic socialism within a moral economy and community. Habermas recognizes that the joining of the productive forces with the social relations of production, the economic base with the political/cultural superstructure, and science with political economy was part of the process of creating a one-dimensional society incapable of finding the social and political space for traditional concepts, reflection, and critique. His goal was to separate these social areas and to view knowledge and science beyond technological and instrumental rationality. McCarthy finds that Marx, like Hegel, had "failed to realize the potential for a radicalization of epistemology" and its "various stages of reflection" rooted in the material world of the productive forces and class reflection (55, 83). McCarthy, like Habermas, argues that with the "repoliticization of the institutional framework of society" in the creation of the welfare state and state interventionism into the economy in advanced capitalism, the political and moral dimensions within society have reemerged as the basis for social critique (38). This forces Marxist theorists to move beyond a narrow range of consciousness and ideology tied to the production process and natural science, thereby viewing capitalism within a broader theory of rationalization of the total social system. This broadening of the sociological analysis of contemporary society is crucial, but these insights also reinforce and reconfirm the power of Marx's theory of social justice and the genesis and evolution of consciousness in terms of the history and dialectic of moral life and ethical ideals (108–9 and 162ff.). However, the real foundation of social critique lies not in language, work, and interaction (Marx and Habermas), with its stress on the metatheoretical language of hermeneutics, psychoanalysis, and lifeworld discourse; but in ethics, work, and politics (Marx and Aristotle), with its stress on the ethical and political consciousness of the ancients and the moderns.

9.   For many years the generally accepted tradition was that Aristotle in his *Politics* favored either a monarchy or aristocracy as the best form of government. However, if one reads Aristotle within the framework of a Socratic dialogue and dialectics, these two forms of government are initially introduced to show how inapplicable and inappropriate they would truly be. Only a democratic polity fulfills the ideal of the best form of political constitution, citizenship maturation, and moral economy.

10. See, McCarthy, *Marx and Social Justice*, note 57, 307–8; Shlomo Avineri, *Karl Marx on Colonialism and Modernization*, and Kevin Anderson, *Marx at the Margins* (Chicago: University of Chicago Press, 2016). For more secondary sources, see the works of Ralph Fox, Edward Said, Shlomo Avineri, Dilip Hiro, Cedric Robinson, Walter Kennedy, John Rodden, Kolja Linder, Salome Lee, Robin Blackburn, Donny Schraffenberger, Eric Foner et. al. mentioned in McCarthy, *Marx and Social Justice*, 307–8.

11. McCarthy, *Marx and Social Justice*, chapter 1, 27–71.

12. This has continued to this day in the Catholic tradition, with the papal publication of *Laudato Si': On Care for Our Common Home* by Pope Francis and contemporary Marxist ecologists like John Bellamy Foster, Paul Burkett, Fred Magdoff, Jason Moore, Michael Löwy, Chris Williams, and Brian Tokar.

13. For an introduction to major works in the field of critical and Marxist ecology, see the following authors and their writings: John Bellamy Foster, Paul Burkett, Wolfdietrich Schmied-Kowarzik, Ted Benton, Gus Fagan, and Tony Burns.

14. For an analysis of the key ideas on the democratic polity in classical Athens in Aristotle's *Nicomachean Ethics*, *The Politics*, and *On the*

Athenian Constitution, see the following: Part 1: virtuous life and happiness in the *Ethics,* books 1–4, 6, 8–10; Part 2: best constitutions of monarchy, aristocracy, and democratic polity in the *Politics,* books 1, 3, 4, and 6ii; Part 3: moral economy and the virtuous life in the *Ethics,* books 4, 5, 7, 8, 9, and *Politics,* book 1; Part 4: political institutions of Athens in *On the Athenian Constitution* including the council (*boule,* chs. 43–49), assembly (*ekklesia,* chs. 89–92), and jury courts (*dikasteria,* chs. 63–69); and Part 5: forms of social justice, including rectificatory or legal justice in the *Ethics,* book 5, ch. 4, particular or economic justice, *Ethics,* book 5, chs. 2 and 5, and universal or political justice, *Ethics,* book 5, chs. 6–9.

Index